THE CATENIAN ASSOCIATION 1908–1983

By the same author
Documents in British Economic and Social History, 1750–1980
British History, 1760–1914
The Industrial Revolution
A History of Post-War Britain
Our Future King
The Queen Mother
Prince Philip
British Social History, 1760–1978
British Social and Economic History from 1760 to the present day

The 'forgotten Bishop' whose vision of an active laity inspired the founders of the Association, Louis Charles Casartelli, Bishop of Salford, 1903–1925. The bust, which stands in the Head Office of the Association, was sculptured by the Bishop's friend, Thomas Mewburn Cook (1869–1949).

The Catenian Association
1908–1983
a microcosm of the development of
the Catholic middle class

[Microcosm, miniature representation
of, any community or complex unity
so viewed. *(The Concise Oxford Dictionary)*]

Peter Lane

THE CATENIAN ASSOCIATION, LONDON

Copyright © The Catenian Association 1982
First published in Great Britain 1982

ISBN 0 9508433 0 X

The Catenian Association,
8 Chesham Place,
London, SW1X 8HP

Printed at the Burleigh Press by Burleigh Ltd. Bristol

Acknowledgements

During the last two years I have become indebted to an almost endless list of people who gave so readily of their time and memories. I am delighted to acknowledge my gratitude to the children of some of the founders of The Chums Benevolent Association – O'Donnell, Gibbons, Holt and O'Brien. They provided that living link with the inception of the Association. I am grateful to the Past Grand Presidents who allowed me to question them and who proved to be mines of information. Two of them died while the book was being written – 'Jimmy' Baker and John Eyre. But the Association still has the living memories of 'Bob' Burns, Alex Carus, Joe McMurray, Frank Lomas, Bernard Daly, George Harris, Douglas Jenkins, Frank Lloyd, John Bowen, Denis Mather, 'Paddy' Forde, Albert Smallbone, Pat Stevens and Dick Last.

I am grateful to the Presidents of the many Circles and Provinces who were kind enough to allow me to talk to Brothers in various parts of the country. In north, south, east and west, in Circles large and small, the welcome to 'the stranger without the gate' was always the same and provided a special insight into the spirit of the Association. I have a particular debt of gratitude to the late Bernard Kirchner, once Editor of *Catena*, whose prayerful wisdom and deep insights made his observations of great value. His successor at *Catena*, Leo Simmonds, was a kindly guide and help who, like so many other Catenians and Catenian wives, put his home at my disposal.

I am conscious of the endless patience and kindness of the many people at Head Office who helped in so many ways. Keith Pearson, Grand Secretary, was always willing to offer advice and guidance; Michael Pick was a cheerfully efficient secretary of the sub-committees chosen to see the work through its various stages; Tim O'Brien and 'Bonzo' Krarup, Viga Bajorek, Mia Dowdall-Brown and Desmond Fitzgerald made the work of research more pleasant than it might otherwise have been.

The Association was fortunate in having a team of men who willingly gave of their time to help the work through its various stages. Bernard Daly, Frank Lloyd and Harry Yates read the script, and their constructive criticisms led to improving amendments. Pat Coker chaired all our meetings with cheerful firmness, while David Nagle undertook the complex task of dealing with printers. I am grateful to all of these and to Herbert Rees, whose 'merciless kindness' ensured that the manuscript was correctly prepared for the printer.

My deepest debt is owed to my patient wife and children, who have allowed me to enjoy the pleasurable privilege of working on this book. Every Catenian knows that one's capacity to enjoy membership of the Association depends, to a large extent, on the co-operation of an understanding wife. I gratefully acknowledge my good fortune.

In the original manuscript I included footnotes and references to the many statements of fact and opinion made in the book. It was felt by the sub-committee that these should not appear in the published work. I have left a copy of the original typescript together with references and footnotes at Head Office. I hope that this may be of help to some future historian, while also serving as a source for the answers to readers who may query some of the statements made in the book.

I have dedicated the book to the countless number of Brothers, past and present, whose names never figure in the annals of their Circles or of the Association, because it is they who have made up, and continue to make up, the Association. It has been, as I have said, a privilege to have written this work. There was a good 'story' to be told and I only hope that readers will think that I have told it as well as it deserved. For its inevitable shortcomings and faults I ask the indulgence of the reader.

PETER LANE

May 1982

The author and the Association are grateful to the publishers, authors and copyright owners for permission to quote from the following:

Andrew Beck (ed.)	*The English Catholics, 1850–1950*
Graham Greene	*A Burnt-out Case*
George Scott	*The R.Cs: a report on Roman Catholics in Britain today*
Evelyn Waugh	*Brideshead Revisited*
Morris West	*The Shoes of the Fisherman*

Bibliography

Adelson, Roger. *Mark Sykes: Portrait of an amateur.* London 1975.
Ashton, T.S. *Economic and Social Investigations in Manchester, 1833–1933.* New edition. Hassocks 1977.
Beck, George Andrew (ed.). *The English Catholics, 1850–1950.* London 1950.
Booth, Charles. *Life and Labour of the People in London.* Three Series. London 1902–1903.
Briggs, Asa & Saville, John (eds). *Essays in Labour History.* London 1960.
Butler, Richard Austen. *The Art of the Possible: The Memoirs of Lord Butler.* London 1971.
Calder, Angus Ritchie. *The People's War: Britain 1939–45* London 1969.
Casartelli, Louis Charles. *The Signs of the Times.* 1903.
Dawson, Christopher. *The Spirit of the Oxford Movement.* London 1933.
Ensor, R.C.K. *England, 1870–1914.* Oxford 1936.
Finan, John J. *Struggle for Justice: A short history of the Catholic Teachers' Federation.* 1976.
Fitzgerald, Percy H. *Fifty Years of Catholic Life and Social Progress under Cardinals Wiseman, Manning, Vaughan and Newman.* London 1901.
Gwynn, Denis. *Cardinal Wiseman.* London 1929.
—— *A Hundred Years of Catholic Emancipation, 1829–1929.* London 1929.
Hickey, John Vincent. *Urban Catholics. Urban Catholicism in England and Wales from 1829 to the present day.* London 1967.
Hyde, Douglas. *I Believed.* London 1951.
Jackson, Brian & Marsden, Dennis. *Education and the Working Class.* London 1962.
Jenkins, Roy. *Asquith.* London 1964.
Leslie, Shane. *Henry Edward Manning, his life and labours.* London 1921.
Longmate, Norman. *How we lived then: A history of everyday life during the Second World War.* London 1971.
McElwee, W.L. *Britain's Locust Years, 1918–1940.* London 1962.
Maclure, J. Stuart. *Educational Documents, England and Wales, 1816–1963.* London 1965
Mendelssohn, Peter. *The age of Churchill:* Vol. I. *Heritage and Adventure, 1874–1911.* London 1961.
Money, Leo Chiozza. *Riches and Poverty.* London 1905.
Mowat, C.L. *Britain between the Wars, 1918–1940.* London 1955.
Newman, John Henry. *Apologia pro Vita Sua.* London 1864.
Norman, E.R. *Anti-Catholicism in Victorian England.* London 1968.
Oldmeadow, Ernest. *Francis, Cardinal Bourne.* 2 vols. London 1940–44.
Pelling, Henry. *The Origins of the Labour Party, 1880–1900.* Oxford 1965.
Perkin, Harold. *The Origins of Modern English Society, 1780–1880.* London 1969.
Pollard, Sidney. *The development of the British economy, 1914–1967.* London 1969.
Reynolds, E.E. *The Roman Catholic Church in England and Wales: a short history.* Wheathampstead 1973.
Rowntree, Seebohm. *Poverty: a study of Town Life.* London 1901.
Scott, George. *The R.C.s: a report on Roman Catholics in Britain today.* London 1967.
Seaman, L.C.B. *Post-Victorian Britain, 1902–1951.* London 1967.

Sexton, James. *Sir James Sexton, agitator: the life of the dockers' M.P. An autobiography*. London 1936.
Sykes, Christopher. *Nancy: the life of Lady Astor*. London 1972.
Thomas, Hugh. *The Spanish Civil War*. London 1961.
Thompson, A. *The Day before Yesterday: an illustrated history of Britain from Attlee to Macmillan*. London 1971.
Vaughan, Herbert. *The True Basis of Catholic Politics: A Pastoral Letter*. Manchester 1883.
Williams, Francis. *Nothing so strange: an autobiography*. London 1970.
Wilsher, Peter. *The Pound in Your Pocket, 1870–1970*. London 1970.
Woodham-Smith, Cecil. *The Great Hunger: Ireland 1845–9*. London 1962.

Newspapers and periodicals
Catholic Directory, 1903–1914
Catholic Herald
Catholic Times
The Tablet

Catenian sources
Catena, vols I–LX
Circle Histories submitted in 1957
Circle Histories as recorded at various banquets
Letters from children of some of the founding 'Chums'
Letters from many Brothers
Scrapbook maintained since 1914 at Head Office

Federation material
I am very grateful to Councillor P.J. Doyle of Hull for his kindness in allowing me to use work – published and unpublished – resulting from his long study of Catholic politics and, in particular, the Federation Movement. These include:
1 The Formation of the Catholic Union
2 Catholic Electoral Registration Societies
3 Catholics and the Social Question
4 Religion, Politics and the Catholic Working Class
5 The Hull Hibernians
6 The Salford Federation (an unpublished MS)
7 The Hull Catholic Federation, 1907–1912

Contents

	Page
Acknowledgements	v
Bibliography	vii
Illustrations	xii
Introduction	xv

Chapter 1 THE CATHOLIC SCENE 1903–1908　　1
    1. 1903 – a watershed
    2. Social make-up
    3. Catholic schools
    4. *The Signs of the Times*
    5. The Salford Diocesan Federation
    6. The Eucharistic Congress 1908

Chapter 2 THE MANCHESTER 'CHUMS' 1908–1909　　16
    1. When did they start?
    2. The original aims and objects
    3. The founding fathers
    4. The early meetings

Chapter 3 OUT FROM MANCHESTER　　28
    1. J. McDermott, J.P.
    2. McDermott, Hogan and London
    3. Leeds and Liverpool
    4. Re-naming the Association
    5. Newcastle and Blackburn
    6. McDermott's sudden death

Chapter 4 THE FIRST WAVE OF EXPANSION　　40
    1. The growth of Manchester and London
    2. Birmingham
    3. 1913, *annus mirabilis*
    4. 1914 and the expansion continues
    5. Aims and Objects
    6. New structures
    7. A taste of the meeting

Chapter 5 WARTIME DEVELOPMENTS　　53
    1. A slow-down in expansion
    2. Some effects of the War
    3. The birth of *Catena*
    4. The value of the magazine
    5. Degrees, Chapter Circles and Past Presidents' Clubs

| Chapter 6 | AMBITIOUS BUT ACTIVE 1919–1923 | 66 |

1. The Hierarchy and Catenian expansion
2. Catenians in action
3. Overwhelming ambitions
4. The Association and the Beda College
5. Plater College

| Chapter 7 | ORGANISATION, RE-ORGANISATION AND STRUCTURE | 81 |

1. The need for a new Constitution
2. The 1923 Constitution
3. The politics of development
4. More re-organisation?
5. Structures and officers

| Chapter 8 | JOE SHEPHERD AND FRANK RUDMAN | 95 |

1. The first paid Secretary 1910
2. The role of the Grand Secretary
3. Joe Shepherd
4. An élitist Association?
5. Expansion and Shepherd's resignation 1923
6. Frank Rudman
7. Expansion during depression 1923–1952

| Chapter 9 | CATENIANS AND THEIR BENEVOLENCE | 107 |

1. Early and voluntary steps
2. Developments 1914–1923
3. The Children's Fund
4. Benevolence in the depression
5. Catena Trustees 1946–1981
6. The covenant scheme

| Chapter 10 | AIMS AND OBJECTS | 121 |

1. The stated, but amended, Aims
2. Attacks and misunderstandings
3. Bigotry and prejudice
4. 'Service'
5. Catenian friendship
6. Link Clubs
7. Helping young people
8. The spiritual dimension

| Chapter 11 | 1923–1939 | 132 |

1. Expansion during depression
2. The Papal Toast 1925
3. Signs and Passwords
4. Catenians and Secondary Schools
5. Public service
6. Catholic Action in the 1930s

Chapter 12 THE ASSOCIATION AND THE SECOND WORLD
            WAR 1939–1945   145
            1. Wartime problems
            2. Catenian activities
            3. Surprising expansion
            4. To be more politically involved?
            5. The Battle for the Schools 1943–1945

Chapter 13 1945–1952   159
            1. The end of the War
            2. Rapid expansion
            3. The move to London
            4. Active Catenians
            5. The Battle for the Schools
            6. Catenian development
            7. Rudman's retirement

Chapter 14 ADAPTATION, AMBITION AND DISAPPOINTMENT
            1952–1965   172
            1. A slow expansion
            2. Changes and adaptations
            3. Active Catenians
            4. The layman in the modern world
            5. The proposed Chaplaincies Scheme
            6. The collapse of the Scheme – and after
            7. To be active?
            8. An activist's appreciation

Chapter 15 THE AFTERMATH OF THE VATICAN COUNCIL
            1965–1975   185
            1. Failure and reality
            2. 'Dressed for dinner' only?
            3. Action for the handicapped
            4. Relations with the Hierarchy
            5. Laurie Tanner K.S.G.
            6. Keith Pearson

Chapter 16 OVERSEAS EXPANSION 1954–1983   198
            1. Ambitions and reality 1919–1954
            2. The Rhodesian Circles 1957–1959
            3. The Zambian Circles 1959–1981
            4. Into South Africa
            5. Ireland, 1938–1983
            6. Australia 1962–1983
            7. Asia, Europe and America

Chapter 17 THE MATURING OF THE EASTER PEOPLE 1975–1983
            1. Internal developments and strains   210
            2. Relations with the Hierarchy
            3. Catenians in Action
            4. Catenian Ladies
            5. Catenian Families
            6. Has the Association a future?

Index   227

Illustrations

Frontispiece: Louis Charles Casartelli, Bishop of Salford

Between pages 44 and 45
The Signs of the Times
The letter of 14 May 1908
The final page of 'the enclosed proposal'
John O'Donnell
John Gibbons
Charles Holt
O'Donnell's daughters
Edward J. Hogan
Joseph McDermott
Frank Pendergast
Joseph Shepherd
Paul Kelly's driving certificate
Edward Fitzgerald-Hart
John Lomas

Between pages 92 and 93
Hogan's letter (29 November 1909) to McDermott
Sir W.H. Dunn
Dunn's letter to McDermott
Liverpool Circle welcomes Archbishop Keating in July 1921
An Annual General Meeting at Birmingham
A Catenian Anthem
Dr George Foggin
Menu card of Blackburn Circle's first Dinner (28 November 1912)
Dan McCabe, prospective Lord Mayor of Manchester

Between pages 156 and 157
Annual General Meeting at Harrogate 1939
The First Communion, by Bro. David O'Connell
Charles Sheill
Bernard Emblem
The Lifeboat Doctor, 'Jimmy' Hall
The Association's own Archbishop
Alexander Bounevialle
R.W. Brosch
Annual General Meeting at Folkestone 1954
Grand Council 1956–57
The new Plater College

A.G.M. banquet 1966
Laurence Bussy
Phil Bussy
Stephen Bussy
The Bussy family
Sir Joseph Molony
Hugh Lee
M.E. King
Bros Everest and Tom McLachlan
Paddy Crotty
Christopher Peterson
Thomas Francis
James Glynn
John Fitzsimmons
F.H. O'Donnell
Tickle family (three generations)

Between pages 204 and 205
Father Hugh Martin, after his ordination
Olimpio Forte, with Pope Paul VI
The Nockles family meet Pope John Paul II
Rex Kirk at the 1976 Dublin A.G.M.
Cardinal Gray at Mass celebrating the 500th meeting of Aberdeen Circle
Haywards Heath Circle at Mass
Albert Smallbone with Maurice Sheehan (Penybont)
David Higgins and Ann Bolton
Brian and Marian Brett
Mark Hickson and Julie Keane
Gerard Wilcox (Stratford on Avon) with Kathryn and their baby daughter Teresa
Bill Ridgers (Purley)
Bernard Kirchner
Cyril Gaskin (Darlington) and his wife, with their newly ordained son
Laurie Tanner at work on the Jumbulance
Swansea Circle's gift of two wheelchairs
Mass at Hosanna House
A caravan rally, August 1978
Brothers of Pretoria Circle 1981
Golf Trophy presented at Zimbabwe Circle 1966
Rowland Young
Bernard Pepper
Bryan Hooton (Melbourne) with Grand President John Eyre
Bernard Sullivan (Hong Kong)
Brothers of Copperbelt Circle
Cliff Holloway and Dr Peter Maguire (City of Perth)
Stan Clark, Founder President of the Malta Circle, with Mrs Clark

Next let us praise illustrious men,
    our ancestors in their successive generations. . . .
Some wielded authority . . ., others were intelligent advisers.
Others directed the people by their advice, . . .
    others composed musical melodies, . . .
    others were rich and powerful. . . .
Some of them left a name behind them,
    so that their praises are still sung.
While others have left no memory,
    and disappeared . . . as though they had never been,
    and so too, their children after them. . . .
But . . . in their descendants there remains
    a rich inheritance born of them.
Their descendants stand by the covenants
    and, thanks to them, so do their children's children.
Their offspring will last for ever,
    their glory will not fade.

(From the Book of Ecclesiasticus 44: 1–13 and appointed to be read on 6 November for the Feast of All Saints of Ireland.)

Introduction

In May 1983, some 11,000 Catenians will celebrate the 75th anniversary of the birth of their Association. There may be, as this book shows, uncertainty as to the exact date of its birth, but there can be little doubt as to its growth and expansion. The signatories of the Association's first official letter (14 May 1908) could never have guessed that their Manchester-based Association for 'Catholic professional and business men' would develop into a worldwide Association, for in 1908 the number of 'Catholic professional and business men' was very small. The growth of the Association to its present strength is a reflection of the growth of a Catholic middle class, a result of the social revolution which has affected society as a whole. But this growth has both affected and been affected by the development of Catholic life in the twentieth century. One of the aims of this book is to show how, when and where Catenians played a part in that development, of which their Association may be seen as a microcosm.

When, where, why and by whom was the Association founded? These are some of the questions to which some of the answers will be found in the early Chapters of this book. The 'where, why and by whom' can be answered with confidence. But no one can say exactly 'when' the Association was formed. Traditionally, members have taken 14 May 1908 as the day of birth – quoting the letter to Casartelli as evidence. But 'the enclosed proposal' told the Bishop that O'Donnell and his friends were asking for his 'approval and blessing' on 'a society which we have already formed'. All the available evidence suggests that the answer to the question 'when' must be, regrettably, 'On a date unknown in 1908'.

But in one sense the question of an exact date is relatively unimportant. Students of history, like thoughtful people everywhere, have long realised that few things happen as of themselves or, as it were, in a vacuum. The formation of the Association was the result of a series of preceding events and developments – in Catholic life, in the nation's economic and social life, and in the lives of a number of individuals who helped form the Association.

For this reason a study of the History of the Catenian Association begins with an overview of life in 1903, the year in which Louis Charles Casartelli became the fourth Bishop of Salford.

CHAPTER ONE

The Catholic Scene 1903–1908

1. 1903 – a watershed

For younger readers the year 1903 may well appear almost prehistoric, so great have the changes been since then. Some older readers may remember it as decisive in various ways. It was, for example, the year in which the Wright brothers made their first historic flight in a heavier-than-air machine which was dismissed by the knowledgeable as 'a foolish experiment, for man will never learn to fly'; in which Marconi was perfecting his new 'wireless', and owners of motor cars went on the seventh London–Brighton run and celebrated the raising of the legal speed limit to an awesome 20 m.p.h.

For the politically-minded the year was noteworthy on several grounds. There were signs of the revival of the Liberals, recently bitterly divided over the Second Boer War (1899–1902) when the majority had, reluctantly, supported the government while the vociferous minority, led by the young Welsh M.P. David Lloyd George, had campaigned against the war. The Liberal revival owed much to the Nonconformist campaign against the Tory Education Act (1902), designed, amongst other things, to help raise standards at Church schools. The campaign against 'Rome on the rates' united the Liberals who came together to make political capital out of the anti-Anglican and anti-Catholic unrest. In October 1903 their unity was further strengthened by Joe Chamberlain's campaign for Tariff Reform. Chamberlain, once the darling of the republican left and more recently the toast of Imperial diehards as he helped organise the Boer War, was vilified in the Press and from Liberal platforms for doing violence to the sacred cow of Free Trade.

Few paid much attention to the electoral pact signed in 1903 by Herbert Gladstone, Chief Whip of the Liberal Party, and Ramsay MacDonald, secretary of the Labour Representation Committee, by which arrangements were made so that in the next Election the anti-Tory vote would not be split. No one foresaw that one result of this pact would be the return in 1906 of 29 Labour M.P.s – a result which gave the infant Party a credibility which it might otherwise not have gained for many years.

Of more immediate importance was the visit by Edward VII to Paris (May 1903) as part of the diplomatic dance which had brought Britain into a formal Alliance with Japan in 1902 and which was to bring France and Britain together in the *Entente Cordiale* in 1904 – both of them signs that some British statesmen were aware of Britain's changed position *vis-à-vis* the rest of the world. The *Pax Britannica* could no longer be imposed on a changing world.

The year 1903 was also important in British social history. About half of those who had volunteered to serve in the Army during the Boer War had been rejected on medical grounds. The report of a government Committee on Physical Deterioration (1903) showed that only 10 per cent of those who had volunteered in Manchester had been accepted for service, and that in the East End of London eleven out of twelve had been rejected. Here was the evidence

1

that a century or more of industrial progress had resulted in urban conditions which produced millions of unhealthy men, women and children. To the socially-involved these findings did not come as a shock. They merely confirmed conclusions which had already appeared in Charles Booth's work on London and Joseph Rowntree's work on York, both of which had shown that about one-third of the British people lived on or beneath a very low poverty line. It is difficult now to imagine a country without the infrastructure of the Welfare State. But in 1903 there was very little such framework; there was no old age pension, no unemployment benefits scheme, no state health insurance or National Health Service. On the contrary, there was gross overcrowding, with about 40 per cent of the population living more than two to a room in dwellings which lacked toilet facilities and adequate water supplies.

The appearance of Booth's final volumes in 1903 makes that year a watershed in the history of social investigation and in the movement towards the creation of a Welfare State. When social insurance was first provided in 1911 for those with annual incomes of £160 or less, few working-class incomes approached that level, while unskilled workers earned well under 50 per cent of that figure. On the other hand, successful barristers earned £20,000 or more, while many living on capital investment had even higher incomes.

Leo XIII had protested against this unfair division of wealth and of income in his *Rerum Novarum* (1891). His death in 1903 made the year a watershed also in the history of the Church. His successor was Pius X, whose pontificate is best remembered for his advocacy of earlier and more frequent reception of Holy Communion, and for his condemnation of that Modernism which had been discouraged by Leo XIII, whose disapproval of the work of Tyrrell, Von Hügel and others had, however, never extended to condemnation. Cardinal Herbert Vaughan had no hesitation in condemning socialism, of which Modernism was the ecclesiastical counterpart. In 1883 Vaughan had declared that socialism was 'the outcome of Satan's teaching'. But Vaughan too died in 1903. His successor, the youngest Bishop in England at the time, was Francis Bourne.

But, for the historian of the Association, 1903 is most notable for the death of Bishop Bilsborrow of Salford, leading to the elevation to the Hierarchy of Louis Charles Casartelli who was, as we shall see, the founder-patron of the Association to which he gave his active support until his death in 1925.

2. Social make-up

Bourne and Casartelli were leaders of a Catholic community very different from that which exists in modern Britain. There were about 1½ million Catholics in England and Wales and another 433,000 in Scotland, socially divided into the very wealthy and the very poor, the middle class being a small fraction of the total membership. Among the wealthy was the handful of aristocratic families which had held on to the Faith through the period of persecution – the Howards, Cliffords, Stourtons and Jerninghams, for example. There were also the much larger number of the ancient squirearchy typified by the Vaughans, the Mostyns, and the owners of such homes as Stonor.

Most of these 'old Catholic' families had a defensive attitude towards the outside world, an attitude similar in many ways to the ghetto mentality of the

Irish poor. Their family histories were a reminder of the cost of being a Catholic. Few of them had yet come to terms with the relatively new freedom enjoyed since Emancipation – the 'marks' of their families' recusancy were too many and too deeply ingrained to be easily ignored. So, while they supplied the Church with a steady supply of recruits to the priesthood and the religious life, they tended to suspect the evangelistic enthusiasm favoured by converts such as Newman, Faber and, above all, Manning. They might have agreed with Mgr Gilbert Talbot, who, albeit a convert, wrote to Manning:

> What is the province of the laity? To hunt, to shoot, to entertain. These are matters they understand. . . . .

In *Brideshead Revisited* Evelyn Waugh wrote of one such 'old Catholic' family:

> The family history was typical of the Catholic squires of England; from Elizabeth's reign till Victoria's they lived sequestered lives, among their tenantry and kinsmen, sending their sons to school abroad, often marrying there, inter-marrying, if not, with a score of families like themselves, debarred from all preferment, and learning, in those lost generations, lessons which could still be read in the lives of the last three men of the house.

Most of these old families as well as those convert members of aristocratic families understood at least one facet of their responsibility to the Catholic community. Many of them subscribed generously to funds for church building; many helped maintain Bishops and local clergy. However, by the very nature of things – their small number, the demands of the expanding Church and the increasing number of Irish immigrants – it was the shillings and the pennies of ordinary Catholics that provided the greater part of the funds needed for the less pretentious churches and for the schools that were essential if the Church was to go forward into the new era of Catholicism.

These 'ordinary Catholics' were, in the main, Irish immigrants. In 1829, the year of Emancipation, there were about 250,000 native-born Catholics in England and Wales with, perhaps, as many Irish immigrants. The increase in the Catholic population – to about 1½ million by 1903 – was due, almost entirely, to two distinct waves of Irish immigration. So great was the Irish influence on the English Church that Manning remarked that he had 'given up working for the people of England, to work for the Irish occupation of England'. Immigration from various European countries had brought a leavening of Italians, Spaniards, French and Austrians to English Catholic life. But it was the Irish who made up some 80 per cent of the Catholic population.

The first wave of Irish immigration took place during and immediately after the Great Famine (1845–49). Even before that tragedy, foreign observers had found in Ireland 'the extreme of human misery, worse than the Negro in his chains'; the German traveller Kohl wrote that 'no mode of life in Europe could seem pitiable after he had seen Ireland'. The system of land ownership and of 'rack rent' has been described as one 'ingeniously contrived, first for the debasement and then for the continuance in that debasement of an entire people'.

Evicted by landlords' agents from their wretched mud cabins, the Irish poor flocked to England – only the better-off could afford the fares to the U.S.A., Canada or Australia. Speaking only Gaelic, unskilled in every technical sense and accustomed to living and working in the countryside, they flocked to Liverpool, Manchester and London in search of shelter and work. Low-paid and willing to accept work at almost any wage, their family incomes allowed them only the poorest of housing. Many lived in lodging-houses, sharing their beds with men working on alternate shifts. Many more crowded together in the worst areas of the expanding cities and towns, sometimes living sixty to a house, thirty to a house being an average; four or five families often shared the one room.

It is hardly surprising that when describing life for the poorest class in the 1840s, Engels should have concentrated on the Irish in Manchester. Nor is it surprising that, around 1900, Booth, Rowntree and other social investigators found a higher-than-expected number of Irish families amongst the most deprived. Nor, finally, is it surprising that the epidemics which ravaged England in the nineteenth century should have affected the Irish more than the rest of the population. In particular there were the outbreaks of typhus in 1885 and 1893, although these merely increased an already high rate of death in general and of infant mortality in particular.

Newspapers carried reports of the Irish community which more than bear comparison with the worst excesses of language used by vituperative critics of coloured immigrants into modern Britain. Like them, the Irish were accused of being dirty, noisy, feckless, overproductive but lazy. Like them, the Irish lived in overcrowded housing and tended to seek each other out, so that, like more recent immigrants, they created an almost recognisable physical ghetto. In Cardiff, for example, 1500 Irish lived in four neighbouring streets.

And even if they were not subject to this physical isolation from the rest of the population, they lived none the less with a ghetto mentality. In part, this was self-created and self-fulfilling; fearful of the pressures from outside – as evidenced in newspaper reports, attacks on Catholic churches, on Mass-goers, on Irish workers who gained a reputation for strike-breaking, and on their homes – the Irish, not unnaturally, crowded together for self-defence and protection. Isolated from the majority by religion and language, they helped sustain one another in a hostile community.

But in part the ghetto mentality was imposed from outside. The majority of the population were suspicious of Catholicism – and had their suspicions fed by politicians and preachers anxious to win popularity. They also believed that the Irish were not 'loyal', a belief reinforced by the Fenian outrages of the '60s and '70s, by the Parnellite movement for Home Rule in the '80s and '90s and by the many reports of attacks on British people, and property in Ireland. To help confirm the majority in this belief, the Irish immigrant community supported such movements as the Home Rule Federation, the Society of United Irishmen and Davitt's Land League. They kept alive their memories of Ireland in songs, poetry, dances and festivals – St Patrick's Day being, it must have seemed to the English, more important for the Irish than Christmas Day itself.

Some writers argue that the ghetto mentality was the self-induced result of 'exclusivity' – an anti-world attitude arising from the assurance that the Catholics alone possessed the True Faith. There is some truth in this, but it is not the whole truth: one has also to consider the attitude of 'the world' to the Catholic Church – in the nineteenth century. When Casartelli became Bishop of Salford in 1903 there were still thousands of Catholics who could remember the Restoration of the Hierarchy in 1850. They would have remembered Wiseman's first Pastoral, *From the Flaminian Gate* (7 October 1850), and the stormy reception it was given by Prime Minister Lord John Russell, *The Times* and the people of this country as a whole. They would tell of the processions ending with the burning of the Pope and Wiseman in effigy, of the attacks on Irish homes and churches by people roused to anti-Catholic fever pitch by preachers and politicians, and of the Ecclesiastical Titles Act which imposed a fine of £100 on any person assuming a title to a 'pretended see'.

Irish Catholics, huddled in their inadequate housing, would also have heard of Lord Randolph Churchill's call in 1886 for Ulstermen to rise in rebellion against Gladstone's Home Rule proposals. 'Home Rule is Rome Rule' and 'Ulster will fight and Ulster will be right' were among the slogans used against that Home Rule which the Irish-in-England favoured and supported. Nor did things improve after 1903 – with Carson leading Ulstermen to the signing of the 1912 Covenant, and Bonar Law and the Conservatives promising to aid the Protestants to prevent Irish Home Rule reaching the Statute Book. As the diarist Greville wrote: '. . . While everything else is in a constant state of change, Protestant bigotry and anti-Catholic rancour continue to flourish with undiminished intensity . . . founded on nothing but prejudice, and ignorance without a particle of reason.' Thus, the handful of wealthy Catholics and the mass of the Irish poor were isolated from the world.

But by 1903 there had begun to emerge a recognisable, though small, Catholic middle class. They were recognisable – in an age when it was possible to distinguish 'the Gentlemen' from 'the Players' – by dress, by housing, by the schooling of their children and, in some cases, by the carriages which they could afford to own or hire to take them to Mass and to business. Some of these were 'self-made' men, children of the poor Irish immigrants who had pulled themselves out of the poverty of their parents by hard work. Others of them were drawn from the second wave of Irish immigration which took place in the 1870s. In this fresh wave there were men with sufficient education to allow them to take their rightful place in industry, trade, commerce and government service.

Many of them had been helped to develop, psychologically, by the formation of a variety of Catholic institutions in which they learned to play a leading part. Some had helped their priests to run classes where the adult Irish were taught English; others ran religious education classes for children for whom there was no Catholic school. Others learned to exercise leadership in Catholic insurance and friendly societies such as the Ancient Order of Hibernians; others ran parish-based Penny Banks; some helped form the St Vincent de Paul Society (1889) and others organised the Catholic Young Men's Society.

Lasting evidence of the emergence of this new class of Catholic is provided by the growth in the number of schools opened to cater for the children of this class – not sufficiently rich to afford the fees to the long-established Catholic boarding schools, but ambitious enough to want for their children something more than the elementary education provided in the parish school. But, as we shall see, the size and number of those new schools also illustrates the limited numbers of this Catholic middle class.

3. Catholic schools

Children of the aristocracy and the landed families were educated at home or at Catholic boarding schools. These schools were run by religious orders or by secular priests; many of them combined the two roles of providing secular education *and* of being seminaries for the training of priests. Stonyhurst (founded 1794) was the first, although the Benedictines quickly followed the example of the Jesuits by founding Ampleforth (1802), and Downside (1814). The Dominicans founded St Peter's College at Hinckley (1823), the Jesuits founded Mount St Mary's (1842) and the Rosminians founded Ratcliffe (1847). Diocesan Colleges which also acted as seminaries were founded at Ushaw (1808), Oscott, Prior Park (1830) and St Edmund's, Ware (1842).

The fees charged at these schools – £42 a year at Stonyhurst in 1794 and 50 guineas at Oscott – appear small to modern readers, but they have to be set against contemporary money values. As a benchmark we might note that when Peel formed the Metropolitan Police Force in 1829 the constables were paid £1 0s.6d. a week. Fees at Catholic boarding schools in 1850 may, then, be seen as the equivalent of something like a police constable's annual income. Later in the century, fees were increased as standards of accommodation improved. At the Oratory (1859) the fees were £80 a year and at Beaumont (1870) some £90.

These schools were inspected in a series of reviews between 1871 and 1878 and were found to be much smaller than their non-Catholic counterparts such as Eton and Rugby, and to be suffering from a shortage of funds which affected both the quality of the staff employed and the facilities which could be provided. The reviews noted, however, that in 'some' of these schools the standard of education, particularly in the Classics, was very high.

George Scott noted that 'Catholic education reflects the social divisions of secular education in Britain' into public schools, grammar schools, and primary and secondary schools. Schools for the Catholic middle class are of more recent origin than the boarding schools. But, like them, most of these schools were founded by religious orders, the Bishops being over-involved and over-committed to the daunting task of providing elementary schools for the 'huddled masses'. The first two middle-class schools were founded in Liverpool in the 1840s: St Francis Xavier's and a school in Rodney Street each catered for about 50 boys, whose parents paid four guineas a year in fees. The next middle-class school was founded by the De La Salle Brothers who opened a school at Clapham (1855), where they provided schooling for day pupils at £9 a year and for boarders at £21 a year. In 1860 the De La Salle Brothers founded a school in Southwark, and the Jesuits founded the Catholic College in Preston. A sign of the growth of the Catholic middle class was the foundation of Xaverian Colleges in Liverpool (1862) and Margate (1868), and the Josephite College, Croydon (1869), the year in which Manning also brought the Oblates to St Charles's, Kensington. Many Catenians will better recognise the Josephite College as St George's, Weybridge.

These schools were inspected in 1870 and were declared to be very successful in terms of their pupils' achievements in the new public examination system. Pupils from these schools were prepared for those examinations which helped the more successful gain entry into the Home or Indian Civil Service, the Royal Military College, Woolwich, the University of London, and medical schools in Britain and Ireland.

Between 1873 and 1896 another sixteen such schools were founded, including St Bede's, Manchester (1875), where Casartelli was later to be Rector. After 1896 there was an increase in the rate of founding such schools – owing to the influx of religious expelled from Republican France by anti-clerical governments, and to the continued expansion of the Catholic middle class. Ten such fee-paying schools were formed between 1900 and 1910, and another three were opened between 1910 and 1914. Most of them were day schools, although a small number offered some boarding accommodation.

But the most striking thing about these schools and a number of similar schools opened by laymen is their size. The *Catholic Directory* for 1913 shows that in England and Wales there were some 380 such schools, catering for 24,518 pupils – an average of about 64 for each school. This reflects the size of the Catholic middle class. But the vast majority of Catholics in 1900 were to be found among the unskilled and poor. To cater for the education of the children of this deprived class, Bishops everywhere collected money to build Catholic elementary schools, so that by 1913 there were 1310 such schools in England and Wales catering for 339,632 children aged between 5 and 12, an average of about 252 for each school.

By 1900, the cost per pupil in the boarding school was about £100; in the middle-class grammar or secondary schools the day pupils paid about £12 and the boarders about £30 a year. In elementary schools the cost per pupil was £1 14s.7d. – compared to the £1 12s.6d. per pupil spent by the local authorities in their Board Schools. Until 1891, parents were expected to pay a weekly fee of 4d. or 5d., but the 1891 Act made elementary schooling free. The Catholic schools – like their voluntary counterparts in the Anglican, Wesleyan, Jewish and other denominations – received their income from the government, based on the results of an annual inspection.

In 1902 the Tory government pushed through an Education Act which, among other things, provided that the voluntary schools, including the Catholic schools, would, in future, receive their income from the newly-established Local Education Authorities. The Nonconformists raised a nationwide protest against 'Rome on the Rates', ignoring the fact that the Anglicans had many more schools than the Catholics had. Over 20.000 were arrested for non-payment of rates; many had their property sequestered by bailiffs, who sold it to raise the sum required. Some L.E.A.s, dominated by Nonconformist councillors, tried to stamp out the voluntary schools – seeking, for example, to withhold that part of the schools' grants which could be attributed to the time taken for religious education. The Liberals, as we have seen, recovered a unity welded in the heat of this religio-educational controversy, and vowed that when they next came to office they would insist that all voluntary schools should be transferred to the L.E.A.s, thus making all elementary schools council schools. The Bishops formed the Catholic Education Council (1905) to help prepare for the defence of the Catholic schools and, as we shall see, Casartelli helped to organise his own Diocesan Federation to wage 'the Battle for the Schools'.

The Catholic school system reflected the social divisions of society at large and of the Catholic community in particular. There were other divisions inside that community, some of which were to have their effect on the growth of the Catenian Association. The 'old' Catholics were, at best, uneasy at the influence of the intellectual converts who followed Newman into the Church. The hostility to Newman himself is well known; less well known, perhaps, is the opposition which Manning faced as he strove to impose order and discipline on the growing Church. Seminaries were better used, schools built for the poor, aid sent to foreign missions and an attempt made to find an increased public usefulness for laymen, who should be, declared Manning, 'downright, manly and decided Catholics, more Roman than Rome, and more ultramontane than the Pope himself', totally opposed to that 'tame, diluted, timid Catholicism' which had tended to mark the 'conservative spirituality of the old Catholic families'.

The old families may have resented Manning's bustling evangelistic policies. But they also resented the Irish influence. Barbara Charlton wrote in her *Recollections,* by 'a Northumbrian Lady', that the Irish were 'filthy people, with whom duplicity went hand in hand with deceit', while they upheld the 'tyranny of the Irish priests'. The Catholic Union, founded in the aftermath of the loss of the Papal States in 1859 and 1870, excluded the Irish by insisting that members pledge their loyalty to the throne, and even today boasts: 'We keep the Micks out'. The old Catholic families, accustomed to practising their religion in isolated privacy, found strange the warmth and enthusiasm of the Irish, who had led a more normal religious life than had been possible in England.

4. The Signs of the Times

But Casartelli had little of such controversy in his small, but densely populated, diocese when he became Bishop in 1903. For here were to be found one-sixth of all the Irish living in England and Wales, drawn to Manchester, the nation's first industrial city in the '40s and '50s, condemned to live in the appalling conditions described by Engels and other more objective observers. Cecil Woodham-Smith writes:

> Very few of the poor Irish who fled from Ireland in the famine emigration were destined to achieve prosperity and success themselves; the condition to which the people had been reduced not only by the famine but by the centuries which preceded it was too severe a handicap, and it was the fate of the Irish emigrants to be regarded with aversion and contempt. It was not until the second or third generation that Irish intelligence, quickness of apprehension and wit asserted themselves, and the children and grandchildren of the poor famine emigrants became successful and powerful. . . .

They had no technical skills, they were not carpenters, butchers, glaziers, masons or tailors, for few men in pre-famine Ireland had had any trade. In Manchester, as elsewhere, they drifted into unskilled, irregular, badly-paid work – cleaning of yards and stables, loading and unloading of vehicles and boats, pushing carts – and forming a mass of underpaid, casual labour.

The *Catholic Directory* for 1913 was the first to carry some detailed analysis of the Catholic population in England and Wales. It shows that in 1911 there were 10,383 baptisms in the diocese of Salford, when Westminster had 8459, and only Liverpool had the greater number than Salford of 15,227. Here lay one major problem for a Bishop: to find the money for the schools and churches required for such an expanding population, and to train priests to serve them. A reminder that Catholics came, in the main, from the lowest rank of society is the fact that in 1903 the large Catholic population of Salford could support only one, small, grammar school – St Bede's.

Few indeed of the Catholic population had emerged from the poverty into which they had been born. Not for them to enjoy the life of the prosperous and cosmopolitan city then enjoying an Indian summer of prosperity. Here was the city in which the German-born Sir Charles Hallé founded an orchestra financed by the prosperous merchants and traders; here too the Free Trade Hall, the memorial of the days when the Manchester-based Anti-Corn Law

League led by Cobden and Bright could force a major change in Peel's economic policy. Here, too, that great Town Hall, the outward sign of that inward civic pride which was a hallmark of late Victorian England, while adjacent to it was St Peter's Field, the scene of that Peterloo Massacre which had marked Manchester out as a hotbed of Radical politics in the first decades of the nineteenth century.

The choice of Casartelli to fill the vacancy at Salford, 'a grim and forbidding See', was at once both fitting and strange. Fitting, for he was already well known in the city as a leading intellectual, well suited to enhance the Catholic name. Born in 1852, the son of an Italian optician living in Manchester, he had gone to the old Salford Grammar School – yet a further reminder that there were few Catholic secondary schools in the 1860s – before going to Ushaw, where he gained a London M.A in 1873. He was sent to Louvain to study theology and, at his own request, Eastern languages. Ordained in 1876, he was placed on the staff at St Bede's School, founded only in the previous year. While teaching there, he also continued his own studies, gaining a Doctorate in Oriental literature from London University in 1884. His thesis was so highly thought of that a Parsee scholar translated it into his native language for the benefit of Parsees in general. In 1891 Casartelli was appointed Rector of St Bede's. In 1903 he was appointed a lecturer in Iranian languages at the new Manchester University – a fitting post for the multilinguist who also spoke and wrote French, German, Italian and Flemish.

And even after he became Bishop he continued to play an active part in the intellectual life of the city. In 1906 he founded the Dante Society in Manchester, arguing that the *Divine Comedy* was a wonderful description of the transition of the soul through Purgatory to Paradise. In 1908 he founded the Manchester–Egyptian Association of which he remained president until 1910. Between 1898 and 1900 he was President of the pioneering Manchester Statistical Society (founded in 1833), filling the chair once occupied by giants such as the economist Jevons and which was to be filled after him by outstanding men such as Professor S.J. Chapman. He addressed the Society on four occasions, demonstrating the breadth of his interests by the variety of topics on which he spoke: Commercial Education (1881), Teaching of Modern Languages (1887), Responsibilities in the East (1892), Town Beauty (1898), Study of Foreign Languages (1918).

In a sense, then, he was well fitted to be the leader of a Catholic community in an enterprising city. On the other hand, as he himself recalled in his first Pastoral (October 1903), he had never served in a parish, nor had he any of the practical experience of the sort one would have assumed to be essential for a man taking charge of such a busy diocese. But the scholar was called from his study, and the polymath was forced to turn his attention to the needs of a wider community than that with which he was familiar from his work at St Bede's. He continued to live in the Lodge at the School and it was from here that he issued his Pastoral, *The Signs of the Times*. This is a radical document, for in Part 2 he called for Catholic laymen 'to go forth to all the interests of the commonwealth of which we are part', going on to say that he wanted the laity to play their role '... in matters social, municipal, philanthropic, educational, artistic, literary in which we may use the powers we enjoy'. He asked his people to give not so much their material wealth, but ... their time and their work in the service of the commonwealth. Such service is to be rendered on city and borough councils, on urban and parish councils, boards of guardians, education committees, committees of hospitals, museums, libraries, art galleries, as well as in the magistracy of the peace. We cannot but feel that it would be a good thing if some of our younger men would strive to render this service for the benefit of both the Church and the commonwealth.

Here was the scholar who had escaped from the ghetto and had seen the wider world of which most of his flock were ignorant. Here was the man who wanted Catholics to throw off the older and traditional defensive attitude, when, if they had been concerned with public affairs, it had been with such things as affected them directly as Catholics, e.g. the schools. But here too was the priest who was aware that too few of his people had the confidence necessary to go out and make their mark as he wished. Asking why it was that Catholics seemed less willing to serve and act as other 'young men and women of education and refinement, but above all of good will, outside the Catholic Church', he wondered, 'Is it that they do not know how to set themselves to work of this kind and need guiding and informing by their ecclesiastical superiors?' For here was the bishop prepared to invite his people to act without priestly leadership, to learn to walk tall in their own right. Manning might have spoken thus – although he may well have wanted to maintain some control over the activities of his flock. Casartelli alone invited his people to play their own full role in the world at large. And when some of them endeavoured to do so – in the Federation – he gave them his full support, knowing, as he did, that their activity and the Federation was opposed by many priests, most active Irish voters and almost all the 'old' Catholics.

5. The Salford Diocesan Federation

That Catholics should play an active role in social and political affairs was still a novel idea. Manning, of course, had pointed the way. He had campaigned for an improvement in the conditions of agricultural workers, for reforms which would sweep away the industrial slums, for social justice as regards wages, child labour and sweated labour, and for shorter working hours for shop assistants. He was a member of the Royal Commission on Housing of the Working Classes (1884) and intervened effectively in the Dockers' Strike (1889). But this work and activity was criticised by many Catholics who thought that he ought not to interfere in what they considered to be political questions. Some condemned him as a socialist.

But Manning was a convert and, in his zeal, out of tune with the 'old' Catholics. His successor, Cardinal Vaughan, was a member of an 'old' family which had contributed sons and daughters to the religious life and the priesthood. He was not a scholar, nor, indeed, an intellectual, but had shown himself to be a truly pastoral bishop in his twenty years as Bishop of Salford when he founded a Rescue and Protection Society, a Voluntary Schools Association, and St Bede's College. During his time at Westminster he founded the Crusade of Rescue, the Catholic Truth Society, the Converts' Aid Society, and the Catholic Social Union; and he had seen the foundation stone laid of Westminster Cathedral which was completed in 1903 shortly after his death.

But Vaughan had also condemned socialism and had made no attempt to follow Manning into the socio-political world. He had campaigned for the Voluntary Schools and had urged his people to use their votes in defence of their schools. To help them do so, a number of Registration Societies had been formed in various parts of the country as early as 1867 when working men first got the vote. The passing of the 1870 Education Act with its hidden threat to the Catholic Schools had led to a surge in registration which was formally taken up by the Catholic Union in 1872 as one of its main activities. In 1873 a Registration Committee had been formed to advise local Societies, and by 1874 there were 52 such Societies in London alone. Members of these Societies visited the homes of Catholic men entitled to vote, persuaded them to take steps to ensure that their names were included on the electoral roll, and advised them as to how to use their vote at election time.

It has to be said that their work showed few signs of success. In 1906 there were in the whole of England and Wales only 12 Catholic borough councillors, not a single Catholic county councillor, and only 52 Catholic Guardians of the Poor out of a total of 824. In 1906 two convergent developments made it imperative that Catholic voters should become more active. The first was the return, with a massive overall majority, of a Liberal government pledged to abolish the Voluntary (including Catholic) Schools. The Catholic body would have to be roused, united and active, to oppose such a move. The second was the growth of the Labour Party with its emphasis on secularism in education and on rationalism as a philosophy. Catholics who supported Leo XIII's concept of social justice and who might normally have been expected to vote for the Labour Party, feared that that Party might move too far to the left. Tom Burns and other trade unionists in Salford, in common with Catholic trade unionists in other parts of the country, urged vigorous and united action to prevent this.

The Catholic Federation began on 1 March 1906, when 'a number of workingmen from Manchester, Salford, Eccles, Royton, Ashton, Liverpool and Warrington met to discuss some means of opposing the policy of the Trades Union leaders and the Labour Representation Committee on the Education Question'.

Casartelli gave the new movement his full support. He devoted a whole pastoral to the subject, selected its title and laboured to bring every Catholic organisation within its ambit; moreover, he helped develop an organisational structure whereby each parish society and confraternity had a voice on the parish branch of the Federation which then sent delegates to the Diocesan Committee. Not all priests supported their Bishop: the Rector of St Joseph's, Halliwell, Bolton, dismisses it as 'practically useless or mischievous . . . ignores the clergy . . .'; the Rector of St Alphonsus' was 'secretly hostile'; the Rector of St Aloysius' '. . . declared that there was no branch in his parish nor would there be . . .'.

Nor did most Irish voters support the Federation, seeing it as an English-based attempt to distract Irish voters from their true interest – Home Rule for Ireland. The Federation was also opposed by many socialist-minded Catholics who saw it as a Trojan horse aimed at weakening the approach to a socialist solution to society's problems. These divisions in the Catholic body were unfortunate in two respects. First, in 1906, despite the activities of the Registration Societies, not many Catholics had the vote. The franchise depended on residential and property qualifications – only the adult male ratepayer was entitled to vote. Too many of the Irish moved too frequently, from one lodging-hovel to another, to earn the residential qualification; again, too many of them were not ratepayers but mere lodgers in overcrowded houses. What disqualified many was that they had been in receipt of Poor Relief – which automatically removed them from the electoral roll.

Thus, in North-West Manchester, out of a total of roughly 10,000 voters there were only about 900 Catholics. And in 1906 the Liberals had declared war on the Voluntary Schools; a united opposition would be needed if the Liberals were to be thwarted.

In London, Archbishop Bourne spoke at a mass rally in the Albert Hall aimed at rousing the Catholics in defence of their schools. On 14 October 1906, Casartelli noted in his diary: 'Deo Gratias. The magnificent demonstration in Belle Vue, organised by our new Catholic Federation, has been a wonderful success this afternoon . . . extraordinary enthusiasm . . .'. One of those who spoke at that rally was a twenty-six-year-old building contractor, Tom Locan. His boyish appearance and evident enthusiasm, combined with the forcefulness and quality of his speech, drew him to the attention of the main organisers of the Federation who included John O'Donnell, a Manchester stockbroker and close friend of Casartelli's. Locan, in his turn, brought his cousin, John Gibbons, to the forefront of the Federation's affairs and in this almost accidental way the founders of the Catenian Association came together for the first time.

But this was still 1906, and the Association not yet even an idea, let alone a reality. The Federation movement spread: Leeds, Middlesbrough, Liverpool and other northern dioceses used Casartelli's scheme as their model. And, of great significance for the student of Catenian affairs, many Bishops turned to men who later were to help form Circles of the Association in their dioceses. There was, for example, the young Leeds solicitor, E. Fitzgerald-Hart, who had long been active in the Leeds Registration Society and whom Bishop Gordon asked to lead the Federation. Brothers of the Leeds Circle will know that this same Fitzgerald-Hart was to be the Founder President of their Circle. In such ways was the Association born of the Federation.

The Federation appeared to go from strength to strength. In 1910 it founded a journal, *The Federationists*, edited by Frank Pendergast, already a member of the Catenian Association. In 1911–12, Tom Burns won a major victory inside the Labour Party, at whose annual conferences there had always been a resolution in favour of 'secular education'. Burns used his power as secretary of the National Confederation of Catholic Trade Unionists – an offshoot of the Federation – to get the motion defeated (1911) and removed from future discussion (1912). But, in fact, for many people the Federation had suffered a mortal blow in 1908 and, while it continued in existence until the 1930s, it was never again the influence that it had been.

To understand this 'mortal blow' we have to go back to the Liberal victory in the 1906 election. Manchester had seen two signs of that victory: in Eastern Manchester, the Tory leader and former Prime Minister, A.J. Balfour, lost his seat, while in North-West Manchester, a young renegade Tory, now a Liberal, Winston Spencer Churchill, defeated the sitting M.P., William Joynson Hicks. During that election campaign Churchill had his headquarters at the Midland Hotel where later the 'Chums' were to meet and where two Manchester Circles still meet. During that campaign Churchill also saw for the first time some of the horrors of that poverty about which, hitherto, he had only written at second hand.

The new government's first Bill, introduced by Augustine Birrell, the President of the Board of Education, on 9 April 1906, was an Education Bill, proposing that all elementary schools receiving aid from rates or taxes should be controlled and maintained by the L.E.A.s. Religious teaching could be given on two days a week but not by the regular teachers, all of whom would be appointed, without a religious test, by the L.E.A.s. This Bill, designed to abolish Church Schools, passed its Third Reading in the Commons in July by 369 votes to 177.

The Bill was drastically amended in the Lords; the Commons rejected the Lords' amendments; the Lords insisted on them and on 20 December the Bill was withdrawn. Birrell became Chief Secretary for Ireland in January 1907, and the next anti-Catholic Education Bill was introduced into the Commons by Reginald McKenna, who became President of the Board of Education in January 1908. His Bill was withdrawn after its second reading in the Commons (February 1908), following which the Prime Minister, Campbell-Bannerman, resigned owing to ill-health. In the ensuing Cabinet reshuffle, Asquith became Prime Minister, McKenna went to the Admiralty and a Liverpool M.P., Walter Runciman, became President of the Board of Education, promising to bring in, and see through, a Bill to satisfy the Nonconformist demand for an end to denominational schools.

Churchill too had been affected by the reshuffle, for he entered the Cabinet as President of the Board of Trade in succession to his friend, Lloyd George, who had gone to the Treasury in succession to Asquith. At that time, promotion to Cabinet rank led (by an Act of 1705) to a by-election. The 1705 Act had been passed by a Commons which resented the way in which the last of the Stuarts had won the support of some M.P.s by giving them 'offices of profit under the Crown' – or 'jobs for the boys'. As a result of that Act, when an M.P. gained Cabinet rank – and a salary as a Minister – he had to go back to his constituency and fight an election. This was changed by the Representation of the People Act 1918, so that if a man was promoted within nine months of a General Election he was exempt from having to fight the seat again. In 1926 the Baldwin government abolished the 1705 Act.

In April 1908, however, Churchill had to go back to Manchester to fight off the challenge of Joynson Hicks. The by-election was made the more colourful because the militant suffragettes were out in force, led by Christabel Pankhurst who was manhandled out of the Free Trade Hall when she tried to put the question: 'What are you going to do about Votes for Women?' There was also a groundswell of unrest among the Irish, who were instructed by John Redmond, leader of the Irish M.P.s, to vote for Joynson Hicks to show their anger at the Liberal refusal to deal with the Irish question. There was also a Marxist member of the Social Democratic Federation standing as Labour candidate, who raised the issue of rising unemployment and inflation – a modern note and a new one, for prices were rising for the first time after having fallen consistently for about thirty years. Dan Irving, however, made little impact on the electorate and had to wait some years before he finally got into the Commons as M.P. for Burnley.

The election campaign was provided with light relief by the Manchester Barmaids' Association, which campaigned against Churchill because the Liberals had introduced a Licensing Bill which threatened to limit the number of public houses as well as opening hours. The Barmaids were led by Eva Gore-Booth, one of the Anglo-Irish squirearchy, who showed her ability as a horsewoman by driving a carriage, decorated with anti-Churchill bills, through the streets of the constituency. She and her more famous sister, Constance, later the Countess de Markievicz (one of the leaders of the 1916 Rising and the first woman to be elected an M.P.) are commemorated in Yeats's poem which ends with the lines:

> Two girls in silk kimonos, both
> Beautiful, one a gazelle.

When Churchill went back to the Midland Hotel in April 1908 to fight the by-election he found that the chairman of the Liberal electoral committee was Alderman James Thewliss, a great-uncle to the future Prime Minister, Harold Wilson. Churchill also had the help and support of the important Jewish community, led by Nathaniel Laski, whose son, Harold, got his first taste of politics at this election. Churchill was also made to realise that the nationwide swing, evident in by-election results, was sufficiently strong in North-West Manchester to compel him and his supporters to set out to garner every possible vote – including the precious 900 Irish votes. Churchill got Asquith to promise that the government would turn to consideration of the Irish question in the next session of parliament. This was enough for Redmond to instruct the Irish to throw their support behind Churchill.

On the other hand, the leaders of Casartelli's Federation were disappointed when Churchill declared his support for the government's proposals on education. They agreed with Joynson Hicks, who declared that the proposed Education Bill 'breathed enmity against the Church of Rome'. Here was the source of untold friction inside the Catholic community – and not only in North-West Manchester but wherever the Federation organised a meeting. Was the Catholic voter to support the Liberal (and Home Rule) and risk the wrath of the Federation's members? Or was he to vote for the Tory (and against the Education Bill) and so anger those who favoured Home Rule? In this Catch 22 situation the Catholic population was bitterly divided in a campaign which brought out **the worst in human nature**. Families were split; congregations quarrelled; meetings of branches of the Federation often ended in brawling.

By the time of the election several members of the Federation were already meeting informally and laying plans for the organisation of a new Association, as we shall see in the next Chapter. But the election (which saw Churchill losing the seat he had won in 1906) led them to include in their discussion a motion that their new organisation would be '... non-political. We shall never permit wrangling nor dissension to mar our harmony or interrupt our proceedings ...'. Members of the Association will recognise part of the charge read to a new man on his initiation into the Catenian Association which had its origins in the thickets of Catholic socio-political developments of 1908.

6. *The Eucharistic Congress 1908*

Almost as a footnote to the twin questions of bigotry and the Federation came the issue of the holding of a Eucharistic Congress in London in September 1908 – by which time, of course, the Association had been formed in Manchester. This Congress was a landmark in the history of the Church in this country; for the first time there would be a Papal Legate in England. There would also be seven Cardinals, and over a hundred Archbishops, Bishops and

Abbots. Bourne, with his usual thoroughness, had made careful preparations and had obtained the approval of the police authorities for the procession of the Blessed Sacrament planned for the last Sunday of the Congress. The proposal that such a procession should pass along the streets near the Cathedral roused the antagonism of some fanatical Protestants and threats were made that the procession would be attacked. The police, however, were confident that they could deal with any trouble. A few days before the procession. Bourne received a message from the Home Secretary, Herbert Gladstone, suggesting that the plan should be abandoned as 'provocative to Protestant sentiment'. The Archbishop wrote to Prime Minister Asquith saying that he would, of course, obey any official order but not a private letter, adding: '. . . and I shall give the matter the fullest publicity in order that my action may be amply vindicated.' Asquith gave the official order and the procession was cancelled. The government was criticised in some sections of the Press but most saw it as a justifiable halting of a 'blasphemous procession'. The Catholic 'upstarts' had once again been put in their rightful place.

CHAPTER TWO

The Manchester 'Chums' 1908–1909

1. When did they start?
A great historian, Herbert Butterfield, warned fellow-historians against looking for 'patterns in history . . . which does not repeat itself'. He said that anyone seeking to unravel the tapestry of history would find himself holding 'ropes of sand' that would disappear as the tapestry was being examined. So, too, with those who look for the date on which the Association was founded. A number of people have provided their own dates. Unfortunately, none of them agree.

The first 'authentic' dating was made in March 1924 by the then President of Manchester (No. 1), the former Alderman Fyans. He was addressing the Circle on the night of a special meeting called to celebrate the fact that their original roll, a vellum document, could take no more signatures. This was, in a sense, the end of an era which had started with the initial fourteen signatures in 1908. Some of those original signatories were present to hear Fyans – O'Donnell (1 on the roll), Gibbons (2), W. J. O'Brien (11); while also present were others who had enrolled in the early days – W. C. Jordan (15), H. F. O'Brien (16), and J. Delahunty (19). Each of these spoke during the course of the evening and none of them disagreed with Fyans, who had said that the Association was formed 'in June 1908'. In fact it had been in existence for some time before O'Donnell wrote to Casartelli on 14 May 1908.

In January 1943 an article appeared in *Catena* headed: 'How the Association started'. It was probably written by Frank Rudman, the Grand Secretary, who had taken over the editorship of the magazine during World War II. He gave a general outline of the early days, explaining that, 'There are no records of the meetings held before the foundation [for which he does not suggest a date], such records as did exist were lost in one of the fires resulting from an air raid.' In criticising Rudman's article, Frank Pendergast (13 on the Manchester roll) alleged that the Association was formed 'as a result of a split among Irish Nationalists and among Catholics with Irish sympathies as a result of the present Prime Minister (Mr Winston Churchill) being defeated by Mr Johnson [*sic*] Hicks at a bye-election [*sic*] when Mr Churchill took the Government side on the Education Question'. But only a month elapsed between the fateful by-election and the writing of O'Donnell's letter of 14 May. Someone had drawn up a Constitution and set of Rules (to which Pendergast refers in his article), and had got these agreed with the other members of the incipient Association before 14 May. No one who knows anything about the politics of forming an Association, still more a Catholic-Irish one, would dare suggest that a mere month was enough for such a task. So, Pendergast's evidence, like that of Fyans, is more than a little suspect.

A letter from the daughter of John Gibbons (2 on the original roll) appeared likely to throw some light on the question of dating. Mrs Catherine Sheehan wrote:

The *very* first meeting was held at my parents' home, Templefield House, Queens Road, Manchester. Those present were my father, his close friend and neighbour, John McMahon (who was Chief Engineer with the Manchester Corporation Transport Dept.), the two Whittle brothers who were Master Printers in Salford and I *think* (I may be wrong) Mr Worswick.

That, one might think, would be a lead from which one might get a clue as to the date – of that '*very* first meeting', until the writer goes on to say, 'As I was only three years of age when the Chums was founded . . .'.

The origins of the Association were examined in the first of a series of articles on 'The Story of the Association', written in 1954–55 by the then Editor of *Catena*, Sydney Redwood. Redwood alleged that

> the Chums Benevolent Association had its beginnings in a tiny group of Catholic businessmen in Manchester, who used to meet and eat together as friends but with no formalities binding them. Then one day they commented on the fact that one of their number had not been seen for some weeks, and they thought it would be a good idea to look him up. It was. He had run into trouble, and the others immediately and generously came to his aid. That, we are told, was the genesis of the Chums Benevolent Association. Whether the story is true or apocryphal matters little.

This last remark is strange, coming from one who claimed to be 'recounting some of the events in the history of the Catenian Association'. It is also regrettable that he did not say by whom 'we are told' of the informal lunches.

However, there is more to this story than apocrypha. For Pendergast also refers to 'informal lunches' at which some Catholic men met together at regular intervals before the Association was founded. That the Catholic men should have sought each other out in this way would not have appeared strange to our forefathers, for, as Rudman wrote,

> The men of the present generation [1943] can have but little idea of the position of isolation in which Catholics lived as recently as 40 years ago. There were then few opportunities for social intercourse among Catholic men, even among those of the same parish. There were parochial concerts and parties at rare intervals; there was usually an annual reunion, at which there was opportunity of meeting people of other parishes, but of organised social intercourse there was not any.

O'Donnell, Locan and Pendergast met from time to time on Federation business; Gibbons was first cousin to Locan, who might have naturally invited him to join the others at lunch. The Whittles were involved in Federation affairs as printers, while Tait (p. 25, below) and Holt (p. 24, below) would have been natural sources of finance for the Federation. Such internal evidence suggests that there was every likelihood that these men might have organised occasional, even regular, lunches.

And that 'internal evidence' is further strengthened by consideration of the relationship between the Association's founders and the Bishop. That they should have asked for his 'blessing and approval' was both natural and prudent. Natural, because they were already working closely with him on Federation affairs, and they had seen him approving the formation of other Federation-based societies – a savings bank, a cycling club, a benefit society, registration societies and an association for Catholic trade unionists. They would have hoped for similar approval for their Association for 'professional and business men', while prudence would have told them that his approval was essential if they were to get the support of other Catholic men.

But it is unlikely that their approach in May was the first indication they had given him of their intentions. Indeed, granted that they met him regularly on Federation business and that the Bishop had a great personal affection for O'Donnell, it would have been surprisingly ungracious if they had not discussed their proposed venture with him prior to the sending of their May letter announcing its formation.

This suggests that the 'original foundation' may have taken place well before May 1908, which would have allowed time for preparing and writing the original Constitution and Rules. Tradition has it that this was the work of J. Whittle (No. 4 on the original roll), a tradition confirmed by Pendergast. This Master Printer, whose brother, Richard, was No. 7 on the original roll, was not present when the Chums met in June. He had committed suicide.

The fact that the first Constitution and set of Rules were based on the rules and constitutions of several existing societies – including those of the Freemasons – coupled with the fact of Whittle's suicide, has led to the speculation that he was a Mason, that the rules and constitution were based on those of the Freemasons and that the unhappy man's suicide was due to the mental strain arising from conflict between his religion and his Masonic allegiance.

But in an article in *Catena,* Pendergast wrote: 'The Constitution and Rules were drawn up by Mr T. A. Locan. . . . It was collated by him from several Friendly Society Rules. . . .'

Whether Whittle or Locan wrote the Constitution and Rules, the fact remains that the author had to study 'several Friendly Society Rules' before submitting his proposals. This task must have taken some time and further confirms the need to date the 'original foundation' back into April or even March 1908.

Indeed, Manchester Circle celebrated its 70th birthday on 17 March 1978. For, according to Past Grand President Joe McMurray, 'there is an old tradition that the start of the Chums was in March 1908'. It would seem fitting that the Association which emerged from the undergrowth of Catholic-Irish politics should have been founded on the feast of St. Patrick. In any event, that is more likely to have been the date than was June, as declared by Fyans when he spoke in 1924, or 14 May, the date when O'Donnell and his friends sent their letter to Casartelli.

2. The original aims and objects

If we do not know exactly when the Association was founded, we have definite clues as to *why* it was founded. In the proposal sent to Casartelli we read:

> Objects: – to promote the interests of the members and their families by the individual and collective actions of its members. To help one another by their influence both directly and indirectly in their various daily walks of life so as to further the prosperity and happiness of each other.

And later in the enclosure, as part of what was described as 'the President's address to the candidate', we read:

> We are united together not only for the wise purpose of helping each other commercially as far as we possibly can, and to assist those who require our aid, but for moderate enjoyment and friendly intercourse and the temperate interchange of social feeling.

It will help us to understand these limited aims if we look again at the occupations of the men who first formed the Association. With the exception of O'Donnell they were not 'professional' but 'business' men. Frank Pendergast pointed out in articles and conversation that professional men did not join 'till it had been in existence for two years'. And while some of these men were engaged in printing and textiles, the main progenitors were Locan and his cousin, Gibbons, both of whom were involved in the building trade. They knew that their tenders for council work were often rejected in favour of tenders submitted by contractors who were also Masons. They, and others, hoped to be able to obtain a monopoly of Catholic business by a system of inter-trading. Indeed, one of the original 'Chums' referred to this in a letter written to *Catena* in 1926. Having wrongly described himself as 'the first Catenian' (he was only No. 11 on the roll), W. T. O'Brien wrote of: 'the sole reason for the existence of the society, viz. The Association was formed as a purely Catholics [*sic*] *Commercial* undertaking'. He complained that there was too little of this inter-trading so that, in his opinion, the Association was betraying its first principles.

The first two deputations to the Bishop after May 1908 went to ask for his help in business affairs. In his diary for Friday, 25 September 1908, the Bishop noted:

> Received a deputation of 'Chums' (five, including Ms. Locan and R. and Wm. O'Brien) re this new organisation of Catholic business men for self-defence and in their common interests. Evidence of unfair competition of Freemasons, Dissenters, re want of support by Catholic architects.

The 'Chums' wanted the Bishop to persuade Catholic architects responsible for the design and building of Catholic schools, churches and halls, to direct business their way. Many other men obviously had the same ambitious expectation of the new Association. For it expanded, as we shall see, fairly rapidly. Men joined only to resign within weeks of initiation. Having hoped for so much, they left the Association when it became clear that Catholic inter-trading offered relatively little, for there were few Catholics in a position to offer business or contracts.

But this 'Catholic Masons' smear has been allowed to stick. Indeed, in November 1923, priests in the vicinity of the Thames Valley. (now Wimbledon) Circle held a public meeting to discuss the proposal: 'Since Catholics cannot be Masons, how can they belong to a Catholic secret society – the Catenian Association?' That the Association was not a secret society, that its members took a pledge and not an oath, that it was 'proudly Catholic' and that its members were well known to their Bishops and priests, did not (and in some places still does not) save the Association from misjudged, sometimes malicious, accusations.

Thus, one of the main aims of the original founders could have been only partly realised. This takes us to the consideration of that 'moderate enjoyment and friendly intercourse and the temperate interchange of social feeling'. The son of a 'Chum', Charles Holt (No. 5 on the original roll), writes: 'The whole idea of the Chums being started was to counteract drinking among Catholic young men in Manchester. Hence their first and golden rule was ONE drink per meeting – this they adhered to strictly.' Gibbons's daughter makes the same point: 'Just a thought – In my father's time, the Catenians were allowed two drinks – no more – at each meeting, and were given two tokens which they presented for each drink. How times have changed! Yes?'

But whether one drink or two, the fact was that the 'Chums' met monthly and also held whist drives and official dinners, as well as dances and smoking concerts. Social psychologists may see in these gatherings a number of unspecified aims, varying from retreat into the assurance of the 'ghetto' to the discovering of a self-confidence which, in time, helped to create a more outward-looking, able and willing Catholic middle class. To help further this development, Casartelli advised the 'Chums' not to allow or invite priests to become members of the Association. There may have been a number of reasons for such advice – that he did not want his priests to be out and about at too late an hour and at purely social functions; that he feared that the expense of membership would either fall on the lay members or force priests to spend overmuch of their small income on 'worldly pleasures'. Whatever the reasons, Pendergast recalled:

> Bishop Casartelli was certainly responsible for the veto on the clergy being members. I was not present at the meeting but I was present at the second meeting with him where comment was made on the wisdom of his suggestion. It was by no means a surprising suggestion to those who knew him. He had found a great deal of opposition to his scheme of Catholic Federation from various parish priests. Time after time he championed the Catholic layman.

Casartelli hoped that, freed from clerical supervision and control, Catholic laymen might the better learn how to act independently. He had supported the efforts of Tom Burns and Catholic trade unionists in their particular field, and he equally supported the 'Chums' in their very different field. For the 'Chums' was formed by, and for, better-off Catholics. This was indicated by the phrase 'professional and business men' and by the annual subscription noted in the original proposal – 21s. per annum.

The Old Age Pensions Act (1908) provided that from January 1909 the over-seventy was to receive a weekly pension of 5s. The 'Chums' asked for a subscription which was slightly more than four times this pension – and in that sense, represented something like £100 in our inflated currency. This put membership well out of the reach of all but the better-off. This has given rise to the accusation that 'the Catenian Association is snobbish'. It may be that, at some times, the conduct of some Circles has justified this accusation. But the majority of Brothers have come from modest or even humble backgrounds – as did most of the 'Chums'. Not all have forgotten their roots; but they have come to see that, in a materialistic society, the Church can be the better sustained in its mission if a staunchly loyal body of educated Catholic laity have greater influence in the professions, business and commerce – and have greater economic power.

The limited aims which the 'Chums' set themselves have been the subject of much debate and many criticisms. They have been re-defined since 1908 and there have been some small additions, but each re-definition, amendment or addition has kept to the spirit of the original proposal. There have been calls for radical changes – some wanting the Association to become part of some ill-defined Catholic Action movement, others wishing it to become the financial backer to voluntary activities, without saying whether the Association should back all, or only some, or merely one, of the many deserving charities which, in their private capacities, most Brothers support. It is worth noting that the debate on 'Aims and Objects' has gone on almost ceaselessly since 1908.

During much of that time the founders of the Association were still actively involved. Casartelli lived until 1925, O'Donnell until 1934, O'Brien until 1946, and Pendergast until 1964. None of them supported moves for radical change; indeed they gave their support to those who fended off demands for change.

And the reason for this is that the main aim of the Association is only to be found in the charge which is read to each candidate on his initiation. This has changed in style over the years. But in 1908 Locan wrote, as part of the President's address to each initiate:

> . . . in your domestic relationship we look to find you if husband affectionate and trustful, if father regardful of the moral and material well being of your children and dependants, as son dutiful and exemplary, and as friend steadfast and true.

In an age which attacks the concept of the family and the morality which was accepted, even if only as a convention, in 1908, in an age which is not merely materialistic but pagan, there can be little doubt that this 'Object' is even more necessary now than when first proposed in 1908. It may be that the Association has many reasons for pride: in its work for the Beda College, in the Battle for the Schools in the 1920s and 1940s and in its work more recently for the handicapped. But even if it had none of these justifications for its 'social intercourse', if it could only claim that at the end of each meeting it had sent men home with their moral convictions reinforced – albeit unwittingly – by an evening spent with like-minded and 'proudly Catholic' men, so that they were able to be the better 'husband', more competent 'father' or dutiful 'son' it would have justified its existence.

3. The founding fathers

John O'Donnell was the President of the infant Association and the first man to utter that initiation charge. His life story is typical of that of many of the Catholic Irish of the time, even if he was of Scottish stock. He was born in May 1863; his father, a Scotsman, was often unemployed, so that the family lived in very poor and distressing circumstances. They lived in Ancoats, Manchester, and O'Donnell went to St Anne's parish school. His mother was a refined and gifted woman who provided the intellectual stimulus to John's early life.

He left school when he was only twelve years old and went to work in a cotton mill. Unlike most boys of his time and age, he had the drive to go to night school where he studied shorthand, at which, later in life, he became a recognised expert with a European-wide reputation. It was this study which enabled him to move from the mill floor to the office of a velvet-making firm where his wife-to-be was a skilled cutter. She, Jane Emily Harding, was the daughter of a decorator (whose grandchildren still remember the fascination with which they watched him mixing his paints). Her mother was an Irish Catholic, who persuaded her decorator-husband to become a Catholic only late in life.

O'Donnell married Jane Harding in 1886, she being anxious for the marriage 'so that she could look after the thin, delicate and underfed young man'. The marriage took place in her parish church, Salford Cathedral, where she was a member of the choir under the baton of Leslie Stewart, composer of such well-known songs as 'She's my lady love' and 'The Lily of Laguna'.

Shortly after his marriage O'Donnell went to work in the office of a Mr

Nicholson, a stockbroker. At that time and for the next thirteen years the family lived in a small house at 2 Albion Place, Lower Broughton, where five of the O'Donnell children were born. By 1898 O'Donnell had taken over the stockbroking business after Nicholson's death and in that year moved house to 372 Lower Broughton Road, while moving his office to 50 Barton Arcade, Manchester. His children remember that he had many periods of great difficulty while building up his business, sometimes having to use his wife's Co-operative savings to tide him over.

In 1906, by which time three more children had been born, the O'Donnells moved to a five-bedroomed Victorian house, Kersal Dale Villa in Higher Broughton. This had a garden running down to the river and a view over the racecourse on the other side. It is the house which the O'Donnell children best remember, where two children were born, the tenth and last, Clare, arriving in June 1908 – one might say, a Catenian child. As a reminder of the changing value of money, it is worth noting that this house cost O'Donnell only £100. Here he had his own library into which the children and their mother were allowed entrance only to dust and clean.

The more prosperous, widely-read and intelligent O'Donnell was a well-known member of the Catholic community and a close friend of Casartelli's. He was a gentle person, who, as one priest recalled, 'reminded me of Cardinal Newman with his combination of gentleness and keenness and breadth of mind'. That breadth of mind was illustrated by his insistence that all his children should go to grammar schools, and by the encouragement he gave his daughter, now Sister Raphael, O.D.C., when she wanted to go to University to qualify as a doctor. The proud father was happy to look after the business side of the medical practice which she set up in Higher Broughton in the 1920s.

There were a number of indications of his intellectual ability. He was an expert at deciphering ancient manuscripts; he read Italian and French; he was keenly involved in politics, as were most intelligent Catholics of the period. But perhaps the most revealing indication of his worth was 'that Bishop Casartelli thought the world of our father'.

It was from his office in Barton Arcade that O'Donnell sent that letter of 14 May 1908. And it was at this office that the Association's founders held some of their first meetings and, for some years, the meetings of the Council of Manchester No. 1. This office is near the Royal Exchange, the source of O'Donnell's business, and is surrounded by reminders of Manchester's history – the statue of Cobden and the Free Trade Hall, the Town Hall and the statues of Bright and Gladstone, St Peter's Field, scene of the Peterloo Massacre, and St Mary's, 'the Hidden Gem'. There is something particularly fitting that a history-making Association, by and for laymen, should have been founded in the district which is itself so steeped in history. And while the first few meetings of the Manchester Circle were held originally at Ingham's Hotel, then at the Albion Hotel, from March 1910 the Manchester men met at the Midland Hotel. This hotel is itself a historic monument, not only to the railway age with its neighbouring station now demolished (a latter-day reminder of the decline of the railway) but to the history of the theatre. For the Banqueting Hall of the hotel is built on the site of the first Horniman Repertory Theatre. Modern visitors to the hotel are reminded of this former theatre by the large alcove on the Windmill Street side – which was the foyer of that theatre.

O'Donnell was a quiet and gentle person, hardly suitable, it seemed, to be the leader of a group of thrusting, self-made laymen trying to form a new

Association. Indeed, as we shall see, Tom Locan was a more important influence than O'Donnell. So too was No. 2 on the roll, John Gibbons. He was born in Chester in 1858 of Irish parents who emigrated from Co. Mayo. His father, Michael Gibbons, and the Australian Cardinal Gibbons were first cousins. John Gibbons came to Manchester from Chester and, in time, his daughter recalled, started his own business, 'I'm sure in a small way', in the building trade. Through 'rough, hard work, determination and with the help of a wonderful wife – my mother – by his side, built up a very successful business as a Public Works Contractor. During his busiest times he had a 100 workforce and had contracts for Manchester and Salford Schools, hospitals, factories, Woolworths, Lewis's, etc., etc., etc.' The prosperous Gibbons became eventually a governor of Notre Dame Convent and a manager of three Catholic primary schools, and was well known in the Catholic community.

His daughter understood that 'the *very* first meeting was held at my parents' home', and, whatever truth there may be in this, there is little doubt that Gibbons was a major force in the formation of the Association, indicated by the fact that he was invited to be No. 2 on the roll. After his death in 1938 his daughter was told: 'My father refused the Presidency three times (not that he boasted about it).' One of O'Donnell's daughters threw some light on this when she told me, and reiterated, 'Father didn't talk "Lancashire" '. One has the picture of the older Gibbons, more prosperous than O'Donnell (who was moreover burdened with a larger family), already in some ways more of a public figure than the shyer stockbroker, but conscious of the fact that he did not have the same 'image' as the more urbane, Newman-like O'Donnell.

'O'Donnell was responsible for keeping us together . . .', wrote Frank Pendergast, but it was Tom Locan 'who did most of the work at the beginning and was really responsible for the beginning. His energy and initiative was [*sic*] amazing.' Locan was a cousin of John Gibbons 'though much younger and a *very* successful business man and was one of the Company of National Road Builders in Britain'. Locan, born in 1880, was another of those self-made Irishmen whose energy and intelligence had allowed him to enjoy the same sort of social mobility as O'Donnell. It was he, as we have seen, who wrote the first Rules and Constitution and who recruited Pendergast, who became joint secretary with him when the Manchester Circle was formed 'because Locan was in a low state of health through overwork . . . for months Locan and I spent several nights each week collecting suitable names, writing some and visiting others'. Not everyone was interested in the new Association; some were satisfied that, without the help of the Association, they had 'made good'. Thus, the very wealthy Alderman Carus of Liverpool was invited, came, but did not join; neither did Dan Boyle, an Irish Nationalist M.P., nor at first did Alderman Dan McCabe, later to be a luminary of the Manchester Circle, of the Association and of Catholic life at large.

For the human element played its part in the development of the Association. Locan's earlier speech in the Free Trade Hall in defence of Catholic Education had annoyed many of the Irish with its plea for support for the Tory candidate. And the Irish were an important part of the original 'Chums'. Indeed, Pendergast wrote of a dinner with the Bishop with

> most of the leaders of the Thomas Davis United Irish League, including Alderman Dan Boyle who had been elected, although a Mancunian, as M.P. for a constituency in Co. Mayo in 1906, and Alderman McCabe, who was afterwards knighted and became Lord Mayor of Manchester some years later; but, alas for our hopes, few

joined and those not among the leaders. Alderman Boyle never joined the movement, but Alderman McCabe joined about the time he was asked to be Lord Mayor in the City,

But the number of Irish in the early Association is indicated by the names on the first roll – the O'Briens, Corrigan (No. 12) and McMahon (No. 24). And the Irish did not easily forgive what they saw as Locan's 'treachery' in opposing Churchill. Maybe they also resented the drive and ability of a young man who may have been the less able to withstand their criticisms because of his own ill-health, made the worse by his activities on behalf of the Association. At one time he threatened to resign but was prevailed on to stay. He remained a member of the Circle until he resigned on 16 January 1913. The records provide no reason for this resignation. One can only regret the loss of such a driving force at such an early age.

Charles Holt (No. 5 on the roll), the first Treasurer, was a representative for a firm of calico printers, and in 1913 became the first foreign representative of the Calico Printers' Association because he could speak French fluently. Travelling extensively on the Continent, the bachelor Holt learned German and Spanish. In August 1914 he was in Germany when war broke out. He was arrested and put into the 'Rulevan' Camp for political prisoners. In 1915 he was released and repatriated to England. He was then appointed to represent the Calico Printers' Association in Egypt, a post which he held for the next seventeen years, coming back to England at six-monthly intervals. For most of this time he retained his membership of the Association which he had helped to found and, as his son writes,

> ... the aims of the Association were always in his mind, even to the extent that he always said that it was his prayer that I would meet my future wife through the Association. As a lad of seventeen years of age, you can imagine my replies!! Nevertheless, his prayers came true and in 1946 I joined Blackpool Circle and, as a Social Committee member, met my present wife who was a devout Catholic.

By this time Charles Holt, the constant traveller, had ceased to be a member of the Association. But his son continues:

> Much pleasure now, as you can imagine, and then I got Dad to come back into the Association. He was a member for a few years and died as a member as he presumably wished to do.

The younger Holt's reference to his wife being 'a devout Catholic' and the elder Holt's prayer for his son's future marriage serve as reminders that another of the aims of the Association, and one that has been more than realised, is the fostering of friendships between members' families.

As part of the preparation for the writing of this book a questionnaire was sent out asking Brothers, among other things, to say what benefit they felt they had gained from the Association. Almost all answered, in one form or another: 'Friendship'; and many with whom the question was discussed made it clear that they felt that they owed a debt to the Association for the many close and dependable friends they had made as a result of their membership. Among those who wrote and spoke in this vein it was possible to pick out certain groups who felt this in a particular way. There were the many converts who had felt a special 'isolation' when they left their former denomination. There were the many immigrants, and particularly the many Poles who had settled in Britain during and after World War II, who had found a welcome into

Catholic life through their membership of the Association. There were also the many who, like Frank Holt, had met their future wives at Catenian functions or who were pleased that their children had met their future spouses at such functions. O'Donnell, Locan, Holt and the rest could never have dreamt of the multifaceted web of friendship which they had started to weave in 1908.

Among 'the rest' was John Tait, who was born in Newry in 1851 and who, like so many Irishmen of the time, had come to find work in industrial England. As a boy he worked as a warehouse porter in Manchester, but by 1908 he had become 'one of the principal men at Daniel Lees, a rather important Catholic firm in the cloth trade in Manchester'. Here was another of those self-made men who had made their ways from humble beginnings. In 1908, Tait lived in Dane Bank, Disley, Cheshire, a reminder that the Association was formed by men from widely separated parishes, in each of which a small number of the emerging Catholic middle class lived in relatively unsplendid isolation. The value of the Association to these men was immense, for it allowed them to enjoy 'social intercourse' in a socially-congenial and Catholic atmosphere.

4. The early meetings

The first few meetings of the Association were held at Ingham's Hotel, Chorlton Street, Manchester, which was partially destroyed during World War II. Members of the modern Association would have found these meetings very different from the formal meetings which they attend today. There were, for example, no opening or closing prayers. The meeting was divided into three parts. First, there was a business meeting. Then there was a social period, usually in the form of a musical session, but interrupted whenever an initiation was due. It makes strange reading now that the 'Worthy President' asked the Brothers to be 'upstanding' and to stop smoking while the initiation took place. Today's newcomers may be glad to know that one original custom was abolished in the 1920s – the one which insisted that the initiate shook hands with everyone in the Circle. When later there might have been over 400 at a Manchester meeting and over 300 at a Liverpool meeting this must have been both an awesome as well as a dangerous practice. The final section of the evening's meeting would then take place – sometimes a discussion, sometimes a lecture by a visiting speaker. In this sense the 'Chums' were, no doubt unwittingly, undertaking a form of adult education.

The early Minute Books carry frequent mention of 'Musical Evenings', 'Musical Programmes', 'Lists of songs to be sung during the social evening' – reminders of a world which has now entirely gone, when men and women alike carried their music with them when they visited friends and when every home had a piano, for which music sheets were bought as young people today buy pop records.

These first Minute Books also remind us that the 'Chums' had to find their way slowly, and that they were influenced by the practices of a number of existing societies, including the Freemasons. The meeting of the Association was called, at different times, 'a Lodge' (30 July 1908), 'a branch' (20 August 1908), 'an order' (15 October 1908), before it finally became known as 'a Circle' (25 February 1909). The term 'Brother' was first used on 22 April 1909, and this led to the Association being described as a 'Brotherhood' (16 June 1909). By this time the Brothers had set up a Committee to devise 'modes of recognition and certain signs' (18 February 1909). These signs and passwords were finally approved at a meeting held on 22 April 1909; new members did not receive these 'modes of recognition' until they had attended their second meeting – presumably to test their resolve to persevere. Older men will remember the last such sign, 'the Salute' used when Brothers addressed their President at the Circle meeting. One placed the forefinger of the right hand outside the lapel of one's coat, the clenched fist being placed against the breast. This was supposed to indicate that one spoke from the heart, to which one was pointing. Its abolition in 1965 was regretted by many traditionalists but one imagines that attempts to bring it back would be greeted with howls of derision.

Certainly that was the reaction of the men at a meeting of the Manchester Circle in 1945 when the aged O'Brien (who was to die in 1946) told them of the original signs and passwords. There were signs to use on business and visiting cards. One wrote one's number (on the roll), the number of one's Circle and the year of one's enrolment, one above the other at the side of the card. This was supposed to alert the recipient, who would then, it was thought, take pains to see that whatever he could do would be done to help the incoming visitor. But there was frequent confusion over their use. Many men continued to use them after resigning or lapsing through non-payment of subscription – which led to the demand for an annual review of these signs. The mind boggles at the complexities into which this might have led us. Even more mind-boggling was one of those 'modes of recognition' which allowed Catenians to recognise each other while walking down the street. One pulled one's tie downward to the left – and, if the oncomer was a Brother, he pulled his to the right. What happened if he was not a Catenian? Presumably he gave one an odd look – while one continued to search for a Catenian along Manchester's crowded Piccadilly or London's Oxford Street, frantically pulling one's tie, until, perhaps, one choked! It is small wonder that the Manchester Brothers of 1945 burst into laughter – deeply though this angered the traditionalist O'Brien, who remembered how important these signs had seemed in the early days.

We would also find strange the names and appearance of the officers at the meeting. From 26 November 1908, 'Worthy Brother President' was the correct mode of address, while from 17 June 1909 there was a 'Master of the Revels' to lead the social part of the evening. To ensure that no strangers came into the meeting there was 'the Tyler' who later was to become 'Brother Guard' until the recent abolition of this office. Only after the first Annual Meeting (17 June 1909) was 'Worthy Brother President' given a collar to wear at the meetings (8 July 1909), while the other officers received clasps and badges.

By this time, June–July 1909, the Association had expanded. Locan and Pendergast had written to and called on 'suitable gentlemen'. In July 1908 an advertisement was inserted in the Catholic Press and copies of this were sent to 'Catholic gentlemen in the district'. In September 1908 the Association laid plans for a 'social evening' to which gentlemen were invited by cards headed: 'Chums Social Circle'. Originally this social was planned for 21 October 1908, but when it was discovered that this was the day of the Municipal Elections, the date was changed to 5 November.

On 30 July 1908, the members of the small Association had agreed 'on the proposition of Bros. O'Brien and Whittle that a Dinner be held when the membership of the Grand Lodge reached fifty'. The growth of membership led to such a dinner being held on 17 December 1908. It was a glittering affair with the Bishop as guest; members were allowed to bring guests and, whether as a result of its success or not, some twenty men asked to join in January 1909. Invitations had also been issued to prominent Catholic men – including Dan Boyle, Alderman Kenny, Mayor of Hyde, and Richard Holden, K.S.G. (who was to become the Founder President of Blackburn in 1910). Tickets were sent to members and to gentlemen whose applications for membership were under consideration – at a cost of 5s., the equivalent as we have seen, of an Old Age Pension.

We also read of other forms of Circle activity which today's Catenians might find naïve. There were, for example, whist drives (28 January 1909), a picnic to Hope and Castleton (10 July 1909) at a cost of 6s.6d. per head, and smoking concerts (4 March 1909 and 12 September 1909). By that time the 'Chums' had approved a new set of 'rules and regulations as compiled by and approved by the Committee' (25 February 1909). These included the Association's motto, 'Each for all, all for each', an outline of the Objects of the Association which is historically interesting because of its reference to 'C' professional and business men and to the interests of 'C' youths entering business or professional life. It is a reminder of the atmosphere of hostility in which our predecessors lived that, while they spelt out 'Catholic' in their letter to the Bishop, they used the initial 'C' in the first rule book, which might, by accident, have fallen into non-Catholic hands. That they were at the same time 'proudly Catholic' is all the more to their credit, since to be such required more courage than is needed in today's very different climate.

The Rules also went on to define 'a Chums Circle' as the place where the Brothers met 'for pleasure and business intercourse'. The government of the Association was to be in the hands of a Grand Council consisting of the officers of each Circle (including the 'Tyler'), all past Grand Presidents and all foundation members – a sign that even then the 'Chums' were aware that their infant might itself give birth to other Circles.

This expansion outside Manchester was, in the first instance, the work of McDermott (No. 32 on the roll) and one of his protégés, Hogan of London, who was enrolled into the Manchester Circle in October 1909. The efforts of these two men were to lead not only to a rapid expansion of the Association but to a change of name and the adoption of a new Constitution and Rules. It may be fitting to conclude this survey of the first months of the Association's history with a note of the elevation of Brother Alderman Thompson (No. 39 on Manchester's roll) to the office of Mayor of Eccles for the year 1909–10 – the first of a long list of Catenian Mayors, and an answer to Casartelli's plea for Catholic men to go out to play their part in the world. The 'Chums' held a dinner to mark this 'elevation' at the Albion Hotel on Thursday, 25 November 1909, by which time the energetic McDermott and the enthusiastic Hogan had laid well their plans for the opening of a London Circle, an announcement which was 'received with applause' at the meeting of the 'Chums' held on 7 October 1909.

CHAPTER THREE

Out from Manchester

1. J. McDermott, J.P.

At the beginning of 1910 it was still dependent on the enthusiasm of a few, but afterwards it became too big for any small group to control, though credit must always be given to those who saw the value of the movement after it had been in being for two years and then gave it a breadth and a background which was truly extraordinary. *I give the credit for the beginnings to Locan, O'Donnell, McDermott and Hogan* [my italics].

So wrote Frank Pendergast in 1943. We have already considered the work of Locan and O'Donnell – and it is interesting that Pendergast puts them in that order. Hogan's role will be considered in this and subsequent chapters and is fairly familiar to London men in particular. But McDermott has received scant mention in previous accounts of the origins of the Association, although he was the main driving force in the initial expansion and was personally responsible for bringing Hogan into the Association.

Joseph McDermott was one of 'a list of names' read out at the meeting of the 'Chums' held on 12 November 1908 and 'laid on the table as being desirous of joining the Association'. With five others he was initiated on 26 November and – a sign that his ability was quickly recognised – on 23 December 'on the motion of Bro. T. A. Locan . . . .it was unanimously decided to ask Bro. McDermott to become a member of the Committee'.

McDermott may well have inherited his drive from his father, Richard McDermott, who had been one of the four founders of the Ashton-under-Lyne Co-operative Society. The first such co-operative had been founded at Rochdale in 1844, and the example of the Rochdale Pioneers had been followed by other self-helping working men, anxious to break the power of the mill-owner's 'tommy shops', where they were overcharged for inferior produce. This is not the place in which to examine the difficulties of founding a co-operative, of getting the necessary capital, or buying and selling the goods – all in the time available to the founders after they had done a normal day's work. Richard McDermott, like the Rochdale Pioneers, must have had special qualities. These helped him become, in time, the President for twenty-five years of the Self-Actor Mule Spinning Association of Ashton-under-Lyne and neighbourhood – a sign that his fellow-workers recognised his ability to organise and run an Association which improved their 'social status' while curtailing the activities of 'the more wild spirits'.

Joseph McDermott did not follow his father into the textile industry. He became an electrician, and, in a short time, an electrical contractor – the firm which he founded still exists in Ashton-under-Lyne. It may help us to understand him if we remember that electrical engineering was still in its infancy, attracting men with more vision, drive and initiative than did the older, well-established and staple industries such as textiles. These were the men who were to carry Britain into the new stage of that continuing industrial revolution – a stage marked by the development of industries such as petrochemicals, food processing, chemicals and electrical engineering.

A J.P. since 1895 and an active worker in local affairs, McDermott was 'one of the signatories of the Articles of Association' when the Electrical Contractors' Association was formed. He became the second President of the Association (1905–6), being No. 8 on the roll of the Association. His fellow-contractors showed their appreciation of his ability by electing him to the Central Board of the Association and making him one of the first delegates to be appointed to the Northern Section, of which he became Chairman in 1910. When he died he was Chairman of the Manchester branch of the E.C.A., and was remembered as 'one of the Association's hardest workers as well as one of the most jovial and kind-hearted of friends'. A thorough man in all that he did, McDermott visited all the branches of the Northern Section in 1910–11, and was the 'means of very considerably increasing the membership', even though he was 'physically unfit and to the writer's knowledge journeying on propagandist work when he ought to have been home in bed'. His wife, who outlived him by many years, confirmed that opinion, adding only that his sudden death at an early age was due to his 'wearing himself out travelling all over the country, at times unfit, furthering the causes of both E.C.A. and Chums'.

In his work as an electrical contractor, McDermott met a number of other Catholics in the same industry, for here, as in the building trades, there were fewer built-in obstacles to the progress of enterprising Catholics. Some of these became important men in the history of the Catenian Association, most notably, perhaps, Hogan, Holden, the Founder President of Blackburn Circle, and Neville, one of the founder members of Leeds. A glance at the occupations of the early members of the first Circles shows that a number of them were members of the E.C.A. or were electrical engineers. Frank Pendergast was one such: born in Bolton in 1880, the son of an immigrant from Co. Mayo, he studied engineering and, after working some time in an office, joined an electrical firm.

This McDermott-induced link with the E.C.A. may help to explain why on 15 January 1909, when the fledgling McDermott nominated six men 'as being desirous of joining the Association', the list included the Mayor of Hyde, Dan Boyle, M.P., and, most significantly for Catenians, Richard Holden, K.S.G., J.P., of Blackburn – which was ultimately to prove significant for the Catholic men of Blackburn, when steps were taken to form a Circle in that town.

2. McDermott, Hogan and London

Through the E.C.A., McDermott had become friendly with Edward J. Hogan who was a Captain (not, as often claimed, a Major) in the Regular Army, and was for some years stationed at the barracks at Ashton-under-Lyne. McDermott knew Hogan's father, who had his own firm, 'Hogan and Wardrop, Merchants and Manufacturers of Electrical Supplies, Charing Cross Road, London W.C.' When his son went to Ashton-under-Lyne around 1901, Hogan *père* asked McDermott to look out for the young Catholic officer, who was a regular visitor to the family home for some years. In July 1910, Hogan wrote to McDermott on notepaper headed: '2nd Battalion City of London Royal Fusiliers'. Hogan asked McDermott to write him a recommendation in support of an application he was making for 'an appointment with the L.C.C.' on the grounds that 'you have known me since [1899 crossed out] 1901'.

In the autumn of 1909, McDermott invited Hogan to be his guest at a 'Chums' dinner. Hogan recalled that evening in an interview he gave to *The Universe* in December 1930 on the occasion of the 21st anniversary of the founding of the London Circle. He said that 'when he made the acquaintance of the new organisation in Manchester he knew only four Catholics in London'. This must, in some sense, have been an exaggeration, for he must have known dozens of Catholic men – in his parish in New Barnet, in the ranks of the Fusiliers, and among his father's workforce. He really meant that he knew only four Catholics of his own class. The Catholic community was still lop-sided – over-represented among the gentry and the working class, and under-represented among the middle class.

Hogan's appreciation of the socio-religious value of the mutual support generated by the 'Chums' was so great that he determined to form a Circle in London. The Manchester Committee readily agreed and invited him to come to Manchester to be initiated at a private ceremony attended by O'Donnell, Pendergast, Gibbons, Locan, Tate and, of course, McDermott. Pendergast later wrote:

> It took place in a private room at the Albion Hotel and the six of us celebrated the ceremony by a private dinner in the same room. Hogan had been introduced to us by Councillor McDermott [he was never a Councillor] and while I have put Locan as the originator of the movement, I have no hesitation in stating that Councillor McDermott was responsible for spreading it out of Manchester. After his initiation he undertook to go up to London to see certain influential Catholics there and the initiation of Major [another error] Hogan was the result.

It is a pity that Pendergast did not provide us with a firm date for that initiation. Writing in *Catena* in July 1955, Grand Secretary Tanner claimed that it had taken place on 9 September 1949! Allowing that the printer's imp made the one mistake, and that Tanner really meant 1909, we might expect to be on firm ground, until we examine Hogan's membership card at Head Office, on which we find that Tanner has written in: 'November 1909. Initiated during dinner following a Circle meeting in Manchester'. It is clear from Pendergast's article that the initiation took place before a dinner and that it did not follow 'a Circle meeting'. As to the date, the then Grand Secretary managed in his two versions to have bracketed the correct date, which was 7 October 1909.

This creation of unnecessary tangles in the undergrowth of our history is, unfortunately, typical of much that has been written – in Circle Histories written to commemorate one or another landmark. One such perpetuated myth is that, prior to the founding of the London Circle, Casartelli wrote to Cardinal Bourne to win his support for the new Association. Indeed, in writing to McDermott on 29 November 1909, Hogan reported:

> Things are going smoothly. I am arranging for a preliminary meeting this week to settle procedure for 13th Decr. We can discuss the larger development *and the Archepiscopal recognition when you come to town* [my italics]. Mr. Malone is 'red hot' on it – he will be a useful member being a J.P., a committee member of the Metropolitan Water Board, etc., etc.

The inaugural meeting of the London (No. 2) Circle took place at the Old Gaiety Restaurant, later pulled down to make way for Marconi House.

O'Donnell, Gibbons, Locan and McDermott travelled south for the ceremony, which was conducted by O'Donnell who initiated a chemist, an export buyer, and Lionel Caunter, an electrical engineer with his own firm at 86 Charing Cross Road, not far from Hogan's father's firm. It was Caunter who was Founder Vice-President of the new Circle until April 1910 when Patrick Bernard Malone who had been 'red hot' on it was initiated (8 March 1910) to become Vice-President in April.

The London Circle grew quickly, ten men being initiated in January and six more in February and March 1910. No. 9 on the roll was John Callaghan, whose sudden death left 'his widow and family in very straitened circumstances . . .'. On 19 April 1910, the Committee of the Manchester Circle voted to send £5 from its Circle funds immediately and resolved that 'the attention of the Brothers should be drawn to same in the May Circular with a request for donations'. The Benevolent Fund had, in a sense, been born.

But before this, the new Circle and its lively President had made their impact on the development of the Association. On 25 January 1910, the Manchester Committee met and heard

> a letter from Bro. Hogan, London Circle, re ceremonial, and Bro. Locan reported on a discussion they had had on this subject and it was decided to adopt as far as possible the system at the next meeting of the Circle on Thursday Feb. 10th, 1910. It was also decided that the committee and officers should meet earlier to practise the same.

It is strange now to recall that the Manchester men had had no ritual until this date and that opening and closing prayers were not said until the 1920s when, again, they were introduced at London's request.

At the Committee meeting of 25 January 1910, 'The Committee then dealt with the question of the post of paid Secretary.' Three men had applied for the post, and Joseph William Shepherd. A.S.A.A., the youngest member of the Circle, got the job. This is not the place to consider the value of his work in these formative years and as the Association's first Grand Secretary. But it is worth noting that 'on the motion of Br. W. O'Brien seconded by Br. Miller it was decided that the secretary should not have a vote nor be permitted to speak except at the request of the President'. The uneasy relationship between the Association's officers and its Secretary – which will be discussed elsewhere – has deep roots.

3. Leeds and Liverpool

The appointment of Shepherd was, we can see now, fortunate, because the Association was poised on the brink of its first wave of expansion. At a Committee meeting in Manchester on 17 February 1910, 'Bro. McDermott reported what he was doing re the proposed formation of a Circle in Leeds which was very satisfactory and met with the hearty applause of the Committee . . .' and O'Donnell, McDermott and Locan were 'authorised to visit Leeds and endeavour to establish a Circle'.

In fact, by 17 February a good deal had already been done. Casartelli had written to Dr Gordon, Bishop of Leeds, who was very ill at the time. It was his Co-adjutor, Dr Cowgill, who replied to the Founder Bishop, assuring him that Dr Gordon 'will be very glad to welcome "Chums" and will give the promotion of the Association every encouragement'. Casartelli had handed that reply to McDermott, who had then written to Dr Gordon to ask

... if your Lordship could advise me of a suitable professional or commercial man capable of bringing together the leading Catholics in Leeds. I have had the name of Mr. E. F. Hart, Solicitor, mentioned to me. I have not the honour of acquaintance with this gentleman and as so much depends on the tact of a local man to bring all sections together your advice would be of great value.

Gordon replied to McDermott directly, confirming that Fitzgerald-Hart was the right man to contact, whereupon McDermott wrote to him. Having explained the nature of the Association, 'to promote the interest of Catholic Youth entering a Professional or commercial career', and having assured him of the support of the Bishops of Salford and Leeds and 'of the Archbishop of Westminster', McDermott asked Hart if he would

bring together a number of Catholic gentlemen, say in the first week in March, when a deputation from our Foundation Circle would attend and explain the aims of the Association and possibly proceed with the formation of a circle at a later date.

Fitzgerald-Hart was an admirable choice. He was the son of a convert solicitor, who became the first Catholic County Councillor for the Soke of Peterborough. Himself educated at Ratcliffe College, he qualified as a solicitor and in 1904 took over the established Leeds practice of Coghlan and Co. He was an active Catholic, working for the S.V.P., solicitor to a number of diocesan organisations and joint secretary of the first National Catholic Congress held in Leeds in 1910. He had been the first secretary of the Leeds Catholic Federation, and in the course of his work for that body had come to know most of the prominent Catholics in the city. He had also acted as registration agent for the Federation, and in 1907 he had succeeded in getting 104 Catholics put on the electoral roll, while in 1908 he got the Revision Courts to accept 3000 claims for registration.

By 1 March McDermott had had a favourable reply from Fitzgerald-Hart and on 10 March the Manchester Committee resolved that a delegation should go to Leeds on 21 March to meet Hart and 'other gentlemen'.

This meeting was so satisfactory that in recent *Directories* it has been taken as the date of the foundation of the Leeds Circle. Indeed, even the Manchester men seemed uncertain as to what had happened, because on 4 April the Manchester Committee resolved 'that the Secretary write London and Leeds requesting full list of members for purpose of Directory also asking that copies of circulars issued by these circles be forwarded to Manchester'.

On 19 April, however, the Manchester Committee resolved that 'the Secretary is authorised to visit Leeds and make the necessary arrangements for calling the first meeting of that Circle'. At that Manchester meeting of 19 April McDermott reported that he was busily engaged in making arrangements for opening a Circle in Newcastle – of which more later.

On 12 May 1910, O'Donnell and McDermott led a deputation of Manchester men to Leeds for the inauguration of the Leeds Circle (No. 3) at the Metropole Hotel. Fitzgerald-Hart was installed as Founder President of the Circle, which included a cross-section of the Catholic community, including V. Neville, an electrical engineer (and one of McDermott's other contacts in Leeds), and G. Jacomelli, 'Restaurateur', who was to play a significant role in the re-naming of the Association.

But by this time the energetic McDermott was already busily engaged on expansion elsewhere. Some time in March he had got Casartelli to write to the Bishop of Hexham and Newcastle 'and also to Dr. Foggin, a leading Catholic gentleman of Newcastle'. McDermott himself had then written to the Bishop explaining the nature of the Association

> composed entirely of Catholic professional and business men for mutual help and the placing of Catholic youths leaving school in situations where they may have an opportunity of rising in the world and for helping members if and when misfortune overtakes them.

He had gone on to say that 'in accordance with our practice we desire to secure your approval before commencing operation in your diocese'.

On 1 April 1910, McDermott wrote to Anthony F. Donald, a prominent Newcastle businessman, explaining the nature of the Association, its approval by various members of the Hierarchy and its expansion into London and Leeds, claiming that 'a branch' had already been 'opened' in Leeds – which, as we have seen, was not quite true. McDermott met Donald in Newcastle on 12 April 1910, when he also met Dr Foggin and, as the Manchester minute book noted,

> these gentlemen had expressed their willingness to take up the matter of forming a Circle in that City. The Secretary was instructed to write to Dr Foggin asking if he could arrange a Meeting for Tuesday the 26th inst. when the deputation from the Manchester Circle would attend.

There is no record of Foggin's reply except that 'arising from Dr Foggin's letter it was decided to leave the fixing of a date for Newcastle Meeting to the delegates appointed to attend'. The slight disappointment that was possibly felt at this temporary set-back must have been more than compensated for by the excitement doubtless felt at the forthcoming opening of the Leeds Circle.

Before examining the further expansion of the Association it is worth noting that on 24 May 1910 the Manchester Committee rescinded the decision taken on 25 January concerning the role of the secretary in their affairs and resolved that 'the Secretary should have the same status in the Association as any other Brother'. In this way did the Manchester men pave the way for the creation of the powerful role of the Grand Secretary. They had little idea of the significance of this decision. Indeed, and maybe rightly, they were more concerned with trying to keep up with McDermott's efforts on their behalf. By the time they met again on 17 June 1910 he had already written to the Archbishop of Edinburgh, enclosing with his òwn letter one to the Archbishop from Casartelli, whom McDermott had asked to help in this expansion of the Association into Scotland. McDermott told the Archbishop that he would be in Edinburgh on business 'on Monday and Tuesday next' and asked him to 'recommend to us a suitable gentleman to assist us in the formation of an Edinburgh Circle'.

McDermott reported to the Manchester Committee on the success of his interview with the Archbishop, who 'had given his consent and approval to the formation of a Circle in his diocese', and the Committee decided that 'the deputation appointed to visit Newcastle should, if convenient, proceed to Edinburgh for this purpose'. It was fitting that at that June meeting 'a hearty vote of thanks [was] tendered to Br. McDermott for his labours in connection with the opening of new Circles', because at that meeting discussions also took place as to the opening of a Circle in Liverpool. To the Salford-based men who had, under Locan's urging, founded the first Circle, it may well have seemed almost too good to be true; London and Leeds were now functioning, and here they were talking of Newcastle, Edinburgh and Liverpool.

The fact that Liverpool, and not Newcastle or Edinburgh, should have been the next Circle to be inaugurated may seem strange. For Archbishop Whiteside of Liverpool had not been as forthcoming as the Bishops of Leeds and of Hexham and Newcastle. He was suspicious of this 'laymen only' organisation, and may have feared that it would divide his people, with the large Irish element preferring to follow the 'old politics' of the clergy-led support for Irish Home Rule rather than the 'new politics' of lay independence favoured by Casartelli. And, although McDermott told the Archbishop of Edinburgh that the 'Chums' 'have arranged to start [a Circle] in Newcastle on the 28th inst. [June]', and O'Donnell and McDermott were appointed 'to interview Mr. Lynskey or any other likely gentlemen in Liverpool with a view to opening a Circle there', the fact was that by the end of June 1910 neither of these efforts had borne fruit. George Jeremy Lynskey was a leading Catholic lawyer in Liverpool, the father of the eminent Judge Lynskey of post-1945 'tribunal' fame, and whose neighbour was a Catholic solicitor, Taggart, the father of a future and outstanding Grand President, Pat Taggart.

At the Annual Meeting of the Manchester 'Chums', McDermott's work received further recognition. He was chosen to succeed O'Donnell as President of the Circle, while O'Donnell assumed, as it were, an even higher office. For the expansion of the Association into London and Leeds had led to the creation of a Grand Council of representatives from each of the three Circles. This met quarterly, its first meeting being at Leeds on 29 July. By this time the Manchester Circle had formed a Benevolent Board and an Entertainments Committee and, under pressure from London, was beginning to come to terms with the need for a more structured ritual.

Meanwhile McDermott pressed ahead with his efforts to get Circles opened in Liverpool, Edinburgh and Newcastle, while also supporting the speedy initiation of R. Wilding of Blackburn 'for the purpose of facilitating the opening of a Circle at Blackburn'. McDermott had nominated the Blackburn electrical contractor, Richard Holden, as 'being desirous of joining the Association' on 15 January 1909, so that when Richard Wilding went back to Blackburn to find 'suitable Catholic gentlemen' he found one, at least, who knew something of the Association and of the enthusiastic President of the parent Circle, McDermott.

At the meeting of the Manchester Committee on 11 October three significant discussions took place. There was, first, one on 'the action of certain Brothers in sending to members circulars soliciting business'. There is no evidence of the decision reached – other than that Shepherd was 'requested to put in the Circular for our next meeting a paragraph on the lines of the matter brought forward by Bro. O'Donnell'. Then the Committee agreed that the 'Directory of all the members of the Association be in the hands of Brothers before January 1910' and through the kind offices of Past Grand President Frank Lomas, I have been able to use this Directory in my work on this book. Finally, it was agreed 'that a *Ladies' Evening* [my italics] be held on the 24th November 1910 at the Midland Hotel. Tickets to be 3/– Single and 5/– double. Evening Dress'. So another Catenian practice was born, with McDermott, his Vice-President Millers and Shepherd being given leave to organise the evening.

At that same meeting, Shepherd reported that he had been in touch with Bro. Byers, already a member of the Manchester Circle (No. 98 on the roll) with regard to his playing a part in the opening of a Liverpool Circle. Byers helped recruit Richard Rankin, a cotton merchant, Lynskey, a Liverpool solicitor, and John Lomas (No. 8 on the Liverpool roll), whose son, Frank, in his Presidential Address to the Brighton A.G.M. in 1963 said: 'I am old enough to remember the foundation of the Association in Liverpool. I recall the tremendous excitement and enthusiasm it engendered in my father and his friends.' That foundation took place on 15 October 1910, Liverpool becoming the 4th Circle – not, as might have been expected, Newcastle, which had unexpectedly switched the proposed date of its inaugural meeting to 26 October and so became the 5th Circle.

But by that time the Association had given itself a new and, some might say, more dignified name than 'Chums Benevolent Association', and the Liverpool roll bears the scars of that change of name, which took place, as we shall see, during a Grand Circle [sic] meeting held in Leeds early in October 1910.

4. Re-naming the Association

'I give the credit of the beginnings to Locan, O'Donnell, McDermott and Hogan.' So wrote Frank Pendergast in 1943. The impact of Hogan on the Association was almost immediate and certainly decisive. It was he, representing the London Circle, who asked for a new set of Rules, a new Constitution, a form of ritual – and, more to the point here, a new name. For while the title 'Chums' may have appealed to Manchester men, it was certainly less attractive to the more sophisticated Londoners, among whom were few of the builder-contractors and businessmen who had formed the first Circle, but more of those 'professional men' of whom there were all too few in the Manchester 'Chums'. By June 1910 the London correspondence was appearing on paper headed: 'Circle Benevolent Association' – allowing the use of the logo 'CBA' also used by 'Chums Benevolent Association'. Shepherd drew the attention of the Manchester men to this change in title and it was resolved 'that the attention of the London Circle be called to this matter and an explanation asked for'.

No doubt this matter was discussed at the meeting of the Grand Circle in July 1910, but nothing was resolved then. The Manchester men, however, heard more of it at their Committee meeting of 28 October – the last at which McDermott was to preside. O'Donnell, now 'Bro. Grand President', was called upon to report on 'the London Dinner, Grand Circle meeting and opening of the Newcastle Circle'. The London Dinner had taken place on 22 October, and one of the guests was Sir W. H. Dunn, who was to become the first Catholic Lord Mayor of London since the Reformation. What is not acknowledged in London's proud history is that Dunn went to that dinner as a result of McDermott's efforts, as is shown by the letter written by Dunn to McDermott: 'On my return to Town [from Blackpool] the end of the week, I will write to Captain [sic] Hogan, stating *as I promised you* [my italics] I would attend the Dinner on the 22nd. I shall have much pleasure in doing so.' O'Donnell's account of this affair must have pleased the expansionists in Manchester, particularly when he was able to report: 'The question of the initiation of Sir W. H. Dunn was under discussion and finally it was arranged *to leave the matter in the hands of the Bro. President* [McDermott] [my italics].'

Equally pleasing to the Manchester men must have been O'Donnell's report of the opening of the Newcastle Circle on 26 October, news which McDermott capped with his announcement that 'he had hopes of making arrangements for our establishment in Hull and Plymouth and within the next few weeks he hoped to have completed arrangements in Edinburgh'.

But less pleasing was O'Donnell's announcement of 'the alteration of the title of the Association to "The Catenian Association"'. Several men spoke 'regarding the change of title'. Some asked whether 'it would not be advisable to obtain approval from the various Bishops since the change of title'. But there is no evidence that anyone carried this idea any further.

So the title was changed. The written and oral 'history' of the Association is littered with errors of commission (and the creation of myths) and of omission. Among the myths is that Casartelli, off his own bat, wrote to all the Bishops of England and Wales trying to persuade them to help spread the Association. The truth, as we have seen, is that the kindly Bishop wrote when McDermott asked him to. And therein lies another myth – that it was O'Donnell who either wrote the letters, visited the various towns, or persuaded Casartelli to act on his behalf. Again, the truth, as we now know, is that it was McDermott who was the driving force – as it had once been Locan. Among the omissions is any acknowledgement to McDermott of his efforts in the 'histories' which have appeared to commemorate various landmarks in the development of Manchester, London, Leeds, Liverpool, Newcastle, Blackburn and Hull, although, as we have seen, it was McDermott who was largely responsible for the foundation of all.

But perhaps the most firmly established myth is that which has been connected with the re-naming of the Association. On 14 November 1945, Cambridge Circle celebrated its silver jubilee with a dinner at which 'after so many years [of war] we donned evening dress. Back to the old days and the old ways at last.' The toast of the Cambridge Circle was proposed by Bishop Leo Parker of Northampton, a good friend to the Association over many years, as befitted a former secretary of Casartelli's. When proposing the toast, the Bishop

> interested us very much by recalling that as Bishop's secretary to the late Bishop Casartelli, he was present when the founders of the Association approached the late Bishop for his views on the formation of such an Association. Our name, he said, originated from the chain of Bishop Casartelli's cross.

Bishop Parker then painted a verbal picture of the Bishop fingering the chain of his pectoral cross while O'Donnell, Locan, Tait and Gibbons listened to his opinions of the aims of the 'Chums' Benevolent Association – with the Bishop inviting them to change the name into something more dignified, suggesting that they should think of themselves as so many Circles linked together in a chain, such as the chain he was toying with. If they thought that this was a good idea then they might call themselves *Catena* or Chain. Everything about the story seemed so right – its author a bishop who had served with our Founder Bishop, the symbolism of the chain of the pectoral cross with its links, and the subsequent adoption of the linked chain as the Association's logo. It is little wonder that this became the received wisdom.

It came as a shock to many people when in 1954 Sydney Redwood wrote: 'Tradition asserts that the suggested use of the word Catena came from a Leeds member named Brother Jacomelli but nothing appears to survive to tell us much of this subject.' Redwood was wrong in his final assumption, although there were many who challenged his version about Jacomelli. In January 1955, Grand Director Wilfred Paines wrote to complain that Bishop Parker 'told me' about the Casartelli inspiration. Pendergast, however, came to Redwood's help in April 1955, when he wrote to point out that in 1908, when 'the founders of the Association approached the late bishop', Bishop Parker was not even ordained. Indeed, his obituary shows that he was ordained in 1915, long after the formation of the Association in 1908 and its re-naming in 1910. Bishop Parker had the good grace to reply to Pendergast. In July 1955 he explained that he had not been there when the founders first came to see the bishop, but that he had heard the story from Casartelli himself.

Now this again seemed highly probable. One imagines the Bishop with his young secretary coming away from some Catenian function with the older man giving the young priest an account of how it had all started. But then in his letter Bishop Parker ruined his own case by claiming that it was in 1912 that the founders of the Association had first approached Casartelli.

So what did happen? And how do we know? It is surprising that no one from London wrote to challenge Bishop Parker's allegations in November 1945. For there must have been Brothers still alive in London who had heard Hogan's speech at their 21st birthday meeting in December 1930. And there must have been others who had read an account of the interview given by Hogan to *The Universe* in December 1930, in which he said: 'It was a member in Leeds, Brother Jacomelli, who, during the Association's second year, suggested the *Catena* idea.' Maybe the fact that no one challenged Parker in 1945 lends support to Frank Rudman's opinion that 'only the wives read *Catena*'. In any event, Pendergast remembered 'Hogan telling me' that it was Jacomelli's idea, while further confirmation appeared in 1967 in a letter written to Redwood, who was then compiling more material for a film on the development of the Association. Miss Elizabeth Notari of Bath wrote on behalf of her aunt, Miss Louisa Jacomelli, then aged 88. She wrote:

> Francis Jacomelli was my aunt's eldest brother who owned a successful restaurant for many years in Boar's Lane, Leeds, in conjunction with his two brothers, Anthony and George. My uncle died in January 1925 [as did Casartelli] at the age of 48. . . . I recollect my uncle telling us that the name of the Association was changed at his suggestion to *Catenian*.

There are still those who like to think that, despite all the evidence, Casartelli must have had something to do with the change of name. They claim that it was almost inconceivable that O'Donnell would have allowed such a change without consulting his friend and our Founder Bishop. They also claim that if a layman had been asked to suggest a word for 'chain' he would have chosen 'vinculum', not 'catena'.

But this is to attribute latter-day schoolboy Latin wisdom to an Italian restaurant owner. For when I rang brothers of Italian descent to ask them which word they would choose to use for 'chain' they all gave 'catena' as the answer. As Pendergast pointed out, this is the Italian, as distinct from the Latin, word for 'chain'.

As to the Bishop's alleged part in the re-naming. Joe Shepherd, who was in Leeds in October 1910 and so knew that it was Jacomelli's idea, said that 'Bishop Casartelli was rather disappointed when the word "Chums" was dropped'. Shepherd did not say why, but his note ought to explode once and for all the myth started by Bishop Parker, in whose defence Pendergast kindly noted 'that it was a lapse of memory understandable in a very learned elderly man'. Like Alfred and the cakes, Bruce and the spider, Canute and the waves, the story of the Founder Bishop toying with his chain while suggesting a new title for the Association belongs to the undergrowth of history. It ought to have happened – but it did not.

5. Newcastle and Blackburn

One interesting by-product of this change of title may be seen by visitors to the Liverpool Circle. The Manchester men had already paid for the preparation of the membership roll and the scroll carrying the Presidential address to new members; and, not surprisingly, they had headed it 'Chums Benevolent Association', with the 'CBA' logo. But the name was changed shortly before the inauguration of the Liverpool Circle. There may not have been time to prepare a new roll; it may be that people were unwilling to spend the money to pay for a new one. In either event, the new name, 'Catenian Association', was pasted over the old title. This is not obvious until one has a photograph made of the document, when the old title and the logo can be seen beneath the new title.

The opening of the Newcastle Circle was to have a more than usual significance. Its Founder President, Dr Foggin, wrote the first Constitution of the enlarged Association (1910), and was to be the third Grand President (1913–16). Foggin became a legend, particularly on Tyneside, and his O.B.E. (1946) was welcomed as a fitting reward for an outstanding man. He was to die on Christmas Day (1946), as was noted in *Catena* in January 1947, when it was promised that 'his work for the Association in its early years will be told in our next issue'. It is to be regretted that this obituary never appeared. For Foggin had a view of the Association which, in many people's opinion, has still to be realised. Writing in 1917 he said:

> It is our wisest policy to content ourselves with leaving the evolution of ideals to come to us from below rather than to expect Grand Council to formulate elaborate plans and thrust them perhaps upon unwilling Circles which would have to carry them out. The way in which you can best achieve success will be to cultivate the spirit of work – Catholic lay work – any interesting Catholic objects, provided of course you can carry your Circle with you. Each Circle could then do a great deal if it takes up work in that spirit so that the interchange of reports and visits between Circles will lead to an emulation in good deeds.

Another early and distinguished member of the Newcastle Circle was Michael Holohan, B.Sc., who joined the Circle in December 1910. He was an outstanding schoolmaster, a long-serving senior master at St Cuthbert's Grammar School until his retirement in 1948. He became Grand President of the Association in 1932 and so impressed his colleagues on Grand Council that he was re-elected for another two terms of office – the only one to have been so honoured in peacetime, although, as we have seen, Foggin also did three years in the Chair, two of them during World War I. Holohan died in November 1958, so that Brothers on Tyneside had a long-lasting link with the early days of the Association.

The Blackburn Circle was inaugurated by O'Donnell at a ceremony held at the Castle Hotel on 16 November 1910. Shepherd, Millers and Wilding went with O'Donnell, who, however, lacked the support of McDermott, by now suffering from his terminal illness. Eight men were initiated, including the previously elusive Holden, who became the Founder President. Wilding did not sign the roll – although he became the Circle's second President.

The high esteem in which McDermott was held by his Manchester colleagues was illustrated by a decision taken at their meeting of 2 December 1910, when for the second time he was absent, and when the Vice-President, Millers, informed 'the Brothers of the continued illness of our President. The sympathy of the Brothers was communicated to the Bro. President by telephone.' On 6 December, O'Donnell went a stage further and sent a telegram: 'Catenians express sorrow your illness and hope early and perfect recovery. President.' He was unable to attend the meetings of the committee which was organising The Manchester Catholic Charity Ball, the joint secretaries of the Committee being Shepherd and Holt, of the Catenian Association – a reminder that members of the Association, even at that early date (14 January 1911), carried their action into non-Catenian fields. Nor was he able to accept the invitation to the third meeting of the Grand Circle, which was held at the Midland Hotel on 25 January. The invitation to the members of Grand Circle noted that 'all members of the Circle were invited to lunch at the expense of the Manchester Circle'. He received Shepherd's Circular of 2 February 1911 advising him that the meetings of the Manchester Circle were to take place on Tuesday, 7 February and Thursday, 16 February – an indication that for many years some Circles held two meetings each month, during each of which, as the Circular shows, it was 'Business 7.30 p.m. Initiation Ceremony 8.30 p.m.'

McDermott was missed in other places than Catenian functions. A Leeds electrical contractor wrote to him on 13 January 1911 to offer sympathy and best wishes for recovery and noted: 'I do not forget your hearty services to the Association [E.C.A.] and have been glad to do what I could as your co-worker. We always miss you when you are absent.' But on Thursday, 23 February 1911, McDermott died, aged 53. His funeral took place at Dukinfield Cemetery on Tuesday, 28 February, and in a notice headed IMPRESSIVE FUNERAL CEREMONY the local newspaper gave a list of the more prominent mourners. The Manchester men were there in force – O'Donnell, Gibbons, McMahon, Shepherd and others; Holden represented Blackburn, Neville represented Leeds. Representatives of various branches of the E.C.A., as well as 'fellow members of the E.C.A.', paid their tribute, as did representatives of various branches of the United Irish League.

The Manchester Circle organised a Requiem Mass said on Thursday, 23 March 1911 at St Mary's Church, Mulberry Street, at which Bishop Casartelli was present in the sanctuary – a tribute from one able and energetic man to another.

For if the Bishop was an essential *sine qua non* of the original formation of the Association, then McDermott has to be seen as the expansionist without whose efforts the Association might not have broken out of its Salford base. It is a matter of regret that he did not live to succeed O'Donnell in the role of Grand President – as he surely would have done. It is, however, fitting that the two Grand Presidents who followed O'Donnell – Hogan and Foggin – were both McDermott's protégés.

CHAPTER FOUR

The first wave of expansion

1. The growth of Manchester and London

In retrospect, many who lived through the last years before World War I, 'the Great War', remember them as idyllic years. Income tax was only a shilling in the pound – even after the 'rapacious' Budget of 1909. Living-in servants could be had for no more than £20 a year.

But a little research shows that these were years of turmoil, years in which many of the current problems of British society had their origins. Nationwide strikes by large, militant unions often led to clashes with the police and, as on 24 July 1912, to massive riots. Demonstration by suffragettes demanding 'Votes for Women' sometimes led to violence – as on 1 March 1913, when they smashed all the windows in shops in Oxford Street, Regent Street and the Strand, while on 3 April 1913 Mrs Pankhurst was sentenced for 'inciting persons to place explosives outside David Lloyd George's House'.

The House of Lords threatened to set the Constitution at nought with its opposition to Liberal socialism, while in Ulster the Protestants, backed by the Conservative party led by Bonar Law, prepared to make civil war against the British government and the proposed Home Rule Bill. With their slogan, 'Home Rule means Rome Rule', they gave new life to that latent anti-Catholicism which at best had only slumbered. Liverpool, for example, became a battlefield with the Conservative forces pledged to support the Orange creed. Organised clashes between Protestant and Catholic took place, particularly on 12 July, when the Orangemen commemorated the victory of William III at the Battle of the Boyne. On major saints' days Catholic men guarded their womenfolk and their streets, as Protestant gangs roamed the Catholic areas armed with buckets of excrement.

Middle-class Catholics escaped this physical violence, but suffered in other ways. There was, for example, the verbal attack on V. M. Durnford (No. 21 on the London Catenian roll) which appeared in a Protestant Truth magazine:

> Mr. V. M. Durnford, an Assistant Controller in the Central Telegraph Office, is the hon. secretary and treasurer of the Catholic Association and he has lately circulated a prospectus formed to acquire the Salisbury Hotel as a Catholic centre and residential club. A correspondent raises the question whether it is desirable that a civil servant of Mr. Durnford's rank should be prominently identified with the work of an organisation which must make a considerable inroad upon the time of the treasurer and secretary.

Sir Mark Sykes, an M.P. and a founder member of the Hull Circle, speaking at the London Catenians' Annual Dinner in 1914, noted:

> Although Catholics enjoy toleration, yet the shadow of the past remained. Things of the past still to a certain extent affected their lives. There was a tendency in English Catholics to fear public life, a tendency to retirement and self-effacement. Their [Catenian] association had many good objects, but the greatest of them was to give to the Catholic young man a social atmosphere which would tend to remove that social isolation and bind the young Catholic more closely to his faith.

The land-owning Sykes had not fallen into the trap created by 'toleration' in which 'an old boy of Stonyhurst' found himself when telling George Scott, 'I think of myself first as a public schoolboy and second as a Catholic public schoolboy.' Nor had the author of the article in *The Federation*, 1913, who noted, 'We are a minority in this country. On all sides latent prejudices and bigotry have erected barriers against our social advancement.'

A deep awareness of these 'prejudices and bigotry' was a major cause of the continued growth of the Manchester Circle which Alderman Dan McCabe finally joined (No. 149 on the roll). Like O'Donnell he was an Ancoats boy, although he had gone to the Christian Brothers school in Livesey Street before starting work as an errand boy. McCabe became a councillor as the Liberal and Irish Nationalist candidate in 1889, becoming an Alderman in 1902, the first Catholic to be so honoured. One of his reasons for joining the Association was that his Party wished him to become Lord Mayor. Joe Shepherd, now Grand Secretary of the Association and already a respected and successful accountant, undertook to organise a Catholic Fund to provide the money needed to maintain McCabe in the Lord Mayor's Mansion. In 1913 McCabe became Manchester's first Catholic Lord Mayor since the Reformation and was so popular that he was chosen to fill that office for a second term. Not surprisingly, the Protestant Press and his political opponents made much of the fact that on Mayor's Sunday he chose to attend his own church rather than the Anglican parish church.

The Catenians backed McCabe. They also backed other Catholics making their way in the world. The *Universe* headline, 'Manchester Catenians give Miss Mary Anderson a splendid reception. Bishop Casartelli's tribute', appeared over a report of a concert given by the rising soprano at the Manchester Hippodrome 'amid scenes of intense enthusiasm'.

Catenians also, as individuals, made their own contribution to Catholic and national life. There was, for example, William O'Dea, once a pupil teacher of St Anne's school in Ancoats, who led the Catholic teachers of the Salford diocese in their opposition to the 1906 Education Bill. These teachers, under Casartelli's inspiration, formed a Catholic Teachers' Guild and their example was followed by teachers in other cities and towns. The upshot of this action was the formation in December 1908 of the Catholic Teachers' Federation, with O'Dea as its President, of whom the Bishops thought so highly that they invited him to become a member of the Catholic Education Council. His parish priest at Ancoats went on to become Bishop Nulty, and it was he who said at O'Dea's funeral in October 1936 that O'Dea was 'the greatest Catholic teacher of his time'. O'Dea was only the first of a number of Catenians who have played a leading role in the educational world and in the C.T.F. Others of whom the Association has a right to be proud are J. J. Finan, President (1947–8), J. Branigan (1952–3), W. A. Exworthy (1962–3), and C. H. Sheill (1972–3), who was to play an important part in the formation of the Catholic Parents and Electors Association movement during the struggles over the 1944 Education Act.

McCabe, Anderson, O'Dea, and the Catenians generally, wished to show that Catholics could hold their own in their chosen fields. This may seem less necessary in more tolerant times – although even today to be a Catholic is a handicap, as medical students find if they try to specialise in gynaecology, or as applicants to Oxford University may find – 'one college, finding it had "too many" Catholics, made Catholicism a disqualification for entry as an undergraduate for the next two years', as George Scott discovered in 1967.

This ambition – to show that Catholics could make their mark and hold their own – helps to explain the insistence on 'style' in the early Manchester Minutes. There was, for example, the funeral of the late Bro. Bushell in October 1911, when the Manchester Committee resolved that 'Bros. Whittle, O'Donnell, Gibbons and Shepherd attend the funeral as a deputation and *engage a carriage for that purpose* [my italics]'. There was also the visit by the Bishop of Sebastopolis to 'our meeting' in February 1912 when 'it was decided that each member should attend in Evening Dress . . .'.

This sense of 'style' was more clearly seen perhaps in the affairs of the expanding London Circle. Hogan had claimed to have known only four Catholic gentlemen in London in 1909. By the end of its first year the London Circle had enrolled 41 members; by the end of its second year, 107; by the end of 1912, 204; by the end of 1913, 312; and by the time of the outbreak of war in August 1914 some 382 men had signed the London roll.

And what men! It is impossible to do justice to all of them, but imperative to say something about some. There was, for example, René Caraman, K.S.G. (No. 34 on the roll), an active worker in various Catholic fields whose private chapel at The Grange, Elstree, served as the local church until a church was built in 1932 – a reminder perhaps of the recent expansion of the Church in this country. Caraman, born in Smyrna in 1877, came to London in 1897, and was a leading member of the London commodities market, and for many years chairman of the London Dried Fruit Trade Association.

Then there was Sir W. H. Dunn (No. 50 on the roll), whom McDermott had helped recruit. A Land Agent, Auctioneer and Estate Agent who lived in style at 9 Gloucester Terrace, Regent's Park, then merely London N.W., he was to become Lord Mayor of London (1916–17), another of those 'Catenian Mayors' who answered Casartelli's call for men to go into public life.

H. T. Sandy (No. 56 on the roll) was a famous architect – with his practice in Stafford. That he should have attended meetings in London is an indication of the thirst that some, at least, felt for a Catholic social atmosphere. Sandy was to become the Founder President of the Birmingham Circle and to be Grand President in 1917–19, in succession to McCabe. Birmingham Brothers commemorate (maybe unknowingly) his work when they support the Father Hudson Homes which he designed.

Francis Skivington (No. 25 on the roll) became President (1913–14) in succession to Hogan, and was perhaps best known as the author of the Catenian Anthem dedicated to Cardinal Bourne. Baines (No. 62) and Hensler (No. 70) were to win greater Catenian fame as the founders of the City of London Circle (59). Charles J. Munich, K.S.G., F.R.Hist.S., (No. 82) was to be instrumental in obtaining for the Association the Apostolic Blessing. Sir Westby Perceval, K.S.G. and K.C.M.G. (No. 279), had been born in Tasmania. He was a solicitor and parliamentary agent who acted as Agent-General in London for New Zealand (1891–96) and Tasmania (1896–98). His niche in Catenian History was assured by the fine document, *The Catenian Association*, which he produced in August 1916 and in which he explained the nature of and need for the Association.

But these, even for the oldest of Brothers, are only names. With Paul Kelly (No. 103 on the roll), however, we have one who will be remembered by many Brothers, for it was only in December 1964 that he died, having long celebrated the fiftieth anniversary of his initiation, 6 December 1911. Kelly was born in the U.S.A. but became a naturalised Englishman. A director of several finance houses and engineering companies, he was a man of many parts. The holder of one of the first R.A.C. driving certificates (1905), at the time of his death he was one of the ten senior members of the R.A.C. Club. In the City he was a Past Master and member of the Court of the Curriers Company. As a Catholic he was a force in the affairs of the Catholic Social Guild, the Catholic Workers' College, the Conference for Catholic Industrialists and the Sword of the Spirit while that movement lasted. He worked for the S.V.P. and other charities, for the Society of St Augustine, which provides the money to maintain the Archbishop of Westminster, and for the Association, of which he became Grand President, 1931–32, and on whose Grand Council he remained a life member until his death.

2. Birmingham

But Hogan was not content with the success of the London venture. Like his mentor, McDermott, he was ambitious for the spread of the Association, and his success explains why Pendergast puts him alongside 'Locan, O'Donnell and McDermott'. It was Hogan who was responsible for the formation of the Birmingham Circle (9). Pendergast wrote:

> Shortly after [1911] I left for Birmingham and Hogan wrote me to arrange a meeting with Archbishop Ilsley [of Birmingham] and to get together a list of suitable names for a new circle in Birmingham. I saw Fr Dennis Shiel [of the Oratory] who suggested Bro. Hutton [No. 8 on the Birmingham roll] as the most suitable man to draw up suitable names and also told me how the interview with the Archbishop should be arranged.

The Birmingham Circle was inaugurated on 29 February 1912 at the Grand Hotel, Birmingham, when 21 men signed the roll. The Founder President was Henry T. Sandy, who signed the roll as No. 21, being already No. 56 on the London roll. He was, as we have seen, a prominent architect and was not, as described in the document issued for the Golden Jubilee of the Circle, 'a Stafford wholesale woollen merchant'. As in London, so in Birmingham the Circle attracted a number of eminent men. There was Martin Melvin, the owner of *The Universe*, who was to become the first Englishman to be awarded the papal decoration of K.C.S.G. There was J. B. Webb, whose printing and publishing experience was to be called upon when *Catena* first appeared in 1917. There was Frank Pendergast, who brought to the Circle that valuable link with Manchester and the 'Chums'. But above all there was Richard Brosch, who was destined to play a major role in the Association's history, one which entitles him to a place alongside Locan, O'Donnell, McDermott and Hogan.

Brosch was the son of a Polish immigrant who had left his native country in 1853 because, as his family recall, 'things were a bit hot for him in Poland but I don't know if he was a "Polish patriot" or just a "revolting peasant" '. The immigrant had settled in Nottingham, where Brosch was born. He went to Birmingham in 1898 and in time became a partner in the family firm of metal merchants which traded under the name of J. E. Meppledeck, and director of several other firms. Brosch had the energy which typified Locan and McDermott, Casartelli and Hogan. He was on the Tamworth Board of Guardians from 1910, and was to become an active member of the

Birmingham City Council after November 1929 – protecting himself from Protestant attacks during election campaigns with 'a local rugby team's forwards as bodyguards'. He was for many years the Chairman of the Public Health Committee of the city which had first been cleansed by Joe Chamberlain. Unlike Chamberlain, Brosch never became Lord Mayor; 'it was suggested that his Catholicity prevented his possible selection.' For Brosch was well aware of that bigotry and ignorance which led a waiter to say, in his hearing, at a Savoy function: 'I didn't know there were so many —— Catholics in the country.' Brosch would have understood the sentiment while deploring the expletive, for he was 'very proper' and 'not too broadminded, as was probably true of most of his generation'.

3. 1913, Annus mirabilis

Long before Pendergast had gone to Birmingham, Hogan, the eager expansionist, had been to see Bishop Peter Amigo of Southwark (December 1910) and explained the nature of the Association, while asking permission to examine the possibilities of founding a Circle in his diocese. Early in 1912 the Bishop gave his formal approval to the opening of a Circle, and in January 1913 Hogan reported to a London meeting that a Circle was to be opened in South London, a fitting accompaniment, he may have thought, for his own recent promotion to Major.

The first meeting of the South London Circle (No. 10) took place on Monday, 3 February 1913 at the Bridge House Hotel, London Bridge. The Founder President, Thomas Baines of the London Circle, along with ten other men from the parent Circle, initiated two new members as recorded in the Minutes kept by the Founder Secretary, Bernard Baines. Most of the Circle's records were lost when Baines's office was destroyed during the 1940 blitz.

Thomas Baines was to become Grand President in 1921, the first in a line of eminent Grand Presidents provided by this Circle – Kelly (1931–32), Stroud 'of Croydon' (1939–41), Sidney Quick (1966–67) and Dick Last (1979–80). The Circle also provided the Association with more than one Grand Treasurer: following Durnford of London there came the Heyburn brothers, Bernard and Edward. Bernard, the Circle's second secretary (1914–20), was Grand Treasurer from 1917 to 1920; and he was succeeded by his brother, E. L. ('Ted'), who held the office until 1949. Other eminent South Londoners were Sydney Redwood, Editor of *Catena* from 1947 to 1958, and Reggie Myers, President 1931–33 and 1941–44, who kept the Circle alive during the dark days of World War II. The historian has reason to be grateful to Redwood, who undertook some preliminary research into the Association's origins which was published in *Catena* in 1954–55. But the Association as a whole owes a debt to Myers, who opposed Grand Council's decision to remove the *De Profundis* from the Circle ritual. Myers led a local movement to include it in the proceedings of South London Circle and eventually compelled Grand Council to reverse its decision. South London went on to become the spearhead of the Association in the south, being responsible for the founding of Brighton (17), Thames Valley (now Wimbledon) (33), Kent (34), which lost its Charter during the War, Mid-Surrey, now Sutton Mid-Surrey (37), City of London (59), Croydon (60), Hastings (66), Bromley (68), Norwood (88) and Blackheath (99). It was also former members of this Circle who were responsible for the formation of the Dublin Circle (247). When one considers that many of these

THE GREAT CITY MEETING AT GUILDHALL.—(EXTERIOR.)

▲
The atmosphere in which the Association was founded. The Restoration of the Hierarchy (September 1850) aroused a frenzy of indignation. A mass meeting at London's Guildhall denounced 'Papal aggression' in violently un-Christian terms.

DIOCESE OF SALFORD.

THE SIGNS OF THE TIMES:

A FIRST

PASTORAL LETTER

BY

LOUIS CHARLES,

BISHOP OF SALFORD.

FIAT TUA VOLUNTAS

SALFORD

The title page of the Pastoral Letter which invited the laity to become 'The People of God on the march'

The letter of 14 May 1908 which accompanied 'the enclosed proposal' informing the Bishop of the formation of The Chums Benevolent Association.

The final page of 'the enclosed proposal' with the signatures of the Association's first officers.

John O'Donnell, the Manchester stockbroker, the Bishop's close friend and the one who 'kept us together at the start'.

John Gibbons, the Association's first Treasurer.

Charles Holt, one of the Vice-Presidents in May 1908; a photograph taken shortly before his death.

▲
O'Donnell's daughters, Sister Raphael (left) and Sister Clare (right) temporarily re-united for a Carmel celebration. Their brother, Francis, became the Franciscan priest, Father Oswald, whose death in 1974 saddened his many Catenian friends.

Edward J. Hogan, who as Captain Hogan, brought the Association to London and who, as Major Hogan, was one of the many Catenians affected by the First World War.

Joseph McDermott, the man who 'took the Association out of Salford'.

Francis R. Pendergast, joint secretary with Locan of 'The Chums', whose death in 1964 broke the last direct link with the men who first approached the Bishop in 1908.

Joseph Shepherd, whose death in 1975 brought to an end another link with the Association's founders.

Paul Kelly's driving certificate, one of the first to be issued. In this, as in so much else, Kelly was a pioneer.

Edward Fitzgerald-Hart, the Founder President of the Leeds Circle, in a reminiscent mood late in an active life. His death in 1966 broke the Leeds Circle's link with its origins.

John Lomas, founder member of the Liverpool Circle. ▼

THE FIRST WAVE OF EXPANSION

Circles have gone on to generate other Circles, it is easy to see why South London claims to be a major force in the development of the Association.

The opening of the South London Circle was the preliminary to the opening of a further nine new Circles which earns for 1913 the title '*Annus mirabilis*'. In April 1913 the Portsmouth Circle was inaugurated, largely owing to the energy of Hogan and the enthusiastic support he received from the secretary to Bishop Cotter, the then Fr King. It was fitting that, as Archbishop King, he should have been an honoured guest at the Circle's Jubilee banquet in April 1963, when he also celebrated Pontifical High Mass for the Brothers of the Circle.

The Southampton Circle, another of Hogan's 'children', was inaugurated the day after Portsmouth. There were fourteen foundation members, including Tickle *grandpère* who was not only to become an active Apostle for the Association but to be the father of 'Teddy' Tickle, who had the pleasure of initiating his own son into the Circle in the presence of his father so that there were three generations of Tickles in the Circle at the same time. The Southampton Circle also went on to help found Circles at Bournemouth, Reading, Plymouth, Exeter, Torbay and Winchester, and so contributed to the creation of a Province which has always looked to Southampton as a leading Circle.

Further north there was the opening of a Circle in Stoke-on-Trent in April and in Preston on 29 May. The Founder President of Preston, a Preston solicitor, O. A. Goodier, brother of Archbishop Goodier, S.J., became Grand President in 1919 – a sign of the high regard in which he was held by the giants who ran the Association in those days. An active Catholic, he was a mainstay of the Bishops during the struggle for the schools in the 1920s and 1930s and was rewarded for his activities with the decoration of K.C.S.G. in 1936. He was also a civic leader; elected a councillor in 1924, he became an Alderman in 1939, having been, in 1937–38, the year in which Preston won the F.A. Cup, the first Catholic Mayor of the town since the Reformation.

The formation of the Bradford Circle (15) bears a great resemblance to the way in which the first African Circle, Bulawayo (187), was formed. For many years Bradford had had its Catholic Club, which was similar in aims and origins to the Manchester 'Chums'. One of its members, W. O. Pepper, arranged for a visit by delegates from the Catenian Association. This took place at the Victoria Hotel, Bradford, on 30 June 1913. O'Donnell and Shepherd came from Manchester, and Fitzgerald-Hart from Leeds. The meeting led to the inauguration of the Circle as from that meeting. The coincidence is that in the '50s Pepper's son lived in Bulawayo, where he was a leading member of the Vinculum, an organisation similar in many ways to the Association. It was, as we shall see, his persistence that finally overcame Grand Council's reluctance and led to the formation of the first African Circle. Like father, ...

Bradford had a number of eminent members. Of the many Fattorinis who became members perhaps the most outstanding was Thomas, a governing director of the family jewel firm, Thomas Fattorini Ltd. He was, at one level, a simple Catholic, being an altar server and President of the Men's Guild in his parish of St Stephen's, Skipton. At another level, he was an active worker in civic affairs, vice-president of the local Divisional Conservative Association, and founder and first president of the Skipton Chamber of Trade. At yet another level, he was a sportsman, being vice-president of the Skipton Cricket

Club. He went on to become Grand President of the Catenian Association in 1927, a fit companion on Grand Council for the great men of that period – Shepherd, Brosch and others, who re-elected him for a second term of office in 1928.

Thomas Fattorini was a generous benefactor to Catholic and civic causes. So, too, were other Fattorini Catenians. There was, for example, J. E. Fattorini, another founder member of the Circle, who was known to have given 'upwards of £30,000' to St Bede's Grammar School, Leeds, and so helped its constant growth. A Chairman of the Governors of the School, he received the K.S.G. for his services to Catholic education, as did his successor in that post, Bro. J. E. Brennan.

Bradford Circle has always been proud of the very active lives led by its Brothers. Bro. G. F. Duval, a founder member, and Bro. H. B. Sullivan were largely concerned in the introduction of the Knights of St Columba to Bradford, Sullivan being the first Grand Knight of the Bradford Council, and Duval being very prominent in the purchase and development of the Columba Club. Later on, it was a Catenian, Bro. J. A. Sullivan, who became the first Chairman of the Catholic Parents and Electors Association. But perhaps the most outstanding Catenian of these early years was founder member Edward Cash. He had been a member of the Bradford City Council since 1903 and went on to become an outstanding fighter for the cause of Catholic education in the very critical years before and after World War I. He became Deputy Lord Mayor in 1915–16, when he was also an active member of the Belgian War Relief Committee for which he received a decoration from the King of the Belgians. In 1918 the Pope rewarded him with the decoration of K.C.S.G. for his services to Catholic education.

One of Bradford's proudest moments must have been the ordination of a former Brother, F. W. Le Fèvre, the first 'Catenian priest' to study at the Catenian-funded Beda College (see pp. 73–78). Maybe one of Bradford's saddest moments was the announcement of the death of Bro. Dr T. Savage, who, after the death of his wife, had gone to study for the priesthood at the Beda. Unfortunately he died in Rome before completing his studies.

The Charter of the Brighton Circle (17) is dated 8 November 1913, and bears the signature of Grand President Foggin, by then playing a leading part in the expanding Association. It is worth recalling that Foggin, Hogan, Shepherd and O'Donnell as well as all the other active and energetic leaders of the Association had, perforce, only a few years of Catenian experience. It is a tribute to their varied capacities that they built so well.

The development of the Association in Scotland began with a series of letters written to the Archbishop of Edinburgh by the indomitable McDermott. But the first Scottish Circle, opened on 20 November 1913, was Glasgow (18); and, although in 1911 Manchester had been given responsibility for development north of the Birmingham region, it was Hogan who was responsible for the opening of this Circle. A frequent visitor to the city in the course of business, he had made a number of Scottish friends in a city where about one-quarter of the population was Catholic. He urged his friends to think of starting a Circle of the new Association in their city and must have been pleased by the news that Grand President Foggin had presided at the inaugural ceremony in November 1913.

The Founder President was a noted convert of those days, a close friend of Chesterton and Belloc, the Professor of Humanities at Glasgow University,

John Swinnerton Phillimore. Under his leadership the Circle recruited what has been described as 'the cream of what may be termed the upper brackets of the Glasgow Catholic community'. Indeed, so high were the standards set that a leading solicitor, John Shaughnessy, was not considered to be fit to be a founder member. There must be a moral in the fact that in 1935–37 the same Shaughnessy was Grand President of the Association.

The Southend-on-Sea Circle was founded on 29 November 1913. Unfortunately, all its records were destroyed during World War II. Originally known as the South Essex Circle, it owes its origins to the growth in the number of commuters. Among these were members of the London Circle who, having noticed the opening of a Circle in Brighton, thought it right to have a Circle in their native town. In any event a petition for a Charter was signed by seven Catenians and the Circle opened.

4. 1914 and the expansion continues

The expansion of the Association continued during 1914. Brosch, who had been born in Nottingham, led the 'missionary team' which recruited a list of suitable Nottingham gentlemen and obtained the permission of Bishop Brindle one of whose successors, Bishop McNulty, was the son of an early member of the Association. The Charter, granted on 5 March 1914, was signed by Grand President Foggin and Grand Secretary Shepherd, and the inauguration was conducted by Sandy of Birmingham, who was assisted by Shepherd, Brosch and Hutton of Birmingham. Twenty-two founder members signed the inaugural roll of the Circle, which in time became the parent Circle to Derby, Leicester, Burton-on-Trent, Chesterfield, Loughborough, Peterborough, Mansfield and Dukeries, and, of course, Nottingham, City of, all of which have over the years helped to make the Provincial Rallies enjoyable and successful affairs.

The St Helens Circle was inaugurated by Sandy and Shepherd on 6 April 1914 at a ceremony held at the Royal Raven Hotel. Three men from Liverpool and two from Wigan supported the presiding officers who initiated eighteen gentlemen, 'a good cross section of the business and professional men of the area'.

The Bolton Circle was inaugurated on 6 May 1914, when twelve men were initiated into a Circle which wins its own place in the Association's history by virtue of its early interest in the work of the Catholic College of Social Studies, which it supported in 1938 long before it became the Catholic Workers' College and won the support of the Association at large.

The opening of the Chorley Circle on 18 May 1914 was due to the illness of a member of the Manchester Circle, Thomas Halliwell Kevill. A solicitor from Chorley, he had a practice in his home town and in Manchester where his office was in that of Joe Shepherd, who persuaded Kevill to join the Manchester Circle in 1912. When illness forced him to close his Manchester office he continued to practise in Chorley – and also decided to organise the formation of a Circle in his home town. He was a well-known figure in the town, being an active Borough as well as County Councillor. He was well known to the Archbishop and his priests, and advised them on the purchase of sites for schools and churches. He had little difficulty in gathering together a group of leading Catholics who included the future Mayor, Alderman

Fearnhead. Kevill went on to become the ninth Grand President of the Association (1923–24) succeeding Synott, the author of the Constitution which became operative during Kevill's year, and preceding Brosch the dynamic leader of the Association in the Midlands. That Kevill was thought fit to take his place in a Chair occupied by such giants speaks of the ability of the man and of the respect in which he was held by his fellow-members of Grand Council.

The North London Circle owes its existence to the work of Hogan and another member of London, Charles Munich. It was they who gathered together the twenty-five men who were initiated at the first meeting, held on 18 May 1914, at the Stanley Hall, Tufnell Park. Its subsequent development has affected, and been affected by, the opening of new Circles – London Charterhouse, Harrow, North-West London, Southgate and District, and London Northern Heights.

The inaugural meeting of the Blackpool and The Fylde Circle took place at the Royal Hotel, Blackpool on 28 May 1914, when O'Donnell, Fyans and Pegge from Manchester were supported by two Brothers from Preston and by Joe Shepherd. Eighteen men were initiated into a Circle which, like many other Circles, played a major role in the development of Catholic secondary schools in the area, and whose debates and decisions on Service Committees are of interest during the current debate on the proposed new form of help for redundant Brothers.

The Bristol Circle was inaugurated on 17 July 1914 at a meeting held at the Grand Hotel, Bristol. Many of those who were inaugurated had 'pondered long and anxiously on the advisability of a Catholic Association for business men being set up in the city'. For, as their historian wrote, 'Bristol at that time was not too partial to Catholics' – a reminder of the atmosphere in which our forefathers lived just before the outbreak of World War I. However, the Circle was formed and in 1919–20 was the Circle which helped form other Circles in Cardiff, Newport and Swansea. In more recent times it has played a part in the development of the Bristol, City of, Circle and the other Circles in the Province which still regards Bristol as its parent Circle. We shall see that its Brothers played an active role in the Catholic life of the City, while several Brothers have made their individual marks on the history of the Association – notably, perhaps, Bob Burns who was Grand President in 1954–55 and who has been a mine of information as the Association's oldest surviving Grand President.

Bristol was the last Circle to be inaugurated before the outbreak of World War I, which, as we shall see, affected the various Circles in different ways. As the *Directory* for 1914 shows, there were just over 1500 members in the Association at that time, with London having 302 members, Manchester having 203, Liverpool 150 and Birmingham 109. When one reflects that the Association had only been in existence for six years when the War started, and that none of its members had any of that 'Catenian experience' which we look for in today's leaders, one can only marvel at the rapidity and success of the expansion. Of course there were mistakes – some men attended only their inauguration meeting and never returned, while others resigned within a short time, as did the Founder Vice-President of the Nottingham Circle. Some who joined and stayed never really became imbued with that 'Catenian spirit' which inspired those who worked for the expansion of the Association. In spite of these mistakes and lack of experience, the Association did expand; it did win the enthusiastic support of most members of the Hierarchy and, by 1914, had created a skeletal framework on which future expansion was to be based.

5. *Aims and Objects*

One reason for the continued success of the Association in attracting recruits as well as the support of the Hierarchy lay in its limited aims. At the third Annual Dinner of the London Circle, the chief speaker was Fr Aveling, Ph.D., who told the assembled gathering, including Cardinal Bourne, what the Association stood for. Having pointed out that it was 'strictly Catholic' and 'entirely *non-political*', Fr Aveling went on to praise the Association for giving 'to Catholic men of business an opportunity of meeting socially on terms of absolute equality. This is not always possible in the existing conditions of parochial life; and the Catenian Association thus provides a large and comprehensive solidarity of united Catholic life and action which could not easily be secured in any other way.' Fr Aveling listed the stated Aims and Objects of the Association as O'Donnell had outlined them to Casartelli in May 1908, and went on to say that these made 'the expansion of the Association a practical certainty'. He prayed that this expansion would become a reality, so that Catholic men and their families would be the better protected against 'the biting fists of "paganism" and the desolating winds of ignorance and prejudice' provided that 'we be true to our faith and to ourselves'.

But, almost from the start, there were those who were critical of these limited Aims and Objects. Brother G. L. P. Dix made a major speech to the Newcastle Circle in 1916, which was reproduced and printed for wider distribution. In the course of his address, Dix referred to the hostile atmosphere in which Catholics still lived, but went on to stress that the laity, preferably led by Catenians, should play an active role in the affairs of the Church. Benevolence, he claimed, ought to be more widely interpreted than the mere material care of a Brother and his family, or prayers for sick or deceased Brothers. It should, he thought, lead to care and concern for the wider interests of the Church. Some Catenians led similar discussions at their meetings, often in the presence of visiting gentlemen who then wrote to the Catholic Press about the new Association. Some, such as 'Carpe Diem' writing in *The Universe*, asked 'What had the Association done?', which led to a correspondence which spilled over into the columns of the *Catholic Times* so that for several months the affairs of the so-called 'secret society' were well aired.

Some Circles, inspired by the best of misguided motives, took the line that, as leading Catholics with more than their fair share of worldly goods, their members ought to support, as Catenians, any and every call on their money and time. We have seen that Brosch was a leading Catholic activist as well as an outstanding Catenian. Yet it was he who, in December 1917, warned the Nottingham Circle against its practice of making a collection for this or that charity at every meeting of the Circle.

At the risk of being misunderstood, one has to say that the Association was not founded as an arm of Catholic Action nor did its founders intend it to be a collecting agency for Catholic charities. It has, indeed, made major contributions to specific Catholic undertakings, notably perhaps the Beda College, the Catholic Workers' College and, in more recent times, the Jumbulance scheme. We will examine these, and other forms of Catenian action, in the course of this book. But the purpose of the Association was best expressed, perhaps, by Archbishop McIntyre, son of an early member of the London Circle (No. 52 on the roll):

> What is the Catenian Association but an Association for friendship, brotherhood and kindness. . . . It exists for the commendable purpose of making its members warm-hearted, human, true to each other and true to their Catholic inheritance. To teach others to be happy is a noble purpose. It will enable you to go smoothly and quietly through the world and quietly out of it.

This approval of the limited role of the Association was echoed by Archbishop Downey, who said of the Association and its members:

> It is not a question of what Catenians do. If they do nothing more than cultivate the great social virtue of meeting together as members of the great Universal Church, that is enough. I admire Catenians because they are chiefly concerned with themselves.

That is not to argue that as individuals and outside their Circles the members of the Association are not deeply involved – in the work of the Church and in civic life. Indeed, it can be shown that membership of the Circle has acted for some as a spur to such action, while many active men have been able to call on the help of their fellow-Catenians when the need arose. But it is to say that, as Catenians, they have not claimed, nor wished to claim, a role in the world of action. One who understood the apparent paradox – of being both active and Catenian – was Dan McCabe, Manchester's first Catholic Lord Mayor and the Association's fourth Grand President.

> The Association [he said] must not be looked upon as an omnibus to overload with the various activities which members may be interested in. It was not founded for that, but to obliterate boundaries and to assist in the social intermingling of its members, to know each other and to help each other, and above all to remember that their success will be all the greater if they do everything for the greater honour and glory of God.

Of course, members of the Association have played their active roles in Catholic life. Fr Plater paid tribute to the work done by Catenians for the fostering of the C.Y.M.S. during its infancy. A Deputy Supreme Knight of the K.S.C. speaking at the dinner of the London Circle in 1930 'thanked the Catenian Association for what so many of its members had done in guiding the infant footsteps of the Knights'. We shall see that the example provided by the early members of the Association has been continually imitated by later members who have supported and worked for a wide variety of Catholic charities – such as the S.V.P., Housing Associations, schools, hospitals, children's homes and so on, almost *ad infinitum*. But, it has to be stressed, they have done this work in their individual capacities and not as members of the Association. That this has often led to misunderstanding and to the opinion that 'Catenians do nothing' is a price that has to be paid, although it is hoped that this *History* may do something to affect that erroneous opinion.

6. New structures

The continued expansion of the Association led to changes in the structure of its government. The formation of the London Circle did not lead to any immediate change, the Manchester Committee continuing to control the government of the Association. But the opening of the Leeds Circle, and the hopes that McDermott had for further expansion, led to the creation of a Grand Council to govern the Association's affairs. This Council consisted of the following officers from each Circle: the President, the Vice-President, both of their Marshals, the Treasurer, Secretary, Chamberlain and Tyler. To these were added all Past Grand Presidents and all Foundation Members of the Manchester Circle – the term referring only to the first 100 members of the Circle.

It was this Grand Council which, meeting in Leeds in October 1910, agreed on the change in the title of the Association.

The first reference to this Council appears in the Manchester Minutes for 11 July 1910, when Whittle and Holt were elected as members. But, to confuse the student, in August 1910 'Bro. O'Donnell reported on the proceedings of the Grand Circle meeting', and it was at a Grand Circle meeting at Leeds that the title of the Association was changed.

The apparent confusion may be resolved if we note that in April 1910 McDermott had met Dr Foggin in Newcastle, and his enthusiasm made it obvious that a Newcastle Circle would be opened in the near future. It is possible that prior to the opening of that Circle in October 1910, Foggin had already begun to play a part in the affairs of an Association which he had not yet joined. For it is certain that by the time the Grand Council (or Circle) met in Leeds in October 1910 the new Constitution of which Foggin was the author had already been accepted.

Foggin's Constitution divided the country into two: (*i*) the Northern Province was to have its headquarters in Manchester; (*ii*) the Southern Province was to be based on London, although the Rules accompanying the new Constitution specifically said that the Association's Head Office was to be in Manchester. It is interesting in view of later developments to notice the first appearance of the word 'Province' in the Association's affairs, although there was none of that decentralisation of powers and finance which followed the re-organisation of 1923.

The term 'Grand Circle' was devised by Foggin, it is claimed, and appeared in the Rule Book for the first time in 1910. Members of this Grand Circle were to be the President, Vice-President and three other members of each Circle, who when they met elected their Grand President and their Grand Officers – Hogan being the first Grand Vice-President, Hart the first Grand Chamberlain, Dunford (of London) the first Grand Treasurer, and Shepherd the first Grand Secretary.

With the continued growth of the Association the number of members of Grand Circle continued to grow, making it an expensive and cumbersome executive body. For this reason Foggin wrote yet another Constitution and 're-organisation of the Rules governing the Association'. These were approved at an extraordinary General Meeting of Grand Circle held at the King's Head Hotel, Sheffield, on 18 April 1914. This cut down the size of the Grand Circle – although 'it was unanimously resolved that all existing officers be entitled to attend the next Grand Circle meeting, but unless such officers are appointed delegates they shall not be entitled to vote'.

We know something of the affairs of Grand Circle and the finances of the Association from a budget sent out by Shepherd on 1 August 1916. In this he referred to 73 delegates who attended the Annual General Meeting of the Grand Circle and the ten members who attended the three meetings of Grand

Council, which had been set up as an executive body to run the Association's affairs in the year between the A.G.M.s of the Grand Circle which were held in July of each year.

Nor was the writing and re-writing of the Constitution and Rules the only pang accompanying the births of new Circles. From the outset the Association had always been concerned with benevolence, as was clear from the original title taken by 'the Chums'. At first each Circle handled benevolence as it saw fit. Manchester, for example, early decided to put 25 per cent of its subscriptions into a benevolent fund to which Brothers might add as they thought right. Each Circle built up its own benevolent fund, administered by its own Benevolent Board. Grand Secretary Shepherd had to fight a hard battle to get these small funds consolidated into one national fund. It took him until 1912 before Grand Council ruled that all benevolent funds should be centralised with Grand Council, which appointed a Grand Benevolent Board to administer the fund. We shall examine the work of that Board and the administration of that fund in Chapter 9.

7. A taste of the meeting

But for the majority of Brothers neither Constitution nor Benevolence was the main consideration. For them, their Catenian membership meant the monthly (or, as in Manchester and Liverpool, the twice-monthly) meeting of the Circle. The records of the early Circles show that after-Circle functions had a very different flavour from those to which modern Catenians go. Some had a high intellectual content, as may be seen from the learned papers, to which reference has already been made, in which Fr Aveling and Bro. Dix examined the Aims and Objects. Circles invited speakers such as Hilaire Belloc to provide some of that intellectual element; others compiled lists of members prepared to speak on topics of general interest or on aspects of the nation's economic or social life. Circles also tended to do things in what can only be described as 'style', evening dress being the norm, and Archbishops and Bishops being regular guests not only at an annual function but at normal after-dinner functions.

But perhaps the thing which would most surprise the Catenian time-traveller would be that almost every Brother was expected to make a contribution to the evening's entertainment – in song or in verse. Older Brothers in Liverpool may recall having a whiff of the taste of such 'happenings' at the 40th Anniversary of their Circle's inauguration, which was also the 25th anniversary of H. D. Bowden's secretaryship. The script for this occasion was written by Jimmy Gaskin, who had written an even more impressive script for the Silver Jubilee celebrations when he was Circle President, and who wrote the local version of the Catenian Anthem which received Archbishop Downey's *imprimatur* on 16 September 1935. A glance at a programme for 'A Smoking Concert' shows five toasts and responses other than the loyal and Papal toasts, ten individual songs and one duet, as well as two items described as violin solos which were intermixed with the toasts in the course of the evening. It is clear that the members of the early Circles were very different from the men who form today's Association – in occupations, tastes and achievements. But their world was swept away in the holocaust of 1914–18.

CHAPTER FIVE

Wartime developments

1. A slow-down in expansion

The nature of the immense gulf which separates us from a recent past is well illustrated by the words with which Rupert Brooke welcomed the outbreak of World War I:

> Now, God be thanked Who has matched us with His hour,
> And caught our youth, and wakened us from sleeping.

And, convinced that they were called to do God's work for the defence of civilisation, thousands of young men volunteered to serve in the forces in battalions with such names as 'The Cardiff Pals' and 'The Manchester Pals' – reminding us that Locan and O'Donnell in naming their Association 'the Chums' were reflecting the relatively unsophisticated mood of their time.

The War affected the development of the Association. There was, for example, a slow-down in that wave of expansion which had marked the years 1913–14. During the War years only nine new Circles were opened. And while the existing Circles continued to enrol new members, they lost the chance to recruit members from among those who left home to serve their 'King and Country'. Nevertheless the Association increased in size from just over 1500 members in 1914 to 1858 by the end of 1916 and to just over 2000 when the Northampton Circle opened on the day after the signing of the Armistice which brought the War to an end.

The Southport Circle owed its origins to members of the Liverpool Circle, who, seeing the growth of their original Circle, determined to form one in their own neighbourhood. Similarly with the South Manchester Circle. George Flynn and Teddy Doran, members of the original Manchester Circle, saw that as it grew to more than 250 members there was a danger of its becoming somewhat impersonal. They persuaded some fourteen members of the first Circle to form a new Circle in South Manchester. Doran was an extraordinary man: a journalist, drama producer and critic, theatrical director, and, as a builder, involved in the development of the early oil industry. He was also a pioneer in the development of X-rays who suffered from his work in the experimental stage of this new branch of science. He took part in X-ray work in wartime hospitals in France, and it was owing to this work that in the first instance he lost some of his fingers, and ultimately suffered from impaired eyesight. He was to play a major role in the development of the Association, although, perhaps regrettably, he never became Grand President.

The opening of the South Manchester Circle revealed some of the difficulties of forming 'offspring' Circles, as well as some of the problems created by the War. Wartime service took some of the original members away, while others felt the loss of old friendships with men in the parent Circle. Indeed, at one time, it seemed as if the Circle might have to close. It was Doran who led a deputation to see Dan McCabe, then President of the parent Circle, to ask for volunteers to come to keep the new Circle going.

53

The opening of the Harrogate Circle was due to the activities of men from other Yorkshire Circles, while the opening of the Middlesbrough Circle was due in part to the work of Dr Foggin, the 'apostle' of the Association in the north-east. The expansionists of the Southampton Circle played a major role in the opening of the Bournemouth Circle, which in time has become the largest Circle in the Province. The first Coventry Circle, later re-named as the City of Coventry Circle, owed its existence to the success of the work of Brosch in Birmingham, while Wimbledon, the first suburban Circle, followed from the development of suburban London. The Northampton Circle owed its existence directly to World War I. Charles Palethorpe became friendly with 'a North Country Catenian who was billeted in the town and being imbued with the spirit of the Association he worked with great zeal and perseverance to obtain the members needed to apply for a Charter' for a new Circle in his home town.

2. Some effects of the War

The opening of the Northampton Circle was one example of that good which sometimes comes from evil. Rupert Brooke had warmly welcomed the War. That attitude soon changed as men were exposed to the murderous slaughter of those battles which will remain for ever a tribute to the 'lions led by donkeys' – Ypres, Messines, Loos, Vimy Ridge, Cambrai and, above all, the Somme. Catenian fathers mourned the death of sons; Catenians, such as Doran, suffered in various ways. Modern Liverpool Catenians may recall George Henry Chamberlain who in later years served their Circle, Ampleforth and cricket so fully. He was an early member of the Circle, which he joined in 1911. In August 1914 he was commissioned in the King's Regiment and served with the Liverpool Irish in France in some of the worst fighting of 1914–15. He rose to command a company, was wounded in the Battle of the Somme in 1916, and spent the rest of the war in a training unit.

Back home, Chamberlain would have seen evidence of the social changes being wrought by the War. Income tax went up to an unprecedented 5s. in the £, and people on fixed incomes suffered a fall in living standards as prices and taxes rose. New industries – aircraft, motor vehicle, food processing and petrochemicals – expanded, creating job opportunities at all levels for men and women of various skills and none. Social mobility, which had been a feature of nineteenth-century England, went on more rapidly, for in this, as in all things, 'the war hastened everything – in politics, in economics, in behaviour'.

For Catenians, as for others, the War provided opportunities for action. Dan McCabe, Lord Mayor of Manchester, organised a Belgian Refugees Committee to find homes for the 2000 refugees who came to Manchester; a Belgian Club was formed to try to provide the victims of war with the double aim of combining the scattered community into a new society and of promoting mutual helpfulness. To help him in this work, McCabe turned to Joe Shepherd, whose success was rewarded by the C.B.E. and by the Médaille du Roi Albert awarded by the King of the Belgians.

Many Catenians helped organise and run the Catholic Huts campaign, started by the Catholic Women's League to provide social centres for Catholic men and women in the forces or working away from home. Caraman of London, for example, was chairman and hon. treasurer of the Catholic Huts Council and also worked actively at the C.W.L. Hut at Westminster.

But perhaps the Catenian who gained most wartime publicity was Sir Mark Sykes, who was much more than 'the well known public figure in Yorkshire', the phrase used in the note produced for the Hull Circle's Golden Jubilee. Sykes was an outstanding politician and statesman. When he died in February 1919, the *Daily Dispatch* carried his obituary under the headline: 'A Future Premier'. Part author of that Sykes–Picot agreement by which Britain and France divided the Turkish Empire between themselves, Sykes was a confidant of Asquith, his political rival, as well as of Kitchener, of Tory leaders as well as of oriental experts, of Jewish leaders as well as of Arab. But Sykes was above all a loyal Catholic, albeit of the 'old' school, who championed the cause of that Irish Home Rule which he saw as a solution fair both to the Irish Catholics and the English imperialists. While he shared platforms with the Rothschilds in support of the 'Palestine Home for the Jews' he was also prepared to face the wrath of the Tory Press as when he protested against the *Morning Post*'s attacks on the Irish in 1917. In a long letter he accused the newspaper of misleading people by pretending that 'Ulstermen, unlike Irishmen,' were supporting the Allied cause, ignoring the thousands of Catholic Irishmen who had already died in the fighting.

Sykes's work in the Middle East during the War marked him out for future promotion. His biographer believes that if he had not died he might well have become leader of the Conservative Party in 1922 when Bonar Law retired owing to ill-health – for he was certainly better-known and more popular than the then little-known Stanley Baldwin.

Sykes did not live to reap the fruits of what he had sown, and the nation at large and the Association in particular was the poorer for his dying. But his name figures in the history of the time. Another name which is remembered, if only locally, is that of the son of Brother Weidner of Newcastle. Weidner, an early member of the Newcastle Circle, had been Sheriff of Newcastle upon Tyne in 1897 and Lord Mayor of the City in 1912–13. One of his sons was killed in action during the War and, in his memory, Weidner presented Haddon House to the Society of St Vincent de Paul.

Many Catenians were of alien origin: for example, René Caraman and Brosch's father. During the War some of these 'foreigners', although long resident in England, suffered under that xenophobia which affects the nation at times of stress. The Brosch family tell the story of the policeman who called on the suspected alien to ask 'Where were you born?' 'Warsaw,' was the answer. 'Ah, Walsall, then you'll be locals.' But there was little light relief for those who were of Irish origin, particularly after the Easter Rising of 1916. The Catholic Irish were, once again, viewed with suspicion because of their well-known support for the United Irish League, for Home Rule candidates and for the Irish cause at large. In Liverpool, for example, as well as in Manchester, the Irish had their own local political party. And if McCabe was a prominent member of the Manchester Nationalist Party, the Lynskeys, Taggarts, Bakers and others now famous in Catenian history were prominent in the ranks of the Irish Party, whose leader was Taggart (father of a future Grand President and himself an early member of the Liverpool Circle) and whose Chief Whip was the father of another future Grand President, 'Jimmy' Baker.

Nor did the activities of some of these Catenian Irishmen give the lie to the accusation that they were more Irish than English. The Bakers remember their home being used as a centre for gun-running to Ireland; the Taggarts remember their help to de Valera when, on the run from Lincoln prison in

February 1919, he used various Catholic homes in Liverpool as a refuge before being smuggled on to a ship bound for the U.S.A.

3. The birth of Catena

In 1916, Brosch became President of the Birmingham Circle, which almost immediately decided to start a magazine for its own members, a sort of 'house magazine' then becoming a feature of life in some of Britain's newer and successful firms. It is hardly surprising that this idea should have come forward in this Circle, which included among its members Martin Melvin, owner of *The Universe*, who was to become a Papal Knight and was to be knighted by George V. Others with an interest in publishing were J. B. Webb, director of the *Midland Counties Herald*, J. Trevor Jones of the *Birmingham Mail* and James Watson, the first editor of *Catena*, who unfortunately died in 1919. All these were outstanding Catholics – Webb, for example, was the founder of Besford Court, the institution for mentally defective children in Worcestershire, at whose funeral Mgr Hudson, founder of the Father Hudson Homes, preached the oration in the presence of two Bishops led by a body of clergy come to do honour to a man whom *The Universe* described as 'an outstanding member of the Roman Catholic community'.

In July 1916, Brosch told Grand Circle of Birmingham's decision and after discussion Doran, on behalf of South Manchester, proposed that 'Grand Circle enquire and report on the possibility of issuing a journal for the Catenian Association'. A Committee from Grand Circle met Brosch and others from Birmingham and accepted their generous offer that the Birmingham Publication Committee should 'undertake publication of a magazine on behalf of the whole Association'. A short history of the South Manchester Circle implies that the subsequent appearance of *Catena* was due to the initiative of Doran and men from South Manchester. It is, however, clear that the magazine was conceived, gestated and born because of the energies of Birmingham men.

The Publication Committee held its first formal meeting at the White Horse, Congreve Street, Birmingham on 20 February 1917, when Brosch read a letter in which the Grand Secretary confirmed that Grand Council accepted Birmingham's suggestion and invited the Committee to 'formulate definite proposals'. It was Brosch who then outlined his idea for the magazine, which was to have 32 pages, a 4-page cover, plus as many advertisements as could be obtained. He claimed that 'we should be able to count on 5 to 10 per cent of Association members to advertise' and proposed that 'the literary matter [should] consist of articles of general and particular interest, contributed by members only'. The magazine was to include 'Reports from Circles, Roll of Honour, Obituary, Correspondence, Miscellaneous Wants (charged), Exchange and Mart (charged), Financial column, New members, Changes of Address, Official Notices'.

Brosch's scheme was 'unanimously approved' by the Birmingham Committee, which went on to elect its officers. It seems strange that they did not elect Vincent Gosling, later a Grand President of the Association. Gosling, a solicitor, had been sent by his firm to Birmingham, where, he said, he knew no Catholics when he arrived. He met a member of the Council of Circle No. 9 who brought him into the Circle, and, as Gosling later remarked, 'I never lacked for Catholic friends after that date'. He was soon made Circle Secretary while he was also Secretary and Treasurer of the Prisoners' Aid Society, for which the Circle had accepted responsibility. During the War he became Secretary of the Belgian Refugees organisation in the city, and, giving the further lie to those who accuse the Catenians of 'doing nothing', he was President of the Wolverhampton Law Society, a member of the Brewood Parish Council, a member of the governing body and one-time Chairman of the governors of Brewood Grammar School – the only Catholic ever a member and the only layman ever to have occupied the Chair.

The Committee under Brosch fixed their advertising charges – 12s.6d. for a quarter page, £1 1s, 0d. for a half page, £1 12s.6d. for a whole page, with £2 19s.0d. for the 2nd and 3rd pages of the cover, and £3 0s.0d. being asked for the back page.

On 2 March 1916, members of the Birmingham Committee met a delegation from Grand Council – O'Donnell, Charlier (of Sheffield) and Sandy (Grand Vice-President) – who agreed with the Publication Committee's proposals. Having stressed that it was 'not a Committee of the Association' and that it had complete editorial freedom, the Committee went on to decide the print-run (2000 copies per month), the title of the magazine which was to be described as 'the organ of the Catenian Association', and the method of distribution ('to post each month free of cost one copy to each member of the Association').

In return for editorial freedom, the Birmingham Committee agreed to accept full financial and other responsibilities, and to meet all costs, claims and losses. The Grand Council delegation agreed that the Council would

> do all in its power to help the Committee by advising as early as possible all Circles to send in notices and other information, and to authorise and encourage all officers of the Association to send to the Committee all reasonable information.

In particular, the Council would encourage members 'to send in, where possible, advertisements'.

On 27 March 1917, the Birmingham Committee lodged £100 in Barclays Bank so that there would be money to meet the initial costs. But its great expectations were soon dashed. At its meeting on 26 April the Committee heard that money received for advertisements totalled only £152, 'of which £122 was received from Birmingham members and he had not received any advertisements from members of the Manchester Circle'. The *Directory* for 1916 shows that Birmingham was only the fourth largest Circle at the time, and it reflects badly on the rest of the Circles that the bulk of advertising should have come from that Circle. It seems odd that not a single advertisement was received from the first Circle of the Association, and one is left to question whether Manchester men resented the way in which their Association was being taken over by men from 'foreign Circles', its name being changed because of Hogan, its Constitution being re-written by Foggin, and now Brosch of 'brash Brummagem' taking the limelight with *Catena*.

At this April meeting, Webb, on behalf of the *Midland Counties Herald*, reported that the estimated cost of production would be 22s.6d. per page, with no charge being made for the covers. In May the Committee resolved to ask Circle Secretaries to have a representative for the magazine appointed for each Circle 'for the purpose of obtaining advertisements, supplying notices, etc.'. On 8 June the Committee agreed to leave the addressing and dispatching of the magazine in the hands of Bro. Sheldon, and, in due course, the first issue appeared and was distributed, copies being sent to all the Bishops and the editors of the Catholic Press. Not surprisingly, Melvin's *Universe* carried an editorial which welcomed the appearance of the magazine and supported the magazine's call for Catholics to play a more active part in the nation's public life. In July the Committee 'heard letters from the Archbishop of Glasgow and the Bishops of Salford and Northampton expressing their thanks for the first copies of *Catena*'.

But all was not well. The bill from the *Midland Counties Herald* was £99 0s.6d., and while in July the Treasurer was authorised to pay £75 on account, he had also to report that the receipts from advertisements had fallen (to about £40 by October 1917) and that the Committee would be faced with the problem of finding the money to keep the magazine afloat. Webb proposed that the *Herald* be asked to produce the magazine on lighter paper which would not only be cheaper but would also be carried by the Post Office at ½d. postage. But in spite of these economies, by January 1918 the Committee heard that advertising revenue was down to a mere £31, that £118 was owed for previous advertisements and that the printing bills for November and December had not been paid. In March 1918, the Committee was compelled to report to Grand Council that it would continue publication until May 1919 only on condition that 'all members contributed 2s.6d. each for the magazine'. Grand Council's offer of £200 was considered at the Committee's April meeting and accepted, but in August 1918 it was revealed that Grand Council had not really passed such a guarantee, but had instead proposed a levy of 8s. on each member of the Association.

But this proved to be only a temporary respite. With the continued growth of the Association ('about 50 per month'), costs of publication and distribution continued to rise, without a corresponding increase in advertising revenue. In March 1919, Brosch told the Committee that it was possible that the magazine would be taken over by the Association and published free of charge. The Committee instructed Brosch to write to the Grand Secretary stating that it had agreed at the end of the first year (June 1918) to continue for twelve months, and asking what arrangements Grand Council proposed to make regarding a third year of publication, due to begin with the June issue with a print order now of 2500 copies a month. There is no record of a reply to Brosch's letter but the Committee carried on producing the magazine at a loss. In February 1920, Grand Council voted £100 to enable the Committee to carry on, but went on to criticise various aspects of the magazine – in particular expressing its resentment at the appearance in *Catena* of criticism of the Year Book, or *Directory* – a Grand Council publication. This and other criticisms led the Committee, pressured no doubt by news of the continuing losses, to decide that

> they no longer possess the entire confidence of Grand Council, and under these circumstances feel that after nearly three years' service the only course open to them is to ask Grand Council to make other arrangements for the publication of *Catena* after the March issue.

But this crisis was overcome, and in April 1920 the Committee went on to prepare estimates for probable expenditure and income over the next twelve months which Brosch was to submit to Grand Council at its meeting in Manchester in April. Estimates put expenditure at £960 and revenue at only

£500. Grand Council accepted the estimates and decided to accept full responsibility for the magazine, and this led the Birmingham Committee to resolve that the magazine should bear the imprint of Shepherd rather than that of Brosch. Grand Council rejected this proposal; as a result, while Grand Council paid the piper, Brosch remained chairman of the editorial board until ill-health forced his retirement in 1947 and Sydney Redwood was appointed to take over.

In January 1948, Redwood published his first *Catena*, different in shape and radically different in approach from the staid magazine which Brosch had produced for thirty years. With its larger and more frequent headlines, 'snappy' items and less reverent language, *Catena* had some of the hallmarks of a popular paper. Nor is this surprising, for, whereas Brosch had been a successful businessman playing at being editor, Redwood was a successful journalist who, later in life, went into business on his own behalf.

Under his editorship, *Catena*, priced at 6*d.* (although inflation soon raised the price to 9*d.*), served the Association well. While there were the traditional features – Notes from Circles and so forth – there were new features apart from its appearance. In particular, Redwood tried to rouse interest in the aims and objects of the Association, and to show members, old and new, what the real purpose of the Association was, and, in 1954 and 1955, he wrote a series of long articles under the banner headline, *Floreat Catena*, in which he traced the origins of the Association and outlined some of the stages of its early development.

The Association celebrated its Golden Jubilee in 1958 and, by pure coincidence, *Catena* had a change of editorship. In January 1958, the magazine came out with Bernard Kirchner as one of two Associate Editors, L. J. Sullivan being his editorial partner. At the same time the magazine changed shape once again. Kirchner believed that Brothers preferred something which they could slip into their pockets, and so there was a reversion from the large-page format favoured by Redwood to the demi-8vo style of the original. The improvement in the country's economic position and the ending of the post-war restrictions allowed Grand Council to decide that the magazine would once again appear monthly.

Bernard Kirchner was a brilliant mathematician, whose studies were interrupted by the war and his enlistment in the Artists Rifles in August 1914. He was twice wounded in battle; after his second injury at Loos he narrowly escaped the amputation of his left arm. After a year in hospital he 'wangled' his way into the Royal Flying Corps, soon to become the Royal Air Force. On his leaving the services in July 1919, he set about compiling the definitive volume, *Artists Rifles 1914–1918 Roll of Honour*. After the book was finished (1920) Kirchner resumed his engineering studies at Imperial College, where a contact led to his appointment to the staff of *The Statesman* in Calcutta. He spent the next twenty-six years in India, in turn being editor of *The Statesman*, *Times* Correspondent in Delhi and, after 1941, Chief Press Adviser to the Government of India for which he was awarded the C.B.E. in 1944. On leaving India in 1948, he became London Agent for *The Statesman*, a post from which he retired in 1954.

Kirchner had joined the West London Circle in 1920 but had left the Association on his appointment to India in 1922. In 1949 he re-joined as a member of the Weybridge Circle and in 1952 also joined the City of London Circle. He edited *Catena* with the style and distinction one might expect from a journalist of vast experience and from a man of manifest goodness, deep faith, philosophical insight and a knowledge of the Association dating back to the 1920s. To have met him while researching for this book was a privilege and a memorable experience. Reading the magazine of which he was editor showed how he made its readers aware of the nature of the changes being put forward at Vatican II, the changing role of the laity in modern times, and the need for a reconsideration of the role of the Association in a changing world. There can be no doubt that he left the magazine in a healthy and well-respected condition.

4. The value of the magazine

Brosch's early hopes were dashed by the unwillingness of Catenians to support the magazine. Frank Rudman, already a member of the Birmingham Circle and later to be an eminent Grand Secretary, had a more jaundiced view than Brosch – both of Catenians and of the magazine. 'It is only the wives who read it,' was one of his comments. In an editorial in October 1980, Leo Simmonds suggested that the magazine was 'a forum for debate. It is a watchdog. It is a notice board. And it records events.' In fulfilling these and other unstated aims the magazine has served the Association well.

One of the aims of the founders of the Association was to break down that parochialism which had been a feature of Catholic life. *Catena* helped to achieve that aim. It is good for men in one Circle to know that they have a common bond of brotherhood with men in various parts of the country and in other countries. Those who enjoy the pleasure of inter-Circle visiting need no reminder of the 'togetherness' of the Association, of that bond which unites its members and which is reflected in the motto of 'Each for all, all for each'.

In the early days the magazine served to remind men that they belonged to an organisation of a certain size, dignity and standing. Perhaps the modern middle-class Catholic does not need that psychological boost – although a letter appearing in *Catena* in January 1981 shows clearly that Catholics in Ross-shire on the north-west coast of Scotland still

> keep quiet about their faith, just as they have done throughout the years. Only when they see that they are not alone (when Catholic visitors arrive and organise a Mass) do some of them emerge to participate in the Sacraments. Many have not heard Mass for years.... We are not talking about some dark Continent but about our own British Isles.

That letter might help us better understand the position in which most Catholics felt they were even as late as April 1919 when an article in Brosch's *Catena* claimed that one of the aims of the Association was to allow men 'from different missions' to meet. The very word 'missions' calls up the picture of the few living in that sort of isolation of which Richard Helmore wrote in 1981 – and in which many Catholics lived in the 1920s. And that sense of fearful isolation, breeding a sense of inferiority, was still a fact of Catholic life in 1932 when the Association held its A.G.M. in Edinburgh. About 400 middle-class Catholic men made their way to Edinburgh where, by their Conference, their procession to Mass and their general decorum they won the praise and thanks of a number of Scotland's leading Catholics. These expressed themselves in language which may sound foreign to modern Catenians, especially those who live in the more tolerant south. Archbishop McDonald, for example, in addressing the delegates, thanked them for 'advancing the interests of the Church and for removing the inferiority complex which still to some extent exists on this side of the border'. Fr Brown, S.J., speaking at the banquet, admitted that before the A.G.M. the Scottish Catholics had suffered from an inferiority complex so that 'they had been rather afraid to show themselves as they ought – no longer'. For now they had seen that Catholics too, like other people, could walk tall, dress well, run meetings, hold banquets – external signs, if one likes, of an inward confidence and social growth.

And *Catena* discharged this 'encouraging' function each time it appeared, by reminding readers of the status reached by some of the Brothers, and of the heights which they too might reach. It was no mere idle boasting when *Catena* recorded the election of this councillor, that alderman, this guardian or that mayor. Not for nothing did Circle secretaries write of the outings, dinners, ladies' nights, collections and activities; one of the aims, intended or otherwise, of such items was to encourage others to imitate those of whom they read and to take a justified pride in the success of their fellow-Catenians.

Today all Circles have so much in common as regards ritual, forms of entertainment and spiritual activities. But little of this might have come about if it had not been for the lead given by one Circle. In 1919 Newcastle had the idea of a President's Sunday. The report of this function led Bournemouth to follow the northern example and, in due course, the idea was to become a feature of Catenian life. Did Southampton Brothers realise that the report that they were to say the *De Profundis* at each meeting would quickly lead to their being imitated by other Circles and that this would become, despite Grand Council's opposition, part of our ritual?

Would the Children's Fund have caught on as quickly as it did had it not been for the enthusiastic support it received from Brosch, who, while being an active Grand President, was also Editor of *Catena* and took advantage of this position to bring the new Fund to the attention of the wider Association? How many men have been inspired to take up some form of action outside the Circle by reading – in an obituary, profile or item of news – that this Brother or that Circle was noted for such and such a form of action? Even as early as October 1919, *Catena* was listing the activities of various Brothers who were running or supporting children's homes in Birmingham, Nazareth Houses up and down the country, helping to build new parishes and churches, organising support for the Crusade of Rescue, running the S.V.P. and the K.S.C., scouts, cubs and generally showing themselves to be local leaders in many other directions. In Chapter 6 we shall see how, through the columns of *Catena*, Brothers learned of the ways in which some Circles were leading the campaign for day secondary schools.

In *Catena* for June 1921 there was a report of the gathering at Scarborough for Brothers from the four Yorkshire Circles – Middlesbrough, Bradford, Leeds and York. Within months of the report of that gathering, *Catena* was carrying reports of similar gatherings in the Midlands (January 1922), of a visit by Cambridge Circle to West Essex (September 1922), from which Cambridge Brothers,

> who had never had their ladies to any of their functions learned the value of the company of the ladies and were resolved to invite their ladies to some of their after-Circle functions in future.

In October 1922, *Catena* reported that the four southern Circles –

Southampton, Reading, Portsmouth and Bournemouth – had all visited each other during the year and that the joint meetings had followed a similar pattern, with a mayoral reception, an outing, tea with the local clergy, and a dinner. And so the pattern was set for the future, and inter-Circle visiting and provincial rallies became a feature of Catenian life.

Reading through the 54 volumes of *Catena* which have so far appeared, one realises the changing nature of the Association and of the Church, of the demands on the Brothers and their families and of their activities. Sometimes this throws a little light on our national social history – as when one reads of the three Brothers of the Cardiff Circle who owned cars offering lifts to the other Brothers on an outing. One is also reminded of the danger of early motoring by the report (September 1922) of the death of Grand Director Fraser from Southampton whose car stopped when going uphill because of some defective mechanism, ran downhill and then overturned. Our social history is also illustrated by the changing charges made for meals, for outings, for A.G.M.s and so on.

But, more pertinently, one sees in the pages of the journal changes in the nature of the demands and activities of the laity. At one time the battle is over Catholic elementary schools. Then – a sign of the growth of the Catholic middle class – the demand is for Catholic secondary, grammar schools. Again, at one time, the benevolence of the Brothers, in their extra-mural capacities, was devoted to orphans and the destitute and other deprived members of the Catholic family.

It was revealing to trace the sudden emergence of Catenians' involvement in work for the mentally and physically handicapped, of the many Brothers involved in helping sick visitors to Lourdes, of the work for prisoners and ex-prisoners by Brothers involved in such societies as St Dismas. But perhaps the most revealing development has been the gradual growth of Catenian awareness in recent times of the changing role of the laity in the modern world.

This, of course, is shown by the changing nature of Catenian activity; but is more significantly, perhaps, seen in the activities of Brothers in parish councils, deanery councils and at the National Pastoral Congress of 1980. We shall see that some people hope that Catenians will realise the significance of their role as leaders of the Easter People – which was what Casartelli and O'Donnell, Locan and Pendergast, Shepherd and Brosch, Foggin and McCabe, and the other giants of the early days meant them to be. For, in their opinion, the social gathering was a means to a greater end and not, as in some cases it has become, the mere end in itself.

5. Degrees, Chapter Circles and Past Presidents' Clubs

Those who believed that there was something 'Masonic' about the Catenian Association had their beliefs strengthened by proposals made in 1918. For Grand Council considered Foggin's suggestion that the Association should adopt a scheme of Degrees of Membership. The discussion at Grand Council led to a revised scheme being put forward at the September meeting of Grand Council, this time the Grand President, Sandy, submitting the 'Revised Draft Scheme for Degrees'.

Fortunately the scheme was rejected. If it had gone through, the membership of the Association was to be divided into different 'degrees of membership', with a man's advancement through the system being marked, at each stage, with a 'Degree Certificate'. The new Brother, 'the initiate', would have had to have 'a verbatim knowledge of rules 1 to 5 and familiarity with rules 6, 7, 45 and 46'. After 'passing the examination of the Court of Interrogation', paying his initiation fee and 'any of those fees which may from time to time be authorised by Grand Circle', a man might then be initiated – although without being allowed any 'Degree'.

The first 'Degree' was to be awarded to a man after he had been a member for six months and attended at least four meetings – and had satisfied the 'Board of Aldermen' that he had a 'thorough knowledge' of a number of stated rules. After a year's membership, provided that he had attended at least half the meetings, a man would have been eligible for advancement to the second 'Degree' if he could satisfy the examiners 'appointed by the Board of Aldermen' that he had a thorough knowledge of another section of the rule book. Only then would a man be eligible for election to the Circle Council – but not for the Circle 'Presidentship'. This latter privilege was extended to the members of the 'Third Degree', which consisted of 'acting and past members of the Circle Council' who had 'achieved the Second Degree for at least one year and a half', always subject to the proviso that they had 'satisfied the examiners', and that they had a 'sound general knowledge' of all the rules of the Association.

'The Board of Aldermen' was to consist of the Circle Presidents, Past and Present, as well as any member of the Circle 'who holds the Super-Degree of Grand Alderman'. This Board was to act as an advisory Committee to the Circle Council, to have the right to examine the fitness of applicants for membership of the Circle, and to examine any proposals by Circle members for 'alteration or addition to existing rules or for any proposed new rule' which had to be sent to the Grand Secretary 'by the Chairman of the Board of Aldermen'.

Back to the Degrees. The 'Fourth Degree' was to be confined to past and serving members of Grand Council, while a Court of Grand Aldermen, consisting of the Grand President and all Past Grand Presidents, was to act as an advisory Board to Grand Council.

For each of these degrees there was to be a 'Degree Fee' rising from 'nil' for the First Degree to 'One and a Half Guineas' for the Fourth Degree. And, the piper having been paid, there was to be a visible reward – other than Degree Certificates and different-coloured sashes. In Circle Meetings, it was laid down, 'the higher degrees shall take precedence of the lower degrees as regards the position of their seats relative to the Presidential chair'. There followed detailed instructions on the seating arrangements which would have taxed the constitutional lawyers among the membership.

Writing in January 1955, Sydney Redwood noted:

> ... the scheme was never seriously pursued and was completely ignored when the whole Constitution was revised in 1923. Yet for some curious reason, our present Rule Book still states under 27(b): Grand Council may. . . formulate, dispense, or revoke Degrees.

Redwood did not allude to the attempt made in 1947–48 to resurrect part, at least, of the Degree principle. Victor Palmer, at that time Provincial President of Province No.2, proposed in September 1947 that there should be 'Provincial Circles' for past and serving members of Provincial Council and for Past and

Present Presidents of Circles in each Province. Palmer believed that such a Council would provide 'a collective wisdom' for the benefit of Circle Councils and Provincial Councils, and would be 'a trained team' able to carry out initiations and to 'supervise' the work of Circle Officers.

The proposal was agreed by Grand Council although its critics pointed out 'with alarm' that the scheme struck at the heart of the Association, in which each Brother was as good as the next. Under the Palmer scheme, it was said, 'we shall have to say that someone is good, but not good enough to know all that goes on in the Circles of the Association'. At the 1948 A.G.M., Grand President Hildred told the Brothers that Grand Council was submitting the scheme for the consideration of the membership, who would be asked to vote on its merits. The discussions preceding the voting in various Circles showed that some members thought that the proposed new Circles would be 'too powerful', while others thought they would be 'powerless to achieve anything'. In the event the scheme was rejected when, with less than 50 per cent of the members voting, 1255 voted against the scheme while 1076 voted for it.

But the combative Palmer was not one to let sleeping dogs lie. In 1957 he became Grand President and in his Presidential Address to the Scarborough A.G.M. he brought up the plea for 'Chapter Circles, or something on those lines, where the "elders" can find a place of honour and continued usefulness'.

He hoped that such a scheme might be pushed through in 1958 as one way of marking the Jubilee celebrations, which were also to be marked by 'the publication of the official history of the Association – now being written in tremendous zeal and with enormous attention to detail by Brother Grand Secretary who merits our very great appreciation and thanks'.

Nine years had elapsed since Palmer first put the idea forward – and not, as stated in 1959, 'twelve years'. A 'Correspondent' wrote a long article re-telling the 1947–49 story and suggesting that there was great merit in Palmer's proposal. Some condemned the scheme because of its Masonic tinge, asking for some other name than 'Chapter'. But Grand Council, without waiting for further consideration, went ahead. A 'Chapter Committee' produced a working paper which outlined a scheme for Chapter Circles, 'designated by Saints' names, e.g. The St Thomas More Chapter, The St Andrew Chapter, etc.', open only to Past Presidents. These Circles would 'be under the direct supervision of Grand Council' and would have 'a special ritual and regalia'.

The Chapter Committee went on to produce numerous drafts in which the scheme was further explained. The officers were to be known as 'The Dean, Sub-Dean, Clerk and Bursar'; the first three were to sit at a table, with the Bursar, at his 'exchequer table', facing them. The members of the Chapter would sit, like monks in choir, in serried ranks on either side of the room.

There was a document which gave a detailed 'procedure for the meeting of the St George Chapter' which bears a resemblance to the normal Circle ritual. This 'pilot scheme' was launched in 1960, the members of the 'experimental Chapter' being members of the Grand Council and, as *ex officio* members, the members of the Chapter Committee. By June 1960, 'the scheme is already under a cloud', although in his Presidential address, Joe McMurray, gave the idea his blessing and asked 'that it should be tried'.

However, the scheme 'failed to secure the requisite measure of support at two A.G.M.s'. Indeed, even while the Chapter Committee was at work, some men, maybe more realistic than Palmer and his colleagues, were formulating a scheme for 'An Association of Past Circle Presidents'. The first Past

Presidents' Club was set up in London in 1960 with the promised support of some sixty Past Presidents. At its sixth A.G.M. in January 1966 it was noted that 'membership now seemed settled at just over the 100 mark', largely owing to the work of George Butcher of London Charterhouse, who had presided at the 1960 meeting and who had continued to act as a recruiting officer. The Club met quarterly and for social purposes only, disclaiming any of those degrees so favoured in 1918, or powers of 'supervision' favoured by Palmer. A second Past Presidents' Club was set up in Manchester. The idea proved a temporary success, since it provided an opportunity for 'old friends to get together to dine and wine and to enjoy a chat with those who occupied the presidential chair at the same time', and with none of the ritual of 'Dean, Sub-Dean, Clerk and Bursar' and no 'ritual and regalia'. Some people think that Past Presidents' Clubs seem admirably designed to fulfil the first two stated aims of the Association, viz: '(*a*) to foster brotherly love . . .; (*b*) to develop social bonds among the members and their families'.

CHAPTER SIX

Ambitious but active 1919–23

1. The Hierarchy and Catenian expansion

During the years 1918–23 the Association more than doubled in size, five Circles being opened in 1919, eighteen in the remarkable year 1920, three in 1921, seven in 1922 and six in 1923. By the end of 1923 there were 74 Circles and 4500 Catenians, compared with the 35 Circles and 2100 Catenians there had been at the end of 1918.

In some cases the demand for new Circles arose because of the continued growth of an existing Circle. In Newcastle, for instance, where the parent Circle had a membership of over 100, the Sunderland Circle (No. 63) was formed by dividing the members of No.5 Circle into odds and evens and transferring the evens into the new Circle which then had a roll of 61. In Birmingham also there was a parent Circle which by 1922 had grown to 'well over a hundred, and meetings were so fully attended that the Circle became cumbersome'. A group which 'thought that meetings should take place in the best possible surroundings and with a certain amount of luxury in which visitors and ladies could be suitably received . . .' decided to form a new Circle, and the City of Birmingham Circle was born. Brosch led a contingent from the parent Circle to their new Circle's first meeting in May 1922 at a time, as their historian records, when 'taxation was light, the purchasing power of money many times what it is today. Wines and spirits were the common drink and meals set out in lavish style.'

In Glasgow, too, 'it was widely conceded that the creation of a second Circle would not be inappropriate' and seventeen men from the parent Glasgow Circle, led by Shaughnessy, formed the Glasgow (Strathclyde) Circle (No. 55), which held its first meeting in November 1920. The development of the Manchester City Circle was due to the growth in the number of Catenians who had businesses in Manchester but lived at a distance from the city and felt unable to enjoy meetings which went on to a late hour. It was these men who decided to form a new kind of Circle, which would hold its meetings at about 6 o'clock so that it could be closed at 9 o'clock, thus allowing 'the good Catenians to get to their homes in reasonable time'.

Central Liverpool, North Middlesex (now known as London Charterhouse) and West London were other examples of Circles which were 'hived off' from overgrown parent Circles. Other Circles owe their origins to that geographic mobility – due to the building of suburban railways – which had gone on in Victorian England but went at a more rapid rate after 1918, when car ownership also provided some men with the opportunity of living at a distance from their places of work. In 1920, Wallasey members of Liverpool Circle had become sufficiently numerous to allow them to apply for a Charter to form a Circle on the Cheshire side of the Mersey. They could not have foreseen that geographic mobility and social development would one day lead a member of their Circle, Tony Bainbridge, to raise the money for the building of a church at Cemaes Bay in Anglesey.

Another suburban Circle was Croydon (No.60), many of whose original members had been members of South London but wanted a Circle nearer their own homes. The Founder President of the new Circle was D. A. Stroud, who had been wounded in the bitter fighting of 1917 during the War, which had interrupted his career as Civil Servant, author and Catenian. This remarkable man, a convert like so many other notable Catenians, was to become Grand President in 1939, when he was to play a major role in holding the Association together during the difficult years of the blitz.

The Croydon historian pays tribute to the encouragement which their Circle received from Canon McLaughlin, in whose presbytery the first meetings were held and, for some years, Council meetings were held. McLaughlin was only one of a number of perceptive priests who realised the value of the Association to their people. The Cardiff Circle was largely the result of the work of Dom Raymond Lythgoe, O.S.B., who persuaded leading Catholic men in the city to form the first Welsh Circle. The Plymouth Circle had been 'in the pipe line' since McDermott reported in October 1910 that 'he had hopes of making arrangements for our establishment in Plymouth'. But Bishop Kiely, who had become Bishop in February 1911, had refused to allow a Circle to be opened until 1923, by which time a former layman, best remembered in Plymouth as the redoubtable Canon Gaynor, had persuaded him of the benefit which a Circle could bring to the city.

And, of course, once a Circle was established in a region, this often led to the demand for another Circle in the area. If Cardiff had a Circle, then Newport men learned that they too might benefit if there was a Circle in their town. And so the Swansea historian records: 'In the early part of 1920 Mr Rotzinger heard of the activities of the Catenian Association in Newport and Cardiff, so his mind began to work to see what Swansea could do.' Similarly in Derby, where Leo Burns, having joined the Nottingham Circle in 1919, 'was immediately filled with the urge to found a Circle in Derby'.

The Association also received the support and encouragement of most members of the Hierarchy – the Irish-born Kiely being one of the very few who were reluctant to give it their blessing. Founded, as it was, under the inspiration of one remarkable Bishop, the Association had, as we have seen, quickly received the support of other Bishops and in particular had the support of the Archbishop of Westminster, Cardinal Bourne. Whiteside of Liverpool, a member of 'an old Catholic family' and always 'cautious in deliberation', had been slow to give his support to the lay-oriented organisation; but once he had seen it at work he gave it his full support. Archbishop Mostyn of Cardiff was another 'old Catholic' who 'had little contacts outside Catholicism', so that it is not surprising that he sympathised with the isolation of his flock in Wales; he both supported the development of the Association and, in turn, called on it for support in his unending battle with the authorities over the Schools question.

The Catholic community still lived in a hostile climate which would seem strange to the modern Catenian. Shortly after the opening of the Carlisle Circle in October 1920, 'the rumour was circulating through the town that the Catenian meetings were the meetings of a Sinn Fein organisation'. It has to be remembered that at that time British troops, supported by the Black and Tans, were trying to suppress the Sinn Fein government which had declared Irish independence in 1918. This makes it easier to understand why 'patriots' should think that any gathering of Catholics was to be regarded with suspicion. But it also reflects something of the atmosphere in which Catholics lived in 1920. In Scotland things were, if anything, worse. The Minutes of the Edinburgh Circle in 1921 give a description of a meeting at the Mound when a Dominican friar had to 'take all the eggs without the ham'.

At a meeting of the North London Circle in 1919 a doctor-member asked why the local convent was employing a Protestant doctor. The surprising reply illustrates the climate of the time:

> ... having regard to the bigotry that still obtains among a section of the population, there was a certain advantage in having a Protestant medical officer attached to a Catholic institution, as in cases which necessitated public enquiry, *the evidence of a Protestant doctor would be more likely to carry conviction* [my italics].

In December 1922, Kevill, later Grand President, addressing the Manchester Circle, asked: 'Why are we so shy and so diffident? Why do non-Catholic friends look upon us as if we were suffering a handicap? – that attitude of mind was a natural consequence of the past history of Catholics in this country and the coming of the Catenian Association was an instrument for destroying that state of things.' It is difficult now to imagine the feeling of isolation felt by Catholics, still living in 'their different missions' when, even in 1922, Brosch could write of the Catholic body suffering because it was 'still too near the penal times; we still feel "in the bones" the effects of those times', and could claim that one aim of the Association was to 'rescue Catholics from this'. Only if we try to understand the hostility, the feeling of isolation and of deprivation, can we understand why a priest could write in his parish magazine in 1922: 'It was a sight edifying to the congregation and to the priests of the parish to see the brothers of the Catenian Association go in a body to the altar rails on Low Sunday. It was a striking act of faith and devotion' and, he might have added, a psychological boost to himself and his people.

Casartelli had realised that this work – of creating self-confidence among Catholic lay people – could best be performed by laymen themselves, freed from clerical guidance. Not everyone understood this. Indeed, in 1918 there was a proposal to allow priests to become members of the Association. This proposal was defeated on the grounds that the aims of the Association, unlike those of the clergy, were limited, and that Casartelli had intended the Association to be a lay-only organisation. Indeed, it was Bishop Dunn of Nottingham who warned the Association against the danger of its becoming 'the milch-cow of the clergy', each of whom would have their own very good reasons for asking for financial and other help.

With this in mind, it may seem strange to end this review of the post-war expansion with a look at the formation of the City of London Circle. Two members of the London Circle had seen how it had grown. They felt the need for a smaller Circle with a membership restricted to men intimately linked with the commercial and professional life of the City, and with a City meeting place. Hensler, a member of the London Stock Exchange, and Baines, a solicitor, also noted the lack at that time of any provision for the entertainment of prominent Catholics visiting London. Archbishop's House had no such facilities in those days, and Bourne was often in a dilemma when Catholic statesmen from abroad had to be entertained. Hensler helped form the City of London Circle with a view to its having the financial resources to meet those calls of hospitality, while also providing the atmosphere of dignified informality in which members might meet. Within a short time of the Circle being formed the Cardinal asked for its help. At his suggestion a committee was set up, in collaboration with London Circle, whose purpose was to consider ways of widening the scope of the annual Low Week dinner given by the Hierarchy. The result was to enlist Catenian support for the function, and this committee was the forerunner of the Five Provinces Committee which in later years organised an annual function. It is small wonder that Bourne showed his appreciation of the City of London's efforts, being a frequent attender at its monthly dinners.

2. Catenians in action

The increase in the number of members of the Association was due, in part, to its expansion into areas where it had never before existed. In this expansion it enrolled many men who would have fitted into the first Circle – self-made men such as Callaghan of Cardiff, a colliery proprietor and the son of Irish immigrants, professional men such as Stroud, Doctor of Law, of Croydon. But the increase in numbers was also a reflection of that social mobility which has been a feature of twentieth-century life. This mobility is the result of the continued industrial revolution which has led to the emergence of a 'salariat' of people employed, in many cases, in tertiary industries such as banking, insurance, finance, distribution, and other service industries. A comparison of the occupations of men in the early Circles with those of men in post-war Circles also shows a decline in the number of self-employed men, often owners of sizeable family firms, and an increase in the number of members of the 'salariat', working in one or another of the increasing number of national firms, in local or central government or, though few at first, in multinational organisations.

This social progress had gone on even more rapidly in the U.S.A., as had been made clear to Bishop Keating when he went there to take part in the Jubilee celebrations in honour of Cardinal Gibbons, cousin to the Association's first treasurer. Keating had seen, at first hand, the influence of the active, and affluent, Knights of Columbus. On his return he asked the Association that its members should take a leaf from the book of the K.S.C. and become the active arm of the Church. If we may move ahead of our story, such an appeal was made even more strongly in 1927 and 1928, when many members of the Hierarchy asked that the Association should unite with the newly-formed Knights of St Columba to form the one, larger and, it was to be hoped, active body. It was fitting that the riposte to the Bishop was delivered by O'Dea, then President of Manchester Circle. As much as, if not more than, anyone else, O'Dea was the embodiment of Catholic action, recognised and honoured by the Hierarchy. Yet it was O'Dea who pointed out that the Association existed for 'social and benevolent purposes' and, he went on, 'not for more than that, in spite of the demands of impatient brothers'. As one man wrote, going to a Catenian meeting was 'an oasis in the desert of the week', an image which was later to be used by the friendly bishop who described the Association's meetings as 'Catholic Action at rest'. O'Dea's arguments against action were supported by other active Catholics such as McCabe of Manchester, Brosch of Birmingham and Grand President Goodier, who argued that, just as the Church had its sodalities and kindred organisations, and the world had its various political and social organisations, so too middle-class Catholics both needed and deserved their own Association. But perhaps the most remarkable tribute to the Association was to come from Keating himself in 1922. In praising the Association for what it was doing for the social life of some Catholic men he warned it 'against outstripping its aims', claiming that there were other organisations which had other and different aims and that a too active Association might lead to a clash with societies such as the K.S.C.

This is not to say that Catenians, as individuals and as members of Circles, were not active. We have seen the support given to the S.V.P., K.S.C. and other societies, while *Catena* continued to list the Circles which were working actively for various homes, convents, and societies for the deprived. And this activity continued. In Birmingham, the Circle undertook to help the Father Hudson Homes by leading the campaign to provide an operating theatre for the St Gerard Hospital attached to the Home there. In Cardiff, as elsewhere, Catenians set up a branch of the Catholic Evidence Guild, providing both the funds and the speakers. In Stoke, the Brothers heard the first Catenian appeal for help for the Catholic Social Guild. They could never have known that this was to become a Catenian-supported movement which would involve the time of many and the money of all. But perhaps the most significant activity undertaken by some Circles lay in the field of secondary education, a topic which forms part of Chapter 11 where it will be seen that Catenians led the campaign to found secondary schools in the inter-war period.

Catenians also realised Casartelli's hopes that Catholic men would play their part in civic and public life. In September 1918, two became M.P.s – Hailwood and Malone – the forerunners of other Catenian M.P.s. So too at a local level: there was a noticeable increase in this period of the number of Catenians who won places on local councils, became aldermen and became Mayors or Lord Mayors. It was a matter of national report when McCabe became Lord Mayor of Manchester in 1915. But there was little other than local attention paid to the fact that the Newcastle Circle provided three Lord Mayors of the city: Weidner (1912–13), Fitzgerald (1914–15) and Lee (1919–20 and 1924–25). And few outside Manchester noted that in 1919 the Circle had two Mayors: Fox, Lord Mayor of Manchester, and H. F. O'Brien, Mayor of Altrincham. In 1921 there were another three Catenian Mayors, including Turnbull of Cardiff, while a future Mayor of Port Talbot, Karl Wehrle of the Swansea Circle, was elected as the first Catholic councillor for that Borough. Cambridge Circle could boast of two Ollards, of whom one became the first Catholic Mayor of Wisbech, and the other attained the chair at a later date, while also becoming the first Catholic Chairman of Cambridge County Council. Derby Circle was no sooner formed than 'one of the first acts of the Council was to submit Vice-President Edmund Peyton's name for the Bench'. The application was successful and he became the first Derby Catholic J.P. for many years.

This determination to play an active role outside the Circle derived, in part, from the nature of the Circle meeting of the time. Manchester City tried to set a fashion by becoming a dining Circle. Most Circles, however, regarded the social side of the evening as merely one small part of their proceedings. The normal evening was divided into three parts. There was, first, the business meeting, much as the modern meeting; this was followed by a half-hour given over to 'social activities' – when most Circles allowed a drink, smoke and sandwich. But the main item of the evening was the post-social hour or so, when there was often a lecture, debate or discussion. It was in this period of the evening that men listened to and discussed proposals for Association development put forward by such men as Dix of Newcastle, Perceval of London, or O'Dea of Manchester. In January 1921 the Cardiff Circle heard a paper read by Dr Ray Edridge of the Bristol Circle on 'The Poetical Works of Francis Thompson', while, as we shall see, a number of Circles had Cardinal Gasquet or Cardinal Bourne as their main speaker.

Modern Catenians would find such an evening more than a strain, for it is not only in our smaller financial resources that we are different from those earlier Catenians. For them 'a char-à-banc outing to Harrogate' was a major event, for they had few of the amenities which we take for granted, such as motor cars. They did, however, set some patterns for us to follow. In August 1922, Wigan Brothers took their ladies on 'a summer outing' and reported that this was the first summer outing that had been successful. They also established the practice of the Brothers (and later their families) supporting their President at an annual mass. Newcastle had an Annual Communion Day in 1919 and planned to have a President's Sunday. In 1919 Bournemouth had a President's Sunday – the first in the south, some three years before the habit was taken up by South Manchester (which chose Rosary Sunday for their first President's Sunday), some of whose modern members like to think that Doran had been the first to suggest this Catenian custom.

In addition to instituting an Annual Communion Day in 1921, Birmingham also held a Retreat for its members as did the Mid-Surrey Circle and so gave the example to other Circles to copy. In 1920, there was the first Mass for Deceased Brothers said at Westminster Cathedral, and many hundreds of Brothers 'in and around' London attended this Mass which was the forerunner of the current Five Provinces Mass, although its date was changed at the request of the Coventry Circle, whose members asked London to arrange for the Mass to be said 'on the Sunday nearest to the holding of the motor-car show at Olympia – i.e. the Sunday following the first Friday in November, the day of the opening of the show'. The popularity of the London – Brighton run by veteran cars which takes place on that Sunday creates a traffic hazard for Brothers from South London going to Mass.

Bradford followed this example in 1921, and in 1922 over 200 men attended the first Mass for Deceased Brothers said at the request of the Manchester Circle. And if it was the London Circle which first asked that Circle proceedings should open with a prayer to the Holy Ghost, it was the Southampton Circle which first said the *De Profundis* at the end of a Circle meeting.

3. Overwhelming ambitions

Some members of the expanding Association let their ambitions run ahead of reality. In the summer of 1918 there was a proposal that the Head Office of the Association ought to be moved from 'provincial' Manchester to the capital, London, where, it was claimed, the officers of the Association would be able to catch the ear of the Cardinal, the attention of politicians and the notice of the Press. Too many opposed the proposal for it to be successful, but it was a straw in a puffed-up wind. Nearer the truth of the real feelings of members was the expression of envy at the £300 a year then being paid to Shepherd, the overworked Grand Secretary.

But the ambitious had not yet had their say, for there was a proposal that there should be a Catenian Club in every town where there was a Circle. When this was discussed in Birmingham, the centre with a large and prosperous Catholic population, reality broke in as men asked whether such a Club would be open to all the laity or only to Catenians, how it would be managed and, most significantly, how it was to be funded. In the autumn of 1918 the Liverpool Circle started a Luncheon Club 'as a means of bringing Brothers together oftener than the monthly meeting and to enable them to know each other better'. This Luncheon Club organised lunches each Friday at the Exchange Station Hotel. London followed where Liverpool led, and started a Luncheon Club which met weekly, but Manchester only considered the matter without taking action.

It was also Liverpool which went ahead with the acquisition of premises 'in Ruddon Chambers, Lord Street, for the purpose of a Club'. This was the building in which the Taggarts and the Lynskeys had their offices, and it was almost natural that the dominant Pat Taggart should become secretary of the Link Club, the capital for which (£2000) was provided by individual Catenians. Here the local Circles held their meetings; here, too, men might meet at other times to play billiards, have a meal, drink or just talk. The Link Club became a major feature of the Catholic life of the city. But no other town or city followed this example, although there was a proposal for such a Club in London which might serve as a home for all the Circles of the newly created Provinces 2 and 7. It was suggested that such a 'home', with all the facilities of a London Club, might be provided by the knocking together of two large houses, and all for the annual subscription of £1.1s.0d. The proposal remained just that.

Equally ambitious was a scheme started by London for the promotion 'of the material well-being of the members by the creation of some machinery by which the large amount of information necessarily possessed by individual Catenians may be utilised for the benefit of the others'. The Commercial and General Intelligence Committee wanted to obtain information from every Circle – on churches, schools, residences, openings for boys, as well as information which would encourage inter-trading. By the autumn of 1919 the idea had been taken up (and over) by Birmingham, where Brosch hoped to use the columns of *Catena* as the medium of exchange of information. But he had to report that there was a lack of support for the Committee's work, while very few employers were writing to offer openings for young men. Even more daunting was the hard fact that, by the time an employer had written via his local Circle secretary and the information had appeared in *Catena*, some time had elapsed and the vacancy had been filled.

By the end of 1919, Grand Council had become critical of the Committee, which it condemned as being 'too commercialised' and as overplaying what was merely one of the aims of the Association and exposing it to that 'Masonic' criticism. Moreover, as was later pointed out, for all the effort and time spent on its work, it had little to show by way of results. London had its own local Committee, and in 1921 Lancashire Circles formed their own Committee hoping to speed things up at their level, and funded by £1000 raised by Liverpool.

But whatever chance of success there might have been for such Committees, local or national, was almost snuffed out by the onset of the economic depression which led to a rapid increase in the level of unemployment and to many business failures. It was this depression which quickly revealed the false nature of some, at least, of the expansion of the post-war years. By July 1922, the Benevolent Fund was dealing with 'many applications', and the members of the Board complained that too many local Benevolent Boards were submitting applications which could not be allowed under the terms of the Fund – to save firms from bankruptcy, and to pay interest on bank overdrafts.

Even as early as the spring of 1921, Grand Council was reporting that 'we are beset with financial problems' arising from the sudden decline in the economy. This was one cause of the decline in attendances, so that at Blackburn, for example, only 25 per cent attended some meetings, although providing in 1922 a Catholic Mayor in E. L. Carus, while Leeds (30 per cent) was hardly any better. There were, of course, other than economic reasons for this drop in attendance. Some people had joined the Association only to find that it did not provide them with what they were looking for; some wanted Catholic action, others wanted inter-trading; some hoped for a job or promotion, others expected to help their sons on; and all of these were bound to be disappointed. It is clear that if they had been better advised before making their application for membership they might never have joined. In that case the Association would not have had that sudden post-war expansion. But, by the same token, it would not have had that equally sudden fall-off in attendances, that appearance of apathy which acts as a canker in Circles and tends to drive away even the enthusiast. The quest for quantity had led over-enthusiastic Catenians to overlook the need for considerations of quality, and the collapse of the economy merely exposed the folly of the continuing search for mere numbers.

4. The Association and the Beda College

It was at this time of financial hardship and when, for various reasons, apathy had begun to affect attendances and interest, that the Association undertook the saving of the Beda College in Rome.

The Beda had its origins in the ambitious hopes of Cardinal Wiseman. He welcomed the many former Anglican clergymen who followed Newman into the Church in what was optimistically called 'the Second Spring'. In 1852, Wiseman persuaded Pius IX to found the Collegio Ecclesiastico in Rome as a house of studies for Anglicans wishing to become priests. In 1897, Cardinal Vaughan persuaded Leo XIII to take an interest in the College and this led to the *motu proprio* of 1898 by which the constitution and rules were sanctioned, the College founded anew, re-named in memory of the Venerable Bede and moved from its first small home to the English College in the Via Monserrato, although retaining its distinctive character.

In 1917 the Congregation of Studies decided upon the total separation of the Beda from the English College because there had been too much friction between the authorities of the two Colleges, each with their different disciplines and separate Rectors, the Beda being confined to the top floor and its students being publicly referred to as 'the inmates'. The Beda then moved to the former Polish College in the Via Pietro Cavallini, but by 1920 this was too small and, in any event, the Poles wanted to reclaim their College now that the War was over. The Beda authorities were told to vacate the College by June 1921.

In the spring of 1920 the English Hierarchy set about the search for premises to which to move the Beda. The Vincentians had recently vacated their

International College, which seemed suitable. The purchase of this building would take up all the existing endowments, and leave the Hierarchy with the problem of finding money for renovation and adaptation. The Cardinal Protector of the Beda refused to sanction any further loans, fearing that these would prove too great a burden for an already overstretched Hierarchical purse. This left the Bishops with an immediate need for £4000 and the knowledge that in the longer run they would need about £20,000.

In June 1920, Cardinal Bourne attended the Annual Dinner of the London Circle, and, having explained the position, said that 'the Bishops had considered the matter and had asked him to put the case before the Catenians and invite them to give their assistance in what was really a great and good work'. Edward Lescher, President of the London Circle, in response explained that he could not speak for the Association but promised 'that the invitation would be put before the Association by the London Circle, with the request that the assistance asked for should be freely given'.

Grand Circle met in Liverpool at the end of July 1920, their meeting coinciding with the holding of a National Congress in that city. On 31 July, Cardinal Gasquet, O.S.B., addressed these assembled representatives of every Circle on the subject of the Beda. Aidan Gasquet was eminently fitted to explain the position of the Beda and the hopes of the Pope in its regard. Born in 1846 and educated at Downside, Gasquet became a Benedictine; ordained in 1874, he became Prior of Downside in 1878, and embarked on his work of re-establishing monastic studies. His first and perhaps greatest work was *Henry VIII and the English Monasteries*, which appeared in 1888 and 1889. These volumes were the first of a string of books from an eminent scholar.

In 1900, he had been elected President of the Benedictines in England, and in 1903, on Vaughan's death, the English bishops put his name on the *terna*, or list of three, submitted for the Pope's consideration as a possible successor to Vaughan. The other names on the list were those of a fellow-Benedictine, Bishop Hedley of Newport, and the relatively unknown and much younger Francis Bourne. The chance intervention at the Congregation of Propaganda of the Archbishop of Sydney, Patrick Moran, who had spent a lifetime 'rooting out all trace of the English Benedictine work in Australia', ensured that neither Benedictine was seriously considered for appointment to Westminster.

But Gasquet was called to serve the Church in other ways. In 1907, Pius X appointed him head of the commission set up to prepare a revision of the Vulgate. In 1914 he was elevated to the Sacred College of Cardinals, becoming prefect of the Archives of the Holy See (1917) and Librarian to the Holy Roman Church (1919). An English Cardinal, his home in Rome, he appreciated the importance of the work of the Beda and its precarious position in 1920.

Addressing Grand Council in July 1920, he explained that no one thought that the Association was so strong or so rich that it could produce all the money needed to buy or establish the College. But he went on:

> I believe that both from the point of view of your Association and of English Catholicism it would be of immense service to Catenians to find themselves practically in the position of founders of such a College ... the Holy Father would regard such work on your part as a great merit and distinction for your society and I believe that it would serve your purpose as well as it would serve the purposes of the Church.

He concluded by expressing the hope that 'the fact would be recorded in marble that it was through the Catenian Association that this hospice for the education of English clergymen was built'.

It was right that he should enter the caveat as regards the impossibility of the Association finding the money from its own resources. For in June 1920 there were only 3000 members in the 47 Circles, and they were beginning to live through the start of the post-war slump. And if there were 3000 nominal members, there were, as we have seen, perhaps half, maybe even less than half, of them who could be called active members.

It is also right for us to consider the money involved, so that we are not misled by the £3000 that was asked for as an immediate necessity. Today this represents less than the average manual worker's wage. In 1920 new houses could be bought for £400, a Ford car for £120, a week on the Broads cost £4, and a ten days' luxury cruise around Scandinavia cost thirteen guineas. To get a correct view of the money required for the Beda we ought to multiply the £3000 by perhaps 40 or more. To get a correct view of the burden on the active members we might then divide the £120,000 by, say, 1500. The Association was being asked to find the modern equivalent of £80 for each of its active members.

Grand Circle, having considered the Cardinal's request, suggested that every Brother might think of giving £1 towards a Beda Fund, while promising that the Association, having made its own contribution, would act on the Bishops' behalf in organising a national appeal. Some Circles responded to the suggestion by setting up a 'Beda Fund' and imposing a levy of 1s. a month for twelve months.

It was fortuitous that the Grand President in July 1920 was Oswald Goodier, a brother of Archbishop Goodier, S.J., of Bombay. It was Goodier who launched the Beda appeal in August 1920 and it became clear that the initial response was favourable. 'I am very glad that the appeal to the Catenians is making progress . . . the Beda College is in urgent need of assistance and the Catenians are the only body in England capable of dealing with such an appeal.' Goodier also received a letter from the Rector of the Beda, Mgr Mann, who had heard of the appeal's success on the eve of his return to Rome. Mann praised the generosity of the Catenians and assured them that 'the Holy Father will sanction the purchase and even advance the money to acquire the premises if he is convinced that what he advances will be duly returned to him'.

On 30 October 1920, Grand Director Munich, Privy Chamberlain to the Pope, was in Rome to perform his Papal duties. Goodier asked him to take a letter to Benedict XV, assuring him of the Association's wish to serve the Church. In reply Goodier received a letter from Cardinal Gasparri, the Secretary of State, dated 21 December 1920:

> The Holy Father has learnt with much satisfaction that the Association of which you are the head, in ready compliance with the wishes of the English Episcopate, is about to make an appeal to the generosity of its members to come to the assistance and promote the well-being of the Collegio Beda in Rome. His Holiness, who has nothing more at heart than the education of worthy priests, is most anxious that the charity of the faithful should more generally respond to your initiative, and he bestows a special fraternal blessing on those who co-operate in so important a work.

In May 1921, Bourne again attended the Annual Dinner of the London Circle. The President, Lescher, explained that because of the economic situation, the financial problems facing many Brothers, and the many other calls on their benevolence and money, the Association had not been able to do as much for the Beda as it had originally hoped. In replying, the Cardinal both acknowledged what had been done and showed that he appreciated the difficulties facing many Brothers and went on to say:

> At a recent meeting of the Bishops it was decided that we should give the Catenian Association a still further proof of our confidence, and a still further testimony of our appreciation of the far-reaching power of the Association, by entrusting to them the organisation of a further collection – not from their own members – but a collection in which they are to take the lead by associating themselves with other Catholic organisations, with the help of the clergy and the assistance of congregations throughout the country; so that, led and inspired by the great example of the Catenians themselves, the whole Catholic body may be led to do their share in the building up and the permanent establishment of the Beda College.

Goodier was not at that meeting, and it was Thomas Baines, then Grand Vice-President, who replied to the Cardinal. Baines, a London solicitor, was another of those polymaths who give the lie to the idea that the Brothers 'do nothing'. Chairman of the Association of Lancastrians in London, he combined his practice as a solicitor with the duties of Clerk to the Justices of the Wandsworth division, and he was a member of the Wandsworth Borough Council who declined to take the mayoral chair in 1908. A close friend of W. G. Grace, he helped form the English Bowling Association and was its first secretary and later vice-president, being a member of the International Bowling Board for many years. Originally a member of the London Circle, Baines became Founder President of South London in 1912, and of the City of London in 1921. He was Grand President of the Association 1921–23 and, with Synott, was largely responsible for framing the 1923 Constitution.

In replying to the Cardinal's speech, Baines went out of his way to explain that in having undertaken the collection of a Beda Fund the Association had gone outside its Constitution. He did not wish this appeal to be taken as a precedent, nor did he wish it to be thought that the Catenians were 'an omnibus charitable association'. Grand Council wished it to be clearly understood that, 'having made our supreme effort, that is the end'.

Meanwhile, Circles made their varied collections for the Beda appeal. On 22 July 1921, Gasquet was guest at the Manchester Circle, where 150 Brothers and their Grand President heard him say that he 'regarded the Catenians as the founders of the Beda College'. Among the other guests was Bishop Casartelli, who spoke in praise of the Association which had now grown well outside of its Salford origins. It must have pleased the Founder Bishop to see how his progeny had grown up to take its honoured place.

By December 1921 it was clear that some Circles were unhappy at the persistence of Grand Circle's appeal on behalf of the Beda Fund. They pointed out that they were being asked, by local clergy, to support the appeals for local churches, schools, orphanages, asylums, seminaries, missions and so on without end. At the same time the economic outlook was growing increasingly gloomier with a downturn in business activity, a decline in profits, a rise in unemployment and cuts in wages, salaries and profits. Grand Circle met for the last time in February 1923 (to make way for the Grand Council which was one result of the new Constitution). It was somehow fitting that the introduction of the new Constitution should be marked by, among other things, the announcement that the Association considered that as regards the

Beda appeal 'we have given all that we can', while agreeing to organise and support that national appeal of which Bourne had spoken in May 1921.

In May 1923, it was announced that the Grand Secretary had been able to send £3000 to the Beda authorities and hoped to be able to send a smaller, final sum when all Circles had completed their local appeals. In September 1923, Grand Council set about drawing up plans for that national appeal which raised a little more than £6000, so that in July 1924 *Catena* could carry the following note:

> *Beda College*
> The Beda College is now established in a home worthy of its purpose. A house has been secured at a cost of £10,000 and an appeal for a further £20,000 is being made. The Association helped to raise the first £10,000, and this is acknowledged by the Cardinal Protector, who, in thanking all generous benefactors, specially mentioned the Catenian Association.

This is not quite the end of the story. In that same July 1924, the Children's Fund was born – a happy innovation of the re-organised Association. One other result of that 1923 re-organisation was the calling of Annual General Meetings, the first of which was held at Birmingham in 1923, the second at Newcastle in 1924, and the third at Bristol at the end of September 1925, before which a party of 110 people, the Catenian Association Pilgrimage to Rome, had been led by Grand Director Paul Kelly. Leaving London on 8 September, they arrived in Rome on the 10th, and there they were joined by Past President Goodier and his brother, Archbishop Goodier, who acted as interpreter during the private audience which the Catenian pilgrims had with Pope Pius XI, who spoke warmly of the work which the Association was doing – for its members by bringing Catholic men together, for their families, for the Church in Great Britain and for the wider Church. He spoke of the value of the work the Association had done for the Beda College and of the generosity of thought which led to the foundation of the Children's Fund. In view of all this he 'blessed the Association and the good work it was doing'.

The pilgrims returned to London on 19 September, and many of the men made their way to the A.G.M. which opened in Bristol on 26 September, when the Grand President, Richard Brosch, 'announced amid applause that the Holy Father had bestowed his Apostolic Blessing upon the Association – upon its members collectively and individually'. So it was that the Association received the first of what has now become the annual Apostolic Blessing. It is to be regretted that a *Catena* article on The Beda College and its link with England written by a past student should have ignored the part played by the Association.

It is a fitting footnote to this part of our *History* to recall that many former Catenians have gone, as mature students, to the Beda to receive their priestly training. There have been some sixteen or so such ex-Catenian Beda-educated priests who have, in a sense, maintained that Association–Beda link in a special way. The first such 'Catenian priest' of whom I have a record was Fr F. W. Le Fèvre, who was a member of the Preston, Bradford and Newcastle-upon-Tyne Circles for 17 years, holding office for eight years and becoming President of the Preston and Bradford Circles. In August 1934, he said one of his first Masses at the Church of Blessed Thomas More, Blessed John Fisher and Companions, Burley-in-Wharfedale, Yorkshire, for deceased members of the Association. In thanking the Association for its work for his *alma mater*, Fr Le Fèvre pointed out:

When the Bishop of Leeds looked with sorrowful eyes on the vast numbers of the faithful who had to tramp long distances to Mass, it was the Catenian Association which took the foremost part in coming to his aid, and that Association had borne the brunt both of the work and money of the activities of the Bishop's New Mission Fund. And it was this child of the Association, the Bishop's New Mission Fund, which, after the purchase of land, mainly by the people of Otley, provided the first funds – £1200 – for the erection of this church at Burley.

That a church could be built, once £1200 had been raised, may help remind us of the changing value of money and may put the £3000 collected for the Beda Fund in a more correct perspective. That the Burley church owed its establishment to the activities and money of local Catenians may also remind us of the many calls made on Brothers' time and money in earlier days. That the Brothers so evidently supported the Beda Fund while also responding to local calls such as Burley may, one hopes, help rebut the charge that Catenians do nothing but 'wine and dine'.

5. Plater College

There is something fitting about the Association's aid to the Beda College: many Brothers have relatives who are priests; some former Catenians have become priests, and one, James Donald Scanlan (No. 56 on the roll of the Glasgow Strathclyde Circle), was to become a priest (1929). Bishop of Dunkeld (1946), Bishop of Motherwell (1955) and Archbishop of Glasgow (1964). Links between the clergy and Brothers is inevitably close.

But there was nothing inevitable or fitting about the Association's involvement with the Catholic Workers' College, now known as Plater College; for this provides higher education for working-class men and women who wish to fit themselves to play a larger role in their place of work, where some, as union leaders, may well come into conflict with Catholic, even Catenian, employers.

The Workers' College had its origins in Leo XIII's encyclical *Rerum Novarum* (1891), in which, having outlined Catholic social teaching, the Pope went on to plead that employers and employees should educate themselves in this teaching so that they might be better fitted to see that social justice was done. The English Hierarchy, concerned as it was with many problems – schools, church building, priestly training and the like – ignored the encyclical. It was left to an outstanding Jesuit, Charles Plater, to show the way. In 1909 he founded the Catholic Social Guild which provided booklets, courses of lectures and conferences, by which Catholic social teaching might become better known.

Plater died in January 1921 when he was in Malta organising workers against exploiting employers. In his memory, and immediately following his death, another Jesuit, Leo O'Hea, founded the Catholic Workers' College with only three students – a weaver, a tinsmith and a railwayman, who lived with him in his Oxford lodgings, while he established them with the University and almost begged their daily bread. The growth of the College was slow: by 1933 there were seven students, and by 1938 thirteen.

O'Hea developed a syllabus of studies which, over two years, enabled students to take either the Oxford University Diploma in Social Studies, or the College Certificate in Social Studies. Some students did so well that they were allowed to go on to take degrees at the University. Most returned to their place of work and became involved in trade union or social reform. A few, such as Maurice Foley, became national figures, Foley himself becoming Chief Whip of the Labour Party and a Minister in the Wilson governments of 1964–70.

What had this to do with the Association? Catenian employers played a major part in the founding of the Conference of Catholic industrialists. A leading figure in this work was Paul Kelly, whose mantle has been inherited by his nephew Christopher Bussy, the youngest of the seven sons of G.F.P. ('Phil') Bussy, No. 351 on the roll of the London Circle, whose sister married Paul Kelly. Five of Bussy's sons became Catenians, the other two becoming priests, and in 1981 the family set a Catenian record when the fourth-generation Bussy was enrolled into the Association.

Paul Kelly quickly realised that there was little point in helping to develop a Catholic attitude amongst employers unless there was a similar development amongst employees. This helps to explain why he and other Catenians became interested in the work of the C.S.G., as speakers, writers, supporters, members of the necessary committees, and governors of the Workers' College.

But this was, in a sense, merely one aspect of the Catholic action of some Catenians. It was hardly the work of the Association as such. Some Circles, such as the one at Stoke, helped set up branches of the C.S.G. in their locality. Others provided some of the financial help needed to pay the fees and provide the living expenses of the resident students. And this action by individual Circles over the years provided the favourable background against which we have to see the 1949 A.G.M. held at Edinburgh. Circles on Tyneside had for several years after 1945 sponsored scholarships from collections organised in their Circles. Two Brothers from the Newcastle-upon-Tyne Circle proposed and seconded the motion that the Association should sponsor an annual scholarship at the Catholic Workers' College. They pointed out that they were asking the Association to raise 'a capital sum of £5000 to £8000, the interest from which would provide one scholarship in perpetuity'. The resolution was passed unanimously, although Redwood, in *Catena*, expressed doubts as to the possibility of raising the money involved.

Grand President Hildred told the A.G.M. that 'any such fund as was being suggested must be collected on a voluntary basis', and it was he who sent the first of those annual letters which go out from the Grand President, urging every Circle President: 'Please commend this charity to the members of your Circle and forward contributions to Bro. Grand Secretary.' While there was no intention to raise the capital sum spoken of at Edinburgh there was the intention to raise, in 1949, the £200 needed to pay for the scholarship. With hindsight it may be seen as a blessing that the Association did not try to raise that capital sum, but decided on an annual collection, since, with inflation, the sum would have been insufficient to have paid for 'one scholarship in perpetuity', while the same inflation has allowed the Association to offer more than the £200 needed for a scholarship in 1949. Indeed, in the affluent 1960s there was, in some years, enough money to pay for two students – even at higher fees and costs – who might otherwise never have had the chance of a Catholic form of higher education.

In the 1970s the Department of Education and Science undertook to provide grants for students at long-term residential colleges. This changed the financial position and diminished the importance of the Catenian Appeal Fund for the College, which, in the mid-1960s, was re-named Plater College. At the urging of the Principal and the governors, the Association agreed to provide funds for the living expenses of needy students – such as married men, whose grants were not sufficiently large to allow them to maintain their families in adequate comfort. Also in the 1970s the College began to plan for a redevelopment which would allow it to build a new College on a site within the city boundary of Oxford. On this site there would be accommodation for 80 students, 72 of them in single study bedrooms. The cost of the overall scheme was £500,000, half of which was provided by the D.E.S., part of which was met by the Hierarchy and another part met by the proceeds of the sale of the original College site at Boar's Hill. But this still left the governors of the College with the task of raising some £200,000. In December 1975, Christopher Bussy, Chairman of the governing body, asked Grand Council to amend the regulations surrounding the Plater College Appeal Fund so that some of the money might go into a College Development Fund, to be used for servicing the necessary loan. Grand Council agreed to do this, although the decision was greeted with hostility by some legalistically-minded Brothers who wanted to stick to the terms agreed in 1949.

Many Circles send their own contributions to the College Development Fund, while also being generous in their response to the annual appeal by the incumbent Grand President. At the present time, this Fund is used to provide living expenses for a small number of needy students and to provide for the fees for one overseas student. Now that the Association has Circles in Zambia, Zimbabwe, Australia, Ireland, Hong Kong and Malta, there may well be an increase in the number of overseas applicants for consideration as Catenian scholars. Until that happens, Grand Council has decided that some of the money standing in the Appeal Fund should be handed to the College for use in its Development Fund. In 1978, £1000 was transferred in this way, and in 1980 £1500. This is in addition to the £885 paid on behalf of the student from the Channel Islands, and unspecified sums paid to help towards the living expenses of a small number of married students. The many Catenian leaders – Kelly, Taggart, Ward, Bussy and others – who worked so hard for the now-defunct C.S.G. would have approved of this continuing and expanding involvement in the work begun by Fr Plater.

CHAPTER SEVEN

Organisation, re-organisation and structure

1. The need for a new Constitution

In 1921 and in the aftermath of the explosion of inaugurations in 1920, Grand Council issued an eight-page pamphlet written by Willian O'Dea of the Manchester Circle. In *The Catenian Association: a Catholic Retrospect and Prospect* O'Dea traced the fortunes of the Catholic body over the previous three hundred years, with its history of persecution and bigotry. Having outlined the social groupings within the Catholic body at the time of the Restoration of the Hierarchy in 1850, with the 'old' Catholic families on their estates, the small band of 'intellectual' converts, and the mass of the Irish, O'Dea showed that the Catholic middle class was of recent origin and that it was growing because of the greater job opportunities in industry, in commerce, in the professions and in government, in each of which there was such a decline in bigotry that Catholics had greater chance of employment and promotion in the middle-class 'salariat'.

O'Dea explained that the Church had always had a variety of societies and sodalities for its various members, and argued that the Association was in the tradition of the medieval guilds – with its attention to the religious and social well-being of its members and with its major aim of affording benevolence for its members and their dependents. Looking to the future, O'Dea saw that there would be a steady, uninterrupted growth of both the Catholic middle class and the Association which had been founded specifically for the needs of that class. Welcoming the emergence of this class and of the Association, O'Dea asked that the latter should create the organisation by which the skills and abilities of Catholic business and professional men might be best applied in the work of the Church.

On more practical and political levels, the expansion of the Association led to calls for changes in its government. With delegates from each Circle, Grand Circle had grown so that in 1921 there were some 90 delegates attending the annual meeting of the Association's 'Parliament', called to amend or add to the rules, to fix the fees and to elect twelve of their number to form the Grand Council which met four times a year and whose committees carried on the day-to-day work of the Association. If expansion was about to take place at the rate indicated by the recent development, then Grand Circle would grow into an unwieldy, costly and inefficient body. At the same time, members of newer Circles – and some of the older ones – felt that Grand Council was unrepresentative of the Association as a whole. There was a natural tendency for delegates at Grand Circle to elect and re-elect well-known men to Grand Council. Who would not have voted for O'Donnell, Hogan, Synott, Foggin, Baines and Brosch? And if some of the older Circles were over-represented, so too were some of the regions, with the preponderance of power being exercised by Manchester and London, and the newly-developed regions of the south coast and Scotland having no voice on Grand Council.

When Grand Council met in Manchester on 25 June 1921, Brosch of Birmingham presented the case for re-organisation and put forward proposals for the Constitution under which, with minor modifications, the Association lives today. Grand President Goodier allowed discussion of Brosch's proposals, and bitter divisions within the Council appeared at once, with Manchester men resenting the major shake-up proposed. But the majority on Grand Council agreed that the existing Constitution would not be able to cope with the greater number of Circles which most people confidently expected would soon be formed. Grand Council, however, rather than try to impose its views on the Association, agreed to wait for the meeting of Grand Circle at which delegates from every Circle would be able to express their opinions.

Grand Circle met in July 1921, and Grand Secretary Shepherd presented the proposals for a new Constitution. This was a wise choice, for Shepherd was well known to most members of Grand Circle. He had attended the majority of the inaugural meetings of the newer Circles, and he was in constant touch with Circle Officers, from whom most of the delegates to Grand Circle were drawn. It was also obvious that he, at any rate, had the interests of the whole Association at heart, while there was a suspicion that some of the supporters of the new Constitution may have been considering local rather than national interests.

In a hard-hitting speech Shepherd examined the state of the rapidly expanding Association – 'no longer a dream as it was only ten years ago'. He criticised Circles which had some 80 or 90 members on their rolls but rarely had more than 30 per cent of them at their monthly meetings. He argued that there had been a mad quest for mere numbers, for quantity rather than quality, little thought having been given to what, if anything, prospective members might be prepared or able to contribute to the Association. He was critical of the ways in which, at local, Grand Circle and Grand Council levels, there was all too little of that 'fraternal love which animates the Brotherhood', self-seeking, back-biting and personality clashes having been allowed to dominate the members' thinking and behaviour. He announced that, when the new Constitution came into operation, he would no longer wish to remain in office as Grand Secretary, although he would continue to support the Association, which in spite of its faults he still admired and which he hoped would flourish.

Shepherd then outlined the proposed new Constitution, under which the Association was to be divided into 12 Provinces relating to the main regions of Great Britain, named as Scotland (based on Glasgow), north-east England (based on Newcastle), north-west England (based on Preston), the north-east Midlands (based on Leeds), the north-west Midlands (based on Manchester), the west Midlands (based on Liverpool), the central Midlands (based on Birmingham), the south Midlands (based on Leicester), the Home Counties (based on London), the central section of the South Coast (based on Portsmouth), and, finally, Wales and the West Country (based on Cardiff). Circles in each of these Provinces were to elect Provincial Councils which would act as a regional tier of government and would elect Grand Directors to serve on Grand Council along with all the Past Grand Presidents, the Grand Secretary and the Grand Treasurer. Replacing Grand Circle, the meeting place for delegates from every Circle, there would be an Annual General Meeting of the Association, open to members of all Circles. It is worth noting that the proposers of the new Constitution talked about the regional division of the Association, and claimed that it would be right and beneficial for Grand Council to be guaranteed the chance of having regional opinion expressed through the Grand Directors. The new Constitution, however, gave Provinces the right to elect Grand Directors, and as the number of Provinces grew, there was a growth in the size of Grand Council to the point where, once again, in the '60s and '70s there was need to consider the cost and efficiency of an over-large Council. If the right to elect Grand Directors had been vested in regions rather than in Provinces, the subsequent growth of the Association would not have affected the size of Grand Council, since the number of Grand Directors would have remained constant – at twelve. But more of this later.

2. The 1923 Constitution

In October 1921, a sub-committee was set up to examine the proposed new Constitution, and delegates were sent to discuss the proposed changes at a series of regional gatherings where there was much criticism of Shepherd's comments and of some aspects of the proposed Constitution. The sub-committee prepared a detailed scheme for presentation to the Association. This work was done, primarily, by Walter Synott of the London Circle. He had been educated at Stonyhurst and Trinity College, Dublin, before being called to the Irish Bar in 1884. On his return to England he practised as a barrister, becoming especially versed in trade union law. He was well fitted to write the new Constitution, which was presented to Grand Council in February 1922.

Synott's proposals followed the scheme earlier outlined by Shepherd. He appreciated the regret felt by many men at the passing of Grand Circle, but argued that the new scheme would be more efficient, less costly and more democratic, since the Circles would have the right to elect Provincial Councillors who would have a voice in the choosing of the Grand Directors who would govern the Association and choose the Grand President. To replace Grand Circle, the new Constitution proposed an Annual General Meeting as a rally of members to be held in a different region each year. Synott proposed that the A.G.M. might make suggestions to Grand Council, which, however, would not be obliged to follow its decisions. This power to accept or reject decisions reached at the A.G.M. became known as 'Grand Council's veto' and to many it seemed to be undemocratic. But Synott realised that an A.G.M. would not be truly representative of the Association; normally there would be many members present from the region in which the A.G.M. was being held, so that an idea favoured in that region might gain overwhelming support at the A.G.M. although it might not appeal to the Association as a whole. Synott proposed that any changes – in rules, fees or structure – might be pushed through in one of two ways. Either, a Circle might put a proposal to Provincial Council, which, if it supported the idea, would send it on for consideration by Grand Council; if Grand Council approved the proposal, it would then put it forward to be voted on by the Association as a whole. If two-thirds of those voting accepted the proposal, it would then be incorporated in the Rules. Or, alternatively, a proposal might be put forward at an A.G.M.; if it was there carried by a two-thirds majority, Grand Council would then decide whether to accept or reject the motion. In fact, Grand Council rarely used its power to ignore an A.G.M. ruling otherwise than by reviving a motion for some desirable change which had been lost at an A.G.M. owing to poor presentation or over-strong local opposition.

But this did not save the Constitution from the charge of being undemocratic, nor did it in the future save Grand Council from the charge of being unrepresentative and dictatorial. Subsequently, Grand Council gave up this right of veto. Another amendment to Synott's scheme was also forced on Grand Council in the name of fairer representation. He had proposed that all Past Grand Presidents should be *ex officio* members of Grand Council. A glance at the current Directory shows that in 1981 there are 15 surviving Past Grand Presidents. If each of these were a member of Grand Council, they could outvote the 12 Grand Directors produced by Synott's scheme, and, now that we have 19 Grand Directors, would form a large minority of 'old hands'. This proposal was attacked from the very start. Birmingham asked that only the three immediate Past Grand Presidents should be *ex officio* members.

After having been considered by Grand Council in March 1922, the scheme was published and distributed to every Circle for wider consideration and debate. Many of the older members were opposed to the changes suggested, and in March and April 1922 there were very heavy losses of membership, due, it was claimed, to this opposition, although others pointed to the downturn in the economy, to apathy and to selfish disappointments at not having gained business benefit from membership, as potent reasons for the many resignations and lapses. The Grand President in this decisive year was Baines of London, who devoted himself to explaining the scheme to almost every Circle on a Grand President visit. One can only admire the energy and devotion of a man who gave so much of himself at a time when travel was not as easy as it is today.

Circle discussions led to the emergence of several general criticisms: there was, as we have seen, the opposition to the life membership of Grand Council given to Past Grand Presidents; there was anxiety at the prospect of having to find a replacement for Shepherd, which would mean the funding of a new Head Office; there were demands that 'Service' be written into the Constitution – a point that was countered by Grand Council's decision that 'Service' was covered in the then Rule 5, which was a disingenuous way of trying to get rid of 'Service' altogether; there was the demand that all Circles should open and close with the same ritual and that cards be printed for distribution to each Circle – with the *De Profundis* being reinstated as one of the components of the Ritual.

In October 1922, Grand Circle met to consider the comments, favourable and unfavourable, that poured in from the Circles. Among those present were O'Donnell and Hogan. It was fitting that this meeting should take place at Manchester, but one cannot help wondering what O'Donnell thought of the way in which his 'infant' had grown. Having considered the proposed Constitution and the many comments that had been received, Grand Circle resolved that Circles should be asked to vote on the scheme and send a delegate to an Extraordinary Meeting of Grand Circle to be held in Manchester on 3 February 1923, when the votes of the members would be counted.

There was a touch of *The Comedy of Errors* about that February meeting. Most delegates assumed, rightly, that there would be a favourable vote; wrongly, that there would be no need for their presence at the last meeting of Grand Circle. When the meeting opened there was not present the required quorum of one-third of the delegates; telegrams had to be sent out to summon men to attend. When finally a quorum had gathered, O'Donnell and Hogan were appointed tellers, and it was one of these who announced that 1561 votes had been cast for the new Constitution and 109 against it. So it was that Grand Circle was brought to its end, that a new General Secretary had to be found, an A.G.M. had to be planned, and the Association embarked on a new stage in its development.

Baines entertained the members of the old Grand Circle to dinner in April 1923 – the month which also saw the death of Tait, No. 6 on the Manchester roll. On 26 May 1923, the new Grand Council held its first meeting, O'Donnell and Hogan being present as Synott took the chair as Grand President. And while plans went ahead for the first A.G.M. (held in Birmingham in September 1923), Synott was telling Grand Council (August 1923) that the value of the new Constitution was already clear. The Grand Council was both smaller and more efficient, while the new Provincial Councils would soon prove their worth (p. 89). He called for the enthusiastic support of the membership for the work and the expansion of the Association.

3. The politics of development

Synott, Shepherd, Baines and the rest were to be disappointed by the failure of the Association to maintain the momentum of expansion. As we shall see, the years ahead did not follow the patterns of 1920 and 1922. If that rate of expansion had been maintained there could have been some 180 Circles by 1939 – whereas there were only 123. In later Chapters, we shall examine the many reasons for this failure, but here we ought to note that one result of this slow-down was that, whereas there might have been fifteen or so Circles in each Province if the expansion had continued, in fact there were rarely more than ten Circles in a Province. And whereas there was some sense of cohesion in Province 1, based on Manchester, in which all the Circles lay within a fifteen-mile radius of the city, there was no such cohesive unity in Province 12, with its Circles in South Wales, the Bristol region and the far South-West It is not surprising that there was soon a demand that the three Circles in the South-West (Plymouth, Exeter and Torbay) should be allowed to break away and form their own Province, in which even the vast distances still to be covered by Provincial Officers and by members going on inter-Circle visits would be an improvement on the scheme which linked Plymouth with, for example, Swansea.

But now the politics which mar much of the Association's history came into play. There was plenty of scope for expansion in certain Provinces: around Manchester, with the increasing development of towns in Cheshire; around Birmingham, a region which escaped the worst ravages of the inter-war depression and saw the steady growth of a Catholic middle class; and to a lesser degree around Liverpool. But there was little chance of similar expansion, for example, in the new Province 13 with its scattered and small Catholic population, or in Scotland (Province 9) with its future also affected by the peculiarity of Scotland's geography.

And if Province 1 grew while Provinces 9 and 13 did not, was it fair that it should be represented on Grand Council by only the one Grand Director who might represent 800 or so men compared with the 100 or so in Province 13? It was this parochialism which led to the demand for the sub-division of Provinces with large memberships. In 1949, Province 8 was divided to allow the formation of a new Province 14. It is interesting to note that it had at first been suggested that the 'new divisions should both retain the old number but that one should be "East" and the other "West". The affected areas decided that it would be preferable to set up entirely new numbering.'

That was the first break with the 'regionalisation' envisaged in 1922–23. In 1950, Province 6 was divided to allow the formation of Province 15, while Rudman's ambition to have his friend, Jock Shaw, on Grand Council led to the division of Province 9 so as to allow the formation of Province 16. The perverse Scots frustrated Rudman by not electing Shaw as their Grand Director.

When Manchester North Circle was inaugurated in 1954, Province 1 contained 16 Circles (with a membership of some 700) compared to Province 13 (with 4 Circles and 150 members), Province 17 (with 4 Circles and 150 members) and Province 15 (with 5 Circles and less than 200 members). Province 1 contained more Circles and had more members than the other three Provinces combined. It was proposed by some 'activists' that the Province ought to divide so as to ensure a more equitable representation on Grand Council. Provincial Council was in bitter disagreement over this suggestion. The debates were many and quite savage, with dominant personalities taking prepared positions for and against the proposed division. In March 1954, Jack Politi of South Manchester and Grand Director for Province 1 had been a candidate in the election for Grand Vice-President, with the almost assured hope that, if successful, he would become the first Grand President from Manchester since McCabe (1916–17). Politi lost the election by one vote, which confirmed the belief of some that the Province ought to be divided; if there had been two Grand Directors from the Manchester area, Politi might well have gone on to take the chair, which would have been fitting, for, like O'Donnell, he was a former pupil of St Anne's, Ancoats, and was one who, like O'Donnell, had made his way via night school to become a leading figure in the textile trade.

Manchester men resented the passing over of Politi, whom they rightly considered to have been an exemplary Catenian and a great Catholic. Grand Council consented to the proposal to divide Province 1, and Politi became Grand Director of the new Province 17. Once again, Manchester men looked forward to his attaining the presidential office. Unfortunately, his health broke down in 1957 when he was Grand Vice-President; he was forced to retire from active participation in the Association's affairs, and he died in July 1958 after a long illness.

For the members of Province 1, the division had some unfortunate results. The economic and social development of the country meant that the chances of Catenian expansion in the now smaller Province was limited, and only three new Circles have been opened since 1954. Province 17 has proved to be a better region for expansion and has added six new Circles to its roll since 1954. At the same time, the Manchester Circle suffered from a Grand Council decision of 1923 and from the decay of the inner city. Up until 1923 there had been no limit on the number of members who might be enrolled in a Circle, and at one time Manchester and London had over 400 on their respective rolls. Although the defects of such a large membership were obvious – with the danger of cliques being formed, with the newcomer finding it an ordeal on enrolment, when he had to shake hands with every member present at his initiation, with the difficulty of getting to know so many men – yet, despite these drawbacks there was a reluctance to put a limit on recruitment. When in 1923 Grand

Council ruled that in future no Circle was to have more than 100 men on the roll, Manchester, like London, faced a crisis which was slow to develop but which has proved to be of major significance. If in 1923, when that rule was made, Manchester had there and then been divided into, say, five or six smaller Circles, things would not have been so bad. But the Circle continued with its over-large membership. Forbidden to recruit new blood, in time it became an ageing Circle. When it eventually became small enough for recruitment to be allowed again, it was not a sufficiently attractive Circle for potential young members, who preferred to join other neighbouring Circles whose membership had a better age spread. On top of this 'ageing' problem Manchester, like all inner city Circles, faces the problems associated with the decay of inner cities. Both the cause and the effect of this decay is the shift of population away from the inner urban areas to pleasanter suburbs, which helps to explain the development of the Association in those suburbs. But what the suburban Circles gain, the inner city Circles lose. With a smaller residential population on which to draw, and with their existing members tending to move out of the city and being increasingly reluctant to come back into the city for Circle meetings, many inner city Circles face a crisis. Some have tackled this by physically moving their place of meeting so that Liverpool, for example, has now moved its base into a new and expanding area of the city.

4. More re-organisation?

Province 17 was not the last to be formed; for Province 18 was formed by the division of Province 7, and Province 19 by the division of Province 11. And as the Association enjoyed a new wave of expansion in the 1960s, it seemed that there could be almost no end to the sub-division of expanding Provinces. And where would such a sub-division leave Grand Council? Vastly expanded, to the point of being cumbersomely inefficient and at great cost, all to little purpose; for the real work of Grand Council would not increase in proportion to the increase in membership or to the increase in the number of Grand Directors. This explains why in the '50s and '60s Grand Council examined a number of proposals for re-organisation. None of these was put to the members as a whole, because Grand Council could not agree on a firm proposal. In general, the Council agreed that, ideally, the Association ought to be divided into roughly twelve regions (as had been proposed in 1923), each with its regional Grand Director, no matter how many Circles or Provinces might be found in a region. But politics again reared its ugly head. Which of the existing Provinces was going to be asked to sacrifice its representation on Grand Council? Which of the 19 Grand Directors was going to lose the privilege of being a member of a reconstructed Grand Council?

The most serious attempt at reconstruction emerged from the work of a high-powered, active and able Commission which sat under Douglas Jenkins's chairmanship and published its Report in May 1970. Its findings – on regionalisation and a smaller Grand Council – were approved by Grand Council, though it rejected similar recommendations earlier in the '50s and '60s. A series of regional meetings were held, so that members could hear one or more of the framers of the Report explain its recommendations. Then the debate was carried on via the columns of *Catena* where a minority of activists put forward ideas for making the Association even more workmanlike. At the 1971

A.G.M., held in Dublin, the Report of the Re-organisation Commission was debated, approved and sent to the Circles to be voted on. The Report was then approved by the votes of the Brothers in their Circles, although there were misgivings about some of its aspects. Attempts, however, to meet criticisms made at Circle level led to a re-drafting of the Report, which was then rejected by Grand Council.

So, at the time of writing, Grand Council remains the unwieldy body which a majority of the Brothers voted to reform in 1971. The continued growth in the number of Circles at home and overseas has made the case for re-organisation even stronger. But it seems that members are as firmly tied to the 1923 Constitution as were critics of that radical change when it was first proposed in 1922–23. Addressing the 1960 A.G.M., Grand President Joe McMurray said:

> I have known old and valued Catenians, men whose membership stretched back prior to 1914, whose expressed opinion was that hell was not hot enough or eternity long enough for Grand Council. Others I have known have suggested that Hitler's inspiration for the Gestapo came from a study of the 1923 Constitution.

But time is a great healer and the 1923 Constitution with its Grand Council has now become the entrenched wisdom, to be defended at all costs.

5. Structures and officers

The most important part of the Association's structure is the Circle, which, as the Jenkins Commission noted, has 'proved to be an impressively attractive means of providing centres of cohesion and mutual encouragement for men living or working within a common neighbourhood'. And, as the Commission argued, 'everything above the Circle is administrative and is justified only as it serves or supplements the work which finds its prime manifestation at Circle level'.

At his initiation a man is welcomed into a 'brotherhood' and is told of the widespread character of the Association. The fact is, however, that each man joins the Association because of some attraction to the local Circle, one or more of whose members will have first invited him to a post-Circle meeting in which he must have come to believe that he would find that friendship of which his sponsors had told him. Maybe he also learned to enjoy the pleasure of the company of men drawn from a variety of occupations and with a variety of interests, finding, as one man said, 'the sort of interchange of ideas such as one might find at the High Table in a College Hall'. And it is from the Brothers of the local Circle that a man receives, when he needs it, that 'mutual support' of which the Association rightly boasts.

It is in the local Circle that the Catholic activist will find the willing recruits to support his own form of action, whether this be at parish level (as with the S.V.P.) or at inter-parochial level (as with the K.S.C.) or involving action on a wider level (as with the many forms of action to help the handicapped).

The success of a Circle depends, in the first instance, on the quality of the officers selected by its members. The President ought to be the Brother to whom the others (and potential recruits) look for leadership in Catenian affairs and in Catholic life outside the Circle. It is he who has to stimulate the Brothers to make the Circle effective and attractive; it is he who has to encourage inter-Circle visiting which serves to widen the interests of Brothers and to cement that 'fellowship' of which the members talk. Other officers – the Vice-President, Treasurer, Chamberlain and so on – have their respective parts to play in the life of the Circle; but it is the Circle Secretary on whom the greatest burden falls.

The *Manual of Procedure* outlines the nature of the Secretary's work, and this, as well as the experience of every Circle, makes clear that a Circle flourishes in direct proportion to the way in which the Secretary tackles his job. One can only admire the selfless way in which so many hundreds of men spend so much of their time acting as the link with Provincial and Grand Councils, Provincial and Grand Secretaries, as well as with their fellow-Secretaries in other Circles.

The Circle is 'at home' to any Brother who cares to attend its meetings, and this helps to explain the standard manner in which the formal proceedings are carried out. The layout of the Circle is both symbolic and functional; it typifies the chain or Brotherhood, while also making it possible for all members to be seen by their colleagues and to be identified when they stand at roll call, so that newcomers become known by name and are the more easily integrated into Circle life. The placing of the principal officers at the arms of the cross both completes the symbolism of the Association's emblem and ensures that business is conducted audibly and openly and is not concentrated around the Chair. That each of these officers has his own table and badge of office serves at least two practical purposes: it enables him to carry out his functions with a maximum of efficiency, while also ensuring that visiting Brothers will know easily to whom they have to go to register, to obtain the visitor's card, to pay the money due for meals and so forth.

The meeting opens and closes with a simple and dignified ceremonial which some find 'attractively medieval' while others find it 'simply Catholic'. This ritual and manner of conducting the business meeting has evolved over many years. At one time the officers' tables were littered with cards relating to the ritual, most of them being additions made over the years. One has to pay tribute to a former Grand Secretary, Laurie Tanner, for the writing of a *Manual* which contains all the prayers and directions for conducting meetings.

The 1923 Constitution made no attempt to interfere with the ways in which local Circles conducted their affairs. It did, however, oblige each Circle to elect a Provincial Councillor to represent the Circle on the newly-established Provincial Council. This consisted of Provincial Councillors from each Circle, plus the four Provincial Officers, the three immediate Past Presidents and the Province's Grand Director. Each Council meets four times a year and is funded from the capitation fee paid by each Circle to the Association's Head Office.

The authors of the 1923 Constitution hoped that they were creating an efficient intermediate tier of administration midway between Grand Council and the Circles, which, they thought, would become too numerous for Grand Secretary and Grand Council to deal with. Provincial Councils had certain tasks allotted to them, some of which, like the collating of Circle voting returns, they fulfil, others of which, as we shall see, they have failed to carry out. In the event, Circles have tended to ignore Provincial Councils; if there is a problem the Circle Officers tend to write to the Grand Secretary or Grand Council.

Since 1923 there have been many attempts to define the rights and powers of Provincial Councils. But the fact is, and has always been, that these Councils have little power. They have little money at their disposal, they have no full-time staff and would be unable to cope with a flood of material if Circles were to send such in. In theory, the Council has powers to 'discipline' Circles in the Province and to insist on standards of ritual, of general behaviour and of the quality of prospective members. In fact, the Council has no power to impose its will on recalcitrant Circles. It does have, however, the ability to call upon Grand Council to withdraw a Circle's Charter.

Provincial Councils were empowered to ensure that potential recruits to the Association were of that 'quality' which would ensure that they would enjoy membership of the Association while also adding to its effectiveness. In fact, it is, almost inevitably, the local Circle which exercises this supervision of the quality of recruits. The Councils were also charged with the task of encouraging inter-Circle visiting. But such visiting had taken place before 1923, while its spread since then owes little, if anything, to Provincial Councils: in one and the same Province one can find Circles which have a proud record of visiting and being visited, and other Circles which neither visit nor encourage visitors. If Provincial Councils wish to claim the credit for the former, they have to accept responsibility for the latter.

Synott, Shepherd and the other authors of the 1923 Constitution hoped that each Provincial Councillor would bring to the Province 'a feel' of his own Circle and would return from meetings of the Council with reports of Provincial matters. This presupposed that each Councillor would have the ability to make notes during meetings and to translate these notes into a meaningful report at a Circle meeting. Councillors who hear, while on a Circle visit, Councillor-colleagues reporting back, have often wondered whether they have attended the same Provincial meetings as the 'reporters'; what one recalls as important may have seemed trivial to another, and what a careful note-taker has been able to recall has been ignored by the less attentive Councillor. It is not surprising that there have been many critical comments on Provincial Councils.

One task laid upon Provincial Councils is that of electing the Grand Director to serve on Grand Council. We have already seen that it was the continued growth of Grand Council which led to the setting up of a number of Re-organisation Commissions between 1956 and 1970. We also saw how Association politics played a part in ensuring that none of these Commissions gave birth to change. Indeed, at the time of writing, there is a heated debate going on in Province 3, where the late Grand Director came from Barnsley in the south of that Province. Men in the north are now claiming that his successor ought, naturally, to come from their half of the divided Province, whether or not there is a better man willing to serve from the south. One understands the reasons for this demand, but may be permitted to regret that such a parochial outlook should prevail.

In some ways the role of Grand Director is an ambivalent one. He is, on the one hand, chosen to represent the Province on Grand Council, where he is to assist in the government of the Association; on the other hand, he is supposed, on his return to his Province, to take a lower place in its affairs than the Provincial President. Again, he is directed to get around the Province, to visit every Circle as often as he can, so that he can fulfil the role of transmitter – of the 'feel' of the Association at its grass roots, which he will take with him to Grand Council, from which, on the other hand, he will carry the thinking of Grand Council on the Association's affairs. If, for example, Grand Council proposes to make a change, say, in rules or subscriptions, or is thinking of a major development such as the adoption of the Chaplaincies scheme, then the

ORGANISATION, RE-ORGANISATION AND STRUCTURE

Grand Director should, if he is doing his job properly, promote discussion of these changes or developments – at the Provincial Council, at Provincial rallies and at Circle meetings – and should be present at as many of these functions as is possible so that he can personally explain the thinking of Grand Council.

There is evidence that in some Provinces at least the Grand Directors do these jobs well. But in other, geographically larger, Provinces the effort to carry out this 'transmitting and propaganda' function involves a great deal of travel and is not always done as well as it is in, say, the Midlands or the North-West. And there is some evidence that, even when the task is properly tackled, the result may be negative. It may be inherent in human nature, it may be that it is a peculiarly Saxon trait, but the fact remains that, having chosen a man to represent them on Provincial Council (presumably because they liked and trusted him) and having then heard that his peers there have chosen him to serve on Grand Council, many Brothers almost instinctively come to suspect him and 'them' on Grand Council of not doing their job as efficiently as they might or of not considering fully the implications of the proposals they are making. For in spite of a good deal of effort by Grand Directors, by the Editor of *Catena*, through whose columns the issues are open to debate, and by Provincial Councils, it is undeniable that all too few men bother to vote on issues sent down by Grand Council, and of the 50 per cent or so who bother to vote a large number, sometimes a majority, turn down the proposals put forward by the Grand Council.

How does a man become a Grand Director? The normal pattern is for a Brother to be chosen by his peers to serve on the Circle Council, to make his way up the hierarchy of offices in the Circle, and then to be elected to serve as a Provincial Councillor. Having attained office in the Provincial Council, he may then make his way up the hierarchy of office there until his peers elect him to serve on Grand Council. Now this process raises a number of questions, the answers to which throw some doubt on whether Brothers get the Grand Council they need – although it may be true that they get the one they deserve. At what age, for example, does the man get on to Grand Council? He has normally to serve for a number of years on lower Councils, at Circle and Provincial level, before getting on to Grand Council. All too often it is a case of 'Buggins's turn' – whether Buggins is up to the job or not. It ought to be borne in mind that each Grand Director should be a potential Grand President. But once he is elected on to Grand Council, is there any check made to see how effectively the man has carried out his role? Or do Brothers not rather, again because of misplaced affection for Buggins, continue to re-elect him time after time so that some serve for over twenty years, and others continue to serve when they are well beyond the task? Is it true that in a Province there has been no one of Grand Director status who might have been chosen to replace Buggins after, say, ten years or so? Does the man who has served for, say, fifteen years still have anything fresh to say to Grand Council or to the Province? It is small wonder that there is evidence that some Grand Directors have not spoken on any issue for years, so exposing themselves to the accusation that they are 'going along for the ride', while exposing the Association to the risk of being, in part at least, mismanaged.

It may be that there should be some regulation by which no one can be elected to Grand Council for the first time if he has passed the age of, say, 65. There might also be a second regulation to the effect that no one should serve on Grand Council for more than, say, twelve years, unless by that time he has reached the office of Grand Vice-President or Grand President. Changes such as these might allow Grand Council to receive an infusion of fresh blood more often than it does today; they might ensure that it is rather younger than it is and thus, it is to be hoped, more attuned to the thinking of the Brothers in their local Circles. To them, as we have seen, everything above Circle level seems at present mere administration, which has to be seen to be justified.

Grand Council meets four times a year – three times in various places around the country and once during the week-end of the Annual Conference. The various Committees of the Council hold their meetings on Friday afternoon and evening, and present their reports to the whole Council on the Saturday. In February 1958, an article in *Catena* outlined the role of Grand Council, albeit in somewhat sonorous and almost over-awed tones. In the first place, the Council is the focal point for the Association; it acts as the co-ordinating body which ensures that local Circles do not go off on some parochial and centrifugal path. It is Grand Council which alone can ensure uniform standards – of membership, of ritual, for example; it is Grand Council which ensures that traditions are maintained and that Circles do not degenerate into mere dining clubs, dependent entirely on the quality of local leadership, but have a continuity and permanency which can override even poor quality in local officers.

With the growth of the Association there was the obvious need for some centralisation; and the continued expansion of the Association has only confirmed this need. It is Grand Council alone which can keep the records, maintain the accounts, administer the benevolent funds, organise the Annual Conference, carry out national ballots of the members, and produce the Directory and *Catena*. Through the Grand Directors, Grand Council is in touch with what is going on in the Provinces and with the climate of opinion on current issues, and ought therefore to be able to watch and direct policy trends. It may also initiate policy, although its freedom to do so is limited by the need to obtain the consent of the members. This is sometimes seen as a hindrance to speedy action, since it means that every change is subject to a referendum in which the Brothers may (as indeed they have done) turn down what Grand Council considers to be a desirable course of action.

It is Grand Council alone which can represent the Association in its dealing with the Hierarchy, national bodies, and internationally. The expansion of the Association into Asia, Africa, Australia and, latterly, into Malta could not have taken place without the Grand Council, which could advise, encourage, supervise, initiate and otherwise process the expansion of the Association.

The active members of the Grand Council – who serve on the Standing Committees and their sub-committees as well as on Grand Council itself – give a good deal of their time and sacrifice a good deal of their leisure on behalf of the Association. This makes it regrettable that from the membership level there is a good deal of criticism of Grand Council, which is seen as remote, costly and not always cost-effective; which in turn makes it surprising that, when Brothers had a chance to make Grand Council smaller, less costly and so perhaps more cost-effective, they should have turned it down.

And so, as it were, to the summit: the Grand President of the Association is chosen by his peers on Grand Council, on which he will have served for a number of years before reaching the Chair. How do we see his role and how, on the other hand, do the men who have occupied the Chair see the role?

Telephone 4053 GERRARD.   Code : WESTERN UNION.   Telegrams : "TRIBORD, LONDON."
(Universal Edition).

HOGAN & WARDROP,

Merchants, and Manufacturers of Electrical Supplies,

Contractors to H.M. Government.

GLOUCESTER MANSIONS, CAMBRIDGE CIRCUS,

CHARING CROSS ROAD,

Subject   Refs { Ours
                                                { Yours

LONDON, Nov. 29" 1909.
W.C.

**SWITCHBOARDS
and
SWITCHGEAR**
of every description.

**CONDUITS
and
FITTINGS.**

ELECTRIC FANS,
of all classes.

**INCANDESCENT
ELECTRIC LAMPS.**
METALLIC and CARBON.

STRUT SWITCHES.

DYNAMOS.
MOTORS.
TRANSFORMERS.
FLAME ARCS.
RADIATORS.
FITTINGS.
MOTOR STARTERS
AND REGULATORS.
MOTOR PANELS.
CABLES, WIRES,
AND ACCESSORIES.

Enc.

Dear Bro' McDermott. —

Yours to hand — Am very pleased to note the presence of the Bishop at your meeting on Thursday last —

I am sorry that owing to Bro. Logan's indisposition, my letter did not reach you — I had a line from him on the 22nd and wrote last Wednesday so that he could report at the meeting —

Things are going smoothly I am arranging for a preliminary meeting this week to settle

Part of Hogan's letter to McDermott indicating the influence of the latter on the development of the Association.

Sir W. H. Dunn, the first Catholic Lord Mayor of London since the Reformation.

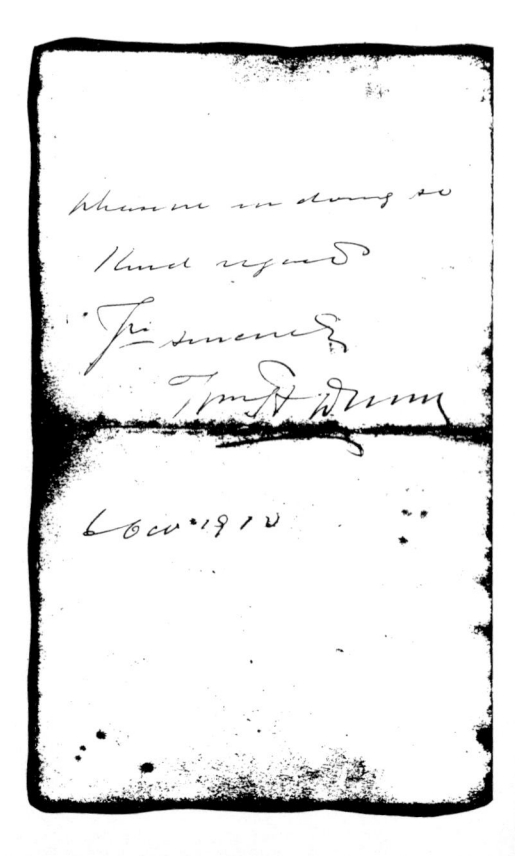

Dunn's letter to McDermott who had persuaded this leading figure to join the Association. Note that Hogan was a Captain at that time. ▸

A photograph taken during the Reception to welcome Archbishop Keating to the Liverpool Archdiocese in July 1921. The Liverpool Circle of those days did things in the dignified style which fitted well into the Adelphi Hotel.

A photograph taken after an AGM in Birmingham when the Association was seen by the Hierarchy as a vital part of Catholic development. The tall figure of Frank Rudman can be seen standing to the left of the picture. Seated were: Mrs de Bless; the Bishop of Northampton; Sir Ernest Hiley; Lady Hiley; the Bishop of Shrewsbury; the Bishop of Plymouth; Archbishop Mostyn of Cardiff; the Archbishop of Liverpool; Alderman T. Williams; the Bishop of Leeds; the Bishop of Brentwood; Mrs T. J. Callaghan;

T. J. Callaghan (founder member of Cardiff Circle), T. F. Molony, Lord Chief Justice of Ireland and President of the London Circle when his son, 'Joe', joined the Association; G. K. Chesterton; Arthur Hungerford Pollen; Mgr Barnes. Then standing were Bishop Vaughan, Alderman Myatt, the Bishop of Southwark and Edward Eyre.

The Catenian Anthem written by J. V. Gaskin to music composed by another Liverpool Brother, D. T. Brookes.

Dr George Foggin, Founder President of the Newcastle Circle and 'apostle of the Association' on Tyneside, was author of the Association's 1910 Constitution.

THE
CATENIAN ASSOCIATION.

FIRST DINNER

OF THE

BLACKBURN CIRCLE,

HELD AT

THE CRITERION RESTAURANT,

BLACKBURN,

NOVEMBER 28TH, 1912.

CHAIRMAN: BRO. R. WILDING.
President of the Blackburn Circle.

The Blackburn Circle's first menu card.

TOAST LIST.

"His Holiness the Pope and His Majesty the King."
BRO. R. WILDING,
President, Blackburn Circle.

Song ... ... BRO. J. SEDGWICK.

"The Catenian Association."
BRO. J. P. BONNEY,
Secretary, Blackburn Circle.
Response—BRO. H. F. O'BRIEN,
President, Manchester Circle.
BRO. J. W. SHEPHERD,
Grand Secretary.

Song ... ...BRO. J. CARRUTHERS.

"Our Visitors."
BRO. HUBERT BLAKE,
Blackburn Circle.
Response —Very REV. PETER CANON LONSDALE,
Rector, St. Alban's, Blackburn.
BRO. R. RANKIN,
President, Liverpool Circle.

Song ... ... REV. T. HENSHAW.

"The Chairman."
BRO. G. GREEN,
Vice-President, Blackburn Circle.
Response—THE PRESIDENT.

Song ... ...BRO. J. CARRUTHERS.
Songs, Recitations, etc., *ad lib.*

"GOD SAVE THE KING."

MENU.

Clear Ox-Tail.

Halibut.   Tartar Sauce.

Chicken Cutlets.

Roast Beef.   Roast Mutton.
Horseradish.   Onion Sauce.
Vegetables.

Boiled Grouse.   Celery Sauce.

Apple Tart and Cream.   Plum Pudding.
Wine Jelly.   Rum Sauce.

Coffee.   Dessert.

DAILY DISPATCH, THURSDAY, AUGUST 7, 1913.
PROSPECTIVE MAYOR OF MANCHESTER

A further stage in the selection of the new Lord Mayor of Manchester was reached at yesterday's meeting of the Manchester City Council, when a private meeting of the councillors was held, at which the Selection Committee was appointed. In accordance with custom, it is this year the turn of the Liberal party on the City Council to choose the new Lord Mayor, and it is quite understood that the Liberals will offer the honour to Alderman M'Cabe, a prominent Irish Home Ruler and a Catholic.

Alderman M'Cabe is well known for his work as chairman of the Markets Committee. Under his administration this department has made splendid progress, and it is now in a more flourishing condition than at any previous period of its history. In addition to serving on other committees, the alderman is a Ship Canal director, and a justice of the peace for the city. He is also a past president of the Catholic Truth Society.

ORGANISATION, RE-ORGANISATION AND STRUCTURE

Ordinary members of the Association see the Grand President as the figurehead who represents them on a variety of occasions: it will be he who will inaugurate new Circles whenever possible, so bringing to the 'birth' a degree of ceremonial and dignity; it will be the Grand President who will meet the members of the Hierarchy when there is discussion about the opening of Circles in new territory such as Australia, Malta or, at the present time, in the U.S.A. He will represent the Association at a variety of functions – meetings of the Hierarchy, Annual Conferences of the K.S.C. and other bodies, and so on.

Catenians may appreciate that he is a presiding officer at Grand Council, a member of the Grand Executive and of the Benevolent Board. If they do understand this, they ought to appreciate that he spends a good deal of his time on Association affairs. Yet they still expect him to attend their Circle function for 500th, 750th or 800th meetings, to attend Provincial Rallies and otherwise make himself accessible to the rank and file. For them, in their own Circles, the particular meeting may have a major significance: a Jubilee of some sort or another; for the Grand President it may well be the third, fourth or fifth such function of the week, during which he may also have had a couple of meetings at Chesham Place to fit in. Perhaps there should be some rationalising of this aspect of his role – in the interests of his own health, in the interests of his family, of whom he can see all too little during his busy year.

Every Past Grand President has been modest in considering the role he has played when in office. Most of them have pointed out that the Grand President is in office only for one year, and that it is impossible in so short a time for a man to make a major impact on the way in which the Association is moving. This is to underplay the role which some, at least, have played. For there can be little doubt that while, as we shall see, Taggart failed to rouse the Association to 'Catholic Action' in 1937 and 1938, Frank Lomas's call for a fresh look at our aims and the adoption of some form of 'action', although made in 1963, is still referred to in discussions on our aims and objects. And there can be no doubt that the financial wisdom which Joe Cox (1968–69) brought to our affairs made a major impact on our development, while the Jumbulance scheme might not have succeeded quite so quickly without the enthusiastic support given it by Denis Mather (1974–75).

Most Past Grand Presidents have seen themselves as having been, as it were, Chairman of a Board with the Grand Secretary as the Chief Executive. This did not mean that there were not clashes between themselves and the Grand Secretary of the time, whether it were Laurie Tanner or Keith Pearson, as is pointed out elsewhere. But the former Grand Presidents could see at least in retrospect, that their role was, by its temporary nature, one which depended on the Grand Secretary playing his role – of continuity. All of them reflected on the great help they received from Grand Secretaries who had, after all, 'seen it all before', and who were able to advise them on what to do or say on a particular occasion.

All of them claimed that they had tried to find out what the thinking of the average Brother was – by frequent visiting and much discussion in Circles and Provinces. If they had any success to report of their year in office it was, they claimed, almost entirely due to their having interpreted correctly the current mood in the Association and then having had the good luck to be able to present an idea which was adopted.

There is, obviously, no single mould into which we pour men and which produces some uniform product called the Grand President. Each has been very much his own man, each bringing to the Chair his own stamp and character. Some have been more learned than others; some have been more active than others; there have been forceful speakers and those less fluent, the ebullient and the more reserved. Each of the Past Grand Presidents to whom I spoke admitted that he had been 'proud' to have held office, and it is clear that an honourable ambition played a part in their advance through the ranks of the hierarchy to the Chair. But none of them gave the impression that he considered himself more important than the Association; all agreed that Brothers honour the office rather than its temporary occupant. There have been very few cases, maybe two or three, of former Grand Presidents who, on leaving the Chair, felt so deflated that they became quarrelsome and overly critical members of an Association which they were once pleased to lead.

One criticism levelled at Grand Council and the Grand Officers is that they have tended to be rather old. The average age of Grand Directors in 1981 was 62 years. In 1965, the City of London Circle sponsored a motion at the A.G.M. which would have widened the field from which Grand Presidents and Grand Vice-Presidents might be chosen. The motion proposed that 'any member of the Association shall be eligible for election as Grand President or Grand Vice-President'. In spite of the support of Paul Kelly and the advocacy of Joseph Molony the motion was lost. Its advocates argued that their proposal would make it possible to bring on some younger person to fill one or other of the high offices; and although the motion was defeated in 1965, it was revived in a modified form in 1966. Provincial Council 8 submitted a proposal to Grand Council that 'any Provincial Council may nominate for this office [of Grand Vice-President] any member who has held continuous membership of the Association for at least the ten years previous'. Grand Council rejected the proposal at its December meeting, and the proposal was rejected by the 1966 A.G.M.

Since then there has been talk of the Association's having a non-Catenian patron such as, for example, the Duke of Norfolk. Those who argue in favour of such Honorary Patrons believe that such a development would enhance the Association's image, making it more attractive to men who at present refuse invitations to post-Circle meetings. Not surprisingly there is widespread opposition to such proposals. Would the Association really be strengthened by the recruitment of men who joined because of a Patron-peer? In March 1981, the General Purposes Committee of Grand Council discussed a letter in which a Past Grand President argued in favour of the need for 'a super Grand President . . . a notable figure in the land [who] would take the Association into different areas of authority, endeavour and council in Catholic and/or Christian affairs'. This, it was argued, 'would be to elevate the Association into a different sphere of influence through the patronage of "noble" persons . . . many influential Catholic men, who now feel that they cannot join the Association, would be encouraged by the names on our letter-heading so to do'. The Committee did not support the proposal, and the matter was not discussed in full Council. Doubtless it will be raised in the future.

CHAPTER EIGHT

Joe Shepherd and Frank Rudman

1. The first paid Secretary 1910

Tom Locan and Frank Pendergast shared the duties of Circle Secretary after November 1908, sending out circulars for the two-monthly meetings, arranging the venue, agreeing such items as menus, and also writing to and visiting 'a number of gentlemen' thought of as prospective members of the Association. When the London Circle was formed, the duties of the two Secretaries were increased, since there was the added burden of communicating with the officers and members of the new Circle; and Locan and Pendergast, looking to the future, saw a constantly increasing burden if the Association spread – as McDermott meant it to.

So it was not surprising that, at a General Meeting of the 'Chums' held at the Albion Hotel in December 1909, 'it was suggested that it would be possible to get a professional man in town, who was a member of the Chums, to undertake the duties of a paid secretary at about £25 a year to commence'. This proposal was carried, with the proviso that 'the whole of the members should have the final decision'. In January 1910, it was resolved that the salary should be only £20 for the first year with the proviso that it 'be reconsidered as the membership increased'. This was carried, as were the motions that nominations for the new post were to be handed to the President or the existing Secretaries. The reduction in salary was probably due to a Committee decision to have both a paid and an honorary Secretary – although there is no evidence of how the two were to share their duties.

At the Committee meeting held at O'Donnell's office on 25 January 1910 there were two nominations for the post of paid Secretary. A Bro. F. Green had applied for the post, and while Locan, Pendergast, McDermott, Delahunty, Barton, Rowbottom and Lees nominated Bro. Denver, there was a second nomination by Bro. Millers of Joe Shepherd. It seems most remarkable that in spite of the powerful group which nominated Denver, Shepherd was appointed 'until the end of the present financial year'. Millers, who had proposed Shepherd for the post, and must have been pleased at his success, then seconded a motion that 'the secretary should not have a vote nor be permitted to speak except at the request of the President'. Here we have the first evidence of that uneasy relationship between the paid Secretary and the Committee – a relationship which subsequently, as we shall see, has often been a stormy one.

The new – and first – paid Secretary of the Manchester Circle became the Grand Secretary of the Catenian Association when Grand Circle was formed at the Leeds meeting in October 1910. At that time there were only three Circles in the newly-named Association, and its headquarters were the offices of the Secretary, Joe Shepherd. By the time that Shepherd gave up the post, in 1923, there were 73 Circles in the Association, and Shepherd's honorarium – for it cannot be called a salary – was £300 a year. In return for this, Shepherd handled all the correspondence that falls on a Grand Secretary, arranged the opening of new Circles, kept the Association's records – and helped the Grand Treasurer with his work. The work was carried out by the staff at Shepherd's private office at 78 King Street, Manchester, and it was Shepherd's telephone, typewriters, filing cabinets and so on that were used to run the growing Association. It is small wonder that many people thought that 'Shepherd *was* the Association'.

Joe Shepherd was born in Preston in 1885, so that he was only 25 when he took on the job of Grand Secretary. He was educated at St Walburga's, Preston, and proved to be not only a very able scholar, but a good sportsman – signing amateur forms with Preston North End. He was the eldest child of a large family, and when he left school he was articled to a Preston accountant. In 1903 he obtained a post with a Manchester firm, which sent him to work in London, Milan and Paris. In 1908 he qualified as an accountant – hence 'A.S.A.A.' which appeared after his name. His firm then offered him a partnership, but he decided to return to Manchester and to set up in practice on his own. He joined the 'Chums', being No. 72 on the roll, and, as we have seen, became the first Grand Secretary in October 1910.

Although the Manchester Circle set up a sub-committee to work out what the duties of the paid Secretary were to be, there is no evidence of their findings. Even if there were, it is doubtful if it would help our story, for the duties obviously changed when Shepherd became, not a paid Secretary to Manchester alone, but Grand Secretary to the whole Association (with its three Circles). And even if someone had devised a job description in October 1910, this would have quickly become outdated as the Association went through that rapid period of expansion after 1912.

2. *The role of the Grand Secretary*

So what were, and are, the duties of a Grand Secretary? How did Shepherd see his job? Obviously a major role is that of administrator – of an office which handles the correspondence with each Circle and with many individual Brothers who write in; there were, and are, Directories to be prepared and updated, membership files to be added to and subtracted from, as men either resign, lapse, or finally die; there are agendas to be prepared for meetings of Grand Council and its various sub-committees, and reports to be issued after each of these meetings; there are contacts to be made with those who may wish to form a new Circle, and arrangements to visit them and their Bishop; if the plans to form a Circle bear fruit, the Grand Secretary will be the one who will organise the opening of the new Circle and watch over it as it takes its first steps along the Catenian road; there are contacts to be made with other organisations with whom the Association may wish to have a working relationship – the Knights of St Columbanus of Ireland, the Knights of St Columba in Great Britain, the C.W.L. and the U.C.M. and so on; there are links to be built and maintained both with the Hierarchy and with the clergy at parochial level. As an administrator to Grand Council the Grand Secretary becomes the best-known member of the Association – to its members and to the world outside.

But there is more; he is the only member of the Association who is in touch with the whole Association. Circle Secretaries and officers know what is going on in their own Circles and should be aware of the waves of support for, or of opposition to, certain ideas and movements. Provincial officers, who came into existence only after Shepherd's retirement in 1923, ought to be aware of the state of play in the various Circles of their Province, although there is evidence that they very often do not know what is going on there. Grand Directors and other members of Grand Council are, in theory, supposed to be aware of what is going on in the Association as a whole. But the theory is belied by practice, as should be obvious when one considers the nature of Grand Council. Here are a number of men who come together infrequently to discuss the Association's affairs. Who draws up the agenda for their meetings? Who decides what they should be told, or read, or discuss? Who alone can see, because of his constant contact with the body of the Association, what the members really want? Here the Grand Secretary exercises a great deal of influence over each Grand Council and over each Grand President.

In talking with Past Grand Presidents it became clear that each was aware of the limited role that he had played in the Association's history – and some of them claim to have been aware of that role when they were in office. For Grand Presidents come to the Chair at one A.G.M., make their speeches, urge the Association to do this or that, and after a year make a farewell speech at another A.G.M. There is no opportunity for them to see any of their ideas through to fruition – so that the urgings of one Grand President are often quickly forgotten as his successor asks the Association to take up some new challenge, whatever it may be. Only the Grand Secretary can provide that element of continuity which an Association needs if it is to develop along any planned line. It is little wonder that all Past Grand Presidents agree that they listened to the Grand Secretary and followed his advice. They would have been foolish not to have done so.

But herein lies a major problem; for the Grand Secretary is a mere employee of the Association, and Grand Council, representing the Association, is his employer. We have seen that Manchester wanted to limit the power of the paid Secretary, not allowing him a vote or a voice unless requested to speak by the President. This proviso was soon abolished as it became clear to the Grand Council that Shepherd alone knew everything that was going on and that his voice had not only to be heard and listened to but even to be welcomed. But what about the employer–employee relationship? Shepherd was an outstanding man, as his subsequent business career proved. It was a mark of the good judgement of the Manchester Circle that such an able man should have been appointed to run their affairs – and, after 1910, the affairs of the Association. But a man of such ability, aware of the nature of his role in the Association's affairs, might not take kindly to criticism from those part-time amateurs who came together to form Grand Council. It is not surprising, then, that there were clashes between Shepherd and successive Grand Councils, nor that many remember him as 'an autocrat'; it is difficult to see how he could have been other if he was to do the job that was asked of him.

3. Joe Shepherd

Moreover, it has to be remembered that, while running the affairs of the expanding Association, Shepherd had also his own business to run. It was the expansion of that business which forced him to retire from the post of Grand Secretary in 1923. He must have felt that he had given the Association some thirteen years of hard work and that he owed it to himself and his family to safeguard the future by paying more attention to his business. He became Deputy Chairman of British Van Heusen, Chairman of the family printing firm of T. Snapes in Preston, and director of a number of other companies. His private practice expanded as well, so that he was able to take on several Catenian partners, and although he left Manchester to live in retirement in North Wales he continued to go to his Manchester office on at least two days every week right up to a few weeks before his 90th birthday.

He was a tall man, always immaculately dressed, with a sharp wit which he could use against those whom he disliked. But he was also a very gentle person, aware of the importance of good relationships with the staff at his office, anxious to help younger men trying to make their way in the business world, and generous in time and money when asked for help. It was typical of him that he should have become the Secretary of the Manchester Belgian Refugee Committee, which was set up in 1914 to help the refugees who wished to settle in this country when the War started, and which also helped the repatriation of those who wished to return to Belgium after 1918. For this work he was rewarded with a C.B.E. and with the Médaille du Roi Albert given him by the King of the Belgians.

Shepherd's interest in the refugee problem had been aroused by the promptings of Alderman Dan McCabe, a fellow-Catenian. McCabe was one who had followed Casartelli's advice to seek public office. In 1911 he became a Catenian – 'the star Catholic of the region', and Shepherd played an important part in helping him to accept the office of Lord Mayor of Manchester in 1913. McCabe, one of the 'ragged Irish' who had made his way in the commercial and political world, could not afford to become Lord Mayor of the city, for he did not have the means to sustain the office. Shepherd organised his fellow-Catenians and other Catholics to put up the money that McCabe needed and so ensured that Manchester had its first Catholic Lord Mayor.

Shepherd, the successful accountant and company director, the decorated Secretary of the Refugee Committee and friend and backer of the Lord Mayor, McCabe, was a well-known public figure. But this only prompted some Catenians to become critical of the man and his office. In *Catena* of September 1918 there were reports of the murmurings against the honorarium of £300 which he was receiving, criticisms which ignored the amount of work he did and the provision of an office which he made available. When he retired and the Association had to find its own office, equipment and staff, it soon realised that it had had a bargain in Shepherd.

In the same issue of *Catena* there is one of the first demands that the Association should move its Head Office to London, a request repeated at regular intervals in the '20s and '30s. Shepherd may have seen the wisdom of such a move, but he was opposed to it, or at least he was opposed to being involved in the Association's affairs should such a move take place. But this demand became involved in other and related demands for a change in the way in which the Association was run. The expansion which had taken place before 1914 had been resumed after 1918, so that it seemed to a number of people that within a few years there might be more than 100 Circles. There would then be a Grand Circle of more than 100 Brothers – which would make the Association's governing body an unwieldy affair. Hence, from 1921 onwards, Shepherd was leading the demand for a reform of the Constitution – a demand which was realised in 1923.

But while welcoming the expansion that was taking place, Shepherd was also aware that some of it was, in a sense, unreal. There were men coming into the Association in the hope that they could get something out of it – a job perhaps, or financial help should they lose a job, as was a distinct possibility once the government had started in 1921 to make the savage cuts in spending which are summed up in the history books as 'the Geddes Axe'. Shepherd knew from his long experience that the Association flourished best when men joined so that they could serve in some way, so that they could contribute something to its life; he had seen hundreds of men give up their membership when they realised it was not a Catholic version of Freemasonry and that it did not prove automatically a chance of a job, of promotion, of increased business and so on. He was aware that many of those joining the Association after 1920 were self-seeking, and in a meeting at Manchester reported in *Catena*, April 1920, he made it clear that he was concerned about the 'quality' of some of the men who had been admitted to membership since 1918. This was a theme to which many Grand Presidents were to refer in later years, for once a Circle gets the reputation of having admitted some people who might in earlier years have been thought unworthy of admission, then it also loses the opportunity of recruiting just those very men for whom the Association had been formed in the first place.

4. An élitist Association?

I have to confess to finding this a difficult topic on which to write. In one sense I can understand and sympathise with the views of Shepherd and his successors. The Association was formed for middle-class Catholic men, and this has to be borne in mind when writing or reading about it. There is little point in asking, as some latter-day critics have done, 'Why does it not widen its membership to allow in any Catholic man who wishes to join?' That would be to ignore the reality of the nature of the Association and of the aims of its founders. Other sections of the Catholic population have, or can have, their own sodalities, societies and confraternities; that the particularly small group of Catholic middle-class men should have their own particular society or Association ought not to be made the subject for attack. And having once allowed their right to have an Association, one has to allow that it has made certain financial demands on its members – to pay for the hiring of rooms, for meals, for entertaining clergy and ladies, for maintaining a Benevolent Fund, a Children's Fund and so on. To be a Catenian does presuppose an ability to pay out certain sums of money. Not everyone can afford to do so, and many Catenians have found it necessary to resign from membership when the demands of growing families have made it difficult or even impossible for them to sustain the financial burden of membership. Many of these have returned to membership when they no longer face the problems of a growing family or when their own financial position has improved. But in the 1920s there was evidence that many men were being admitted who would never be able to support the Association's ventures. It was against this tendency that Shepherd issued his warning.

That the Association may, rightly, be accused of being élitist seems to me to be no serious matter. I have yet to meet a critic of élitism who does not want to get on in his own job, or who does not want his children to get on in school; everyone of any common sense wants to have the services of the best qualified doctors, dentists and mechanics, and supports an educational system which is meant to turn out such well-qualified men. Elitism wins almost universal support in such matters, as it does also in athletics, football and other sports. It remains a puzzle why it should be used to attack the Catenian Association.

5. Expansion and Shepherd's resignation 1923

The Association continued to expand after 1920, taking in men of varying calibre and financial standing. It was this expansion which, as we have seen, led to a demand for the new Constitution which was set up in 1923. At that point Shepherd decided to resign from the post of Grand Secretary, since he saw that with the new system there would be even more calls on the Grand Secretary's time and energies. In March 1923, he announced his intention to resign; in April, reports appeared in *Catena* of the tributes to his work being paid by Circles and officers around the country. It was generally agreed that he had done a difficult job and done it well, that he had carried the Association through a difficult time of constant expansion and had seen it through a period when it might have collapsed under the weight of its own success. Even while applicants for the vacant post were being considered, a Fund was set up to provide some parting gift for Joe Shepherd and in June 1923 it was decided to make Shepherd a Life Member of Grand Council, so that the Association would have the continued benefit of his experience. In 1924, a year after his successor had taken office, Shepherd was chosen to be Grand Vice-President of the Association and it was confidently expected that in 1925 he would become Grand President, a fitting honour for a great Catenian. He declined to take the Chair, however, on the ground that he needed to pay more attention to his own business career. This did not make him any the less an enthusiastic Catenian. He helped to form the Manchester City Circle, he was its President in 1923–24 and he played an active role in the Circle as he did on Grand Council. On the outbreak of war in 1939 he went into semi-retirement and went to live at Rhos-on-Sea in North Wales. Here he met a number of Catenians who had been evacuated from London, and with them he helped to form the North Wales Circle which had its first official meeting in January 1942.

In Rhos-on-Sea, as in earlier days in Manchester, Shepherd started each day with Mass, and his deeply-held religious philosophy set the tone for the rest of his day and life. He died in January 1975, one of the last links with the founders of the Association.

6. Frank Rudman

The search for a successor to the dynamic, if autocratic, Shepherd followed a peculiar path. In May 1923, applications were invited from men who might wish to be considered for the post of Grand Secretary, and in June Grand Council heard that Shepherd had received 20 applications, none of whom was considered suitable for the post which carried the salary of £500 a year. The job was re-advertised and in September 1923 Grand Council heard of the 55 applications. Eight men had been short-listed to be interviewed by a sub-committee which was empowered to make a final short list of three men to be interviewed by Grand Council. Grand Council, however, found that, of the three men chosen, one had withdrawn by the date of the meeting of Grand Council, one had not bothered to turn up, which left only the one short-listed applicant, who was not then interviewed.

In September 1923, Grand Council met at Birmingham, when it had to consider not only the appointment of someone to the post, which Shepherd wanted to vacate as soon as possible, but also the problem of providing an office for the new man. Fortunately, Shepherd was able to arrange for an office to be made available in 78 King Street, Manchester, where he had his own offices. This was convenient since it meant a continuity of address even if it meant a discontinuity of the holder of the office. But it left Grand Council with the problem of finding the equipment and furniture for an office – and appeals had to be made to Circles to make loans to Grand Council for this purpose. It may seem odd that an Association of professional and business men had not previously thought of the problem of providing an office.

It was at the Birmingham meeting in September 1923 that Grand Council appointed Frank Rudman to succeed Shepherd – another oddity, since Rudman's name had not appeared on the short list of eight put forward by the earlier sub-committee. But Rudman was a well-known figure in Catholic circles in Birmingham in particular and in the Midlands as a whole, and it could be that there was a significant link between his appointment and the fact that Grand Council happened to be meeting in Birmingham when the appointment was made.

Frank Rudman was born in Cheltenham where, after school, he joined the clerical department of the Great Western Railway. In 1901 he left Cheltenham for Birmingham and for a job under Martin Melvin, the owner of *The Universe*. Melvin was an early member of the Birmingham Circle and was to become the first Englishman to be honoured with the Papal Award of K.C.S.G. This was a fitting reward for an outstanding Catholic whose worth was also marked by non-Catholic authorities, as can be seen from his appointment as governor of Birmingham University. It was not surprising that the energetic and able Melvin should have recognised the talents of the younger Rudman, or that the latter should have welcomed the chance to work for this leading Catholic. Later they were to quarrel, Rudman being convinced that Melvin failed to honour a mutual agreement.

In Birmingham, Rudman was quickly involved in Catholic life, and in particular took an active role in the emerging Catholic Young Men's Society. In 1910 there were only three branches of the C.Y.M.S. in the city when Rudman decided to take a hand in its affairs. He showed in this role his ability as an organiser, and as a man who could get others to work under his supervision, so that he earned the reputation of being 'a dynamo' who, as many were convinced, would have got to the top of whatever tree he chose to climb. The C.Y.M.S. spread rapidly and in 1912 Rudman became the President of the Birmingham Diocesan Committee of the Society. He was also Hon. Secretary of the Birmingham Retreat Committee and Chairman of the Archbishop's Permanent Committee of Lay Societies. In time he became Chairman of the Committee set up to welcome Archbishop McIntyre to his new Archdiocese. and of the Committee formed to organise the first of the annual processions of the relics of St Chad through the Birmingham streets. This act of piety must have had a particular appeal to the man who, out of his limited income, paid for the priestly education of his brother, Maurice, whose death in January 1951 was one of several blows which marred the last years of Rudman's long tenure of office as Grand Secretary.

So it was no surprise that in July 1916 Rudman was invited to join

Birmingham No. 9 Circle of the Catenian Association. This Circle was then enjoying a period of expansive success under the leadership of men of the calibre of Brosch who had helped to bring No. 9 into existence in 1912; he had been its Foundation Secretary and, having served in that office for three years, was Circle President from 1916 to 1918.

So Rudman, the 'dynamo', felt much at home in a Circle dominated by the energetic Brosch; and in 1919 he was elected Secretary of this lively Circle.

In the summer of 1923, Birmingham was host city to the National Catholic Congress, and Rudman was organising secretary for this mammoth affair. Just prior to this Congress the Birmingham C.Y.M.S. had held its annual meeting in Birmingham Town Hall, and on 18 July, Archbishop McIntyre addressed the gathering of Catholic laymen. At the end of his address he referred to Rudman's work and the example that he had provided for laymen, an example of action and zeal which the Archbishop hoped they would learn to imitate. Then, to everyone's delight, he announced that, as a result of a petition signed by all the parish priests of the city, the Pope had been pleased to make Rudman a Knight of St Gregory.

This, then, was the man who succeeded Shepherd. His appointment meant that he and his family had to move from Birmingham to Manchester. Rudman himself was later to say that he hated Manchester; maybe he resented the break with the city where he had many friends, played cricket and enjoyed a prestige in Catholic circles in which he was so well known. His children, on the other hand, now remember Manchester as 'home', for it was here that they grew up. His son remembers being taken to school each morning by his tall, handsome, 'important' father, who then caught a train into the centre of the city. He also remembers waiting for his father to take him home at lunchtime – for in those less hectic days that was the pattern even in a provincial capital such as Manchester, where from time to time he could watch fellow-Catenians and Test cricketers, Hendren and Sandham. Rudman's daughter recalls the tradesmen, shopkeepers, her schooldays – and her mother, who seemed to have devoted her life to ensuring that 'her Frank' had as much of the best as could be provided. He was a replica of that Victorian paterfamilias once so common even in twentieth-century Britain. The home revolved around the father, who is remembered for always ensuring that his clothes were pressed each evening and his shoes polished each morning, so that he presented the outward image of the successful man. The children remember how he always had a 'nap' after lunch and how thay were constantly being kept in check by their mother so that 'her Frank' could prepare his speech, have his rest, or hold a meeting in the sitting-room with one or more visiting Catenians.

Relations between Shepherd and Rudman seem to have been very uneasy, judging from the recollections of those who heard Rudman refer to his predecessor. One can understand why this could have been so. On reflection, it may be seen as an error to have given Rudman an office in the building where Shepherd had his office. For this put him, as it were, in the shade of his eminent predecessor. Visitors to Rudman must, almost inevitably, have also gone to call on the man with whom, so recently, they had dealt when doing their Catenian work. While there is no evidence that Shepherd interfered in any way with the work of his successor, it may be natural that Rudman may have feared that he was being watched, and perhaps criticised, as he learned to do the job which Shepherd had done so well for thirteen years. It might have been better if a new address had been chosen, so that the dynamic Rudman could have got on with imposing his mark without having to fear immediate comparison with 'the man next door'.

There were Catenians who referred to the fact that until 1923 Shepherd had done it all – and at little cost to the Association. Now, with Rudman at the helm, there were extra costs thrown on the Association: to pay for an office and for equipment, for telephone bills and postage, for clerical help and for Rudman's travel expenses, for which he was allowed £50 a year after a decision reached by Grand Council in January 1924. The Grand Secretary then, as now, was supposed to visit as many Circles as possible, to represent the Association at many functions, and certainly to be present when new Circles were opened. There is no evidence that Shepherd had such an allowance; maybe the much richer man felt that he did not need it; maybe he felt, as one of the early members, that he owed it to the Association to do what he could, at his own expense, to further its interests. But Rudman was not a rich man, and, dependent as he was on his salary of £500 a year, he would not have been able to behave as freely as did Shepherd. Indeed, there are those who remember Rudman's resentful remarks as he watched Shepherd roll up to his office in a chauffeur-driven car, in an era when car ownership was still uncommon.

It must have appeared fitting to most Brothers when Shepherd's resignation was marked by a Life Membership of Grand Council and his election as Grand Vice-President. But it now may be seen as somewhat unwise to have put him into such an exalted position where, in a sense, he was one of those who employed Rudman. In any event, the latter resented criticism and he must have resented even more any criticism by a Grand Council of which Shepherd was an influential and permanent member. And at the end, when Rudman retired, Grand Council did not offer him the sort of reward that Shepherd had been given; there was no Life Membership or Grand Vice-Presidency in 1952. Maybe this was because Grand Council had realised that their predecessors had made a mistake in so honouring Shepherd; maybe they wanted to avoid, in Laurie Tanner's case, the errors of Rudman's early years when he felt under pressure from Shepherd. But, for Rudman, the difference in treatment was one more example of odious comparison between him and Shepherd.

7. Expansion during depression 1923–1952

There are those who today make a comparison between Shepherd, whom they did not know when he was in office, and Rudman, whom they did know. They point, for example, to the great expansion that took place while Shepherd was Grand Secretary, and to the relative slow-down which took place after 1923. If the Association had continued to expand after 1923 as it had done up to that date, then by 1952 there would have been 200 or more Circles with 10,000 or more Brothers. The slow-down, they reckon, was due to Rudman's lack of drive as compared with Shepherd.

But this is to ignore what was happening in the wider world. By April 1921 the government had come to see that inflation was a bogy which had to be exorcised; and – a modern touch – there was set in train those cuts in government spending which were intended to bring inflation under control. Then, as now, such policies led to bankruptcies, unemployment, cuts in salaries and wages and, in general, uncertainty as to the economic future. And while the 1920s were a period of such uncertainty (with unemployment rarely below 1½ million), the 1930s were, as many will recall only too well, an even more horrendous decade. Catenians and prospective Catenians did not escape the general blitz which hit the British economy. And it is not surprising that many men were forced to resign – as they lost their jobs or found themselves with a lower income in succeeding years. Nor is it surprising that there was no large pool into which the Association might dip to draw out new members. Indeed, on reflection, the wonder is that new Circles were opened and that membership in older Circles did not decline more rapidly than it did. But to blame Rudman for the failure to expand is manifestly unfair.

Indeed, one ought to offer Rudman's memory a degree of sympathy. Called to succeed a popular and distinguished man, he had to try to put into effect the new Constitution which was devised by his predecessor, and which then, as now, had its own critics, who quickly learned to blame the Grand Secretary for the failings in the Constitution. He had to cope not only with the problems of the economy but, between 1939 and 1945, with the effects of World War II on the Association. And even when that War ended, there was little improvement in the economy until the Korean War had drifted into an uneasy armistice. Only then did the economy improve – and then Rudman retired. On reflection it may be that we ought to remember Rudman as the man who managed to hold the Association together at a very difficult period of its history.

It was very much he who did hold it together. Grand Council, itself a new body as a result of the changes made in 1923, gave him a very free hand to run things as he saw fit. As with other Grand Secretaries, *he* was the Association, as far as most members and much of the outside world was concerned. It was he who made the first contacts with the Knights of Columbanus at the time of the Eucharistic Congress in Dublin in 1933; it was he who organised the banquet which the Association provided for the Hierarchy at the time of their Low Week meeting in Westminster. Rudman introduced the idea of 'the Group' as the forerunner to the setting up of a new Circle, and the success of the Macclesfield experiment was due in large part to him. It was Rudman who went to see that a new Circle was opened with dignity and due ritual – often telling the officers of the new Circle that he and they would see to things, for they did not want 'them' (i.e. members of Grand Council) coming to 'mess things up'. He was confident of his own ability to do things well – and, it has to be admitted, he did do things well. While A.G.M.s were supposedly organised by the officers of the Province in which the meeting was to take place, it was, in fact, Rudman who saw to everything, so that, as many remember, nothing ever went wrong because Rudman had planned for every eventuality.

The success he enjoyed and the high regard in which he was held by ordinary members were due in no small part to his physical appearance. Everyone who remembers him talks of his aristocratic bearing, his shock of white hair, and his height; there was no doubt that 'when Rudman entered a room everyone was aware of the fact'. Those who did not know him can get an impression of this sense of distinction from the photographs of A.G.M.s, Circle meetings and so on, where Rudman stands head and shoulders above everyone else. But, on the other hand, there was his autocratic character. He would sweep into a Circle meeting, pass Registrar's table and take a seat. If approached by a Guard or Registrar and asked for some identification he would merely snap, 'Don't you know who I am?' He suffered fools – and those who, at least in their own estimation, were not fools – very badly, and this has left the memory of an arrogant man who rode roughshod over anyone who allowed him to get away with it.

This behaviour was less acceptable after 1945, when the Association recruited a new kind of man, more confident than his predecessors, less conscious of being one of a group on whom the rest of the population looked down, more aware of the fact that for him, as for other men, there were greater opportunities for economic and social advancement. The social revolution which has taken place since 1945 had its impact on the quality of men who came into the Association, men who took less kindly to autocracy, arrogance, or control by one who, both in theory and practice, was an employee whose salary they paid. Post-war Grand Councils were less inclined to give Rudman his way and he, for his part, was, after the stresses of war, less zestful, less inclined to impose himself.

The move of the Head Office to London in 1946 was the result of a long-held belief that the Association ought to shed its provincial image and move to the centre where Cardinal, politicians, journalists and image-makers could be more easily contacted. Some believe that Rudman led the demand for this move, ignoring the fact that this demand had been made at least as far back as 1920, when Rudman was not at the centre of things. They are also unaware of the fact that Rudman resented the move, which took his family away from their contacts in Manchester, where they were very much at home, and put them down to live in the London suburb of Worcester Park. A priest-friend recalls the 'frugality' of the Grand Secretary's home, in which, as always, Mrs Rudman worked to provide that background against which Rudman could do his job. Rudman's children do not remember any 'frugality', although they agree that, in the post-war world of rationing and shortages, their mother tried to see to it that the father had the best of what could be got from shopkeepers, with whom they had to make fresh contacts after their move from Manchester.

In 1948, Grand Council decided to provide Rudman with an assistant, and Laurie Tanner entered the Association's history. This is not the point at which to examine the many and valuable contributions which Laurie made to the Association's development. It may be the place to say that relationships between Rudman and the much younger Tanner were, from the first, difficult, so that both of them must have been relieved when Rudman retired in 1952. In honour of his work for the Association Rudman was given promotion in the Order of St Gregory, becoming a K.C.S.G. He and Mrs Rudman moved to the Suffolk village of Southwold, and he joined the Yarmouth Circle. His ill-health did not prevent his becoming a member of the local Town Council, although in time it did limit his activities, so that he rarely attended major functions of the Association. He did get to the A.G.M. at Blackpool in 1958 when the Association celebrated its 50th birthday, but he was then a very sick man. He died on 26 June 1959.

In making an appeal for contributions to a Rudman Memorial Fund, the then Grand President, Joe McMurray, wrote:

> In the name of Rudman lies the history of the Catenian Association for a generation. Appointed Grand Secretary in 1923 at the time of the 'new' Constitution, he made such an impression in his 29 years of office, that to many, both inside and outside, he *was* the Association. No one will ever wield such power or inspire such awe again. Rudmans happen once and once only.

The memorial took the shape of a headstone of Portland stone, over the inscription on which is a striking medallion of the Crucifix, in relief, showing the figure of Our Lord looking upwards. This work was done by Brother Philip

Lindsey Clark, F.R.I.B.A., a distinguished architect and boyhood friend. This headstone over Rudman's grave at Ocklynge Cemetery, Eastbourne, was blessed by Bishop Petit of Menevia on 25 May 1961 in the presence of Mrs Rudman, her children, and many Catenians who had known the great man in his days of power.

CHAPTER NINE

Catenians and their Benevolence

1. Early and voluntary steps
One of the Aims of the Association is 'to establish, maintain and administer benevolent funds'. Members of the Association know this so well that it may come as a surprise to them to learn that it was not always so, as a glance at the original Aims will show. The first Brother to die after the Association was founded was I. Whittle, who had, it is believed, written the first Constitution and Ritual. We know that he died before O'Donnell wrote to Casartelli in May 1908. In January 1910, the Committee of the Manchester 'Chums' considered 'the case of the late Bro. I. Whittle's widow and it was decided to leave the matter in the hands of the President and Bro. Millers's hands to deal with it'. We have no details of 'the case', but we do know that Bro. Millers reported to the Committee in February 'that a situation had been found for Mrs Whittle'.

This was an instance of some active Catholics using their knowledge of the employment market to find a job for the widow of a dead Brother whom they had known and on whose expertise they had relied. But in April 1910 the Manchester 'Chums' faced a different situation. In the Minutes of the Committee we read:

> A letter was read from the London Circle regarding the case of the widow and family of Brother Callaghan of that Circle, who had been left in very straitened circumstances. It was proposed by Bro. Locan and seconded by Bro. McMahon and carried that a grant of £5 should be made from the General Funds of the Manchester Circle in this case, the attention of the Brothers should be called to same on the May Circular with a request for donations.

John Callaghan, a solicitor's managing clerk, had been the ninth member of the London Circle. As was customary for many years after this, he did not get the 'signs and passwords' until the February meeting; initiation was, as it were, only one of the two stages to full acceptance. In March 1910 he died.

Christian charity indicated that the Brothers of the London Circle had some responsibility for the dependents of their dead Brother. But the responsibility of the Manchester men is much less clear. They had not met the late Brother, as they had met and known Whittle. The immediate response of the Manchester Committee may be seen as an acceptance of that interdependence which makes sense of the linked chain which became the logo of the Association.

In July 1910, McDermott became President of the Manchester Circle in succession to O'Donnell. It is significant that at the first meeting over which he presided (11 July 1910) the Committee formed a Benevolent Board, its members being Bros. Shippey, Millers, and Reynolds. Later in July, Grand Council held a meeting at Leeds, where, as we have seen, there was animated discussion on the name of the Association. The expansion of the Association – to Liverpool, Newcastle and Blackburn – led to the writing of the first Constitution for the newly-named Catenian Association, and in this we find that the 'Aims and Objects' were expanded to include a new Aim (*d*) involving the Association with benevolence. Each Circle was empowered to use part of each member's subscription to form a Benevolent Fund.

This was a very untidy scheme, for Circle subscriptions varied from place to place, some charging 2½ guineas, others only one guinea. This meant that the richer Circles built up larger benevolent funds than those Circles which charged a smaller subscription, while, on the other hand, there may have been more calls for benevolence in one of the less well-off Circles than in one of the richer ones. It was Grand Secretary Shepherd who saw the shortcomings in such a locally administered system of benevolence – a reminder of the fact that only the General Secretary can have this overview of the Association, unbiased by membership of a particular Circle.

It was Shepherd who persuaded the Association of the need for a centrally administered fund, and in 1912 the General Benevolent Fund came into being. This meant that decisions about the granting of help were taken by a Grand Benevolent Board of Grand Council; and this might take a decision which was at variance with the desires of the local Benevolent Board which had sent in the application. This led to some misgivings, and Shepherd told Sydney Redwood: 'I was told by some members that I would live to regret the day when I forced this consolidation. But I am happy to say that every year has made me happier over what I actually did force at the time.'

This emergence of Catenian benevolence from uncertain beginnings may be seen, in one sense, as a Catholic application of the generally accepted Friendly Society self-help system of the time. It may also be seen as an extension of the principles of charity which had underpinned the old guilds to which O'Dea thought that the Association was, in part at least, heir and successor. Speaking at the Banquet at Newcastle A.G.M. of 1972, Bishop Lindsay, referring to the work of the Association, said: 'Catenians are trying to do the work of Christ on earth. In your Circles you do this work of charity and kindness especially in the way you rally round when a Brother needs help.' The Bishop also went on to say: 'Everywhere I go I find Catenians involved in the work of the Church. Your Grand President Frank Lloyd is a member of the Hierarchy's Commission for priestly vocations, and in the *Guardian* this morning I read about the death of your Alderman Hugh Lee, former Lord Mayor of Manchester, who had done so much for the Church.' And, as we shall see, the Bishop might have given countless other examples of Catenian activity and extra-Association benevolence. As regards priestly training, there was the work done for the Beda (pp. 73–78), while there is the continuing work done by many Catenians for the various Bishops' Funds and for the Serra Movement (p. 189). As regards benevolence, there is the work of individual Brothers who are members of the S.V.P., the activities of Circles and individuals for local orphanages and homes, and the work of certain Circles and Provinces for Catholic Hospitals, such as the work of the London Circles for the Hospital of St John and St Elizabeth and the work of several Surrey Circles for St Anthony's Hospital at Cheam. In more recent times there have been the activities on behalf of the handicapped, expressed at one level in financial aid for Jumbulance (p. 192) and at another level by the involvement of individuals and Circles in the work of the Across Trust, Hosanna House and the organising of pilgrimages to Lourdes.

Nor, as we shall see, is this all, for Circles and Brothers have founded the Apostleship of the Sea, the Society of St Dismas (p. 175), the St Francis Guild for Leprosy, and the Multiple Sclerosis Society, while also helping local and national activities on behalf of Spastics, Cheshire Homes and so on almost *ad infinitum*. It is necessary to summarise these activities here because of the constant sniping at the Brothers for being 'winers and diners' who 'give nothing of themselves to the work of the Church'.

2. *Developments 1914–1923*

When World War I broke out in August 1914, there were 26 Circles in existence, each paying its voluntary levy into the General Benevolent Fund. The War meant an increase in the claims made to the Benevolent Board from the dependents of men who were killed in the slaughterous battles of that War, or from men so badly injured that they were unable to resume their normal occupations. Many of these claims were from widows asking for help towards the education of the children of dead Catenians, and it is worth noting that there was not yet a separate Children's Fund. So heavy were these claims that Grand Council in 1915 made a special appeal to the members of the Association, an appeal which, it has to be said, failed to bring in anything like the money that had been expected. In 1919 there was a 'Peace Drive' Appeal, and, while this was slightly more successful, the two special appeals raised only £1946 10*s*.11*d*. It is difficult to say what this represents in modern currency, but it may help us to appreciate the generosity of the 3000-odd Brothers if we remember that at that time one could go to the cinema for 6*d*., have a week's holiday afloat on the Broads for £4, or buy a 14/28 h.p. Morris Oxford for £260.

The strains imposed on the Fund were such that in January 1921 the Association agreed to end the haphazard system of membership subscriptions. These were now fixed at two guineas, with half of this going to Grand Council for 'benevolence and administrative purposes'. In 1923 this was amended: Grand Council took 10 per cent of the annual subscription, while each Circle had to pay, in addition, a capitation fee to Grand Council.

This did not end the period of strain, for this was also the period of great post-war expansion: in 1919–22, 33 new Circles were formed, almost doubling the size of the Association. There is plenty of evidence that not all the men who were allowed to join had been sufficiently 'vetted' or instructed. Today, for example, 'Any candidate has given an assurance that he is financially sound and can properly afford the expenses incidental to membership. Implicit in such assurance is confirmation that he is free of financial embarrassment, can adequately maintain any dependents and has made reasonable provision for the future through savings, insurance, pension arrangements or other means'. It was not always so. Many men were attracted to the Association by the idea that it was some sort of insurance society, while others regarded the Benevolent Fund as a bait. With the onset of the depression in 1922, too many of these men became applicants to the already strained Benevolent Fund.

In February 1922, the Grand Council reported that outgoings from the Fund were greater than the contributions received from Circles; two-thirds of these outgoings were helping towards children's education. In 1923, Grand Circle noted with regret that there were too many 'wrong calls' for benevolence, a reference perhaps to applications for help from men facing difficulties at a time noted by Grand Council as 'the awful state of trade'. Such 'wrong' applications were refused, but even so, in September 1923, the Fund had to report that, while the annual income was £755 (inclusive of £204 from interest in investments), the outgoings had been £1072.

The income from investments was a reflection of the work of the Grand Treasurers, who were responsible for handling the Fund. The first Grand Treasurer was Valentine M. Durnford (No. 21 on the roll of London Circle). A civil servant, he held the position from 1912 until 1916. There then came to the office two remarkable brothers, Bernard Heyburn (1916–19) and Edward Heyburn (1920–49). These were two rising stars in the City who became ardent Catenians and founder members of South London (1913). Edward Heyburn went on to become Secretary of a big Investment Trust – a mark of his professional ability. He also went on to become President of South London Circle (1923), and to help form the City of London Circle, of which he later became President (1927–28). It was he and his brother who handled the Benevolent Fund's income, and invested it wisely, so that it helped make up the shortfall in the years of strain; they so administered the Fund and supervised the working of the General Benevolent Board that it is no exaggeration to say that without the Heyburns we might not have had the healthy system we have today. Ted Heyburn died in February 1960, aged 80 – one of the giants of the City of London Circle and of the Association in general.

Heyburn and the Benevolent Board – in 1923 Baines, Perceval and Shaughnessy – made few, if any, claims for expenses, regarding their work as one of those voluntary contributions which the more fortunate were expected to make. They had not learned the modern habit of 'expenses forms and claims'. But even their work was criticised by Brothers of Circles who saw claims turned down. So it was that local Circles set up their own Benevolent Funds. In January 1924, Bradford put aside 5 per cent of the subscription to form such a Fund; in June, Newport set aside 10 per cent and also held regular collections at Circle meetings. In November the habit had become so widespread that Grand Council, accepting the inevitable, gave its official blessing to such local funds. In its Report for 1972, the Committee of Grand Council 'deprecates the maintenance of local funds and recommends that where such funds do exist they should be lodged in the Benevolent Fund Account at Williams and Glyn's Bank, Belgravia'. But the practice continues.

How did – indeed, how does – the Benevolent Board operate? In the first instance, an applicant for benevolence has to approach, or be approached by, the local Circle Benevolent Board. Each Circle Council appoints such a Board annually, comprising the President, the appropriate Grand Director and two other members enrolled in the Circle. The names and circumstances of those on whose behalf application is made are kept confidential to the Circle Board concerned and within the Grand Benevolent Board to whom the submission of the case is made. The local Circle Board ascertains the facts and fills in the form without showing it to the applicant; a supporting letter is usually provided to give the full background and justification for the claim. The form is considered by some members to be irksome and complicated; it is, however, based on a standard approach used by many charitable bodies, and all the information has the important purpose of assisting the Trustees to assess more closely the degree of 'difficulty or need'. This is their legal obligation under the Trust Deed which ordains how Catenian benevolence is administered. There are also the conditions which attach to a Registered Charity responding to the Charity Commissioners to be observed.

Some Circles will meet an emergency situation by giving immediate help from local funds or by raising money amongst their Brothers. Although this is charitable in intent, it contravenes the 1973 Review Board's recommendations which outlawed such payments and asked for recourse to be had to emergency help from Head Office instead. The Chairman of the Grand Benevolent Board and the Grand Secretary in consultation have a delegated power to grant emergency aid to a Brother or his dependents, and this can be done effectively and quickly – even on the basis of a telephone call. The problem with local assistance is that Circles can often lack experience on how to handle emergencies, and a well-meaning but precipitate action can pre-empt the later decisions of the Trustees and may even be unnecessary.

The application form and the letter from the local Board are sent to the Grand Secretary, who very often finds that the local Board has not done its work properly, so that forms have to be returned with a request for more information, and time is wasted while the claimant waits for the help needed. When the form is correctly completed, the Grand Secretary circulates copies to members of the Grand Benevolent Board, which meets every six weeks or so. It is this Board which makes the final decision as to whether help may be provided, either as a grant which will be reviewed each year or as a loan depending on the circumstances and asset holdings of the applicant. A loan is particularly appropriate, for example, in the case of an elderly widow who has a valuable house property and no known relatives but who needs continuing financial help to maintain a reasonable standard of living. The lack of contribution to parental maintenance by the grown-up children can also be a factor in deciding to award a loan rather than a grant – otherwise the grants go merely to preserve the capital asset intact for such children to inherit eventually, and this is considered unfair.

There are certain cases in which the Board will not help – indeed, is precluded from helping. It will not, for example, provide the money to bail out someone whose business is facing bankruptcy, nor will it help meet trading debts. Neither will it provide money to help with house purchase or with applications for help in adding to the capital of a business. Sometimes the Grand Benevolent Board will award more than the local Board has seen fit to ask for; sometimes it will decide that the local Board has not made out a case and will turn down the application; sometimes it will award less than the local Board has asked for. It is this which leads to differences and arguments between the local Board and the Trustees, and there can be anxiety and distress, even anger in the local Board, if an award is declined or held up for any reason. The Grand Secretary gives absolute priority to benevolence matters, but he has responsibility for many other duties in other fields. There may, therefore, be a case for appointing a Grand Almoner, whose responsibility would be to deal promptly and exclusively with benevolence affairs. Nor is the delay always attributable to Head Office or the Trustees; local Boards too often fail to appreciate the need for adequate information and its prompt submission in time for the appropriate scheduled meeting in London. If such a meeting is missed, by a day or so, then the application has to be held over until the next, in six weeks' time – unless there is an emergency situation involved.

It must be said that experience of the work of the Benevolent Board shows that the men involved display a responsible eagerness to help the needy; that they form their judgements with true and kindly wisdom; that they avoid all unnecessary delay and give the recipient the benefit of any doubt that cannot be resolved. What faults there are in the system, and what justifications there may be for the criticisms sometimes levelled at the system, seem to lie rather with the failure of local Boards than with the Grand Benevolent Board.

3. The Children's Fund

It is noticeable that a great deal of the private activities of individual Catenians as well as the activities of Circles and of the Association as a whole have been devoted to helping children. Nazareth Homes, and other similar homes for orphans and deprived children, have always received the support of Catenians who also led the way in the battle for secondary schooling during the inter-war period and after the passage of the 1944 Education Act. In more recent times the plight of handicapped children has almost dominated Catenian activities, with support for the Handicapped Children's Pilgrimage Trust (H.C.P.T.), for Hosanna House and for Jumbulance, which many thought of as a child-centred project.

So it is hardly surprising that the Association's own Children's Fund should have won such massive support that today it is much larger than the older Benevolent Fund. In 1930 the Association produced a small pamphlet, *The Children's Fund, Past and Present*, a pamphlet which was reprinted in 1935 and deserves to be reprinted today because it tells the story of the emergence and development of that Fund.

It may be said to have had its origins in a speech made by the future Grand President Thomas Kevill when he inaugurated the Bromley and Beckenham Circle (No. 68) in December 1922. In the course of that speech he referred to the possible shrinking of the Benevolent Fund. The reasons for that 'shrinking' were recalled by Grand Secretary Shepherd when giving an address on the Children's Fund at Cambridge in July 1929:

> For some years the calls on the Benevolent Fund were in excess of the income arising from contributions, and the Capital of the Fund was being called on to meet the increasing claims. Further, a group of claims which had hitherto not been unduly onerous began to increase considerably, viz., grants for the education and maintenance of the children of deceased members.

To go back to Kevill's address in 1922: The Founder President of Bromley and Beckenham was H. E. Gottelier, whose eldest son, C. L. Gottelier, was to become President of the Bromley Circle from 1934 to 1936 and Founder President of the Beckenham Circle in 1962; another son, L. V. Gottelier, was President of Beckenham in 1965–66. Here is one example of that Catenian family to which reference will be found elsewhere. One does not know what effect Kevill's address had on Gottelier, for he has left no record of his work for the Association. What we do know is that in May 1924 he went to the Annual Meeting of Province No.7 at Tunbridge Wells. At this meeting, West Kent Circle put forward a resolution for the institution of Catenian scholarships. Gottelier argued that this would benefit only the gifted few and suggested that the Association now needed a general fund to help all children, whether clever or not:

> Those who have first call on us are the children of brothers who have died and by force of circumstances leave children whose education must be seen to, and for whom little or no funds are available, also the children of those brothers who, in the

strenuousness of life, have fallen by the wayside either through ill-health or misfortune.

The West Kent resolution was lost. Gottelier's idea was taken up by his own Circle, which, on 22 May 1924, passed a resolution which they forwarded to Provincial Council No. 7:

> That this Circle is of the opinion that a special Fund should be started in connection with the Benevolent Fund to be earmarked for the education of deserving Brothers and suggests that Grand Council be asked to make arrangements to carry the proposal into effect. It also suggests that Presidents of Circles be asked during their year of office to institute a collection for this purpose.

To gain support for their resolution, members of Bromley Circle visited all the Circles in the Province and argued their case. The result was that at its meeting in July 1924 Provincial Council No. 7 resolved:

> That this Council recommend that Grand Council should sanction a collection to be made in each Circle by the President in his year of office for the Benevolent Fund, such collection to be earmarked for the education of the children of deserving Brothers.

The Grand President in 1924 was the energetic and far-seeing Brosch of Birmingham, 'father' of *Catena* and evangelist-successor to McDermott and Hogan. He and Grand Council were keenly aware of the parlous state of the Benevolent Fund, and they fully supported Gottelier's proposals, which would enable Grand Council to overcome their inability to deal as generously as they desired with the calls made on the Benevolent Board. On 4 December 1924, Grand Council sent out a letter to all Provincial Councils which embodied the terms of the resolution from Province No. 7 and went on:

> It is unanimously decided to encourage the suggestion, and, with this end in view, I am requested to bring the same to the notice of Provincial Councils. Grand Council are desirous that such collection shall take place in all Circles for the object named in the resolution, and the Fund to which the collections will be placed will be known as 'The Children's Fund'. I am requested to ask you to do your utmost to make this Fund a success by bringing the matter to the notice of all the Presidents of Circles within your Province. This matter is submitted to you with every confidence, and it is hoped that, as a result of the efforts which you will make, the 'Children's Fund' of the Benevolent Fund will become a great feature of the Association.

It may seem strange that there was a deal of opposition to this new Fund. But it is important to recall that it was launched at a time when the national economy was going into that recession which was to deepen until it became the Great Depression of the 1930s. Many men were already feeling the pinch in their private lives. There were, at the same time, an increasing number of calls upon their generosity: the Benevolent Fund's supporters wanted more so that more men could be better helped; the Cardinal and Grand Council were urging support for the Beda; local clergy expected, and received, monetary help to pay for the many new churches and schools being built, while local charities asked for, and received, generous help. I am reminded of a friend who, after hearing a non-Catholic colleague lamenting his plight in that he was facing a heavy mortgage, commented, 'You're lucky; I'm not only buying my own house, I'm also buying a new church, supporting three schools to which my children go, aiding the Nazareth House nuns in their work, and sending money to the Bishop's Fund, Peter's Pence, etc. etc. I wish I only had one mortgage to worry about.'

Some critics asked why the Fund should not imitate the Benevolent Fund and depend on a universal levy. Gottelier's answer was that to fix a levy might have a twofold harmful effect: those men already under financial pressure might find an extra levy just that straw which would break them; on the other hand, those men who were financially well-placed might be able to and be prepared to contribute much more than might be asked for by a levy. And indeed the evidence of the last fifty years has shown the wisdom of making the Fund a voluntary effort. Whereas the General Benevolent Fund in 1980 had investment assets of £241,174, the Children's Fund had investment assets of £248,457. The Children's Fund has not only benefited from the annual appeal made by Circle Presidents; it has also gained from the funds collected at a variety of activities, by Brothers and by Ladies' Committees, the profits from which have been earmarked for the Children's Fund.

Applications for help for children in need have to be made in the same way as applications for aid from the General Fund. In the first instance, the application is considered by the local Board, which, if satisfied, sends the request on to the Benevolent Board. This considers the plight of the children of deceased or necessitous Brothers and may provide either a grant or a loan to help with children's education and maintenance. The Trustees will not undertake to educate children merely because the father has died or fallen on hard times. The children will not be allowed to suffer, for the Trustees gladly assume liability for their education, but only up to the standard which their parents had intended and had the means to provide. This helps to explain the apparent discrepancies in the amount of help awarded in different cases.

The Trustees of both the General Fund and the Children's Fund rightly surround their work with a high degree of confidentiality, not to say secrecy. Indeed, no one in the Circle other than the members of the local Benevolent Board becomes aware of the fact that a member or his family are receiving help. But in 1933, members of Grand Council received a summary of the way in which the Children's Fund was being used. I reproduce one page from that report as an indication of the people who were helped at that time.

CHILDREN'S FUND

November 1933

The father was badly let down by a Catenian (since resigned) on a deed of partnership which was due for signature when he died, assistance or help of any kind was positively refused to widow by ex-Catenian referred to, she with three children in consequence left absolutely unprovided for.
Position found for Widow as housekeeper to a doctor, she died suddenly in September this year.
The children now 13, 11½ and 10 and have no one but the Association to take care of them. The doctor (non-Catholic) for whom the widow kept house has provided the children with pocket money each term and will continue to do so.
Total cost to date £577: 2: 7

Widow left with nine children (14/3 years), some provision left for her but not immediately available, two eldest boys taken from non-Catholic school and

educated elsewhere, one secured position as a chemist, the other is in employ of the local Corporation.
This is the application where the master at the non-Catholic school enquired – 'Come on H. what were you doing last night, confessing your sins?'
Total cost to date £241: 3: 6

Father died suddenly leaving wife and three young children without means, relatives took charge and are educating two of the children. Wife secured post in Bank and whilst able to maintain herself and one child cannot pay for its education. As a result of Children's Fund undertaking cost of education certain special donations have been made to Fund.
Total cost to date £250: 0: 0

Father was 'killed in action' leaving one boy. Widow was a Convert and under the influence of non-conformist relations, no Catholic school of the type required was available in the immediate vicinity, consequently boy was being educated at a Protestant day school, the widow with a pension of £140 p.a. being unable to afford to send the boy away. Application made to the Ministry of Pensions for assistance was successful, boy removed to Catholic College and the Children's Fund met difference between grant and fees.
Total cost to date £175: 0: 0

Father died aged 36, had set up in business as Architect only three years prior to death. Four children, eldest 10. Estate value £800. Education two daughters completed, wife secured position in Bank and able to look after the other two children.
Total cost £520: 0: 0

In a report to Grand Council in 1944, the Trustees noted that they were then helping 34 boys and 27 girls, and that the total number who had been helped to that date was 235. The report also listed the later careers of some of the children who had been helped:

> Among the professions which have proved attractive are the Church, teaching, chemistry, insurance, nursing, accountancy, engineering, banking, medical, dentistry, the civil service, farming, auctioneering, domestic science. We have not a complete list, but Brothers may be assured that no child who has been under our charge lacks advice and guidance. They have foster-fathers in plenty, of whom the Grand Secretary is the chief.

Moving ahead of our story, I would wish to share with the reader some of the emotion felt when George Harris addressed Grand Council in 1980 on the occasion of his retirement from the chairmanship of the Benevolent Board. He recalled the candidate for membership of the Association who was due to be initiated, when he was told by his doctor that he had a terminal illness. The young man suggested that the Association might not want to 'take him on'. The suggestion was dismissed, the man became a Brother and never attended a second meeting, for he died within the week. Speaking to Grand Council, and visibly moved, George Harris described the deceased Brother's young family. 'And', said Harris, 'we took responsibility for all of them, the older ones now having gone through University, some of the younger ones still being in school.' As a guest at that dinner, I shared, with Grand Council, the corporate grief at the death of a man I had never known, the pride in the way in which the Benevolent Board, my representatives, had dealt with his honourable wish to have his application for membership re-considered, and gratitude to the Benevolent Board for the way in which it had used the Association's money to help the late Brother's children.

4. Benevolence in the depression

Both the Children's Fund and the General Benevolent Fund are administered by the General Benevolent Board. Originally this Board consisted of the principal officers of the Grand Council – the Grand President, Grand Vice-President, Grand Secretary, Grand Treasurer, plus the immediate Past Grand President and two Grand Directors elected by Grand Council. In 1972, the Frank Lloyd Review Board explained that this did not always provide men with the financial acumen needed by the Board which was, additionally, too small to ensure a sufficient attendance at Board meetings. It recommended that in future the Board should consist of the Grand President and Grand Vice-President, Grand Secretary and the immediate Past Grand President, as well as six members elected by Grand Council, of whom two should be Grand Directors, while the others elected should be members of the Association but not necessarily members of Grand Council. This allowed the election of men with the sort of experience and professional wisdom needed by the Board. That Report also recommended that the Chairman of the Board (hitherto the Grand President) should be elected by the Board for a three-year term, as this would provide a much needed element of continuity.

But in the 1930s it was the unreformed Board which ran the two Funds, meeting once every six weeks or so, in great secrecy considering the recommendations of local Boards. The General Fund had to cope with the effects of that Great Depression which overtook the country in the 1930s. It is not surprising, then, to read that in May 1937 Grand Council had to announce an extra 10 per cent levy on members' subscriptions to help make the Fund viable. One feels sympathy for the members of the Board, who, having guided the affairs of the Association through the desperate years of the '30s, then found themselves called on to deal with the effects of World War II after 1939. In another section of this book we shall examine the effects of that War on the Association at large. Here we ought to note that there were many calls on Catenian Benevolence: there were the men whose businesses either collapsed or slumped as a result of the War; there were the families of men killed on active service; there were the many hundreds of men and their families who were affected, in greater or lesser degree, by enemy bombing. No wonder, then, that in 1942 the outgoings from the General Fund (£2042) were much higher than the income (£1037); there was a real danger that the built-up balance (of £10,000) might soon be eaten away.

The members of the Board, coping with this wartime problem, also looked ahead to the days when 'peace would break out'. Like Beveridge and other forecasters, they thought that the country would face a post-war slump. This, after all, had been the experience after World War I and there was no reason to suppose that a greater war, geographically more extensive as well as far more destructive, would not bring a greater slump in its wake. When they looked at the Children's Fund they thought that the future was equally gloomy. There would be the large number of children whose fathers had been killed – a reminder of the large number of younger men recruited to the Association in the latter days of the 1930s, and of the tendency for Catholics to have families larger than normal. The Board also believed, rightly, that the costs of education would rise dramatically after the War. This might, again, remind us that almost all secondary schooling had to be paid for, save by the fortunate few who gained scholarships; and even the Catholic fortunate few might not have their fees paid at a Catholic school if the L.E.A. decided not to recognise the Catholic schools.

In fact, as we shall see, these fears were not realised. There was not that expected post-war slump; members working in post-war Britain proved to be more generous than had been prophesied, so that the two Funds built up larger balances. In particular it has to be seen that the development of State-provided secondary education relieved the Association of much of the expected burden of paying for the children of 'necessitous' or 'deceased' Brothers.

One other development should be noted here. In October 1943, Bristol Circle set up a Wefare Committee consisting of Brothers who agreed to oversee the well-being of Brothers, their families – and their widows. Other Circles have, since then, set up similar Committees, so that, in Bournemouth for example, there is a Committee which has the duty of organising sick visiting, hospital visiting, letters to widows on anniversaries and at Christmas, invitations to widows to attend functions at no charge to themselves, and so on. I am told that Bristol does not have such a Committee today, but it does have a Welfare Officer who has much of the responsibility once exercised by the Committee. And this Officer has one function which is being increasingly exercised by Circle Presidents and Secretaries elsewhere: namely, that of looking after the children or relations of Catenians who are students at the local University or Polytechnics. It must be a relief to Catenian parents to know that, when their children leave for a University, it is possible to write to the nearest Circle and find that Brothers will invite their children to a meal and a social gathering. I have to express my own gratitude to the men of the Swansea Circle for their help to one of my sons.

5. Catena Trustees 1946–1981

There was no formal Trust Deed relevant to the two Benevolent Funds until September 1929, when a Deed referred to 'The Catenian Benevolent Fund'; while it did not name either the General Benevolent Fund or the Children's Fund, it clearly embraced both, since the schedule of investments contained in the Deed specified precisely the investments then held by the two Funds. Legally, therefore, there is only one Fund, although there is a distinction in the use to which its two parts may be put. Contributions collected for the General Benevolent Fund may be used for all the purposes stated in the Deed: (*a*) 'to render assistance to persons being members of the Catenian Association in necessitous circumstances'; (*b*) 'to provide for the material welfare and care of the wives and families and other dependents of the living or deceased members of the Catenian Association who are in necessitous cirumstances'. But money collected for the Children's Fund may be applied only to the maintenance and education of children of living or dead Catenians.

In 1949, Grand Council examined the possibilities of widening the terms of reference of the Children's Fund. But counsel's opinion was that the Trust Deed did not allow the Fund being used for such desirable ends as the education of priests, the founding of Catenian Scholarships at Catholic schools, assistance to research students at Universities, or the provision of an orphanage.

Until 1955, any funds surplus to immediate requirements were invested by the Finance Committee of Grand Council in gilt-edged stocks as laid down by the Deed. In that year the Committee recommended that steps should be taken to allow investment of part of the Funds in equities, which provided opportunity for capital growth. In 1958, Grand Council obtained a court judgement which permitted the Trustees to invest up to two-thirds of the Funds in a limited range of equities. Grand Council then appointed an Investment Committee to advise the Trustees on the investment of the Funds. This Committee was made up, and still is today, of members who are specialists (none of whom are members of Grand Council), plus the Grand President, Grand Secretary, and Grand Treasurer (all *ex officio*), and two representatives of the Trustees, appointed on behalf of the Grand Benevolent Board. The healthy state of the funds at the present day is an indication of the benefit which the Association has obtained from the guidance given by this Committee to the Trustees.

In April 1946, Grand Council decided to form a Trustee Company to hold the Association's investments, in order to avoid the trouble and expense due to changes in the Trustees caused either by death or resignation. The investments of the Benevolent Fund, however, continued to be held by individual Trustees appointed by Grand Council. Only in 1967 did Grand Council seek the permission of the Charity Commissioners to have the Catena Trustees Limited appointed as the sole trustee of Benevolent Funds. From 1 April 1968 the Articles of Association of the Company were amended to make the members of the Benevolent Board *ipso facto* Directors of the Company.

It was fortuitous that the Grand President in 1968–69 was the wealthy Joe Cox, who devoted a great part of his Presidential address to the question of Benevolence. He drew attention to the ominous fact that the income accruing to the Benevolent Fund was less than its expenditure, so that the Trustees were being forced to sell investments. He asked that members of the Association should give more generously to the General Benevolent Fund and to the Children's Fund. The latter had long had the benefit of the competition aroused by the Trophy awarded annually to the Circle which was most generous in its contributions to that Fund. To stimulate interest in the General Fund, Joe Cox contributed a Trophy which is now awarded annually to the Circle which makes the greatest contribution to the General Benevolent Fund in any one year.

The need for larger contributions to the General Benevolent Fund in particular has increased in the years since 1968. In the first place, inflation has tended to lower the real value of the average contribution fixed as a percentage of the members' subscriptions. Then the sharp drop in the share prices in the 1970s lowered the book value of the investments held by the Trustees. But at the same time the depression, of which the fall in share prices was an indication, led to increased calls on the Benevolent Fund. When Joe Cox addressed the A.G.M. in 1968, expenditure from the Benevolent Fund was £11,000. During 1980–81, '92 cases were dealt with and a total disbursement in outright grants or loans amounted to £142,335', and this in spite of the fact that the Grand Secretary was able to help applicants obtain assistance from other sources. This he achieves by being a member of the Association of Charity Officers, comprising nearly 200 other charitable organisations. Contact is regularly maintained with many such bodies in mutually sharing the burden of charitable help. Doctors in need may thus receive Catenian-inspired help from the Royal Medical Benevolent Fund, while solicitors may be helped by the Solicitors' Benevolent Fund.

It is hardly surprising that in 1981 Grand Council proposed an increase in enrolment and capitation fees. Members approved the increased capitation fee, but rejected the proposal for an increased enrolment fee, either because of Grand Council's poor presentation of its case, or perhaps owing to increasingly widespread criticism of the apparent unaccountability of Grand Council, which, furthermore, had recently appeared unable to present its annual accounts in an acceptable form.

6. The covenant scheme

What is surprising is that a large number of Catenians do not use the Covenant System, which allows the Association to obtain tax rebates from the Inland Revenue. The first mention of Covenants appeared in *Catena* in July 1942, when the Epsom Circle claimed that its holding of the Children's Fund Cup was due in large part to the fact that 'the amount of the Circle's contribution has been substantially increased by recovered income tax under the "covenant" scheme, which certain of the brothers have made the channel of their gifts to the Fund. Outgoing President, P. A. Clark Vincent, has been very keen about the adoption of this scheme, and our "landing" of the Cup for another year is largely due to his enthusiasm and zeal.'

Unfortunately there is no evidence that other Circles then followed Epsom's example. In 1945 Bernard Emblem, a member of the Blackheath Circle, retired from his work as a tax inspector and turned his knowledge of the tax world to the benefit of the Church. He knew, of course, that charities paid no income tax, although those who supported the charities did so. Emblem pointed out that this tax, paid on donations to registered charities, could be retrieved, provided that the donor signed a deed of covenant for the yearly sum subscribed.

In 1945, the Methodists already had a scheme in operation. Emblem set out to persuade Bishops, priests and people that it was possible to convert the weekly offering put in the collection plate into an annual figure which could be covenanted: a covenant for £26 a year was the same as one for 50p a week. It took time for Emblem to succeed in his work of 'conversion', and for Archbishop Amigo to allow him to launch the scheme in Southwark. In the first year (1944) the tax refund was 17s.9d.; but by 1945 it was £1211; by March 1958, Emblem had retrieved £240,000 for Southwark and by 1972 Southwark had received some £3,000,000 in tax refund.

Emblem retired from active work in 1957, to be replaced as Southwark Covenant Secretary by Anthony Rice, another Catenian. By this time, too, other dioceses had adopted Emblem's scheme and in many cases had recruited Catenians to act as Covenant Secretaries. Leonard Ross, for example, had started the scheme in Shrewsbury, and it was his son, Peter Ross, then of the Shrewsbury Circle, who in 1965 persuaded representatives of some twenty-seven dioceses to adopt a computer-covenant-clearing house centred on his office.

The Church had been slow to adopt Emblem's scheme, but at least and at last it had done so. The members of the Association, albeit that they are, by definition, 'professional and business men', were even slower, while some have not yet adopted it. In 1947, Emblem made himself available to Circles, offering to come to speak to them about the scheme. But few men signed the requisite forms. In his Presidential address in 1953, Jack Lawler drew attention to this failure to take advantage of the scheme for the benefit of Benevolent Funds. In October 1953, Peter Ross wrote a long and very well presented account of the way in which the scheme worked. Grand Treasurer Brian Coakley handled the small number of Covenants made for the benefit of the Benevolent Funds until 1958, when Herbert Cosgrove was asked to help his colleague, 'and we used to go to Hobart Place on Sunday afternoons to deal with the scheme'. When Coakley died in November 1961, Cosgrove, who had recently retired from the Inland Revenue, took over the scheme which then handled some 200 Covenants on behalf of the Children's Fund.

During Joe Cox's Presidency a drive was made to get members to covenant for the General Benevolent Fund. They merely had to covenant that portion of their annual fee assigned to that Fund. The Inland Revenue agreed this scheme in 1975 and with the appointment of Circle Covenant Officers there was a rise in the number of Covenants. When the Association went over to the computer (1971–72) there were about 1300; when Cosgrove handed the scheme over to Tim O'Brien in June 1976 there were 3000, and in 1981 there were 6189 Covenants. From these the Benevolent Fund benefited by some £11,000 by way of tax refund.

In view of the ease with which members may benefit the Benevolent Fund, at no cost to themselves, it is surprising that some Circles still have no Brothers who have covenanted, that a large number of men in other Circles still refuse to adopt the scheme, and that about half those who do covenant fail to sign the tax certificates. In February 1981, for example, there were some 2770 certificates which had not been returned, worth about £5200 in tax reclaim to the Benevolent Fund.

CHAPTER TEN

Aims and Objects

1. The stated, but amended, Aims

In his letter to Bishop Casartelli, O'Donnell outlined the Aims of the Association for which he was seeking the Bishop's approval. In June 1909, the members of the Association approved the Constitution and Rules in which the Aims were listed as: (*a*) To promote the interests of the Brothers and their families by the individual and collective action of their members; (*b*) The cultivation of a closer acquaintance among 'C' professional and business men; (*c*) To promote the interests of 'C' youths entering business and professional life.

We have seen that the Association was soon called upon to provide help for the widow of a London Brother and for the widow of their own Brother Whittle. This led to the new Aim in October 1910, when a new Constitution was approved in which we find: (*d*) To establish, maintain and administer benevolent funds.

The major reorganisation which took place in 1923 allowed a further change in the list of Aims. The original (*a*) and (*b*) were transposed. There was also the addition of a fifth Aim: (*e*) To sponsor such insurance schemes as from time to time may be considered beneficial to members.

But perhaps the most revealing thing about the 1923 Constitution was that for the first time the Association dropped the 'C' in the original items (*b*) and (*c*) and spelt out 'Catholic'. The fact that they had not felt able to do so in 1908 may help us to understand the atmosphere in which Catholics lived at that time, while the newly-won confidence, derived in part from the expansion of the Association, was reflected in their willingness to spell out their Catholicism in 1923.

These, with slight amendments of language, remained the stated Aims for the next fifty years or so, in spite of the fact that no one was able to devise a system of insurance as set out in (*e*). The major re-writing of the Rules in the late 1960s, with further amendments made in the mid-1970s, has left us with the Aims as stated in the Directory for 1980–81:

(*a*) to foster brotherly love among the members;
(*b* to develop social bonds among the members and their families;
(*c*) to advance the interests of members and their dependents by individual or collective action;
(*d*) to advance the interests of young Catholics and to assist them in the choice or pursuit of a career;
(*e*) to establish, maintain and administer benevolent funds.

There have been many and frequent demands for the Association to amend its Aims so that it might become either a vehicle for Catholic action (which by definition has to be approved by the Hierarchy and controlled by the clergy) or itself lay down forms of action which, while maintaining its independence, would nevertheless make the Association 'more active' than it was from the start and than it is in 1981. While at times demands of this nature have been made by individuals or by individual Circles, there have also been calls for 'action' by Grand Presidents and/or by other influential members of Grand Council. In particular there was the 'call' by Pat Taggart in the late 1930s and the demand for a fresh look at the Aims expressed so forcibly by Frank Lomas during his Presidential address in 1963, when, it was thought, the changes in the Church being generated by Vatican II ought to be reflected by changes in the Aims of the Association. I propose to examine this argument in Chapter 15.

But at this stage it is necessary to look at the Aims as stated in 1908, and to see what they tell us about the thinking of the founders of the Association. What did they intend the Association to be? It seems clear that they wanted to set up a male, lay, middle-class Catholic organisation, in which men could find a social home, through which their families might benefit, and from which the men and the children might gain some benefit in their careers. The fact that the Association prospered and expanded as rapidly as it did in the early years suggests that it fulfilled a need. That it continues to expand in the much changed atmosphere of the modern era, both in Britain and overseas, suggests that it still meets a need. The continued expansion also indicates the wisdom of the founders, for if the foundations which they laid had been faulty then the Association would long since have collapsed. 'Its diminutions and corruptions, and its jeopardy by the follies of its members, were part of the canon of history. There was plenty of ground for cynicism. But over and over again the cynics were confounded by the capacity for self-renewal. . . .' In *The Shoes of the Fisherman*, Morris West was writing about the Church, but, *mutatis mutandis*, we may apply the statement to the Association and pay a deserved tribute to 'the Chums' who had founded so well.

2. Attacks and misunderstandings

That it should be an entirely lay society was in keeping with the major theme of Casartelli's first pastoral letter, which we may take as one of the primary causes for the formation of the Association. It is interesting to note that as early as June 1918 there was a major debate in Grand Circle as to whether we should imitate the American Knights of Columbus and admit priests to the membership. The proposal to do so was lost, in the presence of O'Donnell, Foggin, Shepherd and others of the early members who argued that the aims of the Association were strictly limited – unlike the aims of the clergy who would find membership restricting. During the debate it was recalled that Casartelli had advised against having priests as members – first, because he wanted laymen to 'grow up', secondly, because he approved of the clerical dictum which states that priests should stay out 'rarely after ten and never after eleven', which might have put a damper on the Association's activities and, thirdly, because he saw the danger of his priests being too closely associated in the minds of their people with a particular social group in the Church.

For the Association was manifestly a middle-class organisation. It has often been attacked on that front, most recently by a piece in the *Catholic Pictorial* of Liverpool which in April 1978 carried the following:

> I see from the Archbishop's engagements that he is to – or has – attended a lunch provided by the Equestrian Order of something or other. Ah, a woe on these pale Catholic imitations of secular orders. How I detest titles like Knight of this and Knight of that. How I abhor those knee breeches and toy swords redolent of a

Church I never knew, thank God. How I despise the implied privilege in these empty Vatican titles. How shocked am I by the fact that the full gear for Knighthood costs in the order of £700. For God's sake, chummy, if you're ever offered a Papal knighthood say 'ta, but no' and give the cash for your gear to CAFOD.
Which inevitably, alas, brings me to the Catenians. It would be cheap and nasty to suggest that old snide – that a Catenian was a failed Freemason on the grounds of principle. But then I am cheap and nasty. And the Catenian order seems in many respects to be a sop for those Catholics who would, in the normal course of events, have been Freemasons. The Catenians are outdated. Their society – with cash and social position a prerequisite – was always one of the Church's less savoury limbs. Today the Society is a total anachronism.
Let the Catenians take a leaf from the good Knights – the Knights of St. Columba. Long ago now, or so it seems, they had the good sense to abandon the frolics of secrecy and enter into the work of the Church. And what a great job they made of it too. Perhaps the Catenians could wrest themselves away from solid dinners with solid folk and give something of themselves instead of their cash. It would stop scandal. And think of the warm glow. As cosy as any after-dinner Havana taken under the benevolent eye of a chaplain imported to add dignity to a right old binge.

The snide comment comparing the Asociation with Freemasonry is neither new nor true, for there is nothing exclusive or secret about the Association which is also 'proudly Catholic'. Nor is the comment about snobbery original. As early as December 1919, Grand President Oswald Goodier was pointing out that the Church had a variety of sodalities catering for the interests of various groups within the Church and that working men, in and out of the Church, had their own clubs and organisations. The Association, he pointed out, was merely another such club, catering for a particular group inside the Church. The proof of the need for such an organisation was its rapid growth in Salford, to which men travelled from miles around to enjoy the bi-monthly pleasure of one another's company, and its rapid expansion elsewhere. And the continued expansion of the Association, and more particularly its growth since 1950, is an indication of the way in which the Catholic middle class has grown in line with the social mobility which has been a feature of recent British history.

3. Bigotry and prejudice
To return, then, to the Aims as stated in 1908, which may be seen as the *fons et origo* of Aim (*c*) in the modern Directory. It is important to recall the difficulties which faced Catholic business men and commercial men in 1908, when there was that intolerance towards Catholics which had had its effects on the behaviour of Catholics to one another. In January 1923, Grand Vice-President Kevill, speaking to No. 1 Circle, asked why Catholics were so shy and diffident, so that their middle-class friends looked on them as suffering under a handicap. He reflected that this Catholic attitude, and the consequent attitude of their non-Catholic friends, were the natural consequences of the past history of Catholics in this country. Kevill claimed that the coming of the Association was an instrument for destroying that state of things. Speaking to the Bradford Circle in May 1923 he returned to this theme, commenting on 'the contempt felt by most people for the small Catholic body' and on 'the narrow partisan attitude of some non-Catholics which continued to the present day'. In May 1923, Grand President Synott of London claimed that the Association 'brought men out so that they learned to be confident . . .', which enabled them

to 'go out and prosper . . .'. In September 1928, evidence was revealed of this bigotry on the part of Scottish Protestants acting through three Protestant Associations. In a letter to the Home Secretary they noted that the Catholic population of Scotland was rising, and they asked that the government should take action to prohibit any further 'immigration' from Ireland and Italy.

And in case anyone should think that this intolerance died out during World War II we ought to note a speech made at the inaugural meeting of Worthing (No. 133) on 26 July 1947, in which Past Grand President Percy Briggs (Founder President of the new Circle) spoke of the 'suspicion and scrutiny to which every Catholic business man was subject . . . surrounded by critics . . . made to suffer the attacks of the intellectual scoffer and unbeliever'. Briggs, speaking from the experience of a long membership, claimed that the Association was one bright spot and asked the Brothers to foster friendship amongst themselves. And what of the 1980s? Does anyone believe that hostility to the faith is less than it was? Is the world today less pagan, less materialistic, more moral than it was in 1947 when Briggs spoke? Do Catholic doctors find no opposition to promotion in, for example, gynaecology departments owing to the Church's teaching on abortion? Will they find no opposition to their promotion in geriatric departments when, in the future, we have laws permitting euthanasia? Do London parents not feel themselves under attack when the London Labour Party proposes, in its election manifesto for May 1981, to abolish Catholic schools? In fine, is there less need for this specifically Catholic society today than there was in 1908?

4. 'Service'

To promote the interests of the Brothers and their families by collective action was interpreted in a variety of ways. There was, for example, the fund set up by the Manchester Circle which allowed Dan McCabe to become the first Catholic Lord Mayor of the City in 1913–14 and to serve for a second year in 1914–15. There was the active support given to Brothers seeking public office on local Councils or in Parliament, and the announcement of every success in *Catena* to encourage others to 'go and do thou likewise'. There was the production of the Year Book which was, in essence, a trade directory in which members could be made aware of the occupations of fellow-members in the hope that, in this way, Catholic men might go in for inter-trading. To further this aim, there were also the use of signs, specially embossed cards and Catenian passwords, which, it was hoped, would facilitate contact between members from different parts of the country.

But it was soon realised that there was all too little to be gained from such inter-trading. In the first place there were too few Catholics to support an introverted business, although there was, and is, evidence that some Catenian business does flow to fellow-Catenians. And there was, too, an inbred diffidence which led people to deliberately give work to non-Catholics even when there were perfectly well qualified Catholics available to do the work. In 1919, a certain Doctor J.J. Ryan complained that a convent in North London insisted on employing a Protestant doctor in its home for the aged. In replying to this criticism, as we have seen above (p. 68), another Catenian commented, revealingly, that, if any public inquiry was involved, the evidence of a Protestant doctor would carry greater conviction.

Perhaps the most ambitious scheme adopted as a result of the aim of

AIMS AND OBJECTS

promoting the interests of the Brothers was that covered in the title of Commercial and Intelligence Committee which, in time, became better known as 'Service'. In May 1914, the London Circle had set up such a Committee 'to create some practical machinery by which the large amount of information obviously possessed by individual Catenians should be utilised for the benefit of, and be accessible to members, not only of the London Circle, but of other Circles as well'.

In May 1915, the London Committee issued a Report recommending that the Association should adopt 'a certain number of objects' which were listed and sent for the consideration of Grand Council. Grand Council agreed to allow this Report to be circulated among members of the Association in January 1916, and in January 1917 the London Circle issued a pamphlet, written by Sir Westby Perceval and Walter Synott, which showed that, while only two Circles (Bristol and North London) fully supported the scheme, only four (Newcastle, Glasgow, Southport and Nottingham) were totally opposed to it, with the rest of the Circles being 'partially favourable'. The Perceval–Synott pamphlet then went on to suggest that local Committees be set up for the following purposes:
  (i) to procure information for Members of the Association for business purposes;
  (ii) to procure employment for Members and their dependents;
  (iii) to facilitate business between Members;
  (iv) to give information as to schools, technical training, etc.;
  (v) to find partners, legal representatives or agents for Members;
  (vi) to obtain information for Members when making permanent change of residence as to new parish, neighbourhood, introductions, etc.;
  (vii) to assist Members who require services of a local professional man;
  (viii) to assist Members in starting sons in business or profession by giving information and advice:
    (a) as to selecting such business or profession;
    (b) as to board, lodging, etc.;
    (c) as to apprenticeship or articles.

Brosch at Birmingham agreed that his Circle would act as a clearing house for linking together the various local Committees, and would use *Catena* as a vehicle for promoting their objects. One hardly knows whether more to admire the vision of the authors of the London pamphlet or to wonder at their naïvety. For they were calling for the development of local and national organisations which, in terms of time, money and effort, would have daunted many a larger organisation. They also failed to reckon with the inevitable result that there were more applicants asking for help than offering it. They could not have been expected to foresee the onset of the economic depression after April 1921 which increased the numbers of applicants seeking work and business with no corresponding increase, indeed, rather a decrease, in the number of Catenians able to offer help.

The more cautious members of Grand Council persuaded their fellow-members to oppose the Committees, arguing that it was making the Association too much of a merely commercial organisation to the possible detriment of its other, and more important, aims of social intercourse between Catholic men and their families. By the time of its meeting in June 1921, Grand Council had come to see that the Service Committees were not working as smoothly as Synott and Perceval had hoped. They worked slowly, with the offer of a job (when it came) arriving via the local Committee at the Birmingham clearing house, from whence it was sent via *Catena* and letters to Circle Secretaries. By the time a potential beneficiary had read about and applied for the post some six to eight weeks had elapsed and it had been filled. So there were all too few successes to report, and these largely on the local level at which they might well have been made even before the new Committees were set up.

This helps to explain why, in spite of the arguments of its advocates, 'Service' did not feature in the 1923 Constitution. Local Committees continued to function, with Liverpool, for example, setting aside £1000 in November 1922 to further the work. But some languished and others died, as did the Birmingham Committee. In Lancashire, Circles banded together to form the Lancashire Service Committee which in 1929 issued a series of booklets offering careers guidance to school-leavers. It was all the more ironic, and personally tragic, that when Grand Council decided to bring Service Committees to an end it should have called on Grand Director Teddy Doran to deliver the death sentence at the A.G.M. in Bournemouth in 1931. Doran had been a member of Manchester (No. 1) and founder member of the South Manchester (No. 28) when it was founded in 1915. A delegate to Grand Circle, he quickly made his mark on the Association, starting the practice of President's Sunday in Manchester, organising the showing of the first Ideal Circle on the stage of the Free Trade Hall during the A.G.M. at Manchester in 1926, and becoming an active and popular Provincial President noted for his tireless work for the Children's Fund. In 1929 he was chosen as Grand Director, and in 1934 was first choice as Grand Vice-President. Unfortunately, as it turned out, he allowed Rudman to persuade him to stand down so that Shaughnessy of Glasgow could become Vice-President with a view to becoming Grand President in 1935; Rudman wanted his personal friend, Shaughnessy, to take the Chair so that Scotland might better feel that it had a part to play in the Association. It was unfortunate for Doran that he allowed himself to be talked out of taking his vice-presidential place, for by 1935 his six years as Grand Director were up, and when it came to the election Lancashire men remembered, with some bitterness, the way in which Doran had acted to kill 'Service', which had a special place in Lancashire and the demise of which they regretted. Doran was not re-elected, as he might rightly have expected to be, and he never became the outstanding Grand President which he undoubtedly would have been.

5. Catenian friendship

The original Aim (*b*) – 'the cultivation of a closer acquaintance amongst "C" professional and business men' – has by 1980–81 become Aims (*a*) and (*b*) – 'to foster brotherly love among the members' and 'to develop social bonds among the members and their families'. It would be foolish to suppose that every Circle has been constantly imbued with 'brotherly love'. One sympathises with the honesty of Bro. T.L. Webster, now a member of Brooklands Circle but then of North Cheshire (No. 154), writing in 1955 when the Circle was still relatively in its infancy. Referring to the first six years, he wrote: 'We had our difficulties – most of the sort which arise in any young family – the occasional background grumbles and jockeying for position, misunderstandings, criticisms, forgetfulness, carelessness, wordy impasses. a few resignations

AIMS AND OBJECTS

even.' Which Circle would not have to say something on the same lines?

In the course of researching this book I met a large number of men and have corresponded with even more. At each such meeting, to get the conversation started, I posed the question, 'Why did you join the Association and why, today, would you recommend it to a potential candidate for admission?' In every case the answer could be summed up in one word: 'Friendship', and further discussion revealed how important a part this 'friendship' has played in the Association's history. Converts, such as George Harris, immigrants such as the many Poles now to be found in the Association, members of long-standing Catholic families such as Frank Lomas, Alex Carus and Jimmy Baker, all gave the same answer, that in the Association they had found a friendship which they could not even begin to explain. Of course, as soon became clear, these and the many others got what they gave; for the aim of the Association is the *fostering* of brotherly love, not only its acquisition. They had given freely of themselves, in little ways by attendance at meetings, in larger ways by serving in office; and, as a Provincial President said when opening the Cheshire North Circle, 'We got what we gave', although he might have gone on to add: 'pressed down, shaken together, and running over'.

It is much less easy to find out why, in North Cheshire and elsewhere, there were and are so many 'resignations', for one does not easily meet the men who, once members, have either resigned or allowed their membership to lapse. This has been an unfortunate feature of the history of the Association since its very first days. There were men who joined Manchester (No. 1), who resigned after only one or two meetings in 1908. Why? And why have some 10,000 men lapsed or resigned since then? For some, such as the men who left Manchester in 1908, there was the disappointment they felt when it became clear that the Association was not the Catholic equivalent of the influential Masonic Order. It was not, and could not be, the pathway to jobs, contracts or promotions. The development of Benevolent Schemes and the growth of the Children's Fund, allied with the emergence of the Service Committees, attracted many into the Association after 1919, when there was that rapid expansion which led to the writing of the new Constitution. Some at least of these new members soon showed that they had joined the Association for what they hoped to get out of it. Some joined while unemployed or under threat of being so; and the blame for their admission must be laid at the feet of their sponsors and the officers of the Circles which admitted them. For within weeks or months of joining they were applying to the Benevolent Board for help, and if this was not provided, or not provided on a sufficiently lavish scale, then they left.

But resignations and lapsations are not always due to failures on the part of the defecting member. In some cases men found that they were bored by the Circle they joined, either because too few Brothers turned up at meetings, which were then relatively 'dead', or because the development of cliques made it difficult or even impossible for the new man to feel at home. In some cases, men who had been persuaded to join quickly found that they were temperamentally unsuited for the Association, which is, after all, a club for social intercourse and as such depends on its members being, to some degree at least, 'clubbable'.

Some men have left the Association because their work has taken them to parts of the world or of the country where there is no Circle – although it has to be said that there are very many Brothers who keep up their membership even when 'exiled'. Some have left when, on retirement, their incomes have fallen;

and although the Association has provision for the partial or total remission of fees and subscriptions for the retired, there is an understandable pride which has persuaded some, at least, that they do not wish to belong to an Association in which they can no longer pay their full way. Others leave, maybe for a time or maybe permanently, when the calls of family commitments make it difficult for them to afford the time or money to enjoy their Catenian activities to the full. As the father of five children aged, at one time, between 13 and 8, I felt it necessary to resign as there were simply not enough evenings or hours to cope with the demands of this lively family and, at the same time, to be an active Catenian.

Some have claimed that they were leaving because the ritual was excessive, too childish, not enough, or unnecessary. But, admittedly without proof, one suspects that there must have been other reasons behind these excuses. Some have left because the Association is not 'doing anything' – which shows that they were never properly advised on the nature of the Association in the first place, or that they ignored the many forms of Action in which members of the Association were already engaged and in which they could have joined quite easily. The truth may be that many people want 'the Association' to be more active, while refusing to become personally more active themselves.

6. Link Clubs

In any event, those who resign or lapse have chosen to give up that social intercourse which may now be seen to be the main Aim of the Association. In times past and in pursuit of this Aim, Circles met bi-monthly, a practice that was not given up in Manchester until 1924. They also either proposed to form or actually did form a variety of Clubs. Indeed, in September 1918 *Catena* carried a feature in which there was the optimistic demand for the formation of a Catenian Club in every town, which led Birmingham Circle to consider whether their proposed Club would be open to all Catholics. But at the same time the Circle asked the pertinent question, 'Who would fund such a Club?' Only in Liverpool was there firm action on this front. In December 1922, the Liverpool Circle agreed to form a Limited Company to acquire premises in Liverpool, and by January 1923 it had persuaded other Liverpool Circles to join in the venture, so that a company was registered, £2000 raised as capital, premises acquired in Lord Street, all under the energetic leadership of Pat Taggart. And for some ten years or so the Link Club flourished in Lord Street; Circles used it as a meeting place, non-Catenian members were allowed to use the premises, where there were bars, games rooms and meeting rooms. Various Catholic bodies and cultural societies, such as the Anglo-French Society, used the premises for weekly meetings and the Club seemed a great success. Unfortunately, reports of law-breaking, in the shape of out-of-hours drinking, led to a police raid and to the withdrawal of the Club's licence, and this, in turn, meant that the Club was running at a loss and had to be closed down.

No other Circle or group of Circles ventured to found a permanent Club with its own premises. London, however, saw the formation of a Link Luncheon Club. Members of London Circles used to meet at first bi-weekly, latterly only weekly, for lunch at a restaurant in Holborn, and also held dances from time to time. The London Link Club continued to meet even during wartime, but the continued rationing and other difficulties of post-war Britain saw the ending of this social outlet.

Other Circles, such as Bournemouth, have held, or still hold, occasional lunches for the benefit of older Brothers and their wives, who feel unable to venture out to the regular meetings and Ladies' Nights. These have been enjoyable occasions, at which the older members and their ladies have found almost as much pleasure in the meeting as have the younger men and their wives who go along.

The promotion of social intercourse has taken various other shapes. There has been, for example, the development of inter-Circle visiting and the holding of Provincial Rallies; there is the Catenian Golfing Society and the Catenian Caravan Club in each of which men from a number of Circles and their families can enjoy each other's company. The success of these ventures can be seen in the continued interest and almost constant growth in membership.

7. Helping young people

How successful has the Association been in the pursuit of its original Aim (*c*) – 'to promote the interests of "C" youths entering business and professional life'? Here again, as with the pursuit of Aim (*b*), the Association quickly found that there was all too little that could be done directly to help Catholic youth, for there were simply not enough Catholic men in positions of power able to provide any direct help to young men (and later, women) seeking work. The Service Committees during their lifetime tried to act as a vehicle to further the interests of Catholic young men, but this help also proved to be all too little. Some Circles have provided, and continue to provide, an organised system of careers guidance, the Circle providing from its own strength or from among the Brothers' acquaintances the people who 'staff' one or more careers guidance evenings at local schools.

All this must have been a disappointment to the men who had formed the Association with such high hopes. Against this, however, it has to be pointed out that Catholic youth has been helped in a variety of ways which will be discussed elsewhere in this volume. There are, for example, the various functions held to encourage friendship among Catholic youth – dances, outings, parties, and the meetings of Brothers' families which take place at such functions as the President's Sunday. There was, of major significance, the Catenian support for the foundation of Catholic secondary schools during the 1920s and 1930s, schools at which Catholic youth might get that education which would help them when 'entering business or professional life'. There was, at another level, the help given to the less fortunate Catholic youth found in orphanages and other homes, to the handicapped and to the families of prisoners – and all this in and by organisations, of which some were set up by Catenians and others received constant Catenian support at a local level.

Some Circles in or near University towns have 'adopted' members of the University Catholic Students Association, inviting them to after-Circle functions, helping to find 'digs' and helping students who have found it difficult to adjust to the move away from home. Several Brothers have their own accounts of kindness to their own children: one man had his nurse-daughter 'rescued' from an unhappy situation in a hospital in the U.S.A. through the efforts of a retired Brother living in the States. Elsewhere in this book I have paid my own tribute to the Brothers of the Swansea Circle for their kindness to one of my sons, and many other Brothers have similar stories to tell of unselfish help offered by men whom they have never met but with whom they are linked through membership of the Association.

8. The spiritual dimension

In 1980, I sent out a questionnaire inviting Brothers to send me their views on a variety of topics which I hoped to cover. The response to the questionnaire was, at one level, disappointing, for only a small number of men and Circles bothered to reply. But at another level the response was pleasantly surprising. In particular, I was interested in the response to my question 7, which asked: 'Does the Association have, in fact, a spiritual dimension?' So far as the stated Aims go, it appears not to have one – there is no mention of prayers (and the ritual was slow to emerge), or of Masses (although these were said for deceased Brothers even as early as 1908), or of any other spiritual activity. In reply to the question, some Brothers wondered why I had asked it, fearing perhaps that I was about to launch a charismatic-type crusade aimed at changing the nature of the Association. But others, notably Denis Fitz-Gibbon of Central London, appreciated the point; indeed, saw it so clearly that he chided me for daring to have made this merely question 7, as if it was relatively unimportant. For although there is no mention of spiritual activity in the Aims, it is clear that the Association is a Catholic Association whose underlying, if unstated, purpose is the strengthening and development of each member's spiritual life, which in turn will lead to each one being aware of the need for the expression of that inward state in some form of outward action.

In 1937, *Catena* carried an item in which the writer claimed that the aim of the Association was 'to renew each man's spiritual batteries', so that he felt able and willing to engage in some form of Catholic Action in his individual life although the Association *per se* was not so engaged. And in a masterly document, *Our Relevance Today*, first issued in 1970, Laurie Tanner developed this theme of the sanctifying nature of the Association with the inevitable consequence, it is to be hoped, that its individual members would then go on to engage in whichever form of Catholic Action most appealed to them. Elsewhere in this volume I hope to indicate some of the ways in which members have done this.

It is at least arguable whether or not the Association has lived up to the hopes of its founders as expressed in their original Aims, and whether or not the Association's main function today appears to be that of promoting social intercourse. But it remains true today, indeed it may be even truer today than it was in 1908, that in a world which is increasingly pagan and hostile to Christian principles at work, Catholic men from the commercial, industrial and professional worlds need the support, often unspoken, and the encouragement of their fellow-Catholics if they are to continue to try to put their principles into operation.

In the ceremony of initiation of a new member, the Circle President welcomes the new Brother with a short address in which he reminds him of his duties (where applicable) as husband, father, son and friend. In a world in which the concept of the family is under widespread attack, and in which social workers and psychiatrists preach the doctrine that 'divorce is just as positive a step as marriage while the family is a bourgeois repressive agency of patriarchal capitalism', it may be that the Association plays an undesigned role as the supporter of the family. If each Brother, having attended a Circle meeting, returns home slightly better a husband, father, son or friend, then it may be argued that the Association will be justifying its existence.

There have been, however, and there are still heard, calls from members for the Association as such to take a more positive and obvious stance against the encroaching paganism of our time. In May 1943, Grand Council issued a Circular saying that: 'All Circles should take their full part in the Catholic life of the country, in the furtherance of Catholic principles, or the protection of Catholic interests.' At that time the government was considering the Education Bill and, as we shall see, Circles and individual Brothers played a major part in the new 'Battle for the Schools'.

But in November 1949, C.I. Kelly of West Essex protested that not enough was being done in this 'political world'. Kelly asked that Circles should debate current affairs and 'take appropriate action in the corporate sense as a Circle'. But the danger of such a development was outlined by Bernard Kirchner, who argued that discussion of political matters would lead to the divisions which had marred the development of the Federation in 1908 and which had led Locan, O'Donnell and other founding Brothers to take care to exclude 'wrangling' from their Association. In 1976, some Circles asked that Grand Council should take a positive and public position against possible legislation on euthanasia. Grand Council's decision not to issue a statement on behalf of the Association, leaving it to individual Brothers to make their own protests in whatever way they might choose, was criticised by many Brothers and Circles. When this matter was debated in some Circles, there was just that division of opinion which Kirchner had written about in 1950. But there seems little doubt that with the increasingly evident moral deline, the call for corporate action will be made again, for, as some see it, if the Association is to justify its claim to be a leading Catholic Association then it will have to be seen to be giving a lead.

CHAPTER ELEVEN

1923-1939

1. Expansion during depression

We have seen that the major reason for the decision to formulate a new Constitution was the rapid expansion of the Association, and the confident hope that this expansion would continue. Indeed, at first it seemed that this hope was well-founded. Seven new Circles were opened in 1924 and another eight in 1925. But after this the expansion slowed down, with only three Circles being inaugurated in each of the years 1926, 1927 and 1928, two in 1929, four in 1930, one in 1931 and two in 1932. In 1933 there was no new Circle opened – the first year since 1908 that there had been no addition to the number of Circles. And even after that gloomy year things did not really pick up, with only two new Circles being inaugurated in 1934, three in 1935, two in 1936, four in 1937, three in 1938 and one in 1939.

The history of the Association is, to a certain extent, a reflection of our national history, and the slow-down in expansion after 1922 mirrors that history very clearly, for it coincided with the years when the country suffered from an economic depression. Between 1922 and 1939 the level of unemployment never fell below one million, out of a working force of only eleven million, rising to nearly three million for the years 1931–1933, the years now remembered as the worst of 'the depressed thirties'. But if there was mass unemployment among the working class there was, inevitably, economic hardship for the middle class, for whom the Association existed, with bankruptcies, cut-backs, lower profit margins and cuts in salaries. The areas which had traditionally relied on the older, basic, staple industries became known successively as Depressed Areas, Special Areas and Development Areas; but these euphemisms failed to alter the fact that in these areas there was little economic activity. And this affected the owners or partners in small firms, the self-employed as well as the professional classes in those regions – the very people who had once formed the backbone of the Association. Indeed, rather than wonder why the Association did not expand after 1923, one is left wondering how it managed to keep going. For in those days, which older men will remember, there were no redundancy payments or social security payments (save for the insured workers), and, as the Wall Street Crash showed, there was little comfort to be derived from past investments. When, in 1981, politicians and economists argue that the employment figures (*circa* 2½–3 million) show that the country is as badly off as it was in the 1930s, they ignore the change in the size of the working force (some 8–9 million in the worst of the depression of the '30s and some 23–24 million in 1981) and the social security cushions provided for the redundant in the '70s and '80s.

One is reminded of other differences between our society and that of the '20s and '30s, while reading *Catena*. In 1921, the Circle at York imposed a sumptuary levy of 2*s*.6*d*. (12½p) while the Thanet Circle paid 6*s*. (30p) for the hire of a hotel room for its meeting. In June 1938, the Birmingham Midland

Circle had a clergy night, and the dinner cost 3s. (15p); in July, for its Ladies' Night 'with a Supper Dance' the tickets cost 7s.6d. (37½p). Then there was the invitation to Brothers to visit the Richmond and Twickenham Circle whose meeting place 'is situated only 4 minutes walk from the railway station'. Men had not yet learned that feet were intended to be used on brake pedals and accelerators; indeed, when the Swansea Circle had an outing to Caldy Island in October 1932, the report noted that '. . . those Brothers who had cars very generously put them at the disposal of the majority of the Brothers who did not enjoy this luxury'. And one can almost feel the *frisson* of excitement in the report from the Wandsworth and Putney Circle (now the South West London Circle), which heard, in September 1932, a talk by a Brother on 'The Adventure of Flying'.

The social historian can learn a good deal about our national history from reading accounts of the ways in which the Brothers entertained themselves. In most Circles the pre-1914 'musical evening' continued to be the normal pattern, with Brothers and their guests playing the piano, singing arias and light classical airs. But in May 1924 a series of reports gave a forewarning of the demise of this form of self-entertainment. For in Waterloo, Manchester, Glasgow and Liverpool, the Brothers 'spent some part of their meeting "listening in" to the new wireless'. Newport is the only Circle which reported the holding of a yo-yo championship in December 1932 – a reminder that Catenians like others are affected by popular crazes. And there is something magically nostalgic about the reports of 'the outing by char-à-banc' from many Circles as late as November 1936. For older men no explanation of the 'magically nostalgic' is needed; for the younger men no explanation is possible.

The appearance of the wireless, motor-car and 'flying' in Circle reports helps to remind us that the inter-war period was not entirely one of economic depression. For there were many new, developing industries either emerging or growing during this period. There were large national firms, such as I.C.I.; there were the multinational firms, such as Shell and Esso, Ford's and Hoover; there were the chain stores and large department stores, such as Woolworths and John Lewis. In these and many other firms there were increasing job opportunities, not for the men who had traditionally relied on their brawn (as in mining or shipbuilding) or on 'rule of thumb' technical knowledge, but for semi-skilled workers at one level and for a host of trained workers at another set of levels. At the same time there was an expansion of the role of government at the local and national level, with the creation of new Ministries (of Health, Transport, Agriculture) and greater spending on housing, education, pensions and so on. Here, again, there were job opportunities for educated men and women. But perhaps the most significant development was in the tertiary industries – banking, insurance and the like, which neither produce a primary product (coal, fish or food) nor make manufactured articles, but provide a service.

In each of these fields there was a growth of what has been termed 'the salariat' – the men and women who enjoy a salary rather than a wage, and who enjoy other privileges, in terms of hours worked, holidays, pensions, time off for sickness and so on, as compared with the wage-earners. The 'salariat' embraced both bank clerk and bank manager, lawyer's clerk and High Court judge, costing clerk and company secretary. Many of those who joined the Association in the '20s and '30s belonged to this salariat. They might, in earlier years, have gone into a family firm or been self-employed, as were so many of the Brothers before 1914. But with the managerial revolution and the spread of the influence of the publicly-quoted company, there was a decline in the number of family firms, though an increase in the job opportunities in the managerial field. Some of the older men thought that there had been a decline in quality, since there were fewer men who owned their firms, had their own telegraphic addresses. once taken as *de rigueur* as can be seen from original Roll Books. In one sense they were right, for there was indeed that decline of which they complained. But they were ignoring the greater number of Catholic men working in upper, middle and lower management who formed a new Catholic middle class and who joined the Association.

Many of the new or developing industries tended to site their factories away from the older industrial regions of the North-East, North-West, Scotland and South Wales. The almost continual expansion of Greater London and the major development of industry in the Midlands took place at the same time as the older regions became depressed areas. This led to talk of the 'Two Nations' – one of them, in the booming regions, having a high standard of living, the other suffering from the worst effects of the depression. This change in industrial location was reflected in the way in which the Association developed after 1923. On the one hand, the City of Cardiff Circle (No. 87) lost its Charter – a Catenian indication of the way in which the depression hit South Wales. On the other hand, there was the spread of the Association into the suburbs of London (88, 90, 92, 94, 95, 96, 99, 100, 101, 109, 115, 121, 122). The building of the many suburban lines and of the underground railway system led to the building of middle-class estates in what Betjeman has christened 'Metroland', and the Association found recruits in the new parishes which grew up there. One of the pleasant features of this development was the way in which older Circles helped to found new ones – holding propaganda meetings, allowing existing members to leave parent Circles to get the new one off the ground, and taking care that, having founded the new Circles, they engaged in inter-Circle visiting to ensure the future of the newcomers, which themselves went on to act as 'parents' to other newer Circles.

2. The Papal Toast 1925

In these new suburbs there was little evidence of bigotry, for in the quest for economic and social advance most of our countrymen had become, in the main, indifferent to religion. That is not to say that Catholics were accepted as 'normal' for, as George Scott noted in 1967,

> At Cambridge . . . anti-Catholic prejudice was evident. The English public schools . . . reinforced and perpetuated 'old wives' tales' about the sinister properties of Catholics. If an English public school boy were told that a man was not only a Catholic but also that he had been trained by Jesuits, he would look at him as at some devilish foreigner. The term 'Papist' was in common use at Cambridge, as a description if not as a term of abuse.

Catholics in general, and the Catenians of London in particular, were reminded of the uncertainty of their position by a row which gained national notoriety in March 1925. The Catholic Lord Mayor of London, Sir Alfred Bower, had accepted an invitation to be one of the guests at the London Circle's annual dinner. Then he discovered that Hogan, who was to chair the after-Circle proceedings, was going to toast 'The Pope and the King', whereupon the Lord Mayor returned his invitation explaining that his patriotism would not allow him to attend a meal where the King was placed after the Pope. Articles in the *Daily Despatch,* the *Daily Express* and other national and local papers carried such headlines as 'No Popery here'. The Catholic Press took its own hard line, attacking the Lord Mayor for his lack of respect for the Holy Father, which, in turn, led to a spate of letters to various editors, articles learned and unlearned, as well as vituperation on both sides. The controversy showed signs of dying down, when in June 1925 the Lord Mayor invited the Cardinal and other members of the Hierarchy to a banquet at Mansion House. The national press assured its readers that there would be 'No Popery at the Mansion House' because while the first toast was to be 'The Health of His Majesty' there was to be no toast to the Pope. While the secular press rejoiced at this putting down of the Catholics, our own press attacked the Lord Mayor, noted that many members of the Hierarchy had not accepted his invitation, and by implication criticised the Cardinal for having allowed himself to be used by the errant Lord Mayor. Once again the controversy flared up, with Protestants being reminded of the dangers they were exposed to from the Papists, while the latter were reminded that they were a minority which ought to have regard to their modes of conduct.

The issue was finally resolved by the Cardinal, who devised the ritual which is now commonly used at Catholic gatherings. In this, the prayer for the Pope (but not, in that sense, a toast) forms part of the Grace before Meals, while the first toast in the after-dinner proceedings is 'the Queen'. Thus, in a sense, both sides could claim a victory – since the Pope is mentioned before the Monarch, while the first toast is to the Monarch.

But if this issue had been resolved, albeit after a good deal of newsprint had been wasted, the element of anti-Catholicism did not go away. In Plymouth the virulent Kensitites held their weekly open-air meetings at which they attacked the Church; and maybe the Plymouth Circle's decision 'that at the Corpus Christi procession Brothers will wear evening dress' was by way of being a response to these attacks. In May 1937, the report from the Nottingham Circle noted 'our great surprise that the the Lord Mayor of Nottingham, who is a non-Catholic, should make an extraordinary speech in favour of Catholic attitudes towards marriage and the family'. Maybe the reporter was right to note that this might indeed have been a case of inverted bigotry; maybe, on the other hand, his report merely indicates that Catholics expected to be attacked – hence the 'great surprise' when they were praised. As George Woodcock, later General Secretary of the T.U.C., told George Scott in 1967, 'In early life . . . I was very conscious of being a Catholic and conscious of the disabilities of being in a minority. . . . As a young lad before the first world war I knew that I might get to be a "tackler" but it was inconceivable that I should become a manager. This was something all Catholics accepted as a fact of life.'

3. Signs and Passwords

What were the issues which dominated Catenian thinking during these inter-war years? Some issues we have seen elsewhere in this book – the Children's Fund, the growth of the Benevolent Fund, the help to Beda and so on. But the Association was also concerned with many other issues – some, such as Signs and Passwords, seemingly of little importance today; others of greater importance, such as the widespread interest in the development of Catholic secondary education; and some which may be seen to have a continuing importance, such as the call for Action and the need for concern at the danger from Russian Communism.

In reading *Catena* it is difficult to avoid the conclusion that Circles spent many hours arguing about Signs and Passwords. Experience in present-day Circles, where the arguments are about 'Should we dine or have buffets?', suggests that these arguments may often have become heated, have frequently gone off at tangents and have almost always been inconclusive. Nor was there any Association-wide agreement about Signs and Passwords. Mid-Surrey thought that they were 'inadequate and undignified', while many other Circles wanted them to be retained as important emblems of our national unity and Catenian identity.

In October 1930, Grand Council issued a set of instructions headed: 'Methods of Recognition'. This showed that there were three occasions on which these Methods had to be used:

1. When seeking admission to his own Circle a Brother will give an alarm at the door. He will be challenged by the Guard, who will ask him to produce his current card of membership; if this is not available the Guard will ask: 'Whom do you seek?' The Brother challenged will reply with the number of his own Circle, i.e. 'Number . . .'.
2. A Brother seeking admission to a Circle other than his own will give an alarm at the door and on being challenged by the Guard will produce his current card of membership; if this is not available he will respond to the challenge by giving first the number of the Circle he is visiting and add: 'from Number . . .', giving the number of his own Circle.
3. In correspondence with a Brother, if you wish to intimate that you are a Catenian or, similarly, when sending in your business card to a Brother, put on the face of your letter or card:
   No. of Province   – 6
   No. of your own Circle – 34   i.e. 6/34/17.
   Your No. on Circle Roll – 17
   Note. These figures will be found on your card of membership.

The wise Dr Stroud (Grand President 1939–41) thought that the Signs and Passwords were only used by ex-Catenians who, having learned them while members of the Association, then tried to drum up business or exercise influence after they had left the Association. West Kent had similar thoughts, for in the month when Stroud made this complaint, they argued that the Signs and Passwords ought to be changed annually so that ex-members would not be able to take advantage of their former colleagues. The issue gradually died out as Grand Council ruled, year after year, that the Signs ought to be abolished, until by 1939 the only one remaining was the 'finger in the lapel' to be used when addressing the President during a Circle meeting.

4. Catenians and Secondary Schools

The talk of Signs and Passwords now appears dated. Not so other topics which occupied a good deal of the business meetings at Circles in the '20s and '30s. There were, for example, the complaints of apathy and non-attendance, some Circles reporting only a 25 per cent average attendance; there was the worry expressed at the fact that the number of new men being initiated was, in some years, only just equal to the number lapsing, with a variety of explanations being given to explain the high rate of lapsation; there was the call by Grand Presidents and Provincial Councils for Circles to be on their guard, when enrolling new men, to ensure that men of the right 'quality' were enrolled rather than men in 'quantity'. Certainly the Association enrolled some distinguished men in this dire period: there were the academics such as Bodkin of Birmingham, Tolkien of Oxford, Phillimore of Edinburgh and Dixon of North Lancs, while at a completely different level there were the Test cricketers Andy Sandham of Croydon and 'Patsy' (christened Elias) Hendren of West London, who entertained many a Circle with their cricketing stories. One may be entitled to see the hand of the cricket-loving Rudman in the recruitment of Sandham (who joined Croydon in 1924) and Hendren (who joined West London in the same year). No doubt he also was pleased with Sandham's record innings in the West Indies (which still stands as a record) and Hendren's contribution of a new word to the English language, the 'chinaman'. On the tour of the West Indies, Hendren was bowled by a West Indian of Chinese extraction – Achong, a spinner who bowled 'the wrong 'un' which deceived Hendren. On his return to the pavilion Hendren complained that he had been beaten by 'that chinaman', and the cricketing world had a new word.

But there was one item which interested Circles in this period which, like Signs and Passwords, now seems dated, but for a different set of reasons. Reading *Catena* soon makes it clear that for Brothers in many Circles a major item of interest and of corporate action was the provision of a Catholic secondary school in their districts. It is, perhaps, not surprising that the Brothers should have been interested in the question of schools; after all, the Association may be said to have been born out of 'the Battle for the Schools' in 1908. But that battle had been about elementary schools, the schools to which the vast majority of children, Catholic and non-Catholic, went at that time.

Today we assume that every child will go on to a secondary school; today we assume in many places that the Catholic child will have the opportunity of going on to a Catholic secondary school and that he or she will be taught in the main by lay teachers. None of this was so in 1908 – or in 1923. Until 1902 all secondary schools were privately-run, fee-paying institutions. It was the Education Act of 1902 which allowed the newly-established L.E.A.s to build and maintain fee-paying secondary schools out of the education rate and permitted them to take over any existing secondary school which applied for rate-aid. Only in 1907 did an Act provide that one-quarter of the places in such rate-provided or -aided schools had to be kept as places open to children who had been at the elementary schools from which they could transfer at about the age of eleven. For these children the L.E.A.s were empowered to provide assistance – paying fees, providing books and so on – on a 'means test' basis. So, for the first time, children from working-class homes had the opportunity of getting a full secondary education, in State-provided, fee-paying schools.

During the inter-war period thirty-one such Catholic schools were opened in various parts of the country – again, almost all of them founded by religious orders although four were founded by diocesan clergy. This doubling of the number of secondary schools for children from the Catholic middle class is an illustration of the growth of that class during this period. But the fact that there were still only some sixty such schools throughout England and Wales (with St

Illtyd's in Cardiff being the single such school in the Principality) reminds us of how limited was the size of that middle class for whom the Association existed.

And, as a sign that the Brothers were conscious of their own social progress and were determined to seek even greater opportunities for their children, we have an unorganised but widespread campaign to get Bishops and L.E.A.s to consider the question of providing secondary schools for Catholic children. The result is that individual Catenians and local Circles may claim credit for the founding of some of the thirty-one schools founded during the inter-war period. In July 1921, the Brothers of Wallasey determined to act to get a secondary school for the children of their area. In December 1921, the Brothers of Southampton were reported as having to 'force the local clergy to consider the question of a secondary school', while in the same month the Bishop of Nottingham appealed to that Circle to help him get such a school set up. In March 1922, the Brothers of Hull 'demanded' a secondary school for Catholic boys, while in June and July 1922 the Brothers from Southampton were reported as having interviewed the Superiors of various religious orders with regard to their determination to get a school. In December 1922, the Brothers of the Cardiff Circle were involved in the negotiations to get the De La Salle Brothers to set up St Illtyd's, while in July 1923 two Brothers set up their own Catholic secondary school in Cambridge. Also in July 1923, the Brothers of Burnley were asking for a school, as were the men from Blackpool (March 1924); while in November 1928 the Archbishop of Cardiff asked the men from the Newport Circle to help him get a school for their town. The Brothers of the Bournemouth Circle helped to get the Jesuits set up a school at Southbourne and when the Jesuits moved out in 1947, it was three Brothers of the Circle who persuaded the De La Salle Brothers to take the school over.

So the Association can claim to have played a part in the establishing of a number of secondary schools for Catholic children – all in accordance with one of the main Aims of the Association. It is possible, of course, to argue that there was an element of self-seeking in this activity, for some of the men must have had their own children or grandchildren in mind. But even if this was true, it would also be true to note that, while helping their own, they provided opportunities for many other children for whom the schools would be available. The evidence, in fact, is that the Brothers did not merely seek their own. For in Circle after Circle we find that funds were collected so that scholarships could be provided for poorer children at the fee-paying schools. It is to Manchester's credit that it showed the way in this as in much else, accepting the responsibility for a young man who started his secondary education in 1920 and for whom the Circle paid fees and a maintenance allowance until he had finished his studies at the Manchester College of Art and Design. It was reckoned that by 1925 this venture had cost the Circle some £600. Annual scholarships were provided out of funds provided by Circles in Leeds (January 1922), Southampton (June 1922), Middlesbrough (October 1922), and Liverpool (which set up one such scholarship in 1923 and then expanded their benevolence so that after 1924 they were providing three such free places). Cardiff (May 1923) provided a free place annually at St Illtyd's; Portsmouth Brothers (August 1923) did the same at St John's, as did Circles in Glasgow (February 1924) and Bournemouth (July 1932), while in 1942 Thomas Gordon Hensler left money for the setting up of a Catenian scholarship at Cotton College.

Various functions were organised to raise the money needed to pay for these scholarships: dances in some places, whist drives in others, while in a few places Ladies' Committees were formed to help in this regard. And all this during a period of economic depression with its consequent financial hardship and at a time when the Association was also involved in providing for its own Children's Fund, its Benevolent Fund, the Beda College and, in 1938, for the Catholic Workers' College. It is permissible to pay tribute to the active generosity of the men who saw the Association through a difficult period and whose memorials, such as the men I have met who won a Catenian scholarship in the '20s and '30s, are still living tributes to our predecessors and a pertinent answer to the question 'What do you do'?

5. Public service

In March 1910, the Committee of the Manchester Circle of what was still the Chums Benevolent Association debated a suggestion put forward by the dynamic McDermott: 'that the time was now favourable to place members of our Association in public positions, and further that we might endeavour to have the Bro. President [O'Donnell] created a Justice of the Peace'. The Committee asked McDermott (himself already a Justice of the Peace) and Bro. Councillor A. Craven, J.P., to deal with this question.

O'Donnell never became a J.P., maybe because he did not really want to be one, maybe because the Circle could not find enough people to support an application on his behalf. Nevertheless, the spirit behind the debate, and the resolution to set up a small committee to deal with the question, was indicative of the wish of these first members of the Association to live up to Casartelli's hopes – that Catholic men (and women) would come out of the ghetto and play their part in public life.

This was to be one of the indirect but intended aims of the socialising by the emerging Catholic middle class. As Grand President Synott said in June 1923, 'We bring men out so that they come to the Association where they learn a new confidence which enables them to go out and seek to play an active role.' There were, of course, Catholic men who had learned that self-confidence before the Association came into being – possibly via the still expanding Trade Union movement, possibly via the Irish-based political activity. We know, for example, that an early recruit to the Manchester Circle was an Alderman Thompson, who became Mayor of Eccles in 1909. And there have been Catholic men who have played an active role in public life who have not been Catenians. It would be foolish to suggest that membership of the Association is either a *sine qua non* of public activity or, on the other hand, a sure sign that a man was going to undertake such activity. It remains true, however, that in the '20s and '30s, in town after town, the Circle Secretary was able to report to *Catena* that a member of the Circle had become 'the first Catholic Mayor since the Reformation', or that a Brother had become the second or third Catholic Mayor. Manchester has a special memory for Dan McCabe, while the Association may look back to 1915 as the year in which Catenians were Lord Mayors of London and Manchester, the country's two principal cities. But McCabe and Dunn were only the first of a long line, for there were Catenian Mayors or Lord Mayors for Manchester (1919), Altrincham (1919), Wolverhampton (1922), Cambridge (1921), Shrewsbury (1922), Blackburn

(1922 and 1928), Birmingham (1923), Rochdale (1924), Coventry (1928) and Preston (1937), while the Cardiff Circle could boast of having provided three Lord Mayors for the capital of the Principality – Turnbull, Stone and Purnell. And if the Brothers became Mayors or Lord Mayors it was only after years of service as Councillors and Aldermen, and the columns of *Catena* report the elections of Brothers in local elections in Burnley, Northampton, Bournemouth, Port Talbot, and other towns and cities throughout the country.

Here were some, at least, of the People of God on the move and by their actions, we may think, encouraging other Catholics not in the Association to 'go and do thou likewise'. It must have been easier for Bower to have thought of putting himself forward in London (of which he became Lord Mayor in 1925) once the ice had been broken by Dunn. One is still left asking the question, 'Why did not more people come forward and why, even now (in 1981), are Catholics still under-represented in public life?' An article in *Catena* for November 1936 suggested that the laity were over-conscious of the traditional nature of the Church, in which authority is exercised from above and in which the laity 'pay up and shut up'. The psychological effects of such habits of thought must be, among others, to limit men's willingness to assume a leading role in public life. There was also that 'fear of the world' in which the Church was seen 'as a citadel of Truth, defending and keeping the Faith against the besieging armies of evil and ignorance'. The comfort provided by the knowledge that we alone had the True Faith led to a feeling of exclusiveness which engendered a reserve in one's dealings with the hostile and sinful world. In 1967 George Scott reported that this attitude was still widespread. Casartelli had hoped to break men of this habit of thought, demanding that they should come out of the ghetto, that they should act, as Catholics, without waiting for a clerical lead. In that sense, his first Pastoral and the subsequent founding of the Association may be seen as steps along the road to the emancipation of the Easter People – although, as we shall see, it remains true that neither laity nor Hierarchy seem to have fully accepted the inevitable consequences of that emancipation.

Public life is, of course, much more than representation on local councils. There were many Brothers who played roles – minor but significant, as well as major and hence publicised – in professional associations for doctors, lawyers, teachers and so on. There were Brothers who were active in their unions and political parties without achieving public notice, although the Association was rightly proud of the political success of Sykes (p. 55) and of the two Catenians who won seats in the Coupon Election which followed the end of World War I – Hailwood (M.P. for Ardwick) and Malone (representing South Tottenham), the first of a number of Brothers who have become M.P.s

Less well known may be the participation of Catenian solicitors and barristers in The Society of Our Lady of Good Counsel, set up in 1928 to provide free legal aid to Catholics facing the courts and unable to afford the costs involved. Here we have the seeds of what has now become a national system of Legal Aid, with Catenians sowing some, if not all, of the seeds.

When we consider the part played by Catholic men in public life we have also to take into account the amount of time that the more active men were (and are) expected to give in their local parishes and dioceses. In the '20s and '30s the Church was still involved in a heavy building programme to ensure that enough churches were available for the expanding Catholic population in the expanding towns. And, as Circle reports make clear, individual Catenians as well as local Circles were involved in providing some of the money needed to allow such developments to go on. There were also the calls for what may be best described as local charities organised by Brothers or by Circles. In Reading (1921) and Bournemouth (January 1925), Circles helped the local Nazareth House; in Liverpool the men organised fêtes in aid of the Notre Dame Orphanage; in Birmingham the various Circles were heavily involved in raising money for, and providing the men to help maintain, Father Hudson's Homes. In Leeds, Cardiff, Nottingham and other Circles there were similar annual activities. And on top of this annual involvement there was the more frequent involvement in parish life with Brothers running the local branch of the S.V.P., the C.Y.M.S., the K.S.C., the Crusade of Rescue, church choirs, various clubs, and such more rarefied activities as the Prisoners' Aid Society and the local Bishop's Fund. It is not surprising, then, that when Bishop Burton of Clifton spoke at a dinner organised by the Bristol Circle he should have said that he knew the majority of the Brothers already as he met them in one or more other fields of Catholic activity. He went on to express his gratitude for the work that the Brothers did in their individual capacities, and for the work that the Association did by bringing together Catholic men of different backgrounds and experiences. In their socialising, he said, they learned from one another, each providing the example for the other and providing by that example the support many needed to carry their Catholic principles into practice in their daily lives. In particular, he called attention to the fact that the Association sent the men home from their social gatherings as the better Catholic, the better father and the better husband, so that its value was limitless.

In the autumn of 1934 the Norwich Circle was asked to organise the first Pilgrimage to Walsingham, an activity ignored by the Editor of *Catena* and by Grand Council. Maybe they thought that the Association should not be so closely involved in the Hierarchical venture. So, indeed, thought many of the men in the Norwich Circle, six of whom resigned because of their disagreement with the decision to provide the help requested. The work of Brother Gordon Smith and his committee of four Catenians ensured the success of that first Pilgrimage, when most of the Hierarchy were present, in St John's, Norwich, at High Mass sung with the help of a congregation of over 2000, who then went by coaches and cars to join another 5000 pilgrims at Walsingham. Apart from the war years, the Pilgrimage has been an annual event since 1934. Today, however, the members of the Association join the National Pilgrimage, and it is a matter for regret that this does not appear to receive much Catenian support.

6. Catholic Action in the 1930s

Another who approved of the Association was Cardinal Bourne. Speaking to the Manchester Circle in November 1921, he commented on the Association and the Brothers doing 'good to all men, and especially to those who are of the household of faith'. Some wanted the Brothers to do even more; speaking to the Northampton Circle in February 1919, Bishop Keating called for more action on the part of the Association and the individual Brother. One can sympathise with the energetic Bishops and their hard-pressed priests at a time when *Catena* wrote about Catholics coming together in the Association 'from many different missions'. For we were still a relatively poor section of the community, and the sight of the better-heeled members of the Church at a social function must have led many of the clergy to think that here were the men, with the money, who could best help them in their local problems. It is not surprising that some came to see the Association as a sort of milch-cow. Soon after the Nottingham Circle was opened, it received a visit from Brosch, warning them against getting themselves too heavily involved in 'action'. And in *Catena* in April 1919 there was a warning against 'that restlessness to do other things'. In December 1929, Grand President Percy Briggs sent out a letter to every Brother, reminding everyone that the Association was not an 'active' body, that it ought not, as an Association, to be represented on

> bodies concerned with efforts in the direction of Catholic Benevolence or with other matters of importance to Catholics . . . however praiseworthy they may be, and even though intrinsically they may be of greater import than the unobtrusive social and benevolent objects we have made our own.

Briggs went on to point out that Grand Council was proud of the fact that

> The Catenian Association is looked upon by our spiritual superiors as one of the natural sources from which influential and reputable Catholic laymen willing and eager to co-operate with their fellow Catholics in any field of Catholic effort can be drawn.

Here we have an expression of 'Aims and Objects' as well as of that not always understood distinction between the Catholic activities of the individual Brother and the non-involvement of the Association as such.

The Bishop of Clifton had understood the nature of the Association and would have seen what Briggs was getting at. But even while he was praising the Brothers of the Bristol Circle Pius XI was writing an encyclical which called for Catholic Action. In part, this was a call for the formation of Catholic groups to resist the influence of that militant humanism which was aimed at destroying the Christian fabric of our Western society; in part, it was a reaction to the dangerous growth of Communism with its headquarters in Russia.

There was an immediate Catenian response to this Papal call, best expressed by Pat Taggart, the Grand Director for Province 4, who pointed out (March 1933) that the Association was by its very nature an arm of Catholic action which encouraged the individual Brother to take his own more active role – but as an individual. There was a slower response from the Hierarchy, which, in 1932 as in 1903, had all too little of that vision of lay action which Casartelli had propounded. But, albeit slowly and seemingly reluctantly, the Hierarchy issued its call for the formation of Catholic Action bodies 'under the direction of the hierarchy'. In November 1936, an article in *Catena* pointed out that for such Action to be effective there had to be a definition of aims (the provision of employment for the millions now idle? support for the Catholics in Spain already locked in a struggle with Communist-inspired governments? opposition to Marxism?), with an acceptance of the fact that such Action would be ineffective unless the laity were better educated (in Catholic social teaching, as outlined by Leo XIII and Pius XI) and persuaded to play a more active role in national life.

The article went on to express doubts as to whether in Britain, as distinct from a more Catholic Europe, it would be possible to launch such a movement. Would the Hierarchy really lead the way and in the directions required? Were the laity equipped to play their part in such a movement? Would priests, at the local level, allow the laity who might know what to do (trade union leaders, university lecturers) to play their part? The author of the article doubted whether the Catholic Action movement would get off the English ground.

Some Circles tried to play some part in the national debate. Gloucester issued a pamphlet (November 1937) on Catholic Action; St Helens decided to set up a Catholic Lending Library, by means of which the laity might become more aware of the nature of the Action called for and of the 'enemies' to be attacked. Many Circles organised a series of after-meeting lectures, debates and discussions, some even forming extra-Circle discussion groups to which non-Catenians were invited. In Liverpool, Archbishop Downey set up a Public Services Association to organise Action throughout his archdiocese. This was to do the sort of work done by Casartelli's Federation, in that it was to supervise the setting up of local Action groups. It was to do something more, in that it was to organise a systematic attempt to train and educate possible leaders in the lay community. And he asked a Catenian to be President of this Committee and three other Catenians to form the Committee – a recognition of the value of the individual Catenian, if not of the Association as such.

In June and July 1937, Sydney Redwood, a future Editor of *Catena* and a live-wire Brother, wrote a series of letters to *Catena* in which he asked that the Association should amend its Aims and Objects to take account of the new needs of the Church and of the times, and the new call by the Hierarchy. Pat Taggart became Grand President in 1937, and occupied the Chair for two years. Throughout that time he campaigned for a greater commitment by the individual Brother to Action, while resisting the call for the involvement of the Association. He toured the country to speak to as many Circles as possible; he wrote long and well analysed articles in *Catena*; he invited debate at Circle and Provincial level. Reading *Catena* for the years 1937–39, one can only admire the man's learning, his Catholicity, his hopes for Action – as well as his opposition to letting the Association be drawn into becoming yet one more of those bodies which existed under the protective umbrella of the Hierarchy.

In March 1937, Cardinal Hinsley issued a Pastoral on the need for Catholic Action. In May 1937, Taggart addressed the A.G.M. at Blackpool. In the course of a powerful speech he pointed out that Catholic Action was not a job for the clergy; it was the laity who were the People of God. He proposed the setting up of such administrative machinery as might be needed to ensure that the Action functioned properly, and suggested that the Association might act as a clearing house for the nationwide movement. At this A.G.M., Fr Oldham, a Jesuit, spoke at the Banquet and supported Taggart, saying that the Hierarchy had not given and would not give that guidance which Action needed. The Hierarchy had gone on for too long thinking that they had no need of the laity to help them in the Church's work. Now, said Fr Oldham, they knew differently, but they still did not know how to get that lay support which they needed.

And so throughout 1937, 1938 and 1939 the debate went on, with leaders of the Association urging individuals to become active (as they were in many places), while refusing to commit the Association to adopt a more active role. Many of the Hierarchy were unable to appreciate why this refusal was essential if the Association were to be true to itself; and from this dates the beginning of that cooling in relations between the Association and the Hierarchy. For the next thirty years or so some Bishops tended to view us as mere 'winers and diners', failing to appreciate, as their predecessors had done, the real nature of the Association's worth to the individual member, to his family and to the Church.

CHAPTER TWELVE

The Association and the Second World War 1939–1945

1. Wartime problems
We have seen that from time to time the history of the Association touches our national history. This link between the two histories was nowhere closer than during World War II. That War is now a matter of remote history for under-40s and a dim memory for under-50s. Only the older men can recall the events of those grim years – and even they tend to remember only the lighter side of life in wartime. It is very difficult now to understand the problems facing the Brothers, the officers of Circles and Provinces, and the staff at Headquarters when the country was at war. But some understanding of those problems helps to throw extra light on the nature of the Association, while an examination of the developments that occurred during the unfavourable days of war may help us pay due tribute to the men who ran the Association at that time.

Attendance at Circle meetings was immediately affected by the conscription of men over the age of 18 and by the evacuation of many businesses and government offices from London and other centres to North Wales and other 'safe' areas. Bromley (No. 68), for example, lost most of its 43 members and it owes its continued existence to the devoted work of Sydney Redwood and four or five other men who held meetings so that continuity might be maintained. Mid-Essex (No. 115) was reduced to about six members although it did get the benefit of visits from serving Brothers who found themselves in the district. Sometimes there were too few present to hold a formal meeting, but informal meetings were held so that the Circle might not face the danger of being closed by Grand Council.

Mid-Essex also faced the common problem of finding a meeting place; hotels were unwilling to provide meeting places and meals, especially when the numbers involved were difficult to estimate and might be very small. This led Mid-Essex into the local parish hall until arrangements were made with the Weybridge Country Club. West Middlesex (No. 121) was another Circle which was ousted from its meeting place. This was a relatively new Circle, formed in June 1938, and in early 1939, when the newspapers blazoned the headlines 'There ain't going to be no War', it looked forward with some hope to a period of expansion. But on the outbreak of war many of the 20 Brothers were forced to hold their meetings in a Brother's home at Eastcote.

But this Circle, like so many others, found that there were other problems to overcome. Travel by a much diminished public transport was made even more hazardous by the black-out and by the distances which some Brothers had to travel to get to a meeting. This led the Circle to do as many others did – to hold its meetings on Saturday afternoons. Wives and Brothers would meet for lunch at some hotel, and in the afternoon the Brothers went off to another room to hold their meeting. Forced to go from hotel to hotel, this became known as 'the

Wandering Circle'. This did not prevent the Circle from holding special lunches such as the one held in 1941, when Freddie Deverall was President, at which Grand President Stroud shared the honours with the then Auxiliary Bishop of Westminster, Bishop Myers. The Circle ceased to wander in 1943 when Bro. Owen offered the use of a room in his house which was near to the station and to the routes of three bus services. From 1943 until 1946 the Circle met at Owen's house, managing to entertain Provincial Officers and Grand Presidents in these unusual surroundings.

Attendance at Circle meetings was affected by more than conscription and the difficulties of wartime travel. Most men were called on to do one or another form of voluntary work, once they had finished their normal job. Some were wardens in the A.R.P., others served as part-time firemen; everyone was called on to do a turn at firewatching – in the place of work, in the locality and, for Catholics, at the parish church. Some joined the Home Guard, whilst others helped out at the local hospitals or in the ambulance service. Yet they found time to get to a meeting whenever possible. Southgate (No. 122) recalls in particular the way in which their President, Ross, often came down from Harrogate for meetings, while Dr Coffey was 'always at those meetings, sandwiched in between looking after a practice swollen to three times its normal size and parading as M.O. with the local Home Guard and getting to 9.30 Mass at St Paul's'. Like other Circles, Southgate never missed a meeting, and their historian remembers the swopping of stories – of the destruction of this Brother's house and of that one's business, of the promotion of that serving Brother and the life as prisoner-of-war of that Brother's son.

At the outbreak of War and at various times during the War, the government ordered people and firms to leave cities and towns thought to be particularly exposed to danger from bombing or invasion. These regulations obviously affected membership of city Circles, as we shall see. But it is not so well known that the region most affected by such government regulations was the coastal belt from Yarmouth to Littlehampton. Particularly after the fall of France in 1940, this was the area which was most exposed to the threatened German invasion. Wholesale evacuation left most towns in this belt looking like ghost towns; grass grew in the main street of Margate, while so few people were left in Southend that strangers would cross the street to speak to one another. In 1939, there were a number of Circles in Kent which were already suffering from the problem of falling membership; indeed, Ramsgate (No. 76) and Margate (No. 45) held joint meetings while retaining their individual Charters. But even this failed, since there were often fewer than ten Brothers at a meeting. It is not surprising that the mass evacuation of the towns in the restricted area of coastal Kent led to the death of the Association in Margate, from which the Charter was finally withdrawn in 1945. Hastings (No. 66) had its Charter withdrawn in July 1940, but restored in June 1950. That Ramsgate did not suffer the same fate was due in large part to the energy of Dr Jimmy Hall who has a special place in the Association's history as the longest-serving President – 1929–1948. One reason for this length of service was that in many years there were too few Brothers at meetings to hold elections. But the major reason for his constant re-election was the quality of the man who not only served as the Lifeboat Doctor – and wrote an account of his work, for which he received the O.B.E.; he also acted as choirmaster at St Thomas's Church, Deal, from 1929 to 1968, which helps to explain his Papal Cross Pro Ecclesia et Pontifice and his K.H.S.S.; he founded the Deal Handelian Society, providing

THE ASSOCIATION AND THE SECOND WORLD WAR 1939-1945

it with some of the inspiration which a lifelong study had given him. It was Jimmy Hall who, in days of petrol shortage, cycled the twelve miles from Ramsgate to Deal so that he could get to the monthly meetings. One imagines the puzzlement of the soldiers who challenged the Lifeboat Doctor pushing his bike up some Kentish hill; he was allowed to pass through the restricted areas because he had a military pass signed by the O.C., Military District. Martin Hall of South-West London is right to be proud of his father, to whom the Brothers in Kent Circles owe a special debt of gratitude.

The 'normal' difficulties of wartime travel – the black-out, transport restrictions, petrol rationing and the like – were increased a hundredfold once the towns and cities were exposed to the bombing raids. Coventry Circle (No. 32) lost its meeting place during the devastating raid of 14 November 1940, and most of its records and all its regalia. R.H. Laverty is still alive (1981) to recall the ways in which, along with G. Hains and J.A. Martin, they kept the Circle alive during the period so that it not only survived but became the stronger for the problems it had been forced to overcome. Meetings were held each month – even if they were interrupted and broken off because of the wailing of the air-raid siren and the departure of Brothers to their various tasks in the Civil Defence organisation. Birmingham Midland Circle (No. 65) owes a special debt to its wartime Presidents, Caswell and Glanville, each of whom served for three years; despite bombing and destruction, the Circle never missed a meeting. North Warwickshire (No. 111) was fortunate in that it had moved its meeting place from the Great Western Hotel to the George in Solihull in May 1938. The George escaped bombing, while it enjoyed good public transport facilities, enabling Brothers and visiting Brothers in the Services to attend meetings without serious difficulty. This Circle held few special meetings during wartime, but Archbishop (later Cardinal) Griffin was a guest of honour at a splendid Ladies' Evening early in 1940. In 1943 Founder President Harold Malley became Chairman of the Solihull Urban District Council. He attended High Mass at the Franciscan Friary in his official capacity and to this he invited every member of the U.D.C. They all attended, including a Congregational Minister, an event of some significance in those days.

The historian of the North Warwickshire Circle recalls that travelling in the days of black-out, smoke screens, nightly bombing and petrol shortage

> is difficult to recall for those who lived through it but quite impossible for those who never experienced it. Nevertheless, the Morgan Cup changed hands frequently and North Warwickshire held it on a number of occasions.

Inter-Circle visiting enabled Brothers to find out how so-and-so was getting on, and allowed a widening circle of prayers to be said for men such as Past President John Bowen who was captured by the Japanese in Malaya and suffered the horrors of internment for three years. (The same John Bowen went on to become Grand President of the Association 1973-74.)

Portsmouth (No. 11) was another Circle which suffered during the War. Although reduced in numbers, it was very much alive until the blitz in the winter of 1940-41. Its meeting place, the George Hotel, the Secretary's home, its records, books, regalia, etc., were all lost and the Circle activities ceased. It was impossible to find a meeting place in a town which had been so badly damaged, and some months passed without any meeting. Then, as an experiment, a few Brothers gathered on a Sunday afternoon in the home of a Brother. Similar informal meetings were then held every fourth Sunday. The ladies accompanied their husbands and an informal tea was provided while the men had their meeting. Long journeys had to be made by some men to get to these meetings, which continued to be held throughout the rest of the war. One man had to leave home immediately after Mass and would not get back home until late at night. But he came, as did many Brothers visiting the town – from Scotland and various parts of England. There was even the odd occasion when regalia were borrowed so that initiations might be held. Portsmouth Brothers owe a special debt to Freddie Tindall, whose profile in *Catena*, December 1968, gives some idea of the man who at one time could don a clown's rig and entertain the orphans at Nazareth House while at another he would be examining an enemy mine washed ashore in his role of scientific officer in the Admiralty.

The Southampton Circle (No. 12) is rightly proud of the fact that in spite of the heavy bombing sustained in the town the Circle still carried on. When the bombing and nightly air raids made it difficult for men to gather, a 'valiant few' kept the Catenian flag flying, and it was right that once war was over a small presentation was made to Brother Teddy Tickle in recognition of the work he had done to keep the Circle alive. Teddy's father had been a founder member of the Circle and it was fitting that the son (who died while this book was being written) should have helped keep the Circle going during the difficulties of wartime.

Shrewsbury (No. 113) had its own wartime difficulties, with its Brothers coming from long distances to attend meetings, as did the men who formed the South Bucks Circle (No. 124), which was actually inaugurated on 29 June 1940.

Rationing of food and petrol affected the way in which Circles carried on during wartime. But the records of the Edinburgh Circle (No. 40) provide evidence of a little local difficulty. In 1940 the price of whisky went up to 21*s*.6*d*. a bottle, and two total abstainers proposed that 'we cease to supply whisky at after-Circle meetings'. The motion was lost, so that Edinburgh was able to celebrate the Grand Presidency of one of its Brothers, Thomas Addly, who occupied that Chair for three years, 1941–44. Paisley (No. 118) is another Circle whose records point to the difficulty of finding a meeting place which could also provide a meal. The Circle moved from place to place, Brothers sometimes bringing in supplies of home-made cakes to help matters out. But meetings were held, even in such odd surroundings as the Paisley Ice Rink which for a time managed to supply the needed cups of tea for the afternoon meetings. But the record of this Circle also has its much sadder side with the report of the death of President-elect Dr Skinnider who had been on duty at a First Aid Post which was directly hit by an enemy bomb.

Such bombing attacks affected many Circles. Epping lost its meeting place, while Plymouth recorded over 350 raids, which led to a temporary suspension of meetings. But a gallant few rallied to the Catenian cause and despite all the difficulties meetings were held again and Poles, Canadians, visiting soldiers and sailors were welcomed to meetings. Sheffield suffered from the heavy bombing of that city. In *Catena* for April 1941 one reads of the destruction of homes of many Brothers and of the way in which the Brothers of Leeds rallied to provide refuge for the families of Sheffield Brothers as well as clothes to replace those lost in the bombing. Southampton suffered, as most men lost their homes and offices.

But it was London that suffered more than any other centre. In July 1941,

THE ASSOCIATION AND THE SECOND WORLD WAR 1939-1945

Archbishop Amigo of Southwark, a good friend to the Association, acknowledged the letters he had received when his Cathedral was destroyed during the early blitz. London lost many men to the forces, suffered the sadness of the deaths of others, including a wartime President, H. Lednicki, during air raids, the destruction of successive meeting places and the problems of getting to meetings. South London lost most of its early records with the destruction of the offices of Thomas Baines, the Circle's Founder President 1921-22. This Circle lost eighteen Brothers on active service, so that meetings were occasionally cancelled for lack of numbers during the winter of 1940-41. Meetings were then held on Sunday afternoons under the leadership of Reggie Myers, who had been President 1931-33, and who guided the Circle again during 1941-44, when he was also Provincial President.

North London did not miss a meeting in spite of the bombing – although some meetings took place in odd situations such as that held by a few men gathered around a lamp-post after a savage air raid. London Charterhouse had an equally chequered history with such lamp-post meetings continuing in the bar of a local pub when it had re-opened. Bro. Butcher presided at one meeting held in the Church of St Boniface after the neighbouring Club had been destroyed.

The City of London Circle suffered from the problems of wartime catering, the calling up of many of the younger men, and the bombing. But it continued to meet; it held monthly Saturday luncheons in place of the evening meetings and dinners. In 1940 this routine was varied, Thursday dinners being held in the summer months and Saturday luncheons during the dark winter months. At these functions the Circle entertained members of the Knights of Columbus serving with the Canadian forces as well as members of the Australian forces. In 1941, the Circle entertained Hubert Cosgrove, who had been evacuated to North Wales with his Inland Revenue colleagues, but whom the Circle wished to honour for his eleven years as Circle secretary. The annual Ladies' Luncheon was a highlight; in January 1942, over 200 Brothers and guests heard the chief guest, Cardinal Hinsley, speak of the problems facing the Church.

But the Circle suffered a severe loss in April 1942, when its secretary, Francis Downey, was killed in an accident while travelling home by train in the black-out. In June, Downey's brother-in-law, Reggie Myers of South London, was admitted as a member and immediately elected to the post of secretary, a post which he only gave up in 1963.

Towards the end of the war things became easier so that inter-Circle visiting was resumed; Hubert Cosgrove returned from North Wales and was installed as President in 1944, a year which marked the onslaught by the flying bombs which destroyed the home of Herbert Quick and caused Victor Feeney the loss of an eye. But in spite of all these hazards, no meeting was missed; indeed, in each of the wartime years there were twelve meetings a year compared with the ten a year which had been held during peacetime.

Liverpool, where half the Brothers of the Wallasey Circle lost all their possessions, was another city which suffered from bomb attacks, while Newcastle records the way in which air raids interrupted meetings and forced the Circle to change the time of its meetings. The same story could be told of Circles throughout the country. It is little wonder, then, that one of the things that strikes the historian of the Association at this time was that there appeared to be a great deal of what in another era might be called apathy. The men who then formed our Circles were worn out – by the strain of living in and working through the troubled times: many suffered losses of homes and businesses; others had their lives torn up from the roots by evacuation, by deaths in their families or by conscription into the Services; wartime shortages – of food, clothing, petrol, building material and the like – all affected the reality of life. It is little wonder that one senses a 'greyness' about the people and the country. In *Catena* for January 1941 there are reports of a fall in membership, as men failed to maintain their subscriptions to an Association which to some at least must have appeared to be a luxurious and peripheral affair. We have seen that Circles had their Charters withdrawn when their membership fell to too low a level. Carlisle went through a crisis point owing to evacuation and conscription, and it was proposed by Brother Craven that the Circle should wind up its affairs. Fortunately the motion was lost and the Circle survived – and flourishes. North Glamorgan was another which suffered from a smaller membership because of the demands of the War. But here, as in many other Circles, the tensions of war seem to have acted as a toughening process – as fitted a Circle based on the steelmaking centres of the Welsh valleys, where men knew that from the crucible and the fire the metal emerged the stronger. Although the Circle had only twelve members, these seemed to realise that their presence at meetings was all the more important, and great sacrifices must have been made to ensure that 100 per cent attendance which was normal for wartime meetings. The Circle also inaugurated its practice whereby every Brother breakfasted at the President's home after supporting him at Mass on President's Sunday.

2. Catenian activities

One of the less important victims of the war was *Catena*. The issue of September 1939, which carried no mention of the threat of approaching war, was the last 32-page edition. Government regulations compelled the Association to cut its magazine down to 16 pages. The ending of the so-called 'phoney war' and the fall of France were reflected in more stringent regulations so that after June 1940 *Catena* only appeared as a quarterly.

The Grand President, Douglas Aikenhead Stroud, had taken office at the Harrogate A.G.M. in 1939. Stroud was one of the many converts who have served the Association. He was also one of the most intellectual of the Grand Presidents, being a Doctor of Law and author of several important legal books. Wounded during the bitter fighting of 1917, it was in a sense fitting that he should be the Grand President who led the Association through the period of special difficulties, 1939–41. Through the columns of *Catena*, Stroud called on the members of the Association to become even more active in wartime than they had been in peacetime, reminding them that they had special responsibilities to the families of Brothers who were called to serve away from their home towns.

The Founder President of Croydon in 1922, 'Stroud of Croydon' gave the Association that guidance and inspiration which it needed in 1939–41 and merited the comment that 'his period in supreme office was memorable . . . proved himself more than equal to the task and his work as Grand President will be long remembered'. And the Association responded to Stroud's challenge. Many Circles organised, financed and manned canteens or rest

THE ASSOCIATION AND THE SECOND WORLD WAR 1939-1945

centres for members of the forces. Cardiff reported that its canteen at St David's Cathedral was the chief Catenian activity. Newport Brothers helped run a Catholic Servicemen's Club in partnership with men from the C.Y.M.S. Preston Brothers helped the members of the C.W.L. and the K.S.C. to run a canteen and club where 2000 meals were served in an average week.

Many Circles offered to provide hospitality for serving Brothers and for their serving relations and friends. Glasgow set up a fund to provide for the entertainment of anyone with whom they were put in contact. Portsmouth invited other Circles to supply the names of serving Brothers or sons of Brothers stationed in their district and pointed out that the Circle could be regarded as 'at home' to all such men. Liverpool set up an enquiry office through which local Circles could be put in touch with Catholic visitors to the city and district.

Other Circles undertook similar sorts of activities, notably Leeds, Sheffield and Sunderland. Many priests, wives and parents wrote to express their gratitude for the help which various Circles provided for Catholic members of the forces. Some Forces Chaplains asked for Catenian support 'in cases of difficulty, which arose from time to time, and which required expert aid from laymen for a satisfactory solution'. Many Circles seem to have specialised in helping Catholic members of the Allied Forces. Plymouth Brothers provided various forms of help for the wives and families or relatives of men serving in the Polish navy, based on Devonport. The West Surrey Circle undertook to entertain and to visit the families of Canadian soldiers stationed in the district.

Many Circles made great efforts to retain contact with Brothers serving in the forces away from home. The ladies of the Norwood Circle organised a system whereby every serving Brother from that Circle received a present from time to time. Victor Palmer, then secretary of the Epping Forest Circle and a member of the Home Guard, sent a monthly newsletter, each ending with the letters 'T.H.W.H.' which stood for 'To Hell with Hitler'. These were regarded as great morale-boosters at a time when Catenians in big cities were suffering from the effects of wartime privation and almost nightly air raids. Frank Rudman thought so highly of them that he had them duplicated for distribution to Circles in the north of England.

Perhaps the most outstanding effort was made by the Norwood Circle which sent a letter each month to every 'Brother Exile'. Reading copies of these wartime letters has been one of the privileges attached to writing this *History*, for they gave each Brother a vivid but lively account of life in wartime Norwood, with its black-outs, Brothers on various wartime duties, shortages, bombings and other difficulties. One would have welcomed a chance to have seen the work of David O'Connell, wartime President of Blackheath, who sent out 'monthly jottings, which included a Ladies' Page, and a staggering correspondence with absent Brothers; those in the forces were sent a parcel each month'. O'Connell was one of the most gifted of Catenians, whose religious art won him a worldwide reputation. The walls of many churches carry beautiful examples of his work in the shape of the Stations of the Cross and altar pieces. A founder member of the Chichester Circle, he is remembered there for the Stations of the Cross at St Richard's Church, a fine example of his work. Catenians generally have a constant reminder of him in the design of their Grand President's chain of office.

3. Surprising expansion

Given the difficulties which faced Catenians, in common with the population as a whole, it is remarkable that six new Circles were formed during wartime. Two of them, South Bucks and Macclesfield, were the products of an experiment fostered by Frank Rudman. It was he who realised that in some districts it might be difficult, if not impossible, for a parent Circle to undertake the work of forming a new Circle. He gave his approval to the formation of a group in which one or more Catenians might undertake the recruitment of potential members of the Association. The first such group was inaugurated in October 1938 at Macclesfield, where John Lomas, the first Secretary of the Liverpool Circle, had come to live in 1935. He transferred his membership to the Stockport Circle and introduced several men from the Macclesfield district to the Circle. Rudman proposed through Grand Council that Provincial Council should help form an experimental group at Macclesfield which started with a membership of fourteen but, despite wartime difficulties, had grown to a membership of twenty-four by April 1944, when the Macclesfield Circle was inaugurated, with Frank Lomas as its Founder President.

It was the Macclesfield experiment which enabled the drawing-up of the procedure for the conduct of Group meetings which is still to a large extent in operation, although the formation of Hong Kong and Guernsey owed more to the activities of energetic individuals than to the supervisory work of a Provincial Council.

The example of Macclesfield was followed in a development in the South Bucks area, where Provincial Council appointed H.W. Paines to chair a group which led to the inauguration of the Circle in June 1940. Another such group was formed in Scunthorpe in December 1938 after Brothers Grasar and Stanford had been recruited into the Doncaster Circle. They persuaded Provincial Council that, in spite of the problems facing the formation of a Circle in Scunthorpe owing to the nature of its industry and its isolation, the chances of doing so in due course were reasonably good. Grasar and Stanford held dinner parties each month to which they invited potential Brothers. By 1941 they had recruited six 'reliable members', all of whom attended the Doncaster Circle but who, additionally, formed the Scunthorpe Group (1943). The fact that the Group remained as such until May 1957, when the Circle was inaugurated, does not indicate the efforts that were made to form a Circle. The War accentuated the difficulties in a town which was growing rapidly and whose population was of a very floating character. Whilst every effort was made to contact professional men who came into the town, and many were invited to the monthly dinners, it was found that the lack of suitable Catholic schools and social amenities, together with Scunthorpe's isolation from the stream of Catholic life, caused gentlemen who were likely to prove suitable to leave the district. This problem was further aggravated by a very acute shortage of accommodation. It is only very recently that the population has become more settled and that suitable potential members have settled permanently in the district. It is the proud boast of Scunthorpe Catenians that from 1940 to 1956 only two members *initiated for the Group* have resigned from the Association; both of them left the country.

The North Wales Circle has its origins in the wartime evacuation of civil servants to the area where, by a coincidence, Joe Shepherd had also gone to live. Such exiled Catenians held informal meetings as early as January 1940, and were so enthusiastic and experienced that Grand Council issued a Charter for the formation of a Circle in September 1941. So, although wartime difficulties led to some Circles (Stockton and West Kent) being deprived of their Charters, those very difficulties in the shape of evacuation led to expansion elsewhere. And another Circle which owed its origin, in part, to evacuation was Oxford, where many Colleges were taken over by various government departments. The opening of the Oxford Circle in October 1944 was notable, at least with hindsight, for the initiation of Frank Pakenham (later Lord Longford) and Professor J.R.R. Tolkien, the Founder Vice-President. In the light of the current interest in Tolkien's work, one would have wished for a recording of the speeches at the second annual dinner of the Oxford Circle, February 1945, when Tolkien proposed the toast to Provincial Council 'in a most amusing way which included an actual toast in Anglo-Saxon'. He was a member of the Association until 1956. Pakenham left in 1952. He was disappointed when no Brother came out to support him when he stood as a Labour candidate in the 1945 election, which illustrates his own lack of understanding of the nature of the Association and serves as a warning to those who advocate that the Association should become politically involved. He also explained that, having become a member of the House of Lords after the election, he felt it would not be consistent for him to be a member at one and the same time of the Upper House (and the upper class?) and of an Association which almost by definition was oriented to the middle class, although, he claimed, if there were a Circle formed for members of the peerage he might have to reconsider his position.

There were no such crises of conscience for Peter Kelly, a member of the Carlisle Circle who during the war was stationed in Leigh as an auxiliary policeman. Kelly noticed that there were many Catholics in the town, including a number who were active in public life. It was he who gathered together a number of men who, led by a former Mayor, Kearney, persuaded Grand Council to issue a Charter for the formation of a Circle in January 1945. Kearney died during the Silver Jubilee year of the Circle, of which he had been President from 1945 until 1948.

The War had delayed the opening of a Circle at Weybridge, one of the many suburban districts which developed in the 1930s. Several Catenians moved to the district in 1936, when some of them discussed the possibilities of inaugurating a Circle in the town. The War intervened, however, and the matter was shelved until 1944, when there were a dozen or more Brothers from some seven Circles living in the district. The Circle was inaugurated at 3.30 p.m. on 24 March 1945 – the only Circle to be inaugurated outside opening hours, but not, as was claimed at its 300th meeting, the only Circle to be inaugurated during the War.

4. To be more politically involved?

During the War, Cardinal Hinsley, Archbishop of Westminster, became a nationally known figure, largely because of a series of broadcasts which he did for the B.B.C. Hinsley, a former headmaster of St Bede's College, Bradford, and a former Rector of the Venerable English College in Rome, took great pains to ensure that the Catholic population would not be 'tainted' in the non-

Catholic mind with the neutralism which kept the Irish Free State out of the War. He explained to the country at large, but to his own people in particular, that the British cause was a just one, that the evils of totalitarianism had to be fought and that Christians of good will should unite first to help ensure victory and then to achieve a Christian peace.

One of the by-products of Hinsley's desire for united Christian action was the formation in August 1940 (not October, as George Scott claims) of the organisation called The Sword of the Spirit, which altered its name in the summer of 1965, so that it became the Catholic Institute for International Relations. In 1940 the movement, which became known simply as The Sword, attracted the support of many individual Catenians. It was not surprising that Paul Kelly and others should have helped organise the infant movement. For in many ways it was what Past Grand President Taggart had called for in the years before the War. The Sword organised discussion groups and lectures and issued pamphlets in the hope that these would help in the process of adult formation.

The Sword, however, went further than Taggart's Catholic Action. For Hinsley urged his followers to work with people of other Churches. In 1942 the Church of England, the Church of Scotland, the Free Churches and The Sword of the Spirit issued a joint pledge 'to work through parallel action in the religious field, and joint action in the sphere of social and international ethics'. This 'mixed bathing' won the enthusiastic support of many Catenians, and membership of The Sword grew rapidly. Unfortunately Hinsley had not consulted his fellow-Bishops. These did not share his idealism nor his willingness to work with fellow-Christians. They noted that he himself was reprimanded by Rome for joining with the Bishop of Chichester in saying the Our Father at a public meeting. With Hinsley's death in 1943, The Sword was allowed to rust and owed its later refurbishing to the support of Cardinal Griffin.

Catenians in general, like the Christian population of the country as a whole, shared the wish to restore Christian values in social, economic and political affairs. The Sword was one evidence of attempts to make the wish a reality. Crowded churches, the popularity of broadcasts by religious leaders such as Hinsley, and the expanded sale of religious literature provided other evidence. In the Association, Circle reports told of the higher attendance at President's Masses, at Provincial Retreats and other religious ceremonies. Manchester Circles combined to hold Days of Recollection at the Cenacle Convent, the first being held on Saturday, 9 November 1940. While the arrangements for 'these very enjoyable days, both spiritually and temporally', were in the hands of Politi of South Manchester, the idea of holding such Days sprang from the fertile mind of Frank Rudman. He had discovered that the nuns of the Cenacle had fallen on hard times, because the War had deprived them of the revenue from the retreats and Days of Recollection organised in peacetime for women and girls. In the summer of 1940 the nuns were 'impoverished and literally short of food because of lack of money'. Rudman persuaded Politi and the South Manchester Circle to organise Days of Recollection. A special dispensation was obtained to allow men into the precincts and the War 'was many years finished before a new Reverend Mother discovered the irregularity. In this way the Catenians preserved the Cenacle while also receiving the spiritual help of some of the leading preachers of the day.'

Catenian participation in The Sword, coupled with the upsurge of political debate in the light of publications such as the Beveridge Report, led Grand President Hildred to suggest that members of the Association, and especially those who had been 'informed and instructed' by the material issued by The Sword, had a duty to come forward as leaders. He went on to argue that the Association as such ought to act in a corporate way to promote 'resistance to encroachments on Christian freedom, proposals which violate moral principles deduced from revealed truth'. In May 1943, Grand Council discussed these and similar proposals, and issued a statement which argued that the existing Object (*b*) called for 'the promotion of the interests of the Brothers and their families by the individual and collective action of the members'. Grand Council pointed out that individual members should ensure that they became better informed by study, and that Circles were entitled to adopt a political (albeit not a party political) stance. Grand Council, however, drew back from asserting that Grand Council or the Association as such should be asked to provide a lead in these matters.

Many Circles took Grand Council at its word. Hull, for example, organised meetings of The Sword of the Spirit, while, as we shall see, many Circles undertook to organise local branches of the C.P.E.A. and to play a major role in the Battle for the Schools. But the active and able Victor Palmer of Epping Forest argued against Catenian adoption of a political stance. From his wartime base in North Wales, H.E. Cosgrove argued that if the Association and its members did not provide the leadership so badly needed, then it would deserve to fail to attract the support of the Old Boys of the leading Catholic Schools who preferred to find their Catholic life in other Associations or Societies. But another outstanding Catenian, Walter Keast, 'the father of Province 13', argued that individual Catenians were already playing leading roles in the Societies named by Cosgrove – the K.S.C., S.V.P. and C.P.E.A. Keast argued that the Association's *raison d'être* was to provide that Catholic friendship which would foster both the spiritual and active lives of its members. Support for Keast's point of view (which was also that of Victor Palmer) came from Bishop Bright when he addressed a Rally of Brothers from Province 6 in January 1945:

> He said that he had met Brothers at meetings of other Catholic societies, clubs, groups, etc., which proved that Catenians are playing their part in Catholic action, a part not exclusive and defined, but action in whatever sphere you find yourselves and whenever required by the Church, in every parish, in every group.

5. The Battle for the Schools 1943–1945
Palmer, Keast and Bishop Bright might have pointed to the sterling work being done by Catenians throughout the country in the wartime round of the Battle for the Schools. This particular round may be said to have started with the T.U.C.'s resolution (1943) that the post-war government ought to abolish all the grants made to Catholic schools. Older readers may recall that in 1943 the Coalition government began to make plans for Post-War Britain, with the publication of proposals for Full Employment, New Towns, Population Re-Distribution and, most of all, the Beveridge Plan. Among the debates which went on was the one which was to lead to the passing of the 1944 Education Act with its abolition of fee-paying at secondary schools, its division of such

secondary schools into three – grammar, technical and modern – and its expressed aim that every child should leave a junior school at the age of 11 to go on to a secondary school.

And the T.U.C., speaking for many Labour Party members, wanted the Catholic body to receive no aid. But without aid, what would happen to Catholic children? About half the Catholic children in the country went to Catholic schools and the majority stayed on in these same 'all-age' schools until they left at the age of 14. A small minority were successful in gaining local Council scholarships in an 11-plus examination and went on to secondary schools, most of which were run by religious orders or priests and in which some pupils came from better-off families and paid fees.

What would be the position of such schools when fee-paying was abolished and children went on to compulsory secondary schooling? Would a local council pay the cost of every child's schooling at one of the few Catholic secondary schools? Or would it insist on children attending a council secondary school? What about the majority of Catholic children for whom there was no available Catholic secondary school? Would the L.E.A.s and the government help the Catholic body to provide such schools? Not if the T.U.C. had its way. But even if the T.U.C.'s policy were rejected by the government, how much money would the government or an L.E.A. provide to help in the building of the needed Catholic secondary schools? 25 per cent? 50 per cent? 75 per cent? 100 per cent?

It is difficult now to recall the atmosphere and attitudes of the 1940s. For most Catholic children, and certainly for the majority in larger towns and cities, there is now adequate provision of Catholic secondary schools. But, as we saw (p. 137) this was not the case in Britain before 1939, when Catholic secondary schools were few and far between; most of them were small – far too small to cope with the influx which might be expected if all Catholic children were to go on to a Catholic secondary school; all of them were fee-paying schools, although in some places the L.E.A. had agreed to meet the cost of Catholic pupils who passed the L.E.A.'s own 11-plus examination. This was not always the case; in Liverpool, for example, the L.E.A. was dominated by a virulently anti-Catholic Party which refused to make any concessions to the Catholic case before 1939 and threatened to continue its bigoted policy after the War.

So there was much need for 'action' over the question of secondary schools. And this 'action' might conveniently be divided into two: firstly, there was need to persuade Parliament and councils of the justice of the Catholic argument concerning aid for the provision of schools; and secondly, there was the need for the provision of schools. It is to the credit of the Catenian Association that many of its members played leading roles in both parts of this 'action'.

The Catholic Electors' and Parents' Association was one of the brainchildren of Charles Sheill, once of South London and, at the time of writing, still a member of North-West London. Sheill was just one of a band of Catenian teachers who had followed in the footsteps of O'Dea (p. 41), Exworthy and Finan, who had not only played a part in the Catholic Teachers' Federation but had also devoted their time to their national unions. It was Sheill, as secretary of the London Catholic Teachers' Association, who launched the campaign to amend the 1944 Act, so that Catholic schools became government-aided 'voluntary' schools rather than, as originally

A photograph taken at the last pre-war AGM at Harrogate, 1939. The tall figure was Frank Rudman. On his right were Paul Kelly (partly hidden), Pat Taggart, John O'Donovan, Vincent Gosling, Glen Hildred and a Bro. Parkinson. On Rudman's left were O. Goodier and with paper, Dr Stroud. The bespectacled figure third from the right was 'Tommy' Baines (partly hidden). On his right were Percy Briggs and, in dark suit, M. Holohan. In all there were eleven Past or future Grand Presidents in the photograph.

The First Communion by David O'Connell, whose talents were also used to produce the line drawings of guests at Annual General Meetings.

Charles Sheill, who led the fight for the schools in the 1930s.

Bernard Emblem, who did so much for the Covenant scheme.

The Lifeboat Doctor, Catenian 'Jimmy' Hall of Ramsgate.

The Association's own Archbishop, Dr James Donald Scanlan of Glasgow.

Alexander Bounevialle, of South London Circle, whose daughter Mary, married 'Phil' Bussy whose sister, Beatrix, married Paul Kelly.

The dynamic R. W. Brosch, who did so much to spread the Association in the Midlands.

A photograph taken at the Folkestone AGM, 1954. From left to right, Mrs Lawler with (partly hidden) Past Grand President Jack Lawler, Col. and Mrs Peckston and the then Grand President, 'Bob' Burns.

A photograph of the Grand Council, 1956–57. In the front row (left to right) were: J. Cosgrove, 'Bob' Burns, Victor Palmer, Grand President Cyril Grobel, 'Bob' Richards, Jack Lawler, Laurie Tanner and Walter Keast. Standing at the rear were: W. Paines, Laurie Arnold, B. Litting, T. Addly, Joe McMurray, H. Gallagher, Percy Briggs, Harry Hipkin, and J. Politi. In the centre row were: Joe Corrigan, 'Jimmy' Baker, B. Coakeley, Alex Carus, and (on the extreme right) J. McCarey. In all there were fourteen Past or future Grand Presidents in this group.

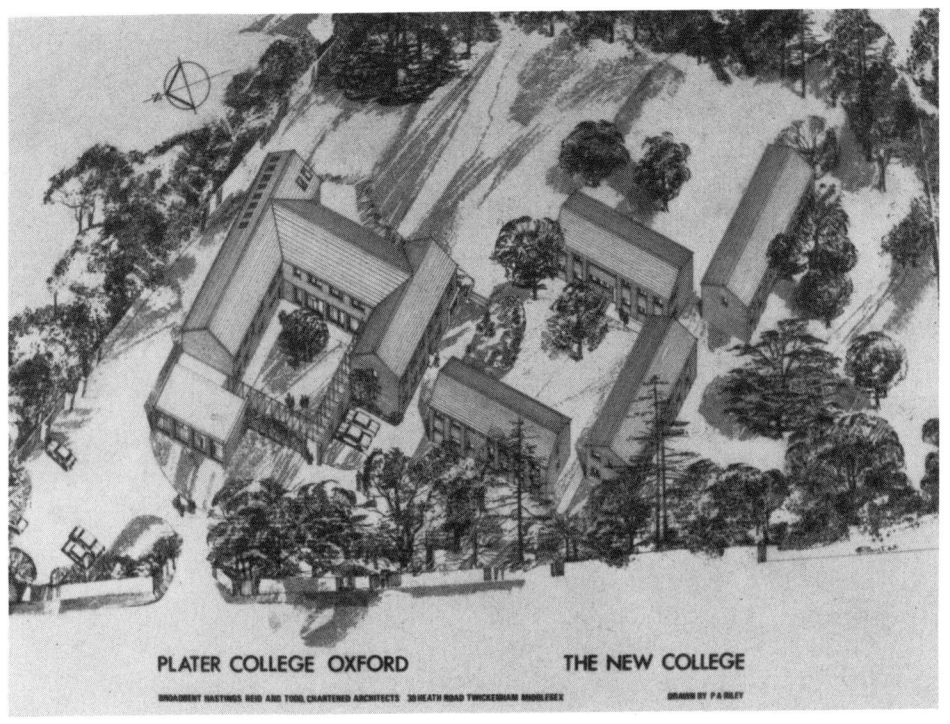

An artist's impression of the new Plater College, Oxford.

Bishop Langton Fox addressing the banquet at the 1966 AGM with Bishop Cashman and Grand President Sidney Quick enjoying the joke.

Laurence Bussy of the City of Liverpool Circle.

Phil Bussy.

Stephen Bussy.

The Bussy family.

Sir Joseph Molony of the City of London Circle, a distinguished lawyer, judge and Circle President.

Hugh Lee of the City of Manchester Circle and one of many Catenians to become 'first citizen'.

M. E. King of the Brooklands Circle, another Catenian Mayor.

Bro. Everest, Catenian Mayor of Westminster, with Christopher Soames, then Minister of Agriculture, and Brother Tom McLachlan at the opening of the Pure Food Exhibition organised by McLachlan in 1960.

Paddy Crotty of the Leeds Circle and Lord Mayor of the City.

Christopher Peterson of the Cardiff Circle on his way to being sworn in as High Sheriff.

Thomas Francis of the Eccles Circle (now known as City of Salford Circle).

James Glynn of Chorley.

John Fitzsimmons of Manchester Circle during his mayoralty.

F. H. O'Donnell of the Leeds Circle and another 'first citizen'.

Three generations of Catenians. Archbishop King of Portsmouth at the meeting of the Southampton Circle in February 1960 with three generations of the Tickle family, grandfather W. Tickle, son 'Teddy' and Teddy's son, Roger, whose early death deprived the Association of a valuable link with the origins of the Southampton Circle.

planned, 'auxiliary' schools. And it was he who succeeded in getting the idea of the C.P.E.A. off the ground.

His campaign bore fruit in many Catenian Circles where men were concerned over the educational future of their children and grandchildren. In Southampton, Bishop King called on the local Circle to help in the formation of a branch of the C.P.E.A. in the city; in May 1943, over 900 Catholics gathered in the Corn Exchange in Leicester to hear Douglas Woodruff re-state the right of Catholics to have their own schools. He was supported by Kimberlin (p. 167), a leading Catenian who was to go on to become the city's first Catholic Lord Mayor, and it was the local Circle which organised the dance for over 700 people which helped provide the funds needed for the local C.P.E.A. It was a Catenian group which organised Catholics to attend and speak at a public meeting called by the anti-Catholic Council for Educational Advance. This Council proposed the abolition of denominational schools. At the Stoke meeting this resolution was not only defeated but replaced with one which called for 'full justice and equality of treatment for Catholic schools'.

In Walsall, the local Circle helped form a branch of the C.P.E.A., while in Leeds the Circle organised a meeting of representatives of all the Catholic societies which led to the formation of a branch of the C.P.E.A. under the chairmanship of a Catenian. The Brothers of Croydon and Norwood share the credit for calling a mass meeting on education at which Past Grand President Stroud took the chair, while in the same month the men of the Harrow Circle organised a similar meeting in Wembley Town Hall.

A Catenian M.P., Bower and his wife, came forward as leading Catholic speakers on the Catholic Schools question. They were invited to address the City of Westminster Circle in June 1943, and this was followed by invitations to address other Circles and public meetings. Not everyone approved of this Catenian link with 'action' and in particular of its involvement with 'political action'. Some, however, saw a link between this 'battle' and the work of the ill-fated Salford Diocesan Federation, and wondered nostalgically whether the Catholics would have fallen on such hard times if they had followed Casartelli's path and had long since formed their own organisations.

But this less than forward view was not in accord with the feeling of the time. So it was that Sutton formed a branch of the C.P.E.A., while the men from the Bradford Circle organised the delegation of the C.P.E.A. which met the local M.P.s to inform them about Catholic anxieties over the 1944 Act. To help organise Catholic opinion, two Catenians of the Bradford Circle – Sullivan and Wilson – formed what was described as 'a flying circus' which went around local parishes to bring home to people the need for a greater participation in public life – by all Catholics and not by the minority which formed the Association. In Middlesbrough, the Circle joined with the men of the K.S.C. to help form a branch of the C.P.E.A., while in Newport the local branch was chaired by a Catenian. Early in 1944 the Brothers of the Southport Circle heard from John Taggart and Bro. Exworthy – who gave a critical analysis of the proposals involved in the Education Bill. They wrote letters to the local M.P.s – Commander Stephen King-Hall and R.S. Hudson. While King-Hall ignored the letter, Hudson invited a delegation from the Circle to meet him in London. After first explaining that 'public opinion is not with the Catholics' he then listened to what they had to say and 'was so impressed with the financial case made out that he promised to have a word with R.A. Butler', the Minister in charge of the Bill.

There is insufficient space even to name the many Circles which took similar action in the cause of the Battle for the Schools. The 1944 Education Act proved much more favourable to Catholics than the T.U.C. would have wished. And if the provision of a 50 per cent grant towards building costs still left the Catholic population with the fearsome task of finding the other 50 per cent of the money needed to provide the many new schools that would be necessary, at least the Catholic body was in a better position than it had been in during the 1930s and than it would have been in if the Battle had not been fought in 1943 and 1944. But the Battle did not end with the passing of the Act. For there still remained the matter of its putting into effect by national and local authorities; and, as we shall see, Catenians remained in the forefront of the Battle in peacetime, as they had been in wartime.

CHAPTER THIRTEEN

1945–1952

1. The end of the War
The council of the Cardiff Circle had fixed the date of their May meeting while the Allied Forces were fighting their way across Germany. The officers were not to know that the day they decided on would prove to be VE Day, when, as older readers will remember, the nation celebrated the end of the European War. It is not surprising that none of the Cardiff officers turned up for their council meeting; their Catenian activities took second place to the national rejoicing.

Not that the 'outbreak of peace' brought an end to the difficulties which had plagued the country, and the Association, since 1939. Rationing continued, and, in the case of food, became even more stringent than it had been during the War. Travel restrictions were slowly lifted so that it was possible to move along the south coast again, but petrol rationing meant that few men were able to use their cars. The damage done to over 3 million homes by enemy bombing would not be remedied for some five years, as imports of building materials were limited in face of the massive Balance of Payments problem facing the country, so that licences had to be obtained for even the smallest repair. Portsmouth and other heavily bombed cities carried the scars of the War for many years into peacetime. Bro. Tindall's home at Portsmouth continued to be the Circle's meeting place until January 1947, when a hotel could at last be found to house the Brothers.

The period from 1945 to 1951 – the period of the Attlee governments – has been well labelled 'the Age of Austerity', with the severity of the grim winter of 1947 being matched by the bleakness of the economic outlook and the constant fear that World War III might well break out over such issues as the Berlin airlift, the Greek crisis and the Korean War.

But there were some signs of improvement, at least on the Catenian front. There were the pleasures of welcoming home former prisoners of war, including some, such as Gerard Rudman, son of the Grand Secretary, who had been reported as 'killed in action'. There were, in particular, the men, who had suffered as prisoners of the Japanese, who brought back news of a world entirely different from that known to Europeans. Circles as far apart as Greenock and North London welcomed their Brothers back from Formosa, Siam and Singapore, while North Warwickshire welcomed back John Bowen who was to on to become Grand President in 1973–74.

The demobilisation of men who had served in the armed forces and the return of businesses and government departments from their wartime bases in the provinces, led to an increase in numbers attending Circle meetings. In April 1946, Norwood reported an attendance of over 40 at its last few meetings – a distinct change from wartime days. Brothers who had served in the forces were joined by new recruits to the Association many of whom, according to the report from Ealing in July 1946, showed an anxiety to serve the Association and the wider community.

Although some Circles continued to find it difficult to find a 'home', others, more fortunate, reported a speedy return to peacetime activities. As hotels were freed by the services which had occupied them since 1939 it became possible again to hold Ladies' Nights and dances. In October 1945, Birmingham held what was described as 'A Young People's Do' and some 500 turned out for the event. In April 1946, Liverpool reported its first peacetime 'Children's Party', while in July 1946 Blackheath reported that it was now possible to continue the Circle meeting until 10.00 p.m. – an improvement on the earlier 'closing time' of 9.00 p.m. which had been imposed on the Circle during the War.

And the Circle discussions threw some interesting sidelights on our national history. In June 1946, the Coventry Circle held a debate on the National Health Service then being proposed by Nye Bevan for the Attlee government, and reported a 'diversity of opinion' – so much for that rule against wrangling! In March the Leigh Circle heard from an expert in the Indian cotton industry, who warned the Brothers from this cotton-town that the Lancashire trade was doomed. In October 1950, the Brothers of the Oxford Circle congratulated their former President, J.R.R. Tolkien, on the publication of *The Hobbit*, but could not have known that they were witnesses to the beginnings of a cult.

2. Rapid expansion

One sign of the improvement in the Association's affairs was the increase in membership and in the number of new Circles being opened. Some of these had developed from a Group, as had the Duchy of Cornwall, where Brothers visited parishes around St Austell in order to find suitable members and where priests gave every encouragement. Some of the new Circles were the offspring of older Circles, as were Glasgow South, Maidstone (where Alan Rye was a driving force), Oldham (which held its inaugural meeting in the Town Hall), Winchester and Tynemouth. Some of the offspring were, it might be said, 'induced' by the rule forbidding Circles to have more than 100 members. It was this rule which led to the formation of the City of Leeds, Preston and District, and Purley Circles. Some of the new Circles were the result of a shift of population into suburbs and of the resultant increase in the Catholic middle-class population of such places as Purley, Tunbridge Wells, Esher, Leamington and the Cheshire region, where in 1950 three new Circles were formed. So it was that the Association spread its net, with two Circles being opened in 1946, three in 1947, two in 1948, five in 1949, twelve in 1950, seven in 1951 and two in 1952. Not everyone welcomed even this modest expansion during the period of the so-called 'Cold War', when crisis followed crisis – from Berlin and on to Korea. Churchill's 'iron curtain speech', Truman's 'doctrine' expressing American determination to halt Russian expansion, and the seemingly worldwide determination of the Russians to organise revolutions and unrest, all combined in these days of economic austerity to persuade many people that World War III could not be long postponed. In 1950–51 the Labour government embarked on a massive re-armament programme, while there were Americans who called for the use of the atomic bomb against the Chinese fighting in Korea.

It is against this gloomy background that one has to read of Rudman's advice to enthusiasts, such as Tom McLachlan, to 'slow down', since there was bound to be an outbreak of a war more savage even than the one from which the country had just emerged. Fortunately, Rudman's advice was ignored and the expansion went on.

We shall see that in the 1960s there was a similar increase in the number of Circles. But this latter-day expansion of Circles has not been accompanied by an increase in overall membership – for reasons which we will consider later. The immediate post-war expansion of Circles was, however, accompanied by a continuing increase in the membership of older Circles. In April 1946, Liverpool reported the initiation of six men on one night, while in October 1946 Burnley had seven initiations on the same night. In April 1946, the Provincial President of Province 13 reported that, whereas from 1933 to 1939 membership of the Province had steadily declined, by 1946 it had increased to the extent that not only had all that loss been made up but a new record of membership had been set. It was the same all over the country. In July 1946, Fleetwood reported 'a crowded meeting with standing room only'; Ealing reported in January 1947 that it had enrolled nine new members already in that Catenian year and had a number of other men 'in the pipeline'. Portsmouth reported 'an influx' of new men, so that in January 1947 the Circle was getting back to pre-war strength and habits.

At the A.G.M. at Worthing in 1950 the incoming Grand President Dermot Walsh was able to report that between the end of the War and the opening of the A.G.M. the membership had increased by 1650, with the number of Circles increasing by eighteen. A slight acquaintance with mathematics will show that the new Circles were responsible for only part of the increase in membership. By the time that he had finished his two years in office, Walsh was able to report that there were now over 7000 Catenians and some 158 Circles, and that there were all the signs of enthusiasm, expansion and a wish to serve.

3. The move to London

At the April 1945 meeting of the Council of Province 12, there was a long, vigorous and at times acrimonious debate on 'the hoary old topic' of the contemplated move to London. The idea of having headquarters in London instead of in Manchester had, as we have seen, been discussed in the 1930s. As the report from Province 12 noted, the subject was 'as antique as those two old favourites, Catholic Action and What's wrong with the Association'. But, as we know, this time this particular issue was not only discussed but resolved.

The arguments in favour of the move to London were fairly strong. London is the communications centre for the country, and it would be more convenient to hold meetings there than in, say, Manchester. London was also the base for the Cardinal Archbishop of Westminster, and if the Association wanted to claim a place in the Catholic world it would be better if its H.Q. was situated near Westminster and the Cardinal who hosted the Bishops during Low Week, when, if at any time, the Association's officers could meet the Hierarchy. Visiting dignitaries tended to stay in or around London, and if the Association wanted to have 'an international face' it needed to be able to meet such people. London is also the H.Q. for the nation's Press as well as for politicians, and if the Association wished to wield any influence then it was better for it to have its H.Q. near the politicians and Press barons. It was also felt that having the H.Q. at Manchester gave the Association a slightly 'provincial' air, which would be lost with a London H.Q. – something which might attract some of those leading Catholic laymen who did not join the Association.

In September 1945, Grand Council 'settled the question of the removal of headquarters by deciding to take a lease of a suite of rooms in Park Lane, London'. In fact, Heyburn the Grand Treasurer and Boniface, Grand Director for Province 11, had fixed on eight rooms at 40 Park Lane 'at a reasonable rent'. This announcement was not greeted with wild enthusiasm; Province 1 expressed the resentment of some men at this move away from 'the roots' in the name of chasing after a will-o'-the-wisp of 'recognition'. Province 12 heard of the decision 'with a Spartan stoical calmness'.

And many men must have had a quiet chuckle when in March 1946 Grand Council had to report that the negotiations for the suite at 40 Park Lane had fallen through – since the Association could not get planning permission to use the rooms as office space. Having counted their chickens before hatching, Grand Council had already negotiated the expiry of the lease on the Manchester office. This meant that after 25 June 1946 the Association would not have an H.Q. at all. 'So much for the business competence of the leaders!' was the attitude of many provincial members.

Thus, *Catena* for October 1946 carried a banner headline informing the Brothers that for the time being the Association's H.Q. was the home of the Grand Secretary at 100 Church Road, Worcester Park, Surrey. And while the Grand Officers of the Association tried to find suitable premises in London, Mrs Rudman had to cope with the domestic problems of moving house, finding friendly shopkeepers in the time of food shortage, and making a home which Frank Rudman could use both as office and home. Now, more than at any other time, Rudman '*was* the Association', with his home its H.Q.

And while the officers travelled far and wide in their search they were inundated by demands from some over-ambitious Brothers who obviously had all too little experience of an Association whose members had refused, in the summer of 1946, to increase their subscription from two to three guineas. These men wanted not only a London H.Q. They wanted also, at various times and from various Circles, 'a hostel for young Catholics living in London', 'a Club which would serve as the centre for Catholic life in London where men might stay when visiting the capital'. Ideas were mooted of a Limited Company which might raise £30,000 to acquire suitable premises, and of a scheme for membership at seven guineas a year – whereas most Catenians had voted down a much smaller subscription.

There was something fitting about the fact that the establishment of the new H.Q. – at 10 Hobart Place, London S.W.1 – should have been announced in *Catena* for October 1947. For this was the last issue to appear under Brosch's editorship. There was an aptness about the coincidence of the ending of his long and valuable work for the magazine with the opening of the London office. For in future, *Catena* would be edited by London-based men – Redwood, Kirchner and Simmonds.

4. Active Catenians

Meanwhile the Association's members, either individually or in their Circles, continued to make their contribution to the life of the Church and the nation. Men of London (No. 2) maintained the practice of being responsible for the collection taken at the Cathedral for the Crusade of Rescue, while the men from South Manchester contributed to the support of the Catholic Blind Asylum in Liverpool. The men of Province 11 raised £1000 for the endowing of a bed at St Anthony's Hospital in Cheam which has continued over the succeeding years in being a favourite outlet for much local Catenian activity. In St Helens the members of the Circle continued their wartime work of raising the money for the huts which were needed by the C.W.L. In April 1946, the Brothers of the County of Gloucester Circle congratulated a founder member, Major Patterson, for the O.B.E. awarded him for his services to the Soldiers', Sailors' and Airmen's Families Association, of which he was County Secretary. In the same month the Brothers of Derby Circle mourned the death of Leo Burns, once a member of Nottingham and a founder member of Derby Circle. He had been the prime mover in founding the Derby Catholic Lay Association, which later became the Derby C.P.E.A., and was its first Secretary. Largely owing to his work the Local Education Committee had granted representation to the Catholic body while, at the same time, Catholics were appointed to the magisterial Bench.

In July 1946, there was a good example of the way in which the 'action' of an individual Brother quickly wins the support of his Catenian colleagues, proving that the Circle is the natural ground for recruiting support. Graham-Green of Wimbledon had been a Major in the war and, as such, had inevitably helped many men with matrimonial difficulties. His wife also, as an active member of the Citizens' Advice Bureau, had come across many cases of broken homes and marriages ending in messy divorces or messier separations. The increase in the number of such cases had led to the formation of a National Marriage Guidance Council, backed by taxpayers' money, through which dedicated men and women hoped to be able to help couples overcome their matrimonial problems. It was Mrs Graham-Green who suggested to her husband that there ought to be a Catholic Marriage Advisory Council, for, as they both knew, there were many Catholic couples with problems and many Catholic marriages ending in the Divorce Courts. Graham-Green approached Cardinal Griffin. who gave the idea his blessing and encouragement. The Brother then found the support he needed in his own and other Circles: Tressider, of the City of Westminster, was a bank manager and arranged the financing of the new Council; Paul Kelly, perhaps the last of the truly giant figures, not only gave his own money to get the C.M.A.C. off the ground but became an active member of its Executive Council, while Boniface of Wandsworth and Everest of the City of Westminster helped with the conversion of the offices kindly provided by a Jewish friend of Graham-Green's. Catenian links with the C.M.A.C. have been maintained and developed. A former national Chaplain, Canon O'Leary. informs me that when preparing for the opening of a new branch of the Council, he always suggests to the local priests that they should approach the Catenians while looking for suitable laymen to train as Guidance Counsellors. He remembered many Brothers who had served the Council well, but in particular drew attention to the Birmingham Centre,

> which was the third one to be started and which had a strong Catenian composition as far as the men Counsellors were concerned. In fact, probably all the men there were Catenians, led by a very strong character, Fred Flynn, whose brother was Bishop of Lancaster.

Here was one example of 'action' – direct, if almost unsung – which might have met the demands of the minority of Brothers who led the campaign for the Association to become more active. In October 1946, John Taggart, who seemed to have inherited the mantle of his father, Pat Taggart, spoke at the Wallasey Circle on the need for such action. The Circle reported 'some interesting and keen discussion, but views clashed as to the most useful forms of action'.

In May 1947, the Association held the first peacetime A.G.M. – at Bournemouth. Here the assembled Brothers heard Grand President John O'Donovan call for 'action' without specifying what form, if any, that action ought to take. Whether by accident or design, this was the theme for the address given to the Nottingham Circle by Bishop Ellis in the winter of 1948 – an address which was published in full in the *Nottingham Catholic Magazine*, and copies of which were sent to every Circle. The Bishop acknowledged that the original Aims and Objects precluded such 'action' and called for a change in these Aims. With a movement against Christianity gaining strength in this country and throughout the world, there was need for all men and all associations to rally to the cause of 'action'. And in February 1948 Archbishop Godfrey, then Apostolic Delegate but later to be Cardinal Archbishop of Westminster, made much the same appeal when addressing the Brothers of Weybridge and District (129) at their Annual Dinner.

It was left to the new Editor of *Catena* to point out that 'Catholic Action' by definition was and must be such action as is directed and controlled by the Hierarchy. Was this what Casartelli had called for in his first pastoral? Was it what O'Donnell and the Chums had set out to achieve? Would such direction and control by the Hierarchy not so change the nature of the Association that many men would leave? And in what direction was the Hierarchy likely to direct such 'action'? The evidence from the 1930s is that they were singularly ill-equipped to direct 'action' other than by insisting on the formation of a structure of committees and sub-committees which achieved little. In *The English Catholics 1850–1950* (pp. 389–392) Professor Beales detailed the sad failure of the Hierarchy in the Battle for the Schools in the inter-war period, when, as he shows, having refused government offers in one year (and so obtained little if anything), the Hierarchy came back, ten or more years later, to ask the government for the very things and conditions which had been refused at the earlier date with Hierarchical contempt. It was little wonder that the Scots Hierarchy went their own way and won for themselves a deal which, says Beales, 'is now regarded as the best in the world', with Catholic education being safeguarded at little financial cost to the laity, whereas the laity of England and Wales were needlessly saddled with the huge financial burden which still lies heavily on us.

Not that the calls by the Bishops had no effect. Grand President Hildred urged Brothers to become more involved in the life of the nation and the Church; some men agreed with Cuthbert Kelly, who asked the West Essex Circle to support the motion that the Association should become involved in the political life of the country – but in a non-party way, defending Christian principles while not supporting, it seems, any particular political party. Most Brothers agreed, however, with Bernard Kirchner's attack on such political involvement, pointing out that it would split the Association and so bring to an end O'Donnell's dream of its being a haven where men might find mutual support in social intercourse, a haven from which they might go refreshed to become better fathers and husbands and, as many men proved, better Catholics and citizens.

Those, indeed, who called for 'action' by Circles and by the Association appeared to have ignored, or to have known nothing of, the manifold activities of Brothers and Circles. There was the C.M.A.C., as we have seen; but there was also the Catholic Teachers' Federation in which, reported *Catena*, a large number of Catenians took a prominent part. There was John Finan, President of Manchester in 1948, Sheill of South London, Critchley of Rochdale and other Catenian officers of the Federation. Indeed, in 1950 nine of the forty C.T.F. Executive were Catenians. In Scotland in 1948, Bro. Barry of Glasgow Strathclyde was President of the Educational Institute of Scotland, the first Catholic to hold this post. Catenians continued to be prominent in the affairs of the Catholic Social Guild – with Paul Kelly and Bro. McClelland being officers of the Industrial Group; there were Catenians helping to run the C.T.S., with men such as Pendergast running the diocesan affairs of the Society. Laurie Arnold was only one of the many Catenians who found outlet for their 'action' in the work of the K.S.C., although he is alone in having achieved the 'double' of being Grand President of the Association and Supreme Knight of the K.S.C.

Other Catenians entered into public life via local councils. When Casartelli became Bishop of Salford there were throughout the whole country only twelve Catholic councillors or aldermen, and there had been no Catholic mayor of any borough since the Reformation. We have seen in earlier chapters how Catenians played their part in altering that state of affairs; and after 1945 they continued that good work – something, it seems, which went on without the knowledge of the Hierarchy, who were free in their criticism of the 'non-active' Association. In the autumn of 1945, two Brothers from the Bournemouth Circle became Town Councillors; in the spring of 1948, Cyril Grobel, later to be a forceful Grand President, became an Alderman of the Borough of Finchley, by which time the Editor of *Catena* had adopted the necessary practice of merely listing the Catenians who had been successful at local elections. In *Catena* for January 1948, there was a list of eighteen such names, with a note that 'this list is probably very incomplete'. In April 1949, *Catena* listed a large number of men standing as candidates – for both Labour and Conservative parties, a reminder that to have turned the Association into a 'political' movement of any sort would have had disastrous effects. As it was, men could share their Catenian activities in common, while differing, outside the Circle, as to their political loyalties. It is to the credit of the Association, which was dismissed in a *History of the Knights of Columbanus* as consisting of conservative ex-army officers, that in 1948 it should have congratulated Bernard Sullivan of Croydon Circle on his election to high office in his Trade Union while welcoming the return to Parliament of the Labour Lord Advocate for Scotland, John Wheatley of Edinburgh Circle.

In *Catena* for August 1949, the list of Catenians who had gained seats in local elections was longer than ever, some 38 Brothers having been successful. And so it went on, with perhaps a Catenian highspot being reached in the report in *Catena* for April 1951 that James Fitzsimons of Manchester Circle had been elevated to the Aldermanic bench in the Manchester City Council of which his son, G.W.G. Fitzsimons, also a member of the Manchester Circle, was a Councillor. There cannot have been many examples of Catenian father-and-son teams on local councils.

Wheatley's success in Parliamentary elections in 1948 was followed by the election of 1950, when seven other Catenians stood without success. That election led to the return of the Attlee government with a much reduced majority. For various reasons which do not concern us in this *History*, Attlee called an election in 1951, when W.T. Wells was re-elected – following which he was initiated into the Hastings (146) Circle, so bringing the number of Catenians at Westminster to three.

A reading of *Catena* for these post-war years shows how much 'action' was done by Catenians in various Federations, Societies and other organisations. But perhaps the most significant list is that of Catenians who became Mayors or Lord Mayors during this period. There were Catenian Mayors in Hornsey (1946), Manchester (1947), Torquay (1948), Scunthorpe (1948) and Wisbech (1949), where Bro. Ollard crowned his life's devotion to public work which had already brought him the honour of being the first Catholic freeman of Wisbech. In 1949, Martin of Doncaster Circle became the town's second Catholic Mayor – the first, Bro. Clarke, also having been a Catenian. There was a similar 'second' at Lytham St Anne's, where Tom Banks of Blackpool and The Fylde (No. 25) became Mayor, an honour which had once fallen to Bro. Urwin, also of the Blackpool Circle. In 1950, Leeds had its second Catholic Mayor in the person of Bro. O'Donnell of the Leeds Circle, and he was present both at the service at Kirkstall Abbey to commemorate the Centenary of the Restoration of the Hierarchy and at the A.G.M. at Harrogate.

In Bournemouth, Frank McInnes, once of the London Circle and a former President of the Bournemouth Circle, became Mayor – and raised a storm of Protestant protest at his insistence that the Civic Service should be held at the Catholic Church. Other Catenian Mayors during this year were Carroll of Salford, Leach of Pontefract, Edmundson of Morecambe, and Pemberton of Bury St Edmunds, whose Civic Service of Solemn High Mass was the first such Catholic Civic Service since the Reformation and did not cause the storm of protest raised in Bournemouth.

5. The Battle for the Schools

In the post-war period Catenians continued to play a prominent part in the continuing Battle for the Schools. For the Battle did not end with the passing of the 1944 Act. In many places there were problems arising from the failure of Local Education Authorities to honour the spirit (and sometimes even the letter) of the Act. In Cardiff the Circle heard a talk from Bro Vincent, headmaster of St Illtyd's School on 'The problems arising from the 1944 Act'. In fact, the Cardiff L.E.A. was particularly generous, and St Illtyd's flourished after the passing of the 1944 Act with an influx of boys whose fees were paid by the Authority.

It was not so elsewhere. In Exeter the Authority refused to agree to the founding of a Catholic secondary school or to the payment of fees for Catholic children who wished to attend a near-by Catholic school outside the Borough boundaries. It was as a result of a debate in the Exeter Circle that a branch of the C.P.E.A. was formed in that city in 1950. In Doncaster there was no Catholic secondary school for boys. In October 1944 they considered the 1944 Act, and wrote to Bishop Poskitt to ask that a school be formed in the town.

The Bishop replied that he was grateful for the interest of the Brothers and assured them that everything would be done to get such a school founded in the area. In Leicester the Circle organised fêtes and carnivals to raise money for the Leicester Catholic Secondary Schools Fund. And it was a Catenian, Kimberlin, who, as a member of the city council, led the attack upon the L.E.A. when it refused to 'grant an application from the Leicester City Council for arrangements to be made to permit Catholic children who qualify for admission to Grammar Schools to enter the Nativity Convent and have their fees paid by the L.E.A.' In Leicester, Croydon, Liverpool and other major towns and cities, L.E.A.s, under the influence of non-Catholic majorities, refused to agree the case for Catholic children to get a Catholic education at the ratepayers' expense, although being prepared to pay for them to go to local Grammar Schools.

Not every town or city had a Catholic school to which Catholics could send their children. And even the small Catholic schools had not always an assured future. In the summer of 1946 the fathers of the Society of Jesus informed the parents of boys at St Peter's School, Bournemouth, that in 1947 they would end their association with the school. It was Brothers from the Bournemouth Circle who then undertook to visit the superiors of other teaching orders to see if they could persuade them to try where the Jesuits had failed. So it was to McInnes, Wutack and others that goes the distinction of having persuaded the De La Salle brothers to come to St Peter's – which has now grown to be a very large and successful school. Not that the Brothers came willingly or without conditions. Knowing that the Jesuits had failed, and fearing that they too might fail to make a success of the school, the Brothers insisted that they would come only on condition that, in the event of failure, they would not be financially penalised. So they asked that the cost of the land and existing buildings should be guaranteed by someone so that, in the event of failure, they could withdraw from Bournemouth without financial loss. Three Catenians provided those guarantees, McInnes becoming personally responsible for a guarantee of £30,000.

One city which had suffered badly from enemy bombing was Coventry. In 1947 it was going through the early stages of post-war reconstruction. The Coventry Circle was made up of Brothers, 'ninety per cent of whom had received their Catholic education in other cities'. This helps to explain the interest shown by the Circle in trying to get a secondary school for their own children. It is a reminder of how late in time Catholic education has been the right of all, that even in 1950 there was still no Catholic secondary school for boys in this thriving city. This was the case in many other places. It is refreshing, then, to read the headline in *Catena* (April 1948): 'Catenians in Education Battles'. The article which appeared beneath this heading outlined the work of the Brothers of the Shrewsbury Circle (113) led by Bro. Leonard Ross after they had heard that the L.E.A. would not agree to the building of a Catholic secondary school, and that Catholic children were to be transferred to local schools at the age of 11 rather than remaining in the all-age schools which they presently attended. There were letters from Cardinal Griffin to the L.E.A., which was threatening to take parents to court if they refused to send their children as directed. Ross and other Brothers agreed to meet the legal costs if such cases were brought; but in the face of such opposition the L.E.A. climbed down, and although it did not agree to the building of a special secondary school, it did allow the children to remain in the Catholic all-age schools. There was a similar fight in Southend, where, though Catholic girls could be accommodated at the Convent of St Bernard, there was no provision for Catholic boys of secondary school age. Again the L.E.A. insisted that at the age of 11 such boys must leave their Catholic schools and go to L.E.A. schools. It was Alderman Brother Sullivan of Southend Circle who led the fight which succeeded in persuading the L.E.A. to agree to consult the Ministry on the possibility of opening a small Catholic secondary school for boys.

In Wales the picture was confused. The Cardiff L.E.A. provided the funds needed to pay for boys to go to St Iltyd's if they passed the 11-plus, while the Newport L.E.A. also agreed to fund such of its boys as gained places at the Cardiff school even though it was twelve miles away. One reason for the favourable treatment given by the Cardiff and Newport L.E.A.s may have been the presence on the Cardiff Council of Catenians such as Purnell and Taverner of Cardiff Circle, and on the Newport Council of Driscoll of Newport Circle. But in Swansea 'with its traditional antipathy to Catholicism again being displayed', and in Glamorgan and Monmouth, there was no such co-operation. It was to be many years before Catholic children in these areas would have their own secondary schools.

It seems fitting to conclude this section of our *History* with a short account of the appeal made in November 1948 by Bishop Beck, then Co-adjutor Bishop of Brentwood and the leader of the Hierarchy's fight on the education question. Speaking to the Catenians of the West Essex Circle (41), he dealt with the nature of the problems facing the Church over the implementing of the 1944 Act, claimed that these problems could be best surmounted by the laity, and then went on to say that he hoped to formulate an Advisory Council which would deal with the problems and propose solutions. The report goes on: 'It was to Catenians that he looked for assistance, composed as they were of men answering to his three main requirements: Catholic, Business and Professional.' One can only wish that it had been so.

6. Catenian development

As the nation's life slowly returned to normal after 1945, so did the Association slowly undertake a process of modernisation which may be seen as in keeping with the move to a London H.Q. In November 1946, Grand Council agreed to ask Circles to vote on three propositions. The first would reduce the *ex officio* element on Grand Council by restricting the number of Past Grand Presidents entitled to sit on that Council. Since 1923 every Past Grand President had been *ex officio* a member of the Council. This was seen as giving an over-preponderance to age, tradition and the past. Not everyone welcomed the exclusion from the Association's governing body of many of those men who had contributed so much in the past, but the majority of voting Brothers came down on the side of a smaller Grand Council, with only the six immediate Past Grand Presidents as *ex officio* members.

At that same meeting Grand Council announced its decision to revive a proposal to increase the annual subscription from two to three guineas, of which Grand Council would take the lion's share, and to charge an initiation fee of two guineas, to be divided equally between Grand Council and the local Circle. This proposal had first been put in the spring of 1946, but had been turned down by Circles, who apparently resented the 'greed' of a 'far away'

Grand Council. This time, Grand Council linked the 'rise' with the need for greater contributions to the Benevolent Fund, and with the cost of acquiring and operating a London office; Circles voted for the increase asked for.

As a sort of placebo, Grand Council proposed to divest itself of the power of the veto (p. 83) which had enabled it to use its discretion concerning motions passed at A.G.M.s. It was still evident that the A.G.M. was not truly representative of the Association; at the second post-war A.G.M., at Buxton, only 102 Circles were represented and, not surprisingly, there was an above-average attendance from Circles in the Midlands. Grand Council had always argued that the A.G.M. was not and had never been intended to be a legislative body composed of delegates or Circle representatives; it was a gathering of such men as wished to attend – and they represented only themselves. In 1947–48, however, Grand Council took a step towards democratic modernisation by agreeing that if a motion gained majority support at the A.G.M. then it would automatically qualify for submission to the Circles, whether Grand Council really supported the motion or not.

At the Buxton A.G.M., the Brothers considered the proposal to abolish the 'Salute' – a lapel-fingering method of mutual recognition – one of the last remaining of those Signs and Passwords which our Masonic-tinged founders had bequeathed to the Association. Many men felt that the Salute was undignified, akin, it was argued, 'to the manner in which certain tribesmen of darkest Africa scratch certain portions of their anatomy when saluting their chieftains'. (The very words are themselves a reflection on our nation's social and international history; one wonders to which legal body one would be reported if using such terms today.) But the majority voted to retain this link with the past, some claiming that it had enabled them to recognise Catenians when on duty in the forces, others claiming that if it lacked dignity that was the fault of the Circles of which the guilty men were members.

At the Harrogate A.G.M. in 1951, a major step towards modernisation was taken when the Brothers voted for a *Compendium* which would contain the Prayers, Circle Procedure, Investiture of Officers and Initiation of New Members. Only older members of the Association will recall the conglomeration of books and cards which littered the desks of Presidents and other officers, many of whom, particularly in new Circles, found themselves caught up in a mess of booklets and cards when trying to conduct a Circle meeting. This is a reminder that our Ritual had grown up haphazard, and that our businessmen Brothers had apparently found nothing wrong with adding yet another card – on, say, the *De Profundis* – to the existing clutter. Grand Council accepted the challenge, and in October 1953 the first Catenian *Compendium* was issued, still couched in slightly archaic language. Older men resented the accusation that the language was 'meaningless' or 'trite'; having lived with it for many years, they had come to understand it, they had been able to gloss over some of the implications seen by some in the terms used, and they wished to retain this link with their own past and that of the Association. So words such as 'worthy' referring to Brothers and particularly to Presidents, and 'honourable Order' referring to the Association, continued to figure in the revised *Compendium*. It would be many years yet before modernisation would radically alter the Charge and other parts of our Ritual.

In a letter to *Catena* for April 1948 Almond of Bromley drew attention to the number of men who 'resigned' or who 'lapsed'. He claimed that in the lists of such ex-members were to be found 'veterans' who had served the Association well but who, in old age or because of sickness or infirmity, found it financially impossible to maintain membership. Almond proposed that 'Honorary Life Membership should be adopted as part of our Constitution to be awarded to old and valued members who cannot continue to attend meetings owing to infirmity, etc.' This would ensure that they would continue to share in the spiritual benefits of the Association even if their physical links with it were broken.

In the subsequent debates on this subject all sorts of snags were revealed. Who would decide which men were 'valued members'? Would their Honorary Membership entitle them to make claims on the Bénévolent Funds – which might in that event be swamped by claims from an ageing membership? The debate has not ended, even at the time of writing, for while we have made some progress in this matter Almond's 'dream' has not been realised. Today, Circles have the right to retain membership for a 'valued' Brother without imposing any financial burden on him – but in that case the Circle has to pay to Grand Council such subscriptions as the Brother might have been expected to make though Provincial Councils may submit to Grand Council applications for waivers of all dues. It is evident that small Circles, or Circles with a large number of ageing men, cannot be as generous in this regard as some might wish. Grand Council now permits our over-65 Brothers to pay a reduced subscription; this is part-answer to Almond's demands although in these inflationary days even this must be a burden to some older men.

7. Rudman's retirement

In *Catena* for October 1948 there is an appraisal of the work Frank Rudman had done for the Association and for the wider Church. He had been Grand Secretary for some twenty-five years and, as the Profile said, 'he *is* the Catenian Association', as far as many people were concerned. But Rudman was not in good health, and the burden of office was greater now that the Association was expanding again. He was also hampered by the serious illness suffered by his wife in 1948 – for, as we have seen, Frank Rudman relied heavily on his wife (p. 102). In December 1945, the Brothers of Province No. 1, gathered in retreat in the Cenacle Convent, had thought that this might be Rudman's last appearance in the Province – with the move of H.Q. to London planned for the immediate future. They had made him a presentation, which pleased him, for he had been, he said, more used to 'kicks than ha'pence'. The Manchester-based men as well as men from other Circles were conscious of the hard work that Rudman had put in, particularly during the War when it might have been so easy to let the Association flicker and, maybe, die out. It was fitting that the Silver Jubilee of his Grand Secretaryship should be marked by a dinner and presentation by Grand Council (December 1948), when Rudman drew attention to the great work of several of the Past Grand Presidents now dead, and to the work of the Heyburn brothers and their work as Grand Treasurers. Shepherd, the first Grand Secretary, made what *Catena* described as 'a particularly interesting contribution' to the round of speeches. One would have wished to hear that 'contribution' from the predecessor to his successor, with whom his relationship had always been thorny.

In 1952 Rudman organised his last A.G.M. at Torquay, where it was announced that he would retire at the end of that August. Grand President Lawler made a warm and touching speech about the value of the work that he had done for the Association, which had almost tripled in size under his guidance. In his reply Rudman showed that he was moved by the warmth of the reception given him by the Brothers although he noted, in a characteristic Rudmanism: 'I thank you for the generous way in which you have shown your enthusiasm for my retirement.' There was another moving moment when the Supreme Secretary of the Knights of St Columba announced that the Knights had decided to make Rudman an Associate Member of the Order and to give him its Long Service Medal, a decoration previously awarded only to members of the Hierarchy. With his retirement the Association had reached a major stage in its history, for without Rudman's guiding hand it would not be quite the same again.

CHAPTER FOURTEEN

Adaptation, Ambition and Disappointment 1952–1965

1. A slow expansion
In 1952 there were some 7000 Catenians in 161 Circles in Great Britain. By 1965 there were some 8500 members of the Association in 228 Circles, including some in Southern Africa and one in Jersey. The expansion of the Association overseas will be examined in Chapter 16. The expansion during this period in Great Britain provides another illustration of the link between the history of the Association and our national history. And the relationship between the history of the Association and that of the Church is clearly seen in the way in which, towards the end of this period, many Catenians were looking for ways in which the Association might come to terms with the Vatican Council's teachings on the role of the laity in the modern world.

The end of the Korean War and the death of Stalin led to 'The Thaw', which lessened, if it did not end, fear of the inevitability of a third World War. Governments needed to spend less on re-armament, so taxation could be cut; nations needed less materials for re-armament, so world prices fell sharply; the industrial re-building which had gone on in Britain after 1945 now began to come 'on stream', so there were more goods available in shops; rationing ended and Britain moved slowly into what became known in the late 1950s as the 'Affluent Society', in which, said Prime Minister Harold Macmillan speaking in July 1957, the British people had 'never had it so good'.

Industrial and commercial expansion provided job-opportunities for a rapidly increasing number of managers, technologists and technicians, for people in secondary and tertiary industries and for the self-employed. And among those who benefited from this expansion were an increasing number of Catholics. It was from among this expanding group that the Association recruited its new members. The expansion of the Association was a direct result of the economic expansion of the 1950s. Like the nation, the Association, too, might have been said to have 'never had it so good'.

An expansion in the number of Circles, however, was not met by a corresponding increase in the number of members. Nor was the ambition of its leaders always matched by eager response from members. One of the problems that faced the Association in this period was an apathy illustrated by the numbers attending Circle meetings. On average, attendance was rarely above 50 per cent. Even during the heady days of the debate on the Chaplaincies scheme, fewer than 55 per cent of the members bothered to attend meetings to vote. There were various attempts to explain this lack of interest, with almost as many reasons being given as there were correspondents.

Whatever the causes of this apathy, one of its effects was a high rate of lapsation, which was made worse when, in 1958, it was ruled that anyone who failed to pay his subscription within the Catenian year should be deemed to have forfeited his membership. Each year many hundreds of men either resigned or allowed their membership to lapse. There were several attempts to explain this 'draining of blood': some left on moving home to an area where there were no Circles; some older men could no longer afford the cost of membership; some men whose family commitments increased as their families grew up could not afford to remain in the Association. But when all these understandable reasons were taken into account there still remained the many hundreds who joined the Association, presumably because they wanted to, only to leave it again for no given reason.

And if there was a problem of lapsation there was also the problem of the Association's failure to attract as many of the thousands of Catholic men in that 'professional and business' class for which the Association had been founded. It would be foolish to expect that every member of that class would join the Association, for not everyone is 'clubbable'. And many potential members of the Association preferred to join other societies and Associations, such as Rotary, where 'action' and 'business interest' could well be combined. That still left the Association manifestly unable to attract many potential members.

2. Changes and adaptations

The period 1952–65 was notable for a series of attempts to adapt the Association's Rules, its Constitution and its Ritual in the hope that such changes would make the Association that much more 'meaningful'. It was, perhaps, fitting that this period of change should have been marked by the appointment of a new Grand Secretary, Laurie Tanner, who had been Rudman's assistant since 1948. His appointment as Rudman's successor was announced at the 1953 A.G.M. Grand President Bob Burns, in paying tribute to Tanner after his first year in office, claimed that 'if you accept that the Grand President is the captain of the ship, then the Grand Secretary is inevitably the pilot'. That 'pilot' Tanner, like his predecessors Shepherd and Rudman, should have often clashed with the 'captains' and, continuing the metaphor, 'officers' on Grand Council, was almost inevitable.

But it was Tanner who supervised the work of Lomas and John Tucker in the re-writing of the Rules and the Constitution in what was described as 'the most sweeping' change in the Association's history. The new Rules and Constitution were promulgated at the 1957 A.G.M. Among the changes was the provision for a larger Grand Council by the inclusion of the six immediate Past Grand Presidents – a quid pro quo for the abolition of the life membership of Grand Council which had previously been the reward for all Past Grand Presidents. The expansion in the number of Circles and Provinces had also led to an increase in the number of Grand Directors. This, in turn, led to the call for a re-organisation of the Association's structure. In 1957 and 1958 Tanner supervised the work of Committees which proposed a regional format which was rejected by Grand Council in 1958. A similar format, proposed by the Jenkins Committee was rejected by the Association as a whole in 1970.

Older members will recall the long debate on ritual in the '50s and '60s, when it seemed that there was almost an obsession with the subject in *Catena* and at successive A.G.M.s. Calls for a change in the language were made in

1952 and answered by the publication of the first *Compendium*, in which for the first time the Association's ritual was laid out clearly. At the same time Grand Council decreed the appointment of Provincial Ritual Officers (later to be called Chamberlains) to supervise the way in which Circles carried out the new ritual. But no sooner had this been done than there were further calls for even simpler forms and language. In 1957 a committee was appointed to produce a more up-to-date ritual, which was put into operation in 1960 only to be met with shrill cries for 'less ritual', 'more ritual', 'simpler ritual', 'no ritual'. In particular, there was a call for the abolition of the last of the 'signs and passwords' so beloved of pre-war Brothers, the Salute. Grand Council resisted this call for change until late in 1964, and it is somewhat fitting that its abolition did not take place until January 1965 – the end of the period under review in this Chapter.

There was also something apt about the Association's acquisition of a new Head Office during this period. When Rudman succeeded Shepherd in 1923 the Association's Head Office had moved to Cross Street, Manchester. Soon after Tanner succeeded Rudman, the Association had to begin to consider moving from its first London office in Hobart Place, the lease on which was about to run out.

In 1964, Grand Council received a tempting offer for the Hobart Place premises while, almost simultaneously, Bill Cunningham (of the City of Westminster Circle) succeeded in negotiating what has been described as 'a knock-down price' for the present Head Office at Chesham Place. The freehold was acquired and the property officially opened and blessed by Bishop Cashman in March 1965, a short two months before the Hierarchy's abrupt rejection of the Association's Chaplaincies scheme.

3. Active Catenians

In the 1960s, in the heady atmosphere created by the Second Vatican Council, there were many calls for the Association to reconsider its Aims and Objects. Of particular importance in that respect were the calls made at A.G.M.s by such Grand Presidents as Laurie Arnold, Frank Lomas and George Harris. But a call for reconsideration of the work of the Association was the subject of the front page of *Catena* in January 1952, with a report that a number of priests who had been invited to a Circle Clergy Night commented of the Catenians, 'Of course, they don't *do* anything'. When asked what they wanted the Association to do they came up with the suggestion 'of financing a scholarship to the local Catholic Secondary School'. One might ask why these priests knew nothing of the work the Association had done for the whole question of Catholic secondary schooling since the 1920s, or of the support they had given to the efforts of Sheill and others in the C.P.E.A. movement to compel L.E.A.s to provide scholarships to 'the local Catholic Secondary School'. Or one might wonder why they were not as much aware of the work of the Association and its individual members as were the members of the Hierarchy, who at A.G.M.s and Circle functions went out of their way to thank the Association and its members for the work being done.

And what was that work? During this period, 1952–65, there was ample evidence that the Association continued to play the role of being, at one level, 'Catholic Action at rest' and, at at another level, 'the instigator of individual action'. For some men their action took political form, so that there were four Catenian M.P.s, a number of Catenian Mayors, and an even larger number of Catenian Councillors and Aldermen. Catenians played a large part in the affairs of the Catholic Managers and Employers Association and in Catholic professional organisations such as the Catholic Teachers' Federation and the Catholic Pharmaceutical Guild. Some confined their 'action' to local activities: Catenians from Sutton, Epsom, Wandsworth and Putney (now South West London) and Croydon were active members of the League of Friends of St Anthony's Hospital in Cheam, a League which had been founded by Bro. Dan Sullivan while he was Mayor of Sutton and Cheam; Brothers in Province No. 6 'are the primary organisers of the now-famous Midlands Catholic Ball held each winter to provide funds for the Little Sisters of the Assumption Nursing Sisters'.

Few Brothers won the publicity that followed the work of Alan Rye, actor and journalist, who produced and wrote plays for local parish performances before being asked to write and direct a series of pageants at Kenilworth, Blenheim and, most important, at Wembley for the celebration of the centenary of the Restoration of the Hierarchy. At Cardinal Griffin's request he organised the revival of the Catholic Stage Guild, organised the appeal which raised £60,000 for the Tyburn Convent, and edited and recorded a commentary on the work of the Little Sisters of the Poor. The convert Rye, a Catenian since 1938, was President of the Brighton Circle, secretary and later President of Province No. 7, the inspirer of the opening of a number of Circles in Sussex and the reviver of the defunct Hastings Circle. Brothers who attend A.G.M.s see a memorial to Rye in the form of the portable altar which he designed for use when there is no church available for the celebration of High Mass.

An increasing number of Catenians were to be found among the ranks of the brancardiers at Lourdes; a few, such as John Rourke of Harrow and Bob Barrett of Bournemouth, having done many years as brancardiers, were later to make pilgrimages as patients. One man who helped organise many pilgrimages to Rome and Lourdes, George Conrad of North London Circle and for over forty years a director of the Catholic Association, was one of the founders of the Multiple Sclerosis Society and while he earned his K.C.S.G. and K.H.S. for various services to the Church, it may well be that his work for the M.S. Society will prove to be his lasting memorial.

Another work which attracted Catenian support was that of helping discharged prisoners. Many men were active in the Catholic Prisoners' Aid Society which had been founded in 1898. Michael Gregory (of Fleet) was a long-serving Chairman of the Society, which also had a long-serving Secretary in Roger Shelmerdine (of Weybridge). Perhaps the best example of Catenian activity in this field was provided by the foundation and development of the Society of St Dismas. This was formed by Fr Patrick Murphy-O'Connor (the son of a Bristol Catenian) with the help of Catenians in Winchester and Southampton. From a small beginning in 1962 the Society grew so that it quickly had five houses in which former prisoners lived while they tried to re-adjust to normal life and find work. While many Brothers played active roles in the work of the Society, none did more than Len Godwin who had already won national fame when, as a member of the Stoke-on-Trent Circle, he had founded the first 'Meals on Wheels Service' which was subsequently taken over by the W.V.S. In 1964 he became Secretary of the Society of St Dismas, and used *Catena* as a vehicle for winning support from many Catenians, notably in the shape of a single gift of £3000 made in 1969 by an anonymous Brother in London. It was sadly ironic that the newly-appointed Bishop Worlock, who had been Secretary to the Cardinal during the debate over the Chaplaincies scheme, should have dismissed Godwin and enforced the resignations of the other Catenians who had done so much to build up the Society. It is, however, pleasant to note that the Society goes on, and that it is now financially supported by grants from local and national governments.

The Association was, as ever, conscious of the religious life of its members, this, after all, being one, if not the main, concern of the founders. Province No. 11 started to hold Provincial Retreats in 1948, so carrying further the work begun by Rudman and Politi who had organised Days of Recollection in Manchester during the War. That other Provinces were quick to imitate No. 11 is a tribute to the wider Association and to the men of No. 11. Less well known is Catenian involvement with the now popular Catholic People's Week Movement, in which husbands and wives along with their children gather for a week's discussion, prayer and social activities. The first such Week was held at the Convent of the Assumption in Ramsgate in 1952, owing to 'the generous co-operation of a few leading Catenians'. The Secretary of this infant movement was Koolhoven of Ramsgate Circle while David Le Jeune of Walsall Circle was another leading light.

Organisers of Diocesan Pilgrimages to Lourdes, participants in Provincial Retreats, upholders of Catholic Education and founders of the modern Beda, the members of the Association provided that climate in which a man's spiritual development might take place. One illustration of that aspect of the work of the Association is the list of men who, having been Catenians, went on to become priests, following in the steps of men such as Archbishop Scanlan (p. 78) and Fr Le Fèvre (p. 77). In June 1955, a former member of the Stockport Circle, J.C.B. Doyle, was ordained at Hazel Grove. In 1956, the ordination of Fr C.G. Reeve was the first such ceremony in the Channel Islands for thirty years. Reeve had been President of Bromley and Beckenham in 1931–32 before entering the Beda as a late vocation in the 1950s. Another ex-Beda Catenian, Bernard Hegarty, was ordained in April 1956 at Putney. His former Brothers in Birmingham (No. 64) were proud to have him to a Circle dinner in late 1956.

4. The layman in the Modern World

However, in spite of the many examples of action being taken by individual Catenians, there was a widespread feeling that, in the more tolerant and more prosperous days of the '50s and '60s, the Association as a whole ought to be seen to be taking some form of corporate action. This was well expressed in a letter written by Thomas Hurst of West Cheshire Circle (No. 152). In December 1960, he noted:

> Many of us are concerned about: 1. The present plight of the spirit of the Association; 2. The apparent lack of interest shown by members . . .; 3. The rise in average age of membership . . .; 4. The wastage by lapsing or resignation . . .

Hurst's proposed remedies were encapsulated by the Editor of *Catena* in his call for 'the need for inculcating a new sense of purpose in the Association'. In subsequent correspondence Victor Palmer asked that Catenians take a lead in the ecumenical movement, while Bernard Woolgar suggested that Circles adopt some form of Action in their own area. In June 1961, Bro. Kane of Newcastle-upon-Tyne Circle (No. 5) summarised all the correspondence and debate by suggesting that 'what we need now is a "cause" '.

This call for a change of outlook and of action was reinforced by the request made by the Hierarchy following their Low Week meeting in April 1961. Cardinal Godfrey wrote to inform Grand Council that while the Bishops appreciated the individual activities of many Catenians, it had been resolved by the Hierarchy 'that the Catenian Association be asked to consider the possibility of widening the scope of their activities'. It was appropriate that the Grand President for 1961–62 was Laurie Arnold, a past Supreme Knight of the K.S.C. and a model of Catholic Action. In his Presidential Address at the 1961 A.G.M. held at Brighton, he recalled that the last A.G.M. held in that town had heard Pat Taggart call for vigorous Catholic Action, only for his call to fall on deaf ears both in the Association and in the Hierarchy. Arnold claimed that if Catenians lived up to the promises they made when they became members of the Association they would both be active as individuals and supportive of the activities of other Brothers. It was left to Bishop Petit, guest of honour at the banquet in Brighton, to ask 'the Association to give serious thought to the problem of University chaplaincies. The problem today was that the Bishops were called upon to provide chaplains for Universities in their dioceses. But it was a *national problem* and would *never be satisfactorily settled unless some influential body took it in hand* [my italics].' This was not the first that the members of Grand Council had heard of this 'national problem', nor was this to be the last that the Association would hear of the Bishop's request that the Association should be the 'influential body' which should act.

The ordinary members of the Association did not know that throughout 1961 and 1962 Grand Council was involved in discussions with the Hierarchy on the Chaplaincies question. Those who read their magazine and the Catholic Press should have known that, following the assembling of the Vatican Council, Catenians were being urged to reconsider the part which the laity should play in the Christian apostolate. Not all members agreed with the radical views expressed by Laurie Tanner in articles in *The Universe*, although he did have his supporters, as letters to *Catena* showed. It was left to Frank Lomas to reveal that the Association was to involve itself in the Chaplaincies scheme. In his presidential address to the 1963 A.G.M., also held at Brighton, Lomas recalled the origins of the Association, the enthusiasm of the early members, including his own father, and the hopes they had of producing Catholic leaders in various fields. He wondered whether modern Catenians were as enthusiastic or as concerned for the spread of their Catholic influence in society; and he claimed that an interest in the Chaplaincies question fell under the Association's third Object: To assist young Catholics in the pursuit of a career.

Lomas's powerful address was described as 'a turning point in our history'. For, as he had pointed out, we were, in 1963–64, living in a society which was very different from that in which Locan, O'Donnell, Gibbons and the others had founded the Association. And in view of the changes that had taken place in society, there was a need to interpret or re-interpret the Objects of the Association. That this call touched a responsive chord was indicated by the many letters appearing in *Catena,* which also carried a series of long and learned articles by Brothers and by outsiders on such topics as 'The Role of the

Laity', all of which showed both the need for lay action and, in general, the wish of many Catenians to be involved in action. There were, it is true, many who wrote to complain that they were already 'active' through membership of other organisations founded specifically for some form of action. Such men claimed that they had joined the Association precisely because it offered them a chance of getting their batteries re-charged and they pointed out that, throughout the 1950s, Cardinal Griffin and other members of the Hierarchy had spoken in appreciation of the value of that social intercourse which was conducive to the development of friendships and, as had been evident, of action by individuals.

The widespread discussions, however, in Press and in church-based meetings, made it clear that there was little point in trying to compare earlier expectations of the Hierarchy with the demands being made on the laity by the Pope and other members of the Vatican Council. We were indeed living in a new society, in which the laity were expected to play a fuller role as the People of God on the march. And it is to the credit of its leaders that, even after the collapse of the imaginative Chaplaincies scheme in 1965, the members of the Association were still asked to consider what the Association and its members ought to do, so that 'Catenian potential' should be fully realised. Many members argued that the very collapse of the Chaplaincies scheme was itself proof that real corporate activity either was not feasible or would not be allowed by a Hierarchy which had not yet come to terms with the decisions of the Vatican Council.

5. The proposed Chaplaincies Scheme

In October 1958, Grand President Alex Carus had an official audience with Cardinal Godfrey. In the course of the meeting, Godfrey asked that the Association become involved 'in work for Catholic youth. . . . Possibly the members could help with the University apostolate. I have in mind that they might assist in the establishment of University Catholic Chaplaincies. I believe that this has already taken place in Birmingham.' The Cardinal seemed unaware of the existing Catenian involvement in University Chaplaincies. The first Liverpool chaplaincy committee had been set up in 1942 under the chairmanship of Bryson of No. 4 Circle. One of its members recalls that it was supported 'consistently by many Merseyside Catenians and indeed without this . . . the continuation of the chaplaincy would be a well-nigh impossible task'. Following the Liverpool example, Rudman had become Chairman of the Committee which founded the chaplaincy at Manchester University, 'ably supported by Br. Basil Kearney of No. 28 . . .'. This Committee met at the Association's Head Office, then in Cross Street, and by 1958, when Godfrey appealed for help, this chaplaincy was 'home' for some 800 students and was still 'in charge of Catenians . . . in their private capacity, of course'.

It was surprising that the Cardinal was also unaware of Catenian response to the appeal made by the then Bishop Heenan during his speech to the A.G.M. held at Harrogate in 1951. Explaining that he had persuaded the Jesuits to provide him with a priest who would act as chaplain at Leeds University, and that he wanted the chaplain 'to be supported with a building in which the students with whom he would be working could hold their meetings', Heenan went on: 'I rely on you Catenians to supply the material side of this project.' The response of the men of Province No. 3 was such that when Heenan again addressed an A.G.M., again at Harrogate, in 1955, he expressed his thanks to the Catenians 'who had responded and were still responding to his Chaplaincies appeal and he was glad to say that the scheme was flourishing and was responsible for the establishment of chaplaincies at Leeds and Sheffield Universities'.

It is outside the scope of this book to explain the need for Catholic chaplaincies, the increase in the number of Catholic students at Universities after 1945 and, after 1965, the increase in the number of Universities and other centres of Higher Education. But it is pertinent to point out that in 1961 there were 22 Universities or University centres in Great Britain, and 10 full-time Catholic chaplains; there were 12 part-time chaplains who combined parish or other work with that of being chaplain, and few of the 10 full-time chaplains had adequate accommodation in which to function. It is also important to note that, apart from the chaplaincies at Oxford and Cambridge, the providing of chaplaincies and chaplains was the responsibility of the local Bishop. This explains Heenan's appeal in 1951. It also helps to explain why Bishop Petit of Menevia in addressing the 1961 A.G.M. should have asked the Catenians to become that 'influential body' which would tackle the question of chaplaincies as a 'national problem'. For how could a Bishop of Menevia find the funds and the priests needed to provide chaplancies at the three University or University centres in his diocese?

Petit's appeal in 1961 followed hard on the receipt of a letter addressed to Grand Council by Cardinal Godfrey, following the Low Week meeting of the Hierarchy. The Cardinal informed the Association through its Grand Council that the Hierarchy was unhappy that the activities of the Association seemed to be 'restricted in large measure to social gatherings', with its interests 'directed almost entirely to the well-being of its members'. The letter went on to ask the Association 'to consider the possibility of widening the scope of their activities, as at present envisaged in their Constitution, in view of the oft-repeated call from the Pope for increased lay action'. There is no evidence that similar letters were written to other Associations and Societies. Was the Newman Association invited to become active in the provision of housing? Was the Catholic Stage Guild, now led by Alan Rye, invited to widen the scope of its self-centred activities? Was the Catholic Teachers' Federation condemned for having limited objectives? And where, in that Hierarchical letter, was there any awareness of the work being done by Catenians in their individual capacities?

Grand Council discussed both Godfrey's letter and Petit's appeal and wrote to the Cardinal to explain the Association's wish to help with the Chaplaincies problem. Grand Council explained, however: 'the problem is one that can only be dealt with nationally . . . your Eminence will realise the difficulties which face us as a national Association in approaching a problem which hitherto has been managed locally.' Grand Council suggested a meeting with representative Bishops to consider the Chaplaincy question.

Bishop Beck, then of Salford, had been appointed by the Hierarchy to oversee the Chaplaincies question. In May 1962, he met a delegation from Grand Council which was armed with a series of questions to put to the Bishop.

INTERVIEW WITH BISHOP BECK RE CHAPLAINCIES

1. *The Problem*
   (a) The Universities, and therefore the Chaplaincies, are unevenly distributed through the Dioceses.
   (b) The catchment area of the Universities has no limit either in terms of Diocesan boundaries or Local Government areas.
   (c) The responsibility for the provision and maintenance of Chaplaincies is the responsibility of the whole Catholic community.
   (d) It is a national problem.
2. *The Size of the Problem*
   (a) How many Chaplains are there: (i) part-time; (ii) whole-time?
   (b) What is the cost of maintaining them?
   (c) How many Chaplaincy buildings are there?
   (d) What is the cost of maintaining them?
   (e) How many new Chaplaincy buildings are required: (i) now; (ii) in the next ten years?
   (f) What is the estimated cost of providing them?
3. *A possible solution*
   (a) The collection of the Funds to be undertaken on a National Basis.
   (b) The distribution of the money to be allocated by a National Committee.
4. *Further information required*
   (a) Will laymen be accepted on a National Committee?
   (b) Will all Dioceses loyally co-operate?
   (c) What would be the future of Diocesan Chaplaincy Committees?
   (d) Are any other Societies, in particular the Newman Association, interesting themselves in this problem?

6. *The collapse of the Scheme – and after*

Following that meeting, Beck promised to consult his fellow-Bishops, who by then were also busily involved in the work of the Vatican Council. In the meantime Grand Council discussed the problem, and proposed the setting up of a Trust Corporation of representatives of the Hierarchy and laity, to be responsible for the whole problem of the chaplaincies and to raise the money for the chaplaincies and the maintenance of the chaplains.

Beck considered the Association's proposals and, in December 1962, replied with a mixture of good news and bad. The good news was that the Van Neste Foundation was interested in being financially involved in the proposed national scheme. The bad news was that the Bishops had made only 'limited progress' in their discussions of the Association's proposals, that the Scottish Bishops had decided to have nothing to do with it at all, while 'several of the Bishops think that they would do better by organising a local or regional appeal for their University chaplaincies and that local interest would be more than offset by the attractiveness of a national appeal'.

Following the 1963 Low Week Meeting of the Hierarchy, however, the Bishops agreed to the setting up of a steering committee which might produce a clearer picture of what was proposed. The outcome of this was a Conference in July 1963 at which Beck presided. Chaplains, University lecturers,

Catenians, representatives from the Catholic Union and from the Van Neste Foundation, discussed the Association's proposals and instructed Past President Cyril Grobel to draw up a draft Trust Deed for the proposed Corporation, the directors of which were to be six Bishops, four representatives appointed by the Association, Dr Stevens of the Van Neste Foundation, and a nominee of the Catholic Union.

But the enthusiasm of the representatives of the Association did not meet with a similar response from the Hierarchy. Beck wrote to explain that he could not get them together to discuss the proposals, and that Bishop Dwyer, then of Leeds, was opposed to any scheme which would cut across local efforts. During the autumn of 1963, three Bishops were appointed to represent the Hierarchy in negotiations with the Association. Bishop Beck of Salford was the chief spokesman, the other two Bishops being Dwyer of Leeds, who had already made known his opposition to the scheme, and Cowderoy of Southwark who was later to refuse to attend meetings or to accept an invitation to be one of the Bishops appointed to serve on the Trust Corporation. This was hardly an auspicious development.

But the Association's enthusiasm appeared boundless. In spite of Beck's warnings, Dwyer's explicit opposition and Cowderoy's lack of support, the Association sent copies of its proposals to each member of the Hierarchy. At the same time Tanner addressed a gathering of chaplains to explain the proposals. Their response was one of delight: one wrote of 'the splendid news', another of 'hopeful expectations', and a third of 'sincere gratitude for the initiative taken by the Association . . . a milestone in the Catholic life of this country . . .'. Grand Council was so confident that the Hierarchy would approve the scheme at their 1964 Low Week Meeting that incoming Grand President, Bernard Daly, planned to make the announcement of the scheme the centrepiece of his presidential address to the 1964 A.G.M. But, in April 1964, Beck wrote to say that the Bishops were unhappy about the Trust Deed and certain details of the proposed national collection. He asked for further meetings before a final decision was made.

Bernard Daly was disappointed, and the Editor of *Catena* was so angry that he accused the Bishops of vacillating and of being unable or unwilling to match the enthusiasm of the representatives of the Association. This did nothing to help win friends or influence the Hierarchy, despite attempts by Tanner and Lomas to smooth ruffled feathers. But further talks were held in July 1964, changes were made in the proposed Trust Deed, and copies were sent to each Bishop. Further changes were made after amicable meetings in September, and, to Catenian delight, Beck telegraphed from the Vatican that the Hierarchy had approved the revised Deed and Regulations. The Association now published its pamphlet, *Catholic Academic Chaplaincies*, which also appeared as a supplement in *Catena* in December 1964.

It was then that the rank-and-file members of the Association learned that the Association was committing itself to a scheme for the raising of 'one to two million pounds'. The main sources of this vague but vast sum were to be:

1. A *National Collection* to be ordered by the Hierarchy;
2. The Van Neste Foundation, which would donate £20,000 a year;
3. *The Catenian Association.* Each Circle would pay over to Grand Council £5 *per capita* for each member on the roll, which would raise some £30,000 a year from the Circles in England and Wales. The Association

would make this contribution for seven years and 'thereafter substantial support for the Trust will be regarded as a regular Catenian commitment'.

Circles were asked to vote on the scheme. In February 1965, Grand Council had the results of the voting. Only about 50 per cent of members had bothered to vote, and some 75 per cent of these had voted to support the scheme. In spite of this 'natural' apathy, Grand Council proposed that its representatives meet Beck and the other Bishop-representatives for a final meeting on 5 May, when Grand Council and other Catenians would be present at a Memorial Service for Paul Kelly. What better preparation could there have been for the launching of this new, bold, imaginative scheme!

7. To be active?

Then, on 4 May, Tanner received a handwritten note from Beck, who, apparently, had not been able to find time either to call on or to telephone the Grand Secretary:

> Dear Tanner,
> I had to leave for Rome on Wednesday morning and did not get back until last night. This is therefore the first chance I have had of writing to you since the Low Week Meeting of the Hierarchy.
> The Bishops were very disturbed to learn that the Van Neste Foundation was unlikely to co-operate in the Catholic Academic Chaplaincies Trust proposals, and are persuaded that the chaplaincies will be financed more effectively by local efforts rather than by a national appeal. They are not disposed, therefore, to proceed with the Chaplaincies Trust scheme.
> I think, however, that we ought to go on with the meeting which has been arranged for Archbishop's House for 2.30 p.m. on Wednesday so that we can get the situation clarified as far as possible.
> I shall be in London from tomorrow morning staying at the Sainte Union Convent, Highgate Road, N.W.5.
> With a blessing and all good wishes,
> yours sincerely,
> G.A. Beck.

The meeting held on 5 May was a gloomy affair and by no means the triumphal start of the new venture. Grand Council met a little later, and wrote to express disappointment at the rejection, at such a late hour, of a scheme to which the Bishops had apparently given their consent. A Press statement was issued on 12 June during the A.G.M., announcing the abandonment of the scheme. The incoming Grand President, George Harris, had to re-write his presidential address, for he had been led to believe that the scheme would be launched prior to the A.G.M.

Ironically, Beck was a guest at that A.G.M. He had a series of talks with Grand Council in which 'the sense of injustice and resentment against the Hierarchy felt by many Catenians' was fully expressed. That 'resentment' lay behind a spate of angry letters to *Catena* throughout the rest of 1965. Some accused the Bishops of 'narrow self-interest'; others wrote of the 'entrenched paternalism' of the Hierarchy, who, said another, 'regard the possibility of an active, educated laity with disfavour or distaste'. Some invited Brothers to 'complain loudly', while others said that such complaints would receive little attention, for the Association would be 'banging its head against a solid brick wall'.

Cardinal Heenan did his best to assuage the anger. In April 1966, he held the first-ever Catenian gathering at Archbishop's House for past and present members of Grand Council and representatives from each Province. In addressing the gathering, Heenan explained the Vatican Council's call for greater lay involvement and for the need for a national effort for University chaplaincies. He went on: 'I believe that Catenians will be the spearhead of the movement. . . . Unhappily mistakes had been made and misunderstandings had occurred; this little party I have given is my way of saying, "We are sorry".'

The collapse of this ambitious scheme did not mean the end of Catenian involvement. Alban Curtis of Circle 47 was Treasurer of the Committee aiming to raise £150,000 for a new chaplaincy at Manchester. Bishop Cowderoy, the opponent of the national scheme, launched an appeal for the Sussex University Chaplaincy. He may not have known that all save one of the Appeal Committee were Catenians, and that Brother Sidney Ohly used his Catenian connections to obtain a loan of £7000 from Catena Trustees to help fund the building of the Sussex Chaplaincy. *Catena* was used as a medium of appeal by men organising appeals for chaplaincies at Oxford and Reading. When a Chaplaincy Management Committee was set up in Nottingham, the President of No. 20 (Michael Donovan) became Chairman of a Committee which contained a number of Brothers and their wives. . . . In 1971 I attended a meeting at Birmingham with my Chaplain. I found that the majority of Chaplaincies which were being run had, quietly and unostentatiously, been run by Catenians.'

8. An activist's appreciation

That same Michael Donovan who was so busily involved in the Nottingham Chaplaincy project also wrote:

> The Chaplaincy nonsense is typical of us. Misled by our dinner jackets we [*sic*] were asked for money, a fairly hopeless task for a Society based on men rearing families, and our other potential contributions in terms of management skills were rejected.

He then wrote an appreciation of the Association which few members would quarrel with and which might help outsiders to understand it the better:

> We are specifically Catholic but we have no emphasised pastoral aims, nor are we 'anti' anything. But where good aims are being effectively pursued you will find us or our wives quietly contributing, but not with their Catenian badges showing. We go quietly to the root of matters in developing in ourselves more profoundly an awareness of the Catholic family. Our social functions appear to be pretentious whether we are by ourselves or with our ladies – our dinner jackets and bedizened wives looking, at least to the superficial eye, horribly smug. We who have attended the Association's functions have sensed that deeply founded and deeply glowing warmth of friendship and deeply secure regard and a quiet joy in life which makes them so enjoyable – in our otherwise deeply insecure and unhappy modern world the quality is very, very elusive. My own reason for joining the Association arose from my initial contact with the late Llewellyn Davies of the West Surrey Circle. He was a very quiet man but a perceptive eye became aware of the sheer spiritual depth, the sheer spiritual grandeur, quiet as it was deep, of the man. I have felt my membership to be of such value because, in many various and often highly contrasting guises, I have met within the Association men of equivalent true and fundamental worth, and can call to mind a host of men, many of them dead but

many living, with whom I have shared the most wonderful friendship and from whom I have received the most priceless example.

O'Donnell and the other original Chums would have approved of that appreciation of the Association which might be taken as sufficient answer to those who would have it change.

CHAPTER FIFTEEN

The Aftermath of the Vatican Council 1965–1975

1. Failure and reality

Few periods in history have been more written about than this, and almost all of the 'documents' reveal a confused world, in which fantasy tended to overcome reality until the last years of the period. In *The Pendulum Years*, Bernard Levin analysed the fantasies of British politicians which led to the printing of ever-increasing quantities of increasingly worthless money and a rise in the rate of inflation until prices were rising at 25 per cent a year. In *The Young Meteors*, Jonathan Aitken gave thumbnail sketches of the young people who, in the 1960s, promised to change, for the better, the face of Britain. To read even the list of contents is to be reminded of the fantasies of the Swinging Sixties.

In education there were 'progressive experiments' in which babies disappeared with the bathwater. Authority broke down in the classroom, in the home and in society at large, as one fantasy was replaced by another. In the Church too, there were recurring crises in the uncertain years following the ending of the Vatican Council. In *Three Popes and a Cardinal*, Malachi Martin analysed the nature of the crisis facing the post-Vatican II era, in which theologians such as Hans Küng (*On Being a Christian*) attacked the power of 'the Montini Pope', in which the English Hierarchy declared in favour of *Humanae Vitae* while at the same time telling people to follow their own consciences, with a seemingly endless number of priests seeking 'liberation' outside the priesthood, some within weeks of being ordained.

It is not surprising that the Catenian Association was affected by the climate of fantasy and by the economic crises through which Britain blundered ever downwards. There was, for example, this portion of a Grand Presidential address, made on the occasion of the Association's sixtieth birthday, in which Joe Cox was explaining the relative stagnation of the Association after 1923:

> There are many factors to consider; any or all of them could have contributed to the pause in expansion. For example: (1) Grand Council came into existence; (2) Provinces were formed, given much authority, and few lived up to their new responsibilities; (3) Bro. Shepherd retired in 1923 when some 73 Circles had been established; (4) Bro. Frank Rudman had taken over the Grand Secretary's position and the head office moved to London; (5) And finally there had been an economic depression and the Second World War.
> That brings us to 1947 when Bro. Laurence Tanner came to the head office.... The graph commenced to climb again.... In the period 1947 to 1967 a further 100 Circles were added bringing the total to 240 with a membership of approximately 10,000. If we accept that the present growth is to continue there would in the next twenty years be approximately another 100 Circles with a further increase of 6000 to 7000 members, giving a total of 340 Circles and an approximate membership of between 15,000 and 17,000.

185

The unfairness of the (maybe unintended) smear on Rudman was matched by the unjustified link between post-war expansion and the fact that 'Tanner came to the head office'. For the immediate post-war expansion took place while Rudman was still in office. Tanner did not take charge of the Association's head office until 1952–53. The dismissal of the 'economic depression and the Second World War' as major factors in the Association's slow development is matched by the fantasy about future expansion.

For the fact is that, while in the period 1965–75 the Association opened 51 new Circles, it showed only a small increase in total membership. When Bernard Daly inaugurated the Fife St Margaret Circle in November 1964, he pointed out that none of the members of this new Circle had been Catenians prior to this inauguration. Most of the other new Circles opened in this decade were offshoots of existing Circles, with a proportion of their membership coming from these older Circles. The failure to attract wider support was tackled by Grand President Harry Hipkin in his address at the 1970 A.G.M. in Torquay. He asked, 'Where does the failure lie?' but he did not suggest that the Grand Secretary was to blame. Nor did Hipkin offer any answers to his own question. Certainly there was an obvious need for the Association. As Rex Kirk pointed out:

> The intention of our founders was that through social contacts, we Catholics should support each other morally and materially in a hostile world. While our social milieu is no longer so openly hostile, it is indifferent, or even contemptuous of all religious or spiritual thought. It is resentful of any restriction on the satisfaction of its material pleasures on any spiritual grounds. *The need then for mutual support is greater than ever before* [my italics].

But in spite of Kirk's words and of the value of the Association to its members, there did not take place that expansion of which Cox had spoken so enthusiastically. In 1971 there was hardly any growth in membership, while in 1974, the last year for which Tanner might be held responsible, there was actually a decline in membership.

Grand Council pushed through a number of major changes during this period, hoping to make the Association somewhat more streamlined and 'relevant' to potential members. Grand President Bernard Daly suggested, in his Presidential address, that the Association's Rule Book should be examined with a view to 'what is of rule being put into a new Rule Book while what is of regulation being transferred to a Manual of Procedure'. Daly recalled that Frank Pendergast had commented many years ago on the fact that God had only needed ten commandments whereas Grand Council required some 77 Rules to regulate a relatively small Association. After three years' hard work a revised Rule Book, about one-third the length of its precedessor, was approved in 1968. A new *Manual of Procedure* also appeared, only to be revised, until in 1972 a new *Manual* was issued which showed several changes with the past. The Ritual was modernised; some of the traditional offices were abolished – who now remembers the functions of the Vice-President's Marshal or of the Guard? The salutation to 'Worthy Brother President' was abolished, while members were permitted to address one another in the Circle by Christian names. Subsequently Grand Council has tried to ban this informal manner of address, but with no success.

This 'turning in on itself' was a feature of this period. There was, for example, the work of the Jenkins Committee on Re-organisation. There was, more important, the financial reforms inspired by Joe Cox before and after he became Grand President. In August 1966, Cox was at a meeting of the South Manchester Circle when Stanley Jones suggested that every Circle should transfer its account to the Belgravia Branch of the National Bank, where Grand Council had an overdraft of £48,000 following the purchase of Chesham Place. Cox 'agreed to place the matter before Grand Council . . .'. The upshot was a Circular from Grand Council in which Cox explained that the National Bank had agreed that, providing that the Association's credit balance totalled at least £48,000, there would be no interest charge on the overdraft. 'An examination of the balance sheets of the Provincial Councils and Circles has shown that this is well within the range of the Association's finances.' In a sense, Grand Council would be borrowing, at *nil* interest, moneys previously standing in current accounts in the banks of Circles and Provincial Councils. As Grand President, Cox was able to report that the bulk of Circles had answered his appeal by transferring their accounts. Cox had other ideas for raising money. He advocated that men be encouraged to purchase Life Membership for £200, claiming that if only one-fifth of the members entered this scheme 'a capital sum of over £400,000 would be available for investment'. To attract support for this scheme, the Association promised to hand the £200 back to the executors of a deceased Life Member, which meant, in effect, that such members had their membership for only the notional interest they might have received from investing the £200. It was fortunate for the future of the Association that fewer than twenty members took up this scheme. Cox also called for higher subscriptions as another means of putting what he described as 'some wool on our backs'. But here too his appeal had limited success. Professional and business men who paid continually increasing fees to their professional Associations or Societies were reluctant to agree to Grand Council requests for higher fees. Only in 1971 did they approve an increase (to £1 per member) of payment into the Benevolent Fund. It is not surprising that the money available for Benevolence, while rising in nominal terms, actually declined in real terms.

The onset of the recession in 1972–73 saw an increase in the work of Provincial Redundancy Officers and in the burden which fell on the shoulders of Grand Council's Redundancy Officer, Jim McNabb. He produced a redundancy scheme which, as he explained, 'depended on the interest and co-operation of the whole membership'. This scheme was not as ambitious as the Service schemes of the 1920s, but the work involved played a part in the decline in McNabb's health which, in 1975, led to his being forced to resign the office of Grand Vice-President, one more victim to the problems facing an Association which, like the nation as a whole, had finally learned to come to terms with reality after so many years of trying to live with fantasy.

2. *'Dressed for dinner' only?*

In addressing the 1966 A.G.M., the newly-appointed Bishop Cashman spoke of the need for a re-thinking of the Association's Aims and Objects: 'The image of the Catenians as a section of the People of God dressed for dinner and dancing is not good enough,' said the Bishop. Few of those at the A.G.M. were annoyed at this appeal for re-thinking. Indeed, the Association had been debating that very topic for some years, with Lomas's Presidential address of

1963 as a high spot in the debate. It was the wider membership which was irritated. Many men pointed to the various Catholic activities in which they were already engaged. Some claimed that the Bishop was either unfortunate in that 'he had not been properly briefed' or else guilty of 'taking improper advantage of his position as our guest'.

Most of those who were present at the A.G.M. took Cashman's 'image of the Catenians' statement as a leg-pull from a Bishop who was well known to be a friend to the Association and to the considerable number of Catenians with whom he worked closely during his many years as Chairman of the Catholic Association. Indeed, it was Cashman who had invited Frank Lloyd to become a director of that Association, where he joined Conrad and Francis Cuss on the Board. Cashman had also been closely involved in the development of the Serra Movement where, again, he met many leading Catenians.

His Brighton speech and the unfortunate reaction to it of many who had not heard him led to a rift in the relationship between the Bishop and some members of the Association. Through the Catholic Association and other organisations, however, he continued to meet many Catenians. Some six months before he died in March 1971, the Board of the Catholic Association held a meeting at St Joseph's Hall, Storrington, instead of compelling the Bishop to travel to London. At a lunch following the meeting, Frank Lloyd pointed out that nine of the ten present were Catenians.

But it has to be said that the Bishop was only expressing an unease felt by many 'activist' members of the Association. Referring yet again to Lomas's address, Kirchner of *Catena* invoked Newman's support for the need for change. Newman had claimed that '. . . a society embodying a living idea must change in time; if it does not it will decay.' Taking up the principle of the need for change, Lomas and another Past Grand President, Palmer, combined to produce *Time for Reappraisal of Catenian Potential*, in which they called for a fresh look at the Association's Aims and Objects in the light of the calls made on the laity by the Vatican Council. Debates in Circles and letters to *Catena* showed that few ordinary members shared their views. Many claimed that 'action' would split the Association, arguing that such a split would have been revealed by the Chaplaincies scheme. Others wrote of 'pretentious leadership and administrative excess of zeal' being responsible for the vain pursuit of an active Association. Such critics pointed out that 'it was folly to assume that because a Brother is a Catenian he has no wish to take part in Catholic action; equally it is folly to assume that unless our Association takes up the cudgels Catholic action will suffer'. Indeed, but surprisingly, this was the theme of an attack on 'activists' made in 1967 by that very Palmer who had called for a reappraisal in 1965. More significant was the comment by Kirchner that those who saw members only at festive occasions got the wrong impression of the work of the members and the value of the Association. This warning was best expressed by Lord Wheatley who, addressing the Jubilee Banquet of 1968, said:

> While by its nature the Association may be limited in the contribution it could make as an organisation, the Hierarchy could rest assured that its individual members would be in the vanguard of activity through those channels whereby the laity can make their most effective contribution.

But, in spite of such warning statements, the quest for 'new targets' continued. There was, for example, the call in one letter for the admission of the clergy to membership and for the admission of non-Catholic husbands of

Catholic wives. Joe McMurray showed how far this would take the Association from the intentions of its founders, while another Manchester man re-stated the main Aim of the Association as being

> for professional and executive Catholic laymen who are well aware that the society in which they live and work is one where the moral and materialistic views which pervade that society are foreign to them . . . they have been greatly helped by the support and example of their Catholic fellow who is sharing the same burden and facing the same problems. This, I feel sure, is the primary object of our Association.

This too was the main theme of the Association's pamphlet on 'Our Relevance To-day' which was produced by a committee over which the active and practical Frank Lloyd presided.

But the call for reappraisal was still heard in 1975. One 'activist' proposed that each Circle should devote part of its meeting to 'the discussion of their Faith and its practical implication in their own sphere of work'. Leo Simmonds, Kirchner's successor as Editor of *Catena*, had suggested something on these lines in 1973 when he compared a Circle meeting to

> the refectory gathering at a University. Men from diverse disciplines meet in hall and inevitably begin to discuss whatever exercises their private consciences. So it is at the gathering after a Circle meeting. Ideas are shared. Points are argued. Resolutions are made.

Simmonds was, in fact, commenting on the work of the Serra Movement, the first lay organisation to be designated for the Pontifical work for priestly vocations founded by Pope Pius XII. This organisation's work was explained in *Catena* in 1965, by which time it had been brought to the south of England by a Catenian, Jim Daly. The first President of the London Club was Frank Lloyd, and 21 of the original 26 members were Catenians. Much of the work of recruiting for the Movement came from within the ranks of the Association, and the spread of the Movement in this country owed a great deal to the formation of The National Council of Serra, the brainchild of Lloyd, Mahon and Conlon, all Catenians. From this quickly grew the National Council of Directors of Vocations under the leadership of Fr Denis Fairclough. After Vatican II and the formation of various Hierarchical Commissions, Serra was represented for many years on the Commission for Priestly Formation by Frank Lloyd. It is currently represented by Gerald Murphy of the City of London, who was to go on to become the first European International President of Serra International. It was Murphy who, after explaining the work of the Movement and the value of the contribution made by individual Catenians, went on:

> I joined [the Association] to meet other Catholic professional men. I knew very few when I joined. In fact, the Catenians took me into Serra and politics. I remain in the Catenians because it enables me, once a month, to enjoy a remarkably good evening with people I have grown to love, and without any responsibility of having to do something, or feel guilty for not having done it. I see this as being the great value of the Association. It contains men, almost all of whom belong to an active Catholic organisation, who enjoy meeting for purely social reasons. It is also a good recruiting ground for these other organisations. . . . I do not want the Association to be other than social because I find that it provides something which my other activities don't and which I need to activate me in them. I believe this gives the Association an important role which should be highlighted because there are many of the Hierarchy, clergy and fellow-laymen who misunderstand our purpose.

The Association is not a section of the People of God dressed for dinner. It is Catholic Action at rest.

3. Action for the handicapped

There was ample evidence of that Action. Publicity about the Society of St Dismas led to articles about Catenian involvement in the longer-established Catholic Prisoners' Social Service (formerly the Prisoners' Aid Society) of which the Secretary was Roger Shelmerdine of Weybridge Circle. Some Brothers undertook the work of visiting prisons as members of the S.V.P., another favourite form of Catenian 'action'. Catenians were active in the St Francis Leprosy Guild, of which the President was Harold Hood, and continued to play an active role in the work of the Plater College, formerly the Catholic Workers' College.

Some were active in the political field and, in addition to the continuing number of Catenians who served on local councils, there were, in 1966 and 1970, a number who stood as candidates in Parliamentary elections. The Association welcomed the victories of Simon Mahon, W.T. Wells, Hugh Rossi and James Dunn while commiserating with Catenians who were defeated, including G.W. Fitzsimons, G.J. Tordoff, J.M. Bowyer, P. Crotty and Leo Simmonds. A less publicised form for some Brothers' activity was the Samaritans. The columns of *Catena* showed that many Circles had other forms of local 'action'. The Axminster Circle 'raised a not inconsiderable sum of money for the benefit of a Cheshire Home in the vicinity'. Brothers from the North Warwickshire Circle raised large sums of money to save the Convent of Poor Clares (Colettines) in Baddesley Clinton before helping to form a Committee of Friends of the Poor Clares in 1973. Wigan Brothers raised money for the local handicapped children's society, while Brothers from the Stoke-on-Trent Circle adopted the Douglas McMillan Home for cancer and other patients as their special charity. Local Nazareth Homes in Cardiff and elsewhere continued to receive the almost traditional Catenian support, while the more recently established Catholic Housing Aid Society, as well as local attempts to deal with the housing problem (such as Abbeyfield ventures), were the outlets for many Catenian 'activists'.

But in this period the work of Catenians for the handicapped overshadowed every other form of action and may, one suggests, be seen as a tribute to the vigour, imagination and initiative of the men of this time. This work took four distinct forms, all of which had the one theme of providing help for handicapped people. There was, first, the Handicapped Children's Pilgrim Trust, which had its beginnings in 1954 when a young doctor took four handicapped children by train to Lourdes. The numbers of handicapped pilgrims increased, until by 1957 forty children and forty voluntary helpers went on the pilgrimage. Catenian interest in the handicapped was already well established: over the years, hundreds of Catenians had acted as brancardiers at Lourdes, some prior to becoming sick pilgrims themselves. It was almost natural for Catenians to become involved in the work of the H.C.P.T., which by 1976 had over 100 groups responsible for sending 1000 handicapped children and 1000 voluntary helpers for the 'Holiday with our Lady'.

Catena carried appeals for financial assistance for the Trust, the Secretary of which was Pat Porter of the South West London Circle, which also provided the Deputy Treasurer, Pat Hall. In 1965, 134 Catenians placed themselves and their cars at the service of the Trust, while hundreds of others worked to provide the £10,000 needed to take children to Lourdes in 1966. Some Circles held special functions to raise money. Others accepted responsibility for the cost of a certain number of children: London Charterhouse 'sent three handicapped children'. Brothers from Bromley and the vicinity were active in support of the Orpington branch of the Catholic Handicapped Children's Fellowship, which in five years sent 350 children to Lourdes. A major force in that branch was Kenneth Seagar, a member of the Bromley Circle. A consultant obstetrician, Seagar has retired from work to look after a handicapped wife, whose illness had been aggravated by having to look after an epileptic son, the experience of which gave Seagar his deep interest in work for the handicapped.

While this work for the H.C.P.T. continued, the attention of Catenians was drawn to the plight of the mentally handicapped. Jean Vanier, the son of a former Governor-General of Canada, was already well known in France for his work for the mentally handicapped when, in 1969, he had the idea of taking some mentally handicapped children on a pilgrimage. News of the proposed pilgrimage reached British ears through the activities of a number of Birmingham Catholic ladies. A National Committee was formed to raise money to take about 400 mentally handicapped British children to Lourdes. John Bowen promised Catenian help, but he could never have envisaged the generosity of Catenian response. The Faith and Light Pilgrimage was so popular that Catenians raised over £10,000 and were responsible for over half the mentally handicapped children who enjoyed their own 'Holiday with our Lady'.

Meanwhile, in 1970, the affairs of the H.C.P.T. had taken a new turn. A group of helpers, including a number of Catenians, while on retreat in Lourdes, came to appreciate that many of the handicapped children who had been taken on pilgrimage between 1954 and 1970 were now too old for the children's pilgrimage, albeit anxious to make another visit to Lourdes. It also became clear that handicapped people needed even more encouragement in their late teens and twenties. There was no provision in Lourdes for such handicapped youngsters; the hotels were built to cater for the able-bodied, the hospitals for the chronically sick.

This was the background to the decision to build a modern hostel specially designed for the handicapped, a decision which led to the opening of Hosanna House. Appeals were made to raise the money needed, and Grand President Frank Lloyd urged members to give the new venture the sort of support they had given to the Faith and Light Pilgrimage. Brothers Sidney Quick, W.A. Ridgers and (author of the whole scheme) Dick Glithero served on the unofficial committee which was set up by Grand Council to further the appeal and was to go ahead with plans to find the £200,000 which would be needed to build the House. In appealing to the generosity of Catenians, members of the committee showed that the Hosanna House scheme was a logical offshoot from the work of the H.C.P.T. which was already the focal point for much Catenian activity.

Inflation led the committee to abandon its original plan of building a new House. Instead, in 1971, a hotel was purchased in the fields of Bartrès where St Bernadette had tended her sheep. The refurbished house was opened in April 1975. Pat Porter became National Secretary of the Hosanna House Trust set up to raise the money to pay for the House and to provide the amenities which would be needed to make it better fitted to take the handicapped youngsters for whom it was intended.

Dick Glithero and his Catenian supporters on the two Trusts carried the work a stage further in 1973 when it became clear that transport by hospital trains was becoming less and less feasible. The Across Trust purchased a 'jumbo' ambulance – which quickly became known as a 'Jumbulance' – for carrying invalids, sick and handicapped pilgrims on cross-Channel ferries and road. The first vehicle was completed in April 1973 and carried ten bed-passengers and ten seated passengers. It was Glithero who coined the slogan: 'As the train can no longer take the strain, why not go Across to Lourdes?' Several Catenians were involved in the launch of the £50,000 Jumbulance service, built with the aid of three interest-free loans from Catenians and, as Glithero wrote, of great trust in God and Our Lady.

In January 1974, Grand President John Bowen invited the members of the Association to adopt the task of providing a second Jumbulance to further the work of the Trust. Laurie Tanner had been an active worker in Lourdes for many years and an active supporter of the work of the H.C.P.T. and Across Trust. Glithero acknowledges his debt to Tanner in getting the idea of a Catenian Jumbulance through Grand Council, which led to his being invited to join the Board of Trustees. The £25,000 needed to pay for this example of Catenian activity was raised in 1974–75. Since then, this Jumbulance has been completely rebuilt by Van Hool of Belgium, who are now responsible for the supplying and maintenance of a fleet of Jumbulances. It is regretted by many members that Grand Council, having urged Brothers to provide a Jumbulance, did not agree to make the maintenance of the vehicle a Catenian responsibility. Some Brothers, such as J.M. Johnson, of Middleton Circle (No. 209), and G.A.N. Harty, of Huddersfield Circle (No. 145), had long been volunteer drivers of the Jumbulance; and many Circles continue to raise large sums of money each year at functions organised for just this purpose, so that Catenian interest in its Jumbulance continues, and so does Catenian involvement with the H.C.P.T., Across Trust and Hosanna House. It may seem fitting that a decade (1965–75) which started with the Hierarchy's rejection of a Catenian offer to provide some £30,000 a year for the proposed Chaplaincies scheme should have ended with such evidence of Catenian involvement and generosity.

4. Relations with the Hierarchy

The critical attitude towards Church authority was taken a stage further by an article which appeared in *Catena* in November 1965. In his article, 'Freedom and Authority – The Wasted Years', Laurie Tanner argued that Popes and Bishops had, since the First Vatican Council, become increasingly authoritarian, anti-intellectual and over-fearful of even the mildest criticism. There was, and is, some evidence for these claims, which were reiterated in later articles in 1976, when the argument was extended to an attack on the Church's teaching on artificial contraception, with Tanner writing: 'The Church will change its teaching because it is coming to realise that its teaching is wrong.'

Few Catenians were willing to go this far down the road of criticism, however angered they may have been by the Bishops' rejection of the Chaplaincies scheme. Some wrote to complain of the 'peculiar' and 'obnoxious' language used in the articles, while one writer referred to the apparent emergence of a new heresy, 'Tannerism', 'obviously ill thought out and at variance with the truth'. In an article, 'On Defending Shibboleths', Tanner defended himself against his critics, who were even further angered by his use of Hans Küng's work in his attacks on infallibility and the current teaching on birth control.

Indeed, some argued that Tanner, and presumably the Editor of *Catena*, were breaking that golden rule which forbids wrangling and dissension. It was, perhaps, fortunate that Bishop Cashman made his statement at the 1966 A.G.M. and took much Catenian interest away from the intellectual argument. There was also a 'turning inwards' as members discussed the call for Reappraisal voiced by Lomas and Palmer which led to the setting up of a committee to examine the role of the Association in the light of the Vatican Council's Decree on the Laity. Individual members of that committee prepared statements on 'Policy – Bearing in Mind the Decree on the Lay Apostolate', which showed a deep knowledge of the Association and the work being done by its individual members and a wish that this knowledge could be somehow better shared with the Hierarchy. Each of the statements used quotations from the Council's Decree to show how the Association was fulfilling the call made by that Decree upon lay people – to be active in their individual lives, to support each other by social gatherings, to make the family the centre of life, and to carry their Christian ideal into their place of work.

These individual statements led to the production of a Report which showed clearly that the Catenian Objects and practice provided a means of fulfilling a positive role in the apostolic mission.

While that Report was at the printers, the Hierarchy invited Grand Council to make known to Cardinal Heenan 'the important ethical subjects on which clear guidance should be given' in a statement which the Bishops proposed to publish. Many other Catholic organisations received a similar invitation on what was 'the first occasion upon which the Bishops' Conference has directly approached so wide a segment of Catholic opinion . . .'. Grand Council invited members to send in their comments, and 103 replies were received. In July 1970, Grand Council submitted a very long Report which presented 'a consensus of opinion under a variety of heads covering broadly every topic that is currently giving rise to concern: education, civil authority, racialism, industrial relations, the under-privileged, humanism, marriage and the family, sexuality, conscience'. Given the wide-ranging nature of the Report and the fact that it was the first time that lay people had been invited to make such submissions, it is not surprising that many Catenians were shocked by what they read. Some accused Grand Council of using language which, instead of merely 'suggesting', tended to offer 'instructions to the Hierarchy'. Others found fault with the declared and implied criticisms of authority and with the almost *ex cathedra* statements made by 'non-specialist laymen' on complex topics such as teen-age sexuality. Christopher Bussy, however, who had played a part in 'the preparation of submissions from three other bodies as well as from our Association', claimed that 'of them all, our submission in its range, its wisdom and the dignity and tact with which it is expressed, is by far the best I have seen, even though it may not be perfect'.

Before that Report had been completed, in June 1970 Cardinal Heenan invited the views of lay organisations on the work of the provisional Ecclesiastical Commissions which had been set up in 1967. Douglas Jenkins chaired a powerful Committee which produced a major document which was sent to Cardinal Heenan in March 1971, along with forty copies for distribution to the Hierarchy before the Low Week meeting.

While analysing the need for and the work of the Commissions, the Report criticised them, pointing out that, for example, there were no laymen on the Education Commission, that the Religious Commission, composed of three Bishops, had only operated during the past year, and that the Seminaries Commission, composed of eight Bishops, had refused to co-operate with the Jenkins Committee. The Report also suggested the formation of two new Commissions – one for Industrial Relations and one to be called the Pastoral Commission. In all this, the Report was forthright and constructively critical.

Having submitted the Report to the Cardinal, Grand Council was disappointed with the Cardinal's reply that he would not be sending the Report to the whole Hierarchy. 'The Committee of five Bishops has had several meetings and will be holding the final meeting within the next few days. We are not burdening the Hierarchy with the voluminous evidence which has come to hand.' Offended by this rebuff, Grand Council then sent copies of the Report to the various Bishops and to various papers. *The Times* gave the Report a good deal of attention, but was outdone by the room given it in the Catholic Press. Headlines such as GIVE LAITY MORE SCOPE: CATENIAN ATTACK ON CHURCH COMMISSIONS appeared above articles carrying favourable comments on the Catenian Report. Bishop Worlock, a member of the Committee considering the lay submissions, wrote:

> As doubtless you will have appreciated, evidence from the Catholic organisations was invited for submission by the end of December last, but apart from this, I was a little surprised to see that a Press Conference had been held and the text of the Comments released to the Press before the Committee's Report had even reached the members of the Review Committee.

Tanner's reply pointed out that when the Association was asked to make its submission there had been no suggestion of a December deadline. Nor, he added, was it the fault of the Association if copies of the Comments had not yet been handed to the members of the Review Committee. It must have been the Cardinal's decision not to allow even members of the Review Committee to have sight of the Association's Report. It was because the Association wanted its voice to be heard that it had sent copies to various newspapers.

That some, at least, welcomed this Catenian initiative was clear from letters, such as the one from Abbot Holman of Fort Augustus to Christopher Hennessy, Editor of *The Universe* and a member of the Committee which prepared the Report:

> Dear Christopher,
> It pleased me to read the report in the Times about the Catenian statement. Of course this report was slanted in order to excite the reader with drama and tension. But I guessed that the Catenians were bent on redressing a balance in lay co-operation with the Hierarchy which was badly needed.
> At last here was the voice of practical and responsible Catholic men of affairs who represented a great body of laity who bore the heat and burden of the day. One had grown tired of hearing the academics, theorizers, and theological speculators – a tiny minority – who seemed to count far more than they should in the counsels of the Bishops and their Commissions.

THE AFTERMATH OF THE VATICAN COUNCIL 1965-1975

In my not inconsiderable pastoral experience the Catenians have always proved to be stalwarts among the laity who could be counted upon for their loyalty to the Church and to the Holy See and to take initiatives to further the mission of the Church at every level. So this new initiative is a delight to me.

Subsequent correspondence, however, showed that not all Catenians approved of either the Report itself or of its presentation to the Press before it had been made available to members in the April edition of *Catena*. Some denied the statement in the Report that the Association 'in some measure can claim to speak for the organised laity', arguing that any attempt to become directly involved in the work of the Commissions would be a departure from the policy of the Association. It was fortunate that the controversy over this Report became overshadowed by the considerations and deliberations over the Jenkins Committee on Re-organisation, for in 'turning in on itself' the Association had a chance to forget the Report which had offended leading members of the Hierarchy.

5. Laurie Tanner. K.S.G

Much of the blame for this rift between the Association and the Hierarchy fell, fairly or unfairly, on Laurie Tanner, the Grand Secretary. Tanner's retirement in 1975 was made the more significant in the Association's history by the death in January of the Association's first Grand Secretary, Joe Shepherd.

Born in 1912, Tanner had gone via the Oratory School, Chelsea, and Mark Cross, to Wonersh to study for the priesthood. He left the seminary to study at King's College for an Arts degree, but returned again to study for the priesthood. In 1940, however, he finally left the seminary to join the Army. He had a distinguished wartime career as a member of Intelligence and Field Security groups. In 1948 he left the Army to find a new career and to provide for his wife and family.

At that time Grand Council was looking for an assistant to Rudman. Among 140 applicants, Tanner was the only non-Catenian; yet he was appointed. In 1953 he succeeded Rudman as Grand Secretary, having learned from 'the master' the nature of the Association and the importance of the role of Grand Secretary. Tanner brought his own gifts to the role. A quick brain, a gift for public speaking, an enviable ability to write and an easy manner which concealed great strength of purpose – all these were put at the Association's disposal.

But not everyone appreciated the gifts. As one of Tanner's friends has written,

> Superiority of mind can have dangerous consequences for those who possess it. It can lead them to hold in contempt lesser minds. It can also lead them to impatience with those who do not share the vision which guides their actions. It is ripe ground for misunderstanding and also for envy. Where intellectual respect absents itself, there is remarkable scope for pettiness. So Tanner's administration was marked by tension and, on occasions, wrangling. The tension was, no doubt, very good for the evolutionary development of the Association. The wrangling vested nobody involved with credit. Sadly, every side believed it was right.

Another of his friends invited me to see Tanner much as John Masters in *To the Coral Strand* saw 'the Brahmin mentality; the calm arrogance, the cold contempt for anyone else's opinions'. Masters explained that when the Brahmins met the British they 'came across perhaps the only other people on earth with the same self-conceit'. Here was the very model of the clashes between Tanner and some members of Grand Council. Tanner both wrote and spoke scathingly of Grand Council, describing the members as 'cardboard men' and 'men of straw' – hardly the best way to talk of one's employers.

He also criticised Church authorities, as we have seen. One Brother compared Tanner to the ex-seminarian, Rycker, in Graham Greene's *A Burnt-out Case*: 'He knows all the answers – six years wasted in a seminary can do a lot of harm.' Certainly they had given Tanner a sense of intellectual superiority even to members of the Hierarchy, of one of whom he claimed, 'I taught him all the theology he knows.' This attitude offended many Catenians who wrote to attack his 'Modernist' views.

The clashes with leading members of Grand Council and with the feelings of traditionalist Brothers came to a head in 1966 when the Grand President was Sidney Quick – like Tanner a physically small figure and like Tanner a 'bonny fighter'. One outcome of this clash was a move at the 1966 A.G.M. to amend the Rules to remove the Grand Secretary from the Grand Council and to make him merely Secretary to Grand Council. The proposer of this motion was persuaded to withdraw it, but only after a long and bitter debate.

Evidence of the results of the clashes with Grand Council and the Hierarchy was provided, for those who bothered to read it, in a short note in *Catena* in November 1968 concerning the informal dinner which some of Tanner's friends had organised to 'mark the conferment on him of a K.S.G.' The Knighthood had been obtained through the efforts of Bernard Kirchner and without the support of Grand Council. Neither the Cardinal nor the Grand President attended the dinner, at which only four members of Grand Council were present. It was not surprising that Tanner refused to publicise his Knighthood which, rightly, he felt had been well-earned but the award of which had been marked by pettiness on the part of those who ought to have been aware of the work he had done.

In 1969, during the debate about Re-organisation, there were suggestions that the Grand Secretary should not be a member of Grand Council, although many Brothers felt that 'a member who devotes himself whole-time to Association affairs has the knowledge and experience that fits him above most for membership of Grand Council'. In Tanner the Association had a powerful, forceful chief executive. But, as one of his friends wrote, 'There was the rub. How easy it was for a Grand Director, even a Grand President to be upstaged. Such worthy men came and went. They wished to be more than figureheads. Inevitably, since they came and went, the minds of Circle officers focussed on the permanent official at head office.' The role of Grand Secretary is a difficult one to fill. All things to all Catenians, the servant of Grand Council and of any individual with time to lift a telephone, the Grand Secretary must yet have the strength of purpose to keep short-term worries in perspective as he gives flesh to long-term policy.

Privacy is not easily enjoyed by Grand Secretaries. Is he an office worker or on call twenty-four hours a day? If he is on duty at an evening meeting, may he compensate with time off from the office next day? Whatever he decides, someone will think him to have erred. If he hits back at criticism, he lacks humility and stands charged with arrogance.

Laurie Tanner came in for his full share of criticism; yet he made rich friendships among the rank and file. He was often heard to complain bitterly that individual Catenians failed to give the Association the best in leadership. But he never faltered in his conviction that the Association is the richest force in Catholic contemporary life, with a huge untapped potential.

The Association's Chaplaincies scheme was a great opportunity to play a vital role in Catholic intellectual life. Laurie felt that the Hierarchy had betrayed the Association, and that its failure to trust the Association had put back the Association's influence on contempory life. Had the scheme come at the time of the Easter People, it would have been a different story, and Laurie's own personal vision would have been realised.

6. Keith Pearson

The Association's fourth Grand Secretary was Keith Pearson. His career with ICI had been interrupted by the War, when he served in the R.A.F. and, as a member of ground staff, took part in the Normandy landings in 1944. By 1975 he had become a senior manager with ICI. His Catenian record was equally impressive. A founder-member of the Orpington Circle in 1962, he had been Circle President in 1968–69 and President of Province 7 in 1974–75. During his year as Provincial President new records were established for Circle visiting in the Province, culminating in an influx of 187 Brothers at Blackheath's February meeting, when Keith Pearson was presented with a ship's lifebelt inscribed with the signature of every Circle President in Province 7.

It seemed that the Association had chosen wisely in appointing a man with experience in multinational administration and an evident enthusiasm for the good of the Association. He was aware of the problems of a Grand Secretary, and made it clear that he hoped to work amicably with Grand Council and its officers. It was agreed that he would not exercise his vote on Grand Council.

Unfortunately neither this good will nor Keith Pearson's evident enthusiasm were sufficient to achieve this. In June 1982, following negotiations which started in November 1981, Keith Pearson resigned after a period of ill health. Grand Council has taken the resignation as the opportunity for a fresh examination of the role of the Grand Secretary. At the moment there are plans for the appointment from the Association of a person who would handle the Benevolent part of the Grand Secretary's work. The time that this is expected to take is approximately two days a week, which is an indication of the amount of time now spent on Benevolent affairs. We may then see the appointment of an honorary Grand Secretary, a counterpart to the honorary Grand Treasurer. The role of chief executive will then be filled by a third person who will quite clearly be an employee of, and subordinate to, Grand Council.

Only the future will tell whether these proposals become accepted and acceptable, and, if they are, whether they will lead to better government. It may be that they leave a number of questions unanswered. Will an honorary officer be able to give enough time to Catenian affairs? Will a mere change of title from Grand Secretary to Office Manager resolve the problem between the all-time professional and the part-time Grand Council? Above all, will an essential continuity be lost in the Association's administration if there is no longer a full-time Grand Secretary at the helm?

CHAPTER SIXTEEN

Overseas Expansion 1954–1983

1. Ambitions and reality 1919–1954
While appreciating the large-scale immigration of recent years, people seem unaware of the mass emigration which was a feature of British history before and after World War I. It was that emigration which led to the request for the Association to expand overseas, yet another link between the history of the Association and the national history.

It was Catenian emigrants to Australia who asked in 1919 that a Circle be opened in their new homeland. This overseas desire was matched in 1921, at least in Burnley (a Circle formed in November 1920), whose members asked that consideration be given to the Association's becoming an 'International Association'. It is difficult to imagine the relatively primitive methods of communication of that time when few emigrants ever thought that they would either visit or be visited by the families they had left behind. It was this which led the practical-minded to pour cold water on such pleas for overseas expansion.

One Catenian emigrant to Australia was a Dr Moran. When the Association refused to found a Circle in Sydney, he helped form the Knights of the Southern Cross, modelled on the American Knights of Columbus. A short history of the Knights of the Southern Cross in *Catena* in April 1971 made no mention of the Catenian link with this organisation, so quickly do we forget our history. In October 1922, Moran visited London, was re-enrolled in London (No. 2) and supported the initiation of a fellow-member of the K.S.C., H.J. Macken of Sydney, who became No. 666 on the Circle roll. But such expatriate enthusiasm did not tempt Grand Council or Grand Circle towards overseas expansion.

Hogan realised that there was business potential in the many Catenians who lived overseas, some as representatives of government or industry, others as permanent emigrants who none the less paid their subscriptions and remained on Circle rolls. In 1923 he asked that a list of such overseas members should be maintained. Until 1954 this list was maintained at Head Office; only in that year was it decided to print the list of overseas Brothers 'as a separate supplement in the Directory'.

In 1925 the officers of Province No. 11 thought that there was a good chance that a Circle might be formed in Jersey and asked Brothers whose business took them to the island 'to do the spade work'. But the opening of that Circle had to wait another thirty years. In Dublin there were a number of resident and retired Catenians. They were led, after 1938, by the enthusiastic Dennis Aspell (No. 618 on the Roll of London No. 2), a former Grand Director. He organised monthly meetings at the Gresham Hotel and reported that there was 'quite a band' which offered a Catenian welcome to visiting Brothers and their families. He also reported, however, that, in view of the strong position of the K.S.C. and of the Irish Hierarchy's opposition to lay-controlled organisations, it would be 'inadvisable to form a Circle'.

There was no such caution in the mind of Badman of Esher who, in 1950, took up an appointment in Salisbury in what was then Southern Rhodesia. He reported that there were so many good Catholics in the city that it would be 'a very easy matter to introduce the first Catenian Circle in that country...'. But, even though Grand Council was willing to help 'in the formation of a kindred organisation' it refused to countenance the expansion of the Association as such. The tide, however, was running against Grand Council. In his Presidential address in 1954, Bob Burns listed the countries from which came requests for the formation of Circles and said that

> Grand Council feel that every consideration should be given to this question. . . .
> There are, however, great difficulties in the way of establishing Circles in those countries. A sub-committee of Grand Council has been formed to investigate the possibilities and your Circles will be advised as to this development.

It is ironic that the next Grand President, Bob Richards, should have reported in his Presidential address that, responding to the efforts of a Brother Parker of Stockton Circle, 'Grand Council had decided to form a Circle in Singapore', where Parker, a solicitor, had met three other Catenians. For there is still (1981) no Circle in Singapore, while Richards seems to have ignored the formation in 1954 of the Jersey Circle which rightly claims to be 'the first overseas Circle'. Jersey was very much the result of the enthusiasm of Brother Leonard Hems, who had been a member of Birmingham Midland Circle since 1939. Hems retired to Jersey and set about forming a Circle there. It was fitting that he should be the Founder President of the new Circle, which has been a very lively Circle and hosted its first A.G.M. in the Association's 74th year.

2. The Rhodesian Circles 1957–1959

In 1953, Grand Council rejected 'an application from Catholics in Rhodesia to be allowed to form a branch of the Association'. In April 1959, the first Rhodesian Circle was opened. What had happened to bring about the change of hearts and minds at Hobart Place? Who were the persistent Rhodesian Catholics who maintained the pressure until they finally broke through?

The expansion of the Association out of Salford depended on dynamic characters such as McDermott, Hogan and Brosch. Rhodesian Catholics were fortunate in having such a character in Bernard Pepper, who had been born in Bradford where his father had been No. 8 on the roll of that Circle. A doctor – not, as recorded in *Catena*, 'a business man' – he had married a South African girl during the War, and after the War had emigrated to South Africa. Early in the 1950s he moved to Bulawayo and entered into partnership wih another Catholic, Dr Shee.

Catholics formed only about 10 per cent of the population of Rhodesia. And, wrote Pepper,

> there are many sectional power groups with influence out of all proportion to their numbers, notably the Masons and the Jews, and to a lesser extent the Dutch Reformed Church, but there has been no Catholic organisation at all *which gives a sense of strength to its individuals* [my italics], mixing as they do freely with all these social, political and cultural groups, and in the Clubs, the political, athletic and agricultural organisations.

Here was the doctor who appreciated the psychological role which the Association had played in Britain.

Pepper knew a good deal about the Association, for, apart from his father, there was a nexus of Tindalls locking him into the Association. Pepper's mother was Blanche Tindall. One of her brothers, J.A. Tindall, was a founder member of Harrogate in 1915. One of his sons, Edward Tindall, had joined the Harrogate Circle in 1936 and is proud of the fact that three of his sons are now members of the Association. In discussions with his partner, Dr Shee, Pepper suggested that the position of Rhodesian Catholics would be improved by the founding of a Catenian Circle. Shee came on leave to England early in 1954 and, at the suggestion of a Jesuit at Mount Street, visited Catenian Head Office to discuss his and Pepper's ideas with Laurie Tanner. Tanner had to explain Grand Council's refusal to allow a Circle to be formed, but encouraged Shee to form something similar to the Association in Rhodesia and to maintain contact with Catenian Head Office, although the fact that they did so came as a surprise to Tanner, judging by his letter to Pepper in March 1957.

On his return to Rhodesia, Shee arranged a meeting of seven 'interested gentlemen', the Rhodesian counterpart of those who had the first meetings at St Bede's and at O'Donnell's office in 1908. A small steering committee was formed, charged to set up an organisation with Aims and Constitutions based on those of the Catenian Association. In June 1955, there was a meeting of a number of prospective members of the 'embryonic Association', and this led to the inauguration of the Vinculum Association. Its logo was a cross surrounded by a linked chain; it organised monthly meetings followed by dinners 'frequently honoured by the presence of local or visiting notabilities . . .'; it set up a Benevolent Fund and Board; its officers had the same titles as their corresponding numbers in Catenian Circles. It was, in everything but name, a Catenian Circle.

Like O'Donnell in 1908, Pepper was delighted with the speedy success of the venture. There was a steady increase in membership with only one resignation in the first two years of its existence. But Pepper realised that his infant Association would be strengthened by a closer link with the larger Association. Following the 1957 A.G.M. of the Vinculum Association, Pepper wrote to ask for 'closer connection with the Catenians'. Tanner replied assuring him that Grand Council would no doubt receive sympathetically an application for 'a closer relationship with Vinculum. It is my personal hope that Grand Council will grant you Circle status, and, as you form other branches, establish you as a Rhodesian Province of the Association.'

Meanwhile, Grand Council had framed a revised Constitution designed to permit the opening of Circles overseas and to meet the special conditions that would prevail in such Circles. As Tanner had predicted, Grand Council in September 1957 agreed to grant a charter 'incorporating Vinculum as a constituent Circle of the Association'. Pepper wrote, 'welcoming this information but asked for clarification of a number of points where conditions in Rhodesia would create difficulties in complying strictly with the Catenian Association and Rules'. Grand Council then asked the Rules Committee to draft the necessary modification to the Rules, following which the forms for application for a Charter were sent to Pepper. Grand President Carus, Grand Vice-President Baker, and Tanner were the Association's representatives at the opening of the Bulawayo Circle (No. 187) on 2 April 1959, and at a banquet held on the following evening, when 'the Bishop of Bulawayo and leading citizens of the city were guests of the new Circle', Carus rightly described its opening as 'a memorable occasion; it is the first time the Association has spread its wings and gone overseas'. In his speech Pepper said that he hoped that 'it would not be too long before Circles were formed in other centres in Rhodesia. The new Circle had its eyes on the Copperbelt and it also looked towards South Africa.' Here was the McDermott of Southern Africa.

Indeed, the second African Circle was opened within the week, with the inauguration of the Salisbury (No. 188) Circle in the presence of ecclesiastical and civic dignitaries. The Founder Secretary of this new Circle was Frank Coggan, son-in-law of Charles Lee of the Hartlepool Circle, and through Lee's sons, who were also Catenians, very much tied into the Catenian network. The Founder President of the new Circle was Sir Philip Gainsford, a distinguished soldier-administrator in India before 1947, who retired to Rhodesia where he continued to play an active role in civic affairs. He was often in England to visit his two Benedictine sons at Worth Abbey and was a welcome guest at many Circles. It was fitting that when he returned 'home' he went to live in Jersey, which claims, as we have noted, to be the first overseas Circle.

At the opening of the Bulawayo Circle, Bishop Schmitt of Bulawayo had said that 'there is a need for Catholic gentlemen in the country's public life'. The members of the Association responded to this call, several of them becoming Members of the Rhodesian Parliament, where at least two also became members of Cabinets. Indeed the contest for the Salisbury Central seat at the 1962 Election saw Bro. Ryan (of the Rhodesian Front Party) succeed a Catenian member of the United Front Party, Cleveland, President of the Salisbury Circle in 1962–63. The wisdom of excluding 'wrangling' from Circle meetings must have been welcome to such political opponents. And not every candidate wins at election time. Among the defeated in December 1962 was Laurence Ayers, a Past President of Bulawayo, who was defeated by a member of the Rhodesian Front in an election in which many people did not vote 'because they had been intimidated'. Here were the seeds for Rhodesia's unhappy future. But here also was the man who was, in some sense, to play Hogan to Pepper's McDermott in the expansion of the Association in Southern Africa.

3. The Zambian Circles 1959–1981

As in Britain, so too in Africa the development of the Association was affected by a wider history. In 1960, before his 'wind of change' speech, Prime Minister Harold Macmillan made a tour of British territories in Central and Southern Africa, including the three territories of Southern Rhodesia, Northern Rhodesia, and Nyasaland, which had been formed into the Central African Federation in 1953. By 1960 it was clear that African nationalists wanted to break that Federation, following years of 'states of emergency' in both Northern Rhodesia and Nyasaland. Nyasaland was allowed to leave the Federation (December 1962), with Northern Rhodesia following suit in December 1963. Southern Rhodesia had a higher proportion of whites than had the other two territories. Since 1923 it had been a self-governing colony, and with the break-up of the Federation it asked for independence. The Conservative government of Sir Alec Douglas Home and, after 1964, the Labour government under Harold Wilson refused to accede to this demand unless the white government agreed to accept policies aimed at ensuring the advance of black democracy. In 1965 the Southern Rhodesian government issued its Unilateral Declaration of Independence, and a long civil war began which only ended when the illegal government agreed to allow free elections which led to the establishment of the Mugabe government in 1980.

It was against this disturbed background that the Association developed in Central and Southern Africa. Pepper had promised that the Catenians in Bulawayo had their eyes on the Copperbelt and although Grand Council reported optimistically of the possibilities of developments in Uganda the next move was made in Lusaka in what was then Northern Rhodesia. In 1959, Geoffrey Alden went to work in Northern Rhodesia. A member of Wimbledon Circle for some ten years, he was 'very soon aware of the true sense of brotherhood'. In Northern Rhodesia there were no Catenians and 'I felt I was losing a valuable part of life'. Northern Rhodesia was a mission country, many of the clergy were from Ireland and had no knowledge of the Association. Nor had the Archbishop of Lusaka, a Pole who had survived Dachau concentration camp. This was unfavourable territory in which to begin a Circle.

Lusaka was a government centre, many men being there as Colonial civil servants, entitled to home leave for six months every three years, and liable to be posted to distant parts of the territory at a moment's notice. This was also true of Catholics with business interests; they were often away from their Lusaka base. It is not surprising, then, that Alden could write of the Catholics: 'Many of us hardly know each other, save as faces at Mass.' He spoke to a number of men, interested them in the Association, held a series of exploratory meetings and informed Tanner of what he was doing. While many priests seemed dubious about the development of an Association from which they would be excluded, Alden found an ally in the Polish Archbishop, who, having read the Association's Rules and having examined the Directory, told Alden: 'Go ahead, with my blessing.'

In the autumn of 1960 and the early months of 1961, Alden went ahead until the inauguration was fixed for 11 August 1961. Pepper flew 600 miles to act as representative of Grand Council and inaugurate this new Circle. Others travelled from Salisbury and Bulawayo by car, the journey taking two days. The event was marred only by the absence from the banquet of the Governor of Northern Rhodesia, Sir Evelyn Hone, who had to absent himself because of the state of emergency then prevailing in the country.

The Lusaka Circle (201) faced many problems, apart from the emergency. Many men were there on contract, usually of three years, following which many left never to return to Africa. A major problem was that of travel. There was the great distance between Lusaka and the Circles in Bulawayo and Salisbury. There was, during states of emergency, travel restriction and the danger of being attacked by terrorists. After the break-up of the Federation, travelling became even more difficult as, for example, the border between Zambia and Southern Rhodesia was completely closed.

It is not surprising, then, that the Lusaka men should have always invited their wives to their after-Circle dinners, so that 'every night was a Ladies' Night', with some men travelling upwards of 90 miles to get to a meeting. And in spite of the difficulties there were visits to Salisbury, some 300 miles away, and Bulawayo, some 600 miles away, with inter-Circle outings planned for intermediate regions such as the Kafue game reserve where 'Brothers and their families at open-air Mass had the company of puzzled hippopotami plodding across the plain to the river'.

Pepper and his fellow-Catenians were pleased at this initial expansion. They were equally pleased with the developments in Salisbury and Bulawayo. In Salisbury, for example, the Governor, Sir Humphrey Gibbs, was a regular guest at the Circle's Annual Dinner and Ball, which became 'the principal social function for the Catholic community in Salisbury'. The break-up of the Federation in 1963 had led to the return to Britain of many civil servants and some businessmen, so that when Grand President Lomas visited Salisbury in April 1964 he found that Salisbury was 'the weakest' of the African Circles, while Bulawayo, 'the Mother Circle of the Rhodesias', was in excellent shape and had 'a fine concept of the Association in all its facets'.

Lomas was also impressed with the state of things in Lusaka, while it gave him great satisfaction to preside at the inauguration of Northern Rhodesia's second Circle, the Copperbelt, when three existing Catenians were joined by twelve other new members of the new Circle. The two main towns of the Copperbelt, Ndola and Kitwe, are forty miles apart, and this was to create a problem for this new Circle as travel became more difficult and dangerous. Some Catenians thought that there might be two Circles, one in each town, but in spite of various efforts this looked-for expansion has not taken place.

Lomas appreciated the sense of isolation which the African Circles felt. His suggestion that each Circle be attached to an English Province was adopted in 1964, but proved of little real value. An improvement was made in 1969, when the Jenkins Committee, in the process of discussions on Re-organisation, suggested the creation of a Liaison Committee for Southern Africa. This has had the effect of making the African Circles that much more conscious of one another and has led to some expansion.

Expansion was far from people's minds during the unrest which followed the Smith government's U.D.I. in 1965. Although most Catenians in Rhodesia had opposed this means of gaining their independence, they had almost all swung behind the government once the announcement was made. Fear of black government was, perhaps, not surprising in the light of the events in the Congo. Despite the increasing difficulties of travel and the withdrawal of many expatriate civil servants, life in Rhodesia seemed to prosper. This, at least, was the report made by Grand President Joe Cox after he had visited each of the Circles.

The continuation of the civil war in Rhodesia, however, and the effects which this had on life in Zambia, led Grand Director Woolgar to present a gloomy report to Grand Council in November 1976, following a private visit to Africa. But there was more light amidst that gloom than Woolgar had seen, and it is pleasant to report that a second Salisbury Circle was opened in December 1980, partly because of the continuing expansion of the parent Circle in that city.

4. Into South Africa

The debate over the question of expansion into the Republic of South Africa was long and many-sided. On the one hand, there was Grand Council, which in 1962 gave its blessing to the attempts being made by the Bulawayo Circle to form a Circle in South Africa. But, after Lomas's visit in 1964, Grand Council got cold feet and decided that in view of the government policy of 'separate development' it would be inadvisable for the Association to allow the formation of what would be seen as 'whites only' Circles. On the other hand, there were the enthusiasts from Bulawayo and Lusaka such as Pepper, Coppinger and Raymond May who, with McDermott-like zeal wrote to and visited many Catholics in Pretoria, Johannesburg, Cape Town and other centres. Some of these men then travelled long distances to be guests at after-Circle functions in Rhodesia or Zambia. One such was Brother Geoffrey Hussey, a wealthy, active and militant Catholic, who used his own private 'plane to fly around the Republic not only on business but in search of potential Catenians.

There were, too, the Catholics in the Republic. They suffered from the militant hostility of the powerful Dutch Reformed Church, so that Catholics in commerce and the professions were subject to anti-Catholic bigotry. When extremists campaigned for the overthrow of Prime Minister Vorster they significantly headed their list of objections to his policy with 'the influx of Roman Catholic immigrants' and used the sort of language once used against English Catholics in the 1850s.

Pepper and others on the spot persuaded Grand Council to reverse its 1964 decision and to allow them to go ahead with their attempts to form a Circle in South Africa, and in 1966 fresh moves were made. Archbishop Garner, a brother of Vic Garner of the Bulawayo Circle, was influential in getting Cardinal McCann and other members of the Hierarchy to give the attempts their blessing. But in December 1966, Grand Council did a second about-turn and decided to call a halt to the pioneering work. Angry letters came from Pepper, Coppinger and others. Their opinions were summed up in a long letter from Laurence Ayers of the Bulawayo Circle:

> The situation in the Republic of South Africa today is comparable with that in England at the time of the founding of Catenianism through 'The Chums' about 60 years ago. Catholicism in South Africa is referred to by the Afrikaner Nationalist Government as 'The Roman Catholic Menace or Danger'.
>
> In Christian charity, how can you in conscience justify your introduction of politics in spite of Rule 2 of our Constitution? Why refuse to Catholic men the right or opportunity to a fuller Catholic and Christian life, because the political party in control of that country is anti-Catholic and has a policy of 'Apartheid'?
>
> If so, would you also refuse to allow the spread of Catenianism in, say, a country governed by Communism or an Atheistic Christian-persecuting dictator?
>
> What would our Lord Jesus Christ do? Similarly prohibit an association of His Christians because He saw they had to live under the Roman persecution of Nero?
>
> I must make my own position clear politically. I was a founder member of the Capricorn Africa Society with Colonel David Stirling (a multi-racial Society). I stood for Parliament against the Rhodesia Front some 5 years ago (a hopeless seat), and lost of course. I electioneered for our African member in two elections, Mr Behane, who is still a sitting member in this present Parliament.
>
> I am *not* a member of the party which forms the present 'Rhodesia Front' government under Smith.
>
> I am opposed to 'apartheid'. I fought my own election campaign with the platform of advocating the abolition of the Land Apportionment Act in Rhodesia.
>
> I cannot accept it as Christian, just and as Catenianism and as *charity* and *brotherly love*, that Catholic men are to be now denied an opportunity of being Catenians, just because they are under a political yoke.
>
> Please reconsider the whole matter Brother Grand President.
>
> May I also say that Geoffrey Mark Hussey was the man selected by *me*. I have known him for years. He is a convert, a very active and publicly *brave* Catholic. After the last war (rank of Major) was a foremost member of the Torch Commando (opposing Afrikaner Nationalism), was under danger and threat of being 'picked

Olimpio Forte in a private audience with Pope Paul VI. ▼

Father Hugh Martin photographed after his ordination at the Beda, March 1964. He was joined by many of his Catenian friends. From left to right standing were Algernon Rotham (Winchester), Stephen Gaskell (Exeter – of which Circle Fr Martin had once been a member), Paul Edwards (another former Catenian, who went on to ordination in 1965), John Heal (Doncaster), John Martin (of the Southampton Circle and a brother to Fr Hugh). Seated were Gilbert Butcher (Exeter), Col. Griffin (London), Father Hugh Martin and Teddy Tickle (Southampton).

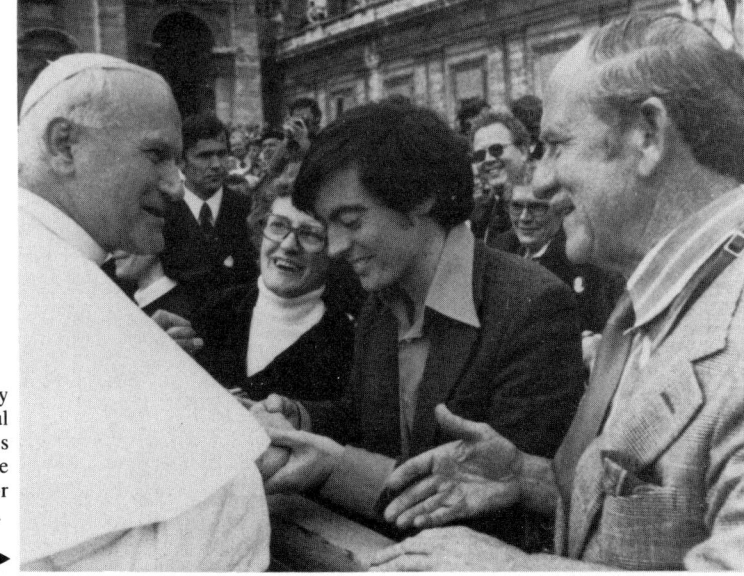

The Nockles family meet Pope John Paul II. Maurice Nockles is President of the National Council for the Lay Apostolate. ▶

Grand President Rex Kirk bowing to Bishop McGill before Mass at the Dublin AGM, 1967.

Cardinal Gray accepting the Offertory Gifts from Aberdeen Brothers at the Mass celebrating their 500th meeting.

The opening Mass at the *Harvest '69 Exhibition* organised by the Catenians of the Haywards Heath Circle.

Grand President Albert Smallbone presenting the General Benevolent Fund trophy to Maurice Sheehan of the Penybont Circle.

David Higgins and Ann Bolton.    Brian and Marian Brett.    Mark Hickson and Julie Keane.

Some of the marriages which united Catenian families.

Gerard Wilcox (of the Stratford Circle) and his wife Kathryn with their newly-baptised daughter, Teresa, whose grand-aunt, Dame Mary Frances Wilcox (left), Abbess of the Benedictine Abbey, Colwich, allowed her nephew, Fr Anthony Wilcox, to use the normally enclosed Abbey for the christening.

Bill Ridgers of Purley and Coulsdon, one of the many Catenians involved in work for the handicapped.

Bernard Kirchner, the distinguished editor of *Catena*, who died as this book went to press.

Cyril Gaskin of Darlington and Mrs Gaskin with their newly-ordained son – a reminder of another Catenian contribution to the life of the Church.

Laurie Tanner at one of the less glamorous tasks involved in the operating of the Jumbulance.

From left to right: Swansea Circle President Cliff and Mrs Booth, Mrs Jean Hopkins, Mr Daly of the HCPT, Mr and Mrs Wall at the presentation by the Circle of two wheelchairs in memory of the late Brother Luke Hopkins who died in 1976 and the young son of Mr and Mrs Wall who died in 1974.

Mass in the garden of Hosanna House.

Part of a caravan rally, August 1978.

Pretoria Circle Brothers and guests at a week-end get-together, 1981.

Golf in another climate; Brother President P. Brett presenting the Golf Trophy to Vice-President Cyril Dewhirst at a Zimbabwe get-together, 1966.

Rowland Young addressing Brothers and guests at the Golf Championship dinner.

Bernard Pepper, the founder of the Association in Africa, addressing the Brothers and guests at the dinner which followed the inauguration of the Lusaka Circle.

Grand President John Eyre (seated) sorting out papers with Bryan Hooton before the inauguration of the City of Melbourne Circle.

Bernard Sullivan, Founder President of the Hong Kong Circle.

Brothers of the Copperbelt Circle with their ladies in the company of their Bishop (seated centre).

The twin-inspirers of the development of the Association in Australia, Cliff Holloway (nearest the camera) and Dr Peter Maguire, at a meeting of the City of Perth Circle.

The Founder President of the Malta Circle, Stan Clark, with Mrs Clark.

up' by the Apartheid Nationalists and his telephones regularly tapped, etc.
This man *is* a Catholic, but now it seems there is to be 'no Catenianism' for him or his like, as he is under the heel of a political system of Government that is out to suppress Catholicism.
Am I to be the one to go and tell him now, after the written authority and encouragement from Grand Council, that Catenianism is not for him or any other Catholic gentleman living in South Africa, because Grand Council has 'changed its mind' on the grounds it has just found out after all these months that the ruling party politically in South Africa sponsors the 'apartheid' that he (Hussey) has and is fighting actively?
No, Brother Grand President, as a Catenian – no, no. I value Catenianism too highly and all I understand it represents and stands for.
I pray and hope and trust that only a temporary mistake has been made, and that soon we shall hear from you that it will be possible to expand our brotherhood to the Glory of God.
In distress and anxiety and hope, I extend my fraternal and respectful greetings to you, our Grand President and all our Brothers.

To its credit Grand Council changed its mind and was persuaded to allow the work to go ahead. Unfortunately, the reality of things proved that much of the enthusiasm of the Rhodesian and Zambian Brothers was misplaced. For in spite of their work and that of Hussey it was some two years before the first Circle was opened. And where they had once glowingly written of opening Circles in several cities and centres, in the event they managed only to form the one Circle in Pretoria. This was inaugurated in March 1969 by Grand President Cox who, as one Brother reported, 'put the seal on what is hoped to be the beginning of a great development of the Association's bonds in the Republic of South Africa'.

That no further development has taken place since then would have saddened Pepper. Unfortunately, early in 1970, he, his wife and daughter were killed in a collision with a bus near Bulawayo. His Brothers wrote movingly of the work that he had done and of the fact that, at the age of 54, he was a 'leader whose place will be hard to fill'.

5. Ireland, 1938–1983

Ironically, while arguing over expansion into South Africa, the Association was planning to form a Circle in Ireland, or rather in Eire, for there has been no attempt to found a Circle in Northern Ireland.

Dennis Aspell had organised informal meetings of retired Catenians living in Dublin since his own retirement there in 1938. In 1958, Grand Council took the first steps to the forming of a Circle in Dublin. The powerful Knights of Columbanus were approached and, unofficially, they told Grand Council that there would be no objection on their part to the promoting of a Circle for 'leading members of the professions and those holding influential positions in industry and commerce' who might not feel at home in 'their own more widely-based organisation'.

But in 1960, when Grand Council appeared to be taking active steps, the K.S.C. wrote to say that 'their organisation would oppose the establishment of a Circle in Dublin'. Visits by Grand Presidents became a feature of the 'informal' but regular meetings of the Dublin 'Group'. Aspell made friends of the K.S.C., while Peckston won support from the Irish Hierarchy which had also expressed opposition to the formation of a Catenian Circle in Dublin. The upshot was the opening of the first Dublin Circle in November 1968, when 28 enrolled Catenians were joined with 15 new recruits at the inauguration conducted by Grand President Joe Cox. In Ireland, as elsewhere, expansion in one city led to a demand for similar expansion elsewhere. Cork men had their first Circle inaugurated by Grand President Gallacher in April 1970, the month which also saw the death in Southern Africa of Bernard Pepper.

This second development alarmed the K.S.C., and Tanner was obliged to write to assure them that the Association had no plans for further expansion in Ireland and 'in fact does not normally concern itself with the establishment of new Circles anywhere'. This last statement was somewhat misleading. Indeed, Tanner's letter went on to explain that, in spite of the disclaimer in the opening paragraph, 'it seems likely that there will soon be application to establish a second Circle in Dublin'.

The opening of the second Dublin Circle by Grand President Jenkins in May 1972 was carried out with the 'minimum of publicity' following opposition, inside Dublin's first Circle and among the K.S.C., to the formation of the new Circle. Indeed, 'the situation in Ireland has deteriorated', wrote a leading member of the Irish Liaison Committee. This was nothing new. For with the Irish facility for finding trouble where none exists, there had been 'difficulties with Dublin Circle for one reason or another since its formation'. So too with the Cork Circle, where the Circle's affairs had been run in an alarmingly haphazard fashion, with its financial affairs being, for a time, in some disarray. In addition, rivalry between the cities of Cork and Dublin was reflected in an unfraternal relationship between the two Circles, reminiscent, for the historian, of the relationship between Lancashire and Yorkshire, Manchester Catenians and London men, and the men of the now divided Province 3. All in all, the development of the Association into Ireland has not been the success which Aspell and Peckston must have hoped for.

6. Australia 1962–1983

The development of the Association in Australia was similarly marred by the inter-State jealousy which is a feature of Australian life. In 1961 there were eighteen Catenians living in Australia, retaining their membership of 'home' Circles and meeting from time to time at the old Wentworth Hotel in Sydney. In 1963, Dr Plunkett Sweeney of the Hove Circle emigrated to Sydney. In June 1967, he wrote to ask Grand Council about the possibility of opening a Circle in Sydney. Tanner explained that there was little such possibility because of the likely opposition from the Hierarchy and from the powerful Knights of the Southern Cross. The Australian K.S.C., a once secret society, set up to provide a Catholic counterweight to the Masonic Order, was widely supported by the Hierarchy.

In spite of this far from encouraging reply Sweeney organised meetings of 'The Association of Catenians and Friends' preferring not to use the term 'Group' because of its 'political connotation in this continent'. Among Catenians at such meetings was Norbert de Roma who, with Sweeney, was to provide that McDermott–Hogan drive which success requires.

Dining meetings were held at more or less monthly intervals in 1967 and 1968 and a Ladies' Night was held in November 1968. Guest speakers – from Serra, the Stockmarket, Alcoholics Anonymous, the Catholic Education Council – were asked to address the 'Group', which also approached 'potential

Friends' who were invited each month to put questions about the Association. In March 1969, Grand President Joe Cox attended a meeting of the 'Group' and also had an interview with Cardinal Gilroy, who stated that 'he saw no reason why the Association should not be established' in Australia. This Presidential visit and Hierarchical approval encouraged the 'Group', which recruited more members and, although its first application was rejected by Grand Council in 1969, persisted with attempts to form a Circle until in January 1971 Grand Council approved a second petition.

Grand Council attempted to form a working relationship with the Australian K.S.C., agreeing that Knights might attend Circle meetings when in England. This friendly attitude towards the Knights did not always please Australian-based Catenians, either before or after the inauguration of the first Circle in that continent; the Knights had made no secret of their antagonism to the development of what they saw as a rival. That development was seemingly assured after May 1971, when Cardinal Gilroy met the officers of the 'Group', 'wished them well and gave his blessing to the establishment of the Association in Sydney'. On 7 July 1971, the 'Group' held its final meeting; on 22 July Grand President Jenkins inaugurated the City of Sydney Circle, eight existing Catenians being joined by nineteen new members enrolled at that inaugural meeting. The Cardinal celebrated Mass for the Circle on the following Sunday, as a further sign of his approval of a development which won headlines in the Catholic and secular Press.

In his address to the Brothers and guests at the inaugural dinner in 1971, Sweeney expressed his confidence that 'the Australian environment... would be greatly enriched by the establishment of the Association on these shores'. In 1981 he wrote that 'with a total of six Circles... the prospects for the future are very bright'. One of those Circles was Ku-Ring-Gai, Sydney's second Circle, a sign of the progress of the Association in that city. This was Australia's third Circle, for in February 1977 the City of Perth Circle had been inaugurated by Grand President Jack Browning.

As with Sydney, so with Perth. There were several Catenians living in the 'most isolated city in the world' when Dr Peter Maguire (Past President of Sheffield) came to live in Western Australia in 1962. After some years he was transferred to Perth and in 1968 arranged a meeting with Catenians living in Perth – Jim Tonks (Sheffield), Joe Swift (North Cheshire) and Paddy Healy (Barnsley). They agreed to hold meetings which, as more Catenians emigrated to Western Australia, became larger and more regular and led to the invitation of non-Catenian guests. In 1971, Douglas Jenkins visited the city on his way to inaugurate Sydney's first Circle; in 1974, John Bowen encouraged the 'Group' during a visit and, in spite of the mobility of the population and the frustration which many potential members felt at the long wait, a Charter was approved in 1976 and the Circle inaugurated in February 1977.

Maguire was Founder President of the new Circle which found its McDermott-like figure in its Secretary, Cliff Holloway, a convert who had joined the Bournemouth Circle prior to emigrating to Perth in 1974. Holloway has proved to be as enthusiastic a Catenian as he is an ardent Catholic. It was owing to his drive that in February 1981 Grand President John Eyre had the pleasure of inaugurating two new Circles in the Perth Metropolitan area, within a week of having inaugurated Melbourne's first Circle. Western Australia is 'the fastest growing state in Australia both in population and economically' and one looks forward to further expansion of the Association in that State.

Students of history are aware of the almost rabid nature of inter-State rivalry in Australia where, above all, other States have always resisted imagined and real attempts by New South Wales to dominate Australian affairs. It is not surprising that this tendency should be reflected in the short history of the Association in Australia. One result of this has been the setting up of separate Liaison Committees for Australia (East) and Australia (West). If, as many hope, the Association expands in this expanding continent, one may hope to see a number of separate Provinces being set up to accommodate the 'ambitions, suspicions and fears of Catenians living in the most over-governed country in the world'.

7. Asia, Europe and America

The expansion of the Association into Asia had seemed assured after Bro. Parker and other Catenians living in Singapore had persisted in their petitions for a Charter. But Grand Council, having approved in principle the establishment of a Circle in Singapore, accepted the verdict of the men on the spot in 1960 that the political situation in Singapore had convinced them that their ambitions could not be realised.

There were a number of Catenians living in Hong Kong and, led by Bernard Sullivan (Croydon Circle), some six or seven held informal meetings before setting up a 'Group' to which non-Catenians were invited. Ladies' Nights were held, minutes were kept of meetings and these were sent on to London for approval. Unlike development in Africa, the expansion in Hong Kong was not marred by racial overtones. The existing Catenians felt free to invite Chinese and Eurasians to their meetings and when Jack Browning inaugurated the Circle in February 1977 he initiated a number of them into the Association.

There had been those who had hoped that the first 'foreign' Catenians might be Europeans. Catenians living in Paris, Dieppe and Calais had at different times since 1920 suggested that it might be possible to form a Circle in one or other of these centres. In 1963, for example, there were some fifteen Catenians meeting informally but regularly in Paris. But Grand Council wanted to be assured that the first European Circle would not be seen as a club for expatriates alone. On the other hand, few Frenchmen seemed interested in the Association. If its purpose was social they had other outlets; if its purpose was to further business interests, why the formal meeting?

There were those who hoped that the opening of the Guernsey Circle in June 1977 might become another Channel Island bridgehead into Europe. But, in the event, it was in Malta and not until 1981 that the Association opened its first European Circle. Only the future will tell whether it will be possible to expand on to the mainland.

Over the years, a number of Canadians and Americans have become members of Circles while working and living in Britain. The Vale of Evesham Circle may be the only one to have had an expatriate American as Circle President, but there are at present a number of Canadians and Americans now back in their home countries who have shown a willingness to help form Circles in those countries. There are already a number of expatriate English Catenians living there, and it is possible that there may be developments on the American continent. If that should happen one might well see a rapid expansion of Circles so that, as one Grand Director hopes, 'there will be more Catenians outside Britain than inside'.

CHAPTER SEVENTEEN

The Maturing of the Easter People 1975–1983

1. Internal developments and strains

In June 1975, *Catena* announced Keith Pearson's appointment to succeed Tanner. Six months earlier the Association's first Grand Secretary had died, illustrating the continuity of the Association. And it was that very continuity which ensured that little changed with Pearson's appointment.

The collapse of the Heath government in February 1974, coupled with the first of the major increases in oil prices, provided the backdrop to the free-for-all pursuit of wage increases allowed by the Wilson government in 1975 and 1978, and to the jacking-up of the rate of inflation to an annual rate of 27 per cent. In retrospect this final period of Wilsonian government may be seen not only as the end of his self-regarding fantasy world but as the last gasps of that 'swinging' world in which the new was always better than the old and the future always seemed to be rosily attractive.

Under the Callaghan government, unions and the nation as a whole co-operated reluctantly to lower the rate of inflation. At the same time, government and local authorities stopped tearing down town and city centres to make way for tower blocks; ecology and conservation ceased to be words inviting the scorn of the 'progressives', and the reality that the world's resources were limited became accepted wisdom.

But the price paid for lowering the rate of inflation, under both Callaghan and Thatcher, was a cut in public and private spending while the rate of improvement in the national standard of living first slowed down and then declined. It was against this economic background that the Association developed after 1975. barely maintaining that slow rate of expansion which had marked Tanner's last years. In 1976 the Association opened two new Circles, in 1977 four (two of them overseas), in 1978 four more (one being overseas) and in 1979 three Circles. In 1980 only the Salisbury North (Zimbabwe) Circle was inaugurated, and in 1981 there were four new overseas Circles as compared with only one new Circle in Britain.

Even the small increase in the number of Circles was not matched by a corresponding increase in overall membership. In 1975–76, there was a net increase of only 11 members although the opening of four new Circles brought in some 70 new members. This led to the decision to appoint Circle Membership Officers responsible for developing local schemes for recruitment. But these had to be made against a backcloth of economic decline, which led Joe McMurray to write of 'the lost opportunities over the last twenty-five years. The management and executive class has grown enormously, but I question whether the Association has reaped its full share of the potential.' McMurray went on to argue that the Association was wasting its time and energies on overseas expansion instead of pursuing expansion at home.

210

One result of the relative failure of Circles to expand was that many consisted of ageing men which made them that much less attractive to younger potential recruits. Equally, the older men had less drive, which led Grand President Smallbone to complain of 'the apathetic non-participation of a substantial portion of our total membership' indicated by voting returns and 'the meagre attendance at Masses for deceased Brothers'.

In fact, this apathy was not a new feature of the Association's history; previous leaders had often complained of such non-involvement. Nor did that apathy prevent some Catenians from calling for some magnificent gesture. In August 1976, one wrote of 'the desirability of a Catenian social centre within six miles of Crystal Palace which might serve as a meeting place for local Circles and a centre for social functions'. Modestly, the writer went on: 'Raising the money would be a complex issue.' Indeed! This sort of proposal had been made at various times in the Association's history; with the exception of the ill-fated Liverpool Link Club, it had never led to any concrete development. Even as Douglas Browne was writing of his social-centre dream, Grand Council's appeal for an increase in capitation fees was rejected. Between 1971 and 1976 the general price level had gone up by 120 per cent, while membership fees had only gone up by 50 per cent. Members, however, refused to accept such evidence as justifying a call for an increase in fees, largely, it was said, owing to widespread opposition to the extravagances of Head Office.

This sniping at Head Office continued to be a feature of the Association's affairs throughout this period. In 1981, for example, a proposal for increases in capitation and enrolment fees was subjected to heavy criticism as members ignored the reality of the rise in costs and chose instead to direct their censure at expenditure on such 'costly luxuries' as Grand Presidential visits to overseas Circles. In their own defence, many men argued that, in common with most other people, they had to make personal economies, as government attempts to curb inflation led to rising unemployment, lower public spending and a slow-down in business activity.

It was this government policy which led to strains on the Benevolent Fund. A sharp rise in the number of Brothers suffering redundancy led, in 1975-76, to the Fund having a deficit of over £5000, leading to the sale of investments just as share prices fell sharply. This led Grand President Paddy Forde to call for increases in the voluntary contributions and to an appeal for all Brothers to covenant their contributions. It must be seen as an indication of apathy that in 1976 only 3000 of the 10,000 men were covenanting, and, in spite of repeated appeals and the appointment of Circle Covenant Officers, only some 5000 were covenanting in 1981.

Concern for the redundant led to the development of the Redundancy Scheme long associated with the names of Jim McNabb and Stan West, the Association's first Redundancy Officers. Their work was the background to the production of a Redundancy Scheme which was laid before the Association at the 1981 Conference. This envisaged the setting up of a new charitable trust and the employment of a full-time careers adviser to help unemployed Brothers by careers counselling, introductions to potential employers, and contacts with employment agencies. This full-time officer would be helped by area careers advisers from within the ranks of the Association.

It is too early to say what the fate of this scheme may be. The brainchild of Province No. 17 in general and of Tony Weir in particular, it is reminiscent, in some ways, of the 'Service' schemes of the 1920s which had a poor record. Many Brothers consider that existing agencies already provide a national network of experienced advisers to assist the redundant, and that the Association's scheme would be either a very costly addition to the existing network, or a poor relative and hence a failure. There are, however, those who ignore the membership's apathy and unwillingness to face financial reality. These call for the Association to 'buy up or buy into' firms of career counsellors, considering, rightly, that the proposed area advisers would be only 'well-meaning amateurs'. But in view of the membership's past voting record, one wonders where the finance for such a venture would come from.

2. Relations with the Hierarchy

During this period there was an improvement in the Association's relationship with the Hierarchy. The clouds which had appeared as a result, on the one hand, of their rejection of the Chaplaincies scheme and, on the other hand, of the alleged excesses of the Association's comments on the Laity Commissions, disappeared. In part this may have been due to the coming to terms, by both parties, with the nature of the Church in the Modern World: the newly-appointed Cardinal Hume invited a Catenian participation in the life of the Church; and the Association showed that it had come to realise that there was no room for the extravagant claims on behalf of the laity which were made in the 1960s.

This reappraisal of the role of the Association formed part of the continuing debate on Aims and Objects, with evidence of the persistent awareness that the Association existed 'against a national background of a growing atheistic humanism – a rejection of traditional Christian values . . .'. It was this which led Faupel of Kingston to ask that 'Circle meetings, or groups of members, give some time to the discussion of their Faith and its practical implications in their own spheres of work'. Others asked that the Association 'take positive action to defend the basic beliefs of our religion'.

The demand for some corporate action led to a discussion paper on 'Moral Issues' being introduced to the 1977 A.G.M. by John Eyre. This urged members to join certain organisations (such as S.P.U.C. and Life) to write to their M.P.s and to support parish-based and national organisations which aimed at providing wider adult education. But, the pamphlet claimed, Grand Council had no authority to speak or write on behalf of the wider membership on moral issues.

The debate at the Torquay A.G.M. was disappointing; the majority indicated that they wanted no change in the Aims and Objects and rejected arguments for giving Grand Council powers to speak on behalf of the membership on moral issues.

There then took place a debate on a proposal to change the Rules so as to allow the appointment of a Committee empowered to concern itself with 'issues before Parliament' and to report to Grand Council, which would then 'make such public pronouncements as it deems appropriate'. Pat Coker, proposing the motion, argued that it was time that the membership had to 'take up our responsibilities and act like Catholics'. His proposal was supported by men who maintained that in an age of 'moral decline we must do something about it and that the Association had a voice that can be heard'. The majority, however, having rejected John Eyre's call, were in no mood to accept Coker's proposals. None the less, the debate – in *Catena*, in Circles and at the A.G.M. – had served to bring the concept of action clearly before the Brothers.

There were several end-products of this wide debate. There was, for example, the reminder that the Catholic Evidence Guild still existed as an outlet for Catenian action. There was the Presidential address by Pat Stevens at Blackpool in 1978, in which, having disavowed any intention of re-opening the Moral Issues debate, he went on to remind the membership of the continuing moral decline and the boast that 'we are proudly Catholic', and to claim that 'the time will come when as an Association we speak collectively as well as individually' in support of Hierarchical statements and action in defence of our faith and morals.

And there was, significantly, Catenian involvement in the Renewal Movement, sometimes wrongly called the Charismatic Movement. In *Catena* there were calls for more men to join the weekly prayer groups in their localities. In the Manchester area, in Newport, Basingstoke and the South generally, there was a good deal of involvement in prayer groups which have, as a prime object, 'a really live commitment to an active faith'. For, as the journeyings of John Paul II showed, 'there is a hunger for spirituality' so great that *Catena* argued, 'We need to urge ourselves to greater prayer.'

There was also the evidence that many individual Catenians had become heavily involved in the formation of Pastoral Councils as well as of parish and deanery councils. In Middlesbrough, for example, Bishop McClean 'when he formed a Pastoral Council relied much on brothers of the Circle'. The Association was asked to nominate members to the Justice and Peace Commission and to present evidence to a Hierarchical working party on marriage. This led to the issuing of a questionnaire to members, and to the production of a body of evidence for the working party. At the same time, in March 1978, the Association was preparing a document for the Commission on Priestly Formation. The quiet constructive tone of this document is in marked contrast to the over-critical attitude of documents prepared in the 1960s, and this must have been instrumental in helping to improve relationships with the Hierarchy.

Evidence of this improvement was widespread. At the 800th meeting of the Blackburn Circle, for example, Bishop Holland 'congratulated the Circle on its achievements and asked Brothers to have courage in upholding the faith in these difficult times'. The special relationship which has always existed between the Scottish Bishops and the Association was highlighted in February 1977, when Cardinal Gray said a special Mass for some 300 members and their families as part of the celebration of the centenary of the restoration of the Scottish Hierarchy. And then there was the National Pastoral Congress. Archbishop Worlock, as Chairman of the National Committee of the N.P.C., called together the lay organisations of his archdiocese and asked them to form an organising committee. It was noticeable that he did not invite representatives of the Catenian Association to this first meeting; he had, it seems, not forgiven it for the 'misunderstandings' over the Chaplaincies scheme and for the criticisms of the Hierarchical Commissions. But it was ironically noticeable that he invited Michael Sampson to chair the committee. Sampson was, and is, a member of South Liverpool Circle, and Sampson, not surprisingly, turned to men he knew, so that Jack Molyneux, Hugh O'Roake and Jack Cooper (all of Liverpool No. 4 Circle), John Mercer of No. 74 Circle and Bob French, Raymond Ahearn and Terry Moorhead (all of South Liverpool Circle) were prominent in the organising of the Congress. There was Jim Morris of St Helens who, as Provincial President, recruited Brothers to act as marshals at the final session, when some 50 Bishops from all over the world assembled with all the delegates, among whom were a number of Catenians appointed to represent their various dioceses as well as two delegates appointed by Grand Council. It was a hopeful portent for the future that the Association should have been instrumental in organising this Congress which was meant to emphasise the role of the laity in the Modern World. As Sampson wrote, 'How sad that the Association is not called upon as a national lay organisation more often; perhaps our own aims are too inwards.' Maybe, too, some members of the Hierarchy have not yet come to terms with the very statements issued on their own behalf in the documents produced after the Congress as they continue to fail to realise the importance of the laity.

There were some Catenians who thought that the laity had a role to play as supporters of 'the priests who seem to become more and more confused'. Grand President Jack Browning suggested that

> we could act as a sounding board for conveying to the Hierarchy the views and criticisms of the lay body on the conduct of religious affairs. Would not the Bishops be encouraged to have the active interest of responsible lay folk in their concerns? Isn't this precisely the new concept of the Church which the Bishops themselves formulated at Vatican II in that phrase 'the people of God'?

Not everyone welcomed the attempt to draw the Association more closely into the work of the Church. Some thought that there was a danger of the Association's becoming 'a cross between the Little Sisters of the Poor and Opus Dei', while, in opposing Coker's motion at the 1977 A.G.M., Past Grand Treasurer Eddie Maltby brought the 'cold sponge of pragmatism upon the ambitions of the membership'. Maltby argued that the Association, as such, had not the capacity to carry through effectively any ambitious plans; it had neither the money, nor the leaders with sufficient time to spare, to promote such plans. He conceded that some individual Catenians might have the time and that other Catenians might have the money, and suggested that Catenian action be left to such individuals. Long and painful experience had taught Maltby that the Association could not yet act as a spearhead for the new laity, although, in these changing times, the Association could well undergo a major change of emphasis so that, in the future, it might adopt just that forceful role.

3. Catenians in Action

Meanwhile the Association's members were active and it is a matter of regret that one can give no more than a glimpse of some of that Catenian activity. If, in the following lines, there are references to this Circle or that undertaking some action, it should be understood that almost every other Circle can justifiably claim that its members also were doing precisely the same. The fact that only a few Circles are named or a few individuals picked out for mention should not be taken as an indication that only they were active. Rather should their activity be seen as typical of the work and activity of most Circles and Brothers.

Although Hugh Rossi's promotion to the Shadow Cabinet led to his resignation from the Association, he had the good wishes of many members who, later, were to be pleased at his elevation to Ministerial rank in the Thatcher government. Catenians continued to occupy Mayoral chairs. In St Helens, Charles Martin had a Catenian councillor-colleague in Tom Harvey and two other Catenian magistrate-colleagues in Basil Shacklady and Gerry Griffiths, while Reg Thorndike of the West Middlesex Circle was mayor's consort to his wife, Betty Thorndike, one of whose first civic functions was a civic Mass at Hayes to which Reg, President of the Circle, led his brother Catenians. Mike King of Brooklands Circle became the first Catholic Mayor of Trafford and Tom Francis of the Eccles Circle became Mayor of the City of Salford, while James Glynn became Mayor of Chorley within a week of his being inaugurated in the Chorley Circle. And as support for these and other Catenian Mayors, there were a host of Catenian councillors and magistrates, the Birkenhead Circle setting a splendid example by providing two members of the Wirral Council and two members of the Merseyside County Council.

Members of the Association were also active in a number of child-centred societies. Michael Bell of the Bournemouth Circle was responsible for the formation of the Lawyers for Life organisation in 1977, and could write in February 1979 that Brothers from some 50 Circles were members of the new organisation numbering about one-third of its total membership. Catenians in many parts of the country undertook work on behalf of Life and S.P.U.C. in their individual capacities and, on occasions, as Circles. Banbury Catenians, for example, are aware of the work of Frank Davis for the local Life and Care Housing Trust which provides practical help for mothers-to-be and mothers and young children in the North Oxfordshire area. Douglas Browne of the Croydon Circle was more than the advocate of an ambitious scheme for a Catenian social centre and a constant attender at singing competitions in Croydon and Leeds. He was also chairman of the Southwark Catholic Children's Society and, as such, an active promoter of Cabrini House, a short-stay home for physically and mentally handicapped children in Forest Hill. This was founded by the Southwark Diocesan Catholic Handicapped Children's Fellowship, in which Reg Cornwell of the Orpington Circle was active as a manager of Cabrini House, while his wife, Peggy, was diocesan secretary of the Fellowship. Other Catenian 'activists' in this Fellowship included Will Farrelly of South London and Bill Ridgers of Purley and Epsom Circles.

On the Isle of Wight, Eddie Minghella was chairman of the island branch of the Save the Children Fund which, in 1978, held a fair which raised around £5000. The London Belgravia Circle was praised by the Association for Spina Bifida and Hydrocephalus for 'kindness and practical help in raising funds to help our work along'. Brian Glynn of the Ashton-under-Lyne Circle, having spent most of his adult life in one form or another of Catholic action, became president of the S.V.P. in 1979, and 'was personally responsible for sending two spina bifida children and their parents to Lourdes'. That he was made a J.P. in 1978 was a fitting reward for a man who followed so faithfully in the footsteps of his fellow-townsman, the great McDermott.

Many Circles continued to raise money for the servicing of the Catenian Jumbulance, which by 1978 had become 'regionalised and based in Grimsby where it is looked after by the Grimsby and District Across Support Group. Of eight members of the group, five are Catenians.' Other Circles adopted the Hosanna House as their special charity. Few Circles can have bettered the success of the small Exeter Circle, which in 1974 raised £600 to endow a room at the House, a room now known as The Exeter Room, and in 1976 raised another £600 to help furnish it and then raised some £1000 for the House in 1978.

Many Circles supported the work of the Handicapped Children's Trust. Cardiff Brothers raised money both for the H.C.P.T. and for the local Nazareth House. The Brothers of the Swansea Circle presented two wheelchairs to the H.C.P.T. in memory of a former Brother, Luke Hopkins, and of the young son of Brother John Wall and his wife. The Preston South Circle also made the H.C.P.T. their main objective, raising some £400 at 'a rave up' in 1978. Plymouth, Torbay and Exeter Circles combined to support a Plymouth venture to take ten handicapped people to Lourdes. Each of the twenty helpers travelled at their own expense and raised the money to pay for the patients' fares. This form of help for the handicapped was, in a sense, a spin-off from the H.C.P.T. and Across. It was also the latter-day version of the work which Catenians had done for many years as brancardiers. For many years the Chief Brancardier of the English National Pilgrimage has been a Catenian – George Farrell of the Southend-on-Sea Circle, succeeding Agnew Reid of the City of London Circle when, in 1974, he retired after twenty years' service. Another Catenian, David Lewis of the Cambridge Circle, was Chief Brancardier for the Catholic Association Pilgrimage Trust, whose annual pilgrimage attracts much Catenian support. Indeed, there were so many Catenians at Lourdes during some Septembers that Catenian meetings were held. In 1980, for example, John Morrison, of the City of Westminster Circle, took the chair at a meeting in Lourdes on the night when his Vice-President took the chair at the regular monthly meeting of the Circle in London. Gerard Wright suggested that the Lourdes branch of the City of Westminster Circle be presented with a silver snuffbox to be given to the Circle which provided the largest number of men at a Lourdes meeting. In 1980 such an award would have gone to the City of London Circle.

Brothers of the Halifax Circle continued to support the local Cheshire Home which was founded after Cheshire had spoken at the Circle's dinner in 1956 and had inspired Richard Blackburn to take the initiative. Blackburn was used to action, having been one of the founders of the local C.P.E.A., the founder of a Catholic bookshop in the city, and a worker for the Halifax Flowers Fund which 'solicits donations from mourners at funerals instead of flowers', using the money to build houses for the elderly.

If the Oxford Circle is 'proudly committed to help run the Nazareth House bus', the Association as a whole should be proud of the admirable record of the North Glamorgan Circle, which 'although small in numbers has a fine record when it comes to the President's annual charity dance'. In 1977 this event raised £220 for the H.C.P.T., while in 1978 it raised £404 for the Little Sisters of the Assumption at Dowlais, who work among the sick and poor of the area. Individual Catenians in the Manchester area have been associated with the Morning Star Hostel since 1963, when it was founded 'with the valuable assistance of Mr Joe Cox and his family, amongst others in the Catenians'. This hostel caters for men who, owing to alcohol or other reasons, cannot be housed in other hostels. There is a chapel where Mass is said on Sundays and Tuesdays, while a prayer meeting is held on Thursday. The founders of the Association, with their 'one drink only' rule, would have approved of this particular Catenian activity.

We have seen that members of the Association have a close link with the

Serra Movement and that, in the past, members had gone on to study for the priesthood. The ordination of Fr Dan O'Connor, for many years an active member of Stratford-on-Avon Circle, was notable for the fact that one of his sons, Fr Liam, assisted Archbishop Dwyer at the altar, while another son, then studying for the priesthood, acted as cantor. Late in 1977, John Farrelly of the Mid-Herts Circle entered Allen Hall to study for the priesthood and was ordained by Bishop O'Brien in 1979 at the church of SS. Alban and Stephen, St Albans. In 1978, the Leicester Circle was represented at the ordination of Fr Sylvester Cotter, who had been a member of the Circle before going to the Beda, thus providing a link betwen Catenian activity and its spiritual base.

4. Catenian Ladies

The claim that the development of the Association is a reflection of a wider social history is well borne out by the evolving treatment of the wives of members. In March 1977, John O'Callaghan of the Southport Circle wrote a powerful letter in which he suggested ways in which the Association might behave to protect members and their families from the inroads of pagan humanism. The final paragraph of his letter is relevant to this section of our *History*:

> ... Thirdly, to form Catenian women's councils. Circles have their occasional functions and invite wives and daughters.... I suggest the setting up of a completely separate ladies' council.... This would bring together Catenian women with a common bond, where the social and moral affairs of the day, as they affect them and their families, could be discussed at some length. There is here a powerful and untapped Catenian linked source of moral rearmament without directly involving Grand Council itself.

O'Callaghan's proposals were at odds with the views of many Brothers. But, as we shall see, there has been a slow development of the concept of a closer relationship between the Association and its members' wives than would once have seemed possible.

The Manchester (No. 1) Circle held its first Ladies' Evening on 11 October 1910 and provided an example which has been followed ever since, albeit reluctantly in some places. The members of the Bristol Circle (founded in 1914) resisted requests that wives should accompany their husbands at the Annual Dinner until 1933. The Swansea Circle (founded 1920) did not have a Ladies' Night until 1923, and did not invite wives to the Annual Dinner until 1925. The members of the Edinburgh Circle (founded 1919) resisted pressure to allow wives to attend the Annual Dinner until 1937, in which year, oddly, the Preston Circle (founded 1913) welcomed the formation of a Ladies' Committee.

It may seem strange that members should have been so reluctant to have the company of their wives at even an annual function. But this was merely the reflection of the social history of the period when society was almost entirely male-dominated. And if some Circles, such as Preston, seemed to be adventurous in allowing wives to play a part in social functions, it has to be said that they did so with self-interest in mind. The members of the Wigan Circle (founded in 1913) took their wives with them on a summer outing in 1922 and noted that this was the first-ever really successful outing. Circles which encouraged members' wives to help in organising social functions did so because it had become clear that this involvement helped ensure the success of the Young People's dance, the Benevolent Fund Evening or other similar functions. Portsmouth, for example, reported that its Ladies' Committee was largely responsible for ensuring the success of the Circle's work for the Children's Fund, a comment which was repeated by the Nottingham Circle.

But this was only 'fringe action' with Ladies being 'allowed' to help the various Circles in their members' activities. This is not what O'Callaghan called for. Moreover, it must be said that even this 'fringe' involvement was not universally welcomed. It is said that that outstanding Grand President, Pat Taggart would not attend any function where ladies were present, while even in 1981 members of some Circles were angry when their circular was used as a vehicle to advertise inaugural meetings of Ladies' groups. But the emergence of such groups is a fact of history and the result of social development, for modern society is no longer as male-dominated as was the society in which Pat Taggart grew up.

Wives of members of Doncaster Circle (founded 1927) have held regular monthly meetings since 1950, and these meetings have 'proved a very worthwhile thing, for not only do they enjoy themselves, but get to know each other so that when they meet together with the Brothers at a Dinner Dance or other social function, they are not strangers to one another'. Similarly, informal meetings, but only of a few ladies, were held in Plymouth in the 1950s and have led there to the emergence of a very active and much larger group of Catenian wives. In 1965, the ladies of the Bournemouth Catenians went a stage further. Led by Maureen, the wife of President Sid Dabinett, the ladies formed the first fully established 'Catenian Ladies Association' in the country. They chose the name 'Catalinks' for the club, whose aim is to foster closer relationships between Catenian wives and families, widows of Catenians and others with Catenian connections. The members normally meet once a month in members' homes, where various demonstrations, slides and discussions take place. Visits to the theatre and other outings are regular features of the annual programme. The Catalinks have been notably active in visiting the sick at home and in hospital, while each Christmas a charity is adopted and donations are sent. The membership has been 'encouragingly constant' and the atmosphere at all gatherings pleasantly relaxed. Firm friendships have been formed and 'we like to think that helpful support is given to the bereaved'.

The question of helping the widows of deceased brothers formed the centrepiece of John Smith's Presidential address in 1981. Smith pointed out that if a Catenian's wife dies, 'he should be able to resume a normal Catenian life'. This is not the case for a deceased Catenian's widow. 'Although Circles should invite widows to some of their annual functions, many of these dear ladies find the personalised attention a little embarrassing and find loneliness even in the crowded rooms and amongst the friends they have been happy with in the past.' Smith then spoke of the widows' club organised by the Knights of the Southern Cross and suggested that a similar organisation might be developed for Catenian widows.

It is noticeable that only in the recent past has concern for widows really developed. In his Presidential address at Blackpool in 1979 Dick Last referred to the

> custom for a member of Grand Council to keep in touch with the widows of our past members, and his report forms an important item on our agenda. I commend some such appointment at Circle level where it does not exist. I know that many Circles

have excellent systems for keeping in regular contact not only with the widows but also with their sick and elderly Brothers, but I have been impressed with one in particular. A very active welfare committee of the Bournemouth Circle seems to me to tackle the whole subject in a practical and caring way that deserves consideration by others.

It is hardly fortuitous that the Bournemouth Circle developed not only the welfare committee but also the Catalinks; for in a sense they are complementary. The welfare committee is made up of some five or six volunteers who meet monthly. When a Brother or a member of a Brother's family is in hospital, flowers are sent, visits arranged with Brothers who are special friends of the sick person (so involving in time everyone in the Circle), and Masses are said if the sick person is to have an operation. There is a well-developed 'taxi-service' to take non-driving wives to hospital for visits to husbands or children. The committee has divided the Brothers into groups of eight or nine, largely on a geographical basis, and has appointed a 'warden' in each group. Brothers are asked to let the 'warden' know about any illness in their families. He is expected to notice when any of 'his' group are absent from Circle meetings and to find out whether the absence is due to illness. He keeps in touch with the parish priest of his area, so that he soon finds out when a Brother or a member of a Brother's family is ill. He thereupon telephones the secretary of the committee, who then calls on other Brothers to help in whatever way may seem best.

When the sick person is a Catenian lady, then the Welfare Committee naturally calls for the help of members of the Catalinks, who, additionally, have their own antennae already alerted for news of the well-being of their own members. In this way the two organisations complement each other, and more than fulfil the aims which Smith had in mind. The Welfare Committee arranges for the widows to be taken to the lunches which the Circle organises on a bi-monthly basis for members and their wives who find it difficult to come to evening meetings during the winter months. It also invites them to various after-Circle functions – Ladies' Nights, Carol Concerts and the like, and to Circle Masses. On the other hand, membership of the Catalinks ensures that when the widow goes to such functions and meetings, she goes as a member of a ladies' group in which she is well known. If Dick Last could recommend the Bournemouth Welfare Committee to other Circles, it may be that the Catalinks should also be seen as the means of fulfilling obligations to Catenian widows, or, as Bournemouth prefers to describe them, 'the wives of our deceased Brothers'. In 1981 and 1982 there were signs that other Circles were taking an interest in this Catalink concept, which would also be a method of fulfilling O'Callaghan's hope that ladies' groups might provide that 'source of moral rearmament' so badly needed in modern times.

5. Catenian Families

O'Callaghan's concern for the well-being of Catenians' families is a reminder that the first stated Aim approved in June 1909, 'To promote the interests of the Brothers and their families . . .' has developed into the two Aims: 'To develop social bonds among the members and their families' and 'To advance the interests of members and their dependents by individual or collective action'.

In a sense everything done in and by members, Circles and the Association at large may be seen as being family-orientated. When a man is enrolled he has the words of the Charge to remind him that he is expected, as a result of his membership, to be a better son; a better husband and a better father. Circles have over the years organised a variety of functions for members' families – dances for teenagers, inter-Circle rallies, Christmas parties and so on.

For a minority the development of 'social bonds' has led to membership of the Catenian Golf Society. It is a reflection of our social history that this Society was first mentioned at the 1928 A.G.M. There were local Catenian Golfing Societies catering for the enthusiasts in different Circles and Provinces. Only in 1929 was the nationwide C.G.S. inaugurated to link these local Societies together, and a competition held for the Catenian Golf Trophy. For many years the golf competition took place after lunch on the Saturday of the A.G.M. in 'a mad scramble' before men went to dress for the evening's festivities. Two provincial Societies organised the first 'modern' Catenian championship in April 1968 at the Mere Golf Club in Cheshire. Since 1974, Rowland Young, the national secretary, has organised the championships at Royal Birkdale, Wentworth, Killarney, Turnberry and other famous courses. Since 1977, the meeting has also included a Catenian Ladies' championship, one more sign of the social change which affects the Association's development. As a result of these meetings 'many new friendships are formed among men (and later women) from all over the country brought together by their love of golf who find on closer acquaintance that they have other things in common too'. The Circles in Southern Africa also used golf as a means of bringing Catenian families together.

> The Bulawayo and Salisbury Circles hold an Annual Charter Function when they meet for a weekend in August. The men play for the Henry Beddy Golfing Trophy, the wives talk over tea under the trees of the hotel grounds, while the children have a 'super' time. In the evening a Joint Circle Meeting is followed by a Dinner/Dance and we finally have Holy Mass in the hotel on Sunday morning, before Catenians disperse to their homes.

Another example of social development and the growth of new activities is provided by the Catenian Caravanning Fellowship which grew out of a suggestion made in 1969 by Phil Scott (of Birmingham No. 64 Circle), one of the many Catenians who have held high office in the K.S.C., of which he was Supreme Knight. Scott invited caravanning and camping enthusiasts to meet for a weekend at Alton Towers. Other enthusiasts arranged *ad hoc* weekends, and it was fitting that for many years a late summer rally was held at Besford Court, a school which owed its foundation to the work of that outstanding Birmingham Catenian, J.B. Webb. By 1976, Catenian caravanning was known beyond the Midlands, owing to notices in *Catena*. Bill Mitchell (Preston), Fred Wilkinson and Desmond Jennings (Broughton-in-Craven) and others organised similar events in Province No. 10. The Caravanning Fellowship was formed in 1979 and now has over one hundred members. There are normally about forty caravans at each of the two national events, while smaller numbers attend the weekends arranged by Provinces or Circles. As one enthusiast wrote, 'Truly, the opportunity to meet Catenians from all parts of the country in an atmosphere of such informality and relaxation with their families provides the finest possible example of true Catenian spirit.'

Cyril Gaskin of the Durham Circle hoped that this *History* would deal with:

1. Fathers, sons and brothers (including brothers-in-law) being members;
2. Sons and daughters of Catenians marrying;
3. Families (or members rather) of Catenians entering religious life;
And in all of these I have a vested interest, in that my father and two brothers are members, as was my father-in-law and his son, and both my brother and I married into Catenianism. I also have a son a priest, and my wife's sister is a nun.

The Gaskins and their in-laws provide one example of that Catenian nexus which has been a mark of the Association's development, and which may be seen both as a natural outcome of the desire to strengthen social bonds and part-answer, at least, to O'Callaghan's hope that the Association may provide a bulwark against ever-encroaching paganism.

If there were a prize for 'the outstanding Catenian family' the award might go to the Bussys, for they provided, albeit only for a short time, the first example of the fourth-generation Catenian. There are, as the Directory will show, five Bussys of the third generation – Roger (enrolled in 1927) now a member of Westerham, Philip (born 1898) still a member of South London, Lawrence (born 1906) a member of City of Liverpool, Stephen (born 1909) a member of both City of London and Orpington Circles, and 'baby' Christopher (born 1914) a member of City of London and Colchester Circles. It was Christopher who wrote:

> The Bussy family has a long Catenian history. My maternal grandfather, Alex Bounevialle (born 1839) and my father, Phil Bussy, joined South London on the same night (10th July 1913). Paul Kelly was my uncle (his wife Beatrix was my father's sister). I was introduced to the City of London by Paul Kelly in 1952 but am also a member of Colchester of which I was founder President. Is there any other family with five brothers in the Association? Between us, we have ten sons and five sons-in-law of Catenian age, but apart from Anthony, none of them has followed in our wake,

although he had the confident belief that one of his own sons would do so 'when he is no longer weighed down with the cost of a young family. My nephew, the son of Stephen, was the first fourth-generation Catenian, but regrettably he left the Association after some nine years' membership.'

Another family which might claim parity with the Bussys is that of Alexander Carus, Grand President 1958–59, if only on the grounds that via 'cross connections of father, son and nephews we could possibly claim a fourth-generation connection'. The Carus family is one of Lancashire's 'old Catholic' families, tracing descent from Sir Thomas Carus of Kirkby Lonsdale and Halton, who died in 1571. One ancestor fought for Charles I in the Civil War, another forfeited the family estates for his part in the 1715 Rising; another, John Leyburn, was Vicar Apostolic of England from 1685 to 1702. We have already seen that 'The Chums' tried but failed to enrol Alexander Carus, 'a leader of the cotton industry and the first Catholic Mayor of Darwen' – the grandfather of the Past Grand President, who wrote:

> James Alexander Carus (now of the Leigh Circle) is descended from a William Carus who was lost at sea in 1841–42 off the Cape of Good Hope. John Machon Carus, my grandfather's younger brother, joined Manchester in November 1910 and was 139 on the roll. His son, Arthur Dawson Carus, joined Manchester in 1917, being 346 on the roll. He is still alive, aged 96 years. Edmund Louis Carus, a nephew of John Machon and my uncle, was a member of the Blackburn Circle until he died in 1927. His son, Alexander Francis Hubert Carus, also joined the Blackburn Circle (1946) but left the Association in 1967. Finally there is John Healy Carus, younger

brother of Edmund Louis, who joined Blackburn Circle in 1913 and who died in 1918, leaving a son, Anthony Carus, who joined the City of Liverpool Circle in 1948 but who resigned in 1975.

The Lomas family would also be in contention for the proposed award, partly because direct Catenian links go back to the origin of the Liverpool Circle and partly because through intermarriage it has created its own 'Lomas–Kearney–Miller–Vickerstaff' nexus. John Lomas (born 1875) was a founder member of the Liverpool (No. 4) Circle, being No. 8 on the roll. His son, Frank (Grand President 1963–64), joined the Stockport Circle in 1936 and, when his father moved to Macclesfield, helped him form the Macclesfield Group. Frank was the Founder President of the Macclesfield Circle, of which his father was President in 1950. Frank's three sons, John, Thomas and Peter, are all members of the Macclesfield Circle. John's father-in-law, Miles Miller, is a Past President of that Circle, while Miller's father-in-law, William Kearney, was Founder President of the Leigh Circle and one-time Mayor of the town. Peter's father-in-law, William Vickerstaff, was another Lomas-linked President of the Macclesfield Circle, into which Michael Vickerstaff, Peter's brother-in-law, was enrolled in 1981. There are a number of younger Lomas children, none yet of Catenian age; but one looks forward to the family providing a fourth generation of members.

Another family with many-sided Catenian links is that of Peter Sandham, a former President of North Lancashire Circle, whose uncle, Andy Sandham, the record-holding Test cricketer, was once a member of the Croydon Circle, and who wrote:

> ... my grandfather, Brother W.J. Atherton and my great uncle, Bro. C.F. Gardner were both founder members and subsequent Presidents of North Lancashire. My father, Frank, was President in 1955–57, my cousin, Roy Gardner, was President in 1969–71 (when he enrolled me) as I am currently President (1980–81). My grandfather, father and myself have continuous membership since foundation. Unfortunately, I have no sons to carry on the tradition. The family has contributed three Presidents to the Circle, a fact of which I am rather proud.

Southampton Brothers respect the memory of Ted Tickle, who died while this *History* was being written, and whose father was a founder member of the Southampton Circle which Ted joined when he was only twenty-two years old. The Circle later enjoyed the pleasure of having grandfather and father present at the initiation of Ted's son, who unfortunately died in 1970. Brothers from Circles in Glasgow, Sheffield and Perth (Western Australia) might nominate the Maguires for the proposed award. Dr Peter Maguire was a founder member of the Glasgow Circle. His son, also Dr Peter Maguire, was enrolled into the Glasgow Circle, later transferring to Sheffield where he became President. More significantly, he was the Founder President of the City of Perth Circle, which was inaugurated in February 1977, some five months before his father died, aged 95, when a third Dr Peter was enrolled into the City of Perth Circle during the inauguration ceremony, thus creating a link between the founding of the Glasgow Circle and the founding of the Circle in Perth.

Dennis Munro, of The Duchy of Cornwall Circle, is the grandson of Charles J. Munich who, as we have seen, was largely instrumental in obtaining for the Association the first Papal Blessing in 1920. Munich was the son of an immigrant named Munch, a Prussian farmer who came to live in England. He changed the name to Munich before 1914, and it was Dennis Munro's father who further changed the name of his branch of the family during the war. But not even a link with Munich and the Papal Blessing would bring Dennis Munro into contention for the award.

It might be that the historian of the Association's affairs would offer the award to the Charlier family, not because it has a longer history than others, for it has only a third-generation record. But it has prepared a family tree which is a model of its kind and is reproduced on page 225 as an encouragement to other Catenian families to 'go and do thou likewise'. Andrew C.J. Charlier was an early member of the Sheffield Circle (founded 1912) who later became the Founder President of the Thames Valley Circle in 1918. One of his sons, Alexander, was a member of the Sheffield Circle, a second son, Oswald, was initiated by his father into the Thames Valley Circle in June 1919, and a third, Bernard, was a member of North London and a founder member of the North West London Circle. It is his son, Anthony, of the Purley Circle who has supplied the family tree.

This tree also serves to fulfil another of the expressed wishes of Cyril Gaskin, namely that the *History* might show the members of Catenian families who have become priests or entered the religious life. Unfortunately, space does not permit such a record. It can, however, be said that there are very few Circles which do not have what might be termed 'a Catenian priest or religious', with the O'Donnell family having provided the example from the outset. Likewise there have been very few years when *Catena* has not recorded the ordination or profession of sons or daughters of Catenians. That the Association has, in this way, made an indirect contribution to the well-being of The People of God may be seen as yet another justification for its existence.

6. Has the Association a future?

Many indeed are the reasons justifying the existence of the Association. Over the years many members of the Hierarchy have expressed their admiration for the Association because of its aims to sustain family life. They, and many priests, have also spoken or written of the value of that 'friendship' which is one of the marks of the Association. It was, as we have seen, 'friendship' which was most often given in answer to one of the questions set out in 1980, 'Why did you join the Association and why would you recommend it to others?'

The visible proof of that 'friendship' has taken varied forms. Brothers of different Circles have their own particular examples to offer. For one Brother it was best illustrated by the manner of the death of Jack Gormley, a highly successful if retired businessman who was killed in an accident 'as he was taking a bottle of Guinness to a sick Brother'. A priest in Bournemouth said that he had best seen what the Association really meant when at an Annual Banquet he had seen Ray Faulkner feed Bob Barrett with a spoon. Barrett, a former President of the Circle, spent nineteen years in hospital with multiple sclerosis. Faulkner had had his car specially 'cannibalised' to take the hoist needed to get Barrett in and out of the car for an occasional visit home or to a Circle function. And seeing the helpless Barrett, his head in a vice-like contraption, being fed by the caring Faulkner was to see the Association in action, so far as one perceptive priest was concerned. 'Inasmuch as you do it to one of these . . .'.

Some might think that the Association's worth is proved by some spectacular success such as the raising of the money for the Beda or for the Jumbulance. Others claim that the 'long-haul' work involved in the constant Battle for the Schools, or for such charities as the H.C.P.T. and Across, shows the Association at its best. There are similar claims for the multi-varied activities of Circles and individuals in their localities – for Cheshire and Nazareth Homes, for Life and S.P.U.C., for the S.V.P. and the K.S.C., and so on almost *ad infinitum*. And there is something in those claims.

But the 'Aims and Objects' puts the emphasis on the value of the Association for the individual Brother and his family. In a society which has become increasingly paganised – with Parliament and the judiciary legalising the murder of the unborn child and, more recently, condoning the 'allowed-to-die' attitude taken by some paediatricians when dealing with the handicapped baby, with psychiatrists and psychologists teaching that the family is outmoded or even an obstacle to individual 'growth', with pre-marital sex and adultery being treated as 'the norm' by playwrights, social workers and an increasing proportion of the population – in such a paganised society the value of a body such as the Catenian Association may be seen as even greater now than it has been at any time during the past seventy-five years. For the existence of the Association seems most justified, not by the spectacular event or the 'long-haul' work or the activities for various charities. Its real value ultimately lies in its prime function, namely, to help a man to be slightly the better father, husband and son, fitted to make more of a success of the work of developing that family on which, 'proudly Catholic' as its members claim to be, they know that both the Church and society depend.

And that would have been the end of this book, had I not received a letter early in 1982 when the manuscript was in the hands of the printer. It came from a Brother who, for obvious reasons, will have to remain nameless, living in a country which equally obviously will also have to be left unidentified. It gives the best résumé of the need for, and the spirit of, the Association:

> We are in a Marxist state ... economically, socially and religiously we are being subjected to increasing harassment. This has forced people like us to turn inward ... we tend to arrange ourselves and our social lives so that we can live in an atmosphere free from petty recrimination, where our children can grow up and develop in an atmosphere of love and peace, where we can just be ourselves without having to defend the social and economic position we are in. This has heightened our concept of family and brotherhood. We now look to our own for companionship, family contact and social activity. The Catenian Association is the perfect vehicle for this, and my joining it could not have come at a better time. The sense of brotherhood, the Catholic atmosphere of our social gatherings, the whole family feeling with other members, these are for us very precious. To know that there are others just like yourself with whom you can socialize, who care, and who want you, not for what they can get out of you, but for what you are, really provides a sense of security in very troubled times. Where Catholics are in a minority, this Catholic contact is vital to give oneself and one's family an island of Catholic peace and friendship in a sea of hate and bitterness.

O'Donnell, Locan, Gibbons, Tait, McDermott, Hogan, Brosch, O'Dea, Perceval and the other giants of the Catenian past would have understood this, and would also have been justifiably proud to find that their Association was so valued in its 74th year. If our worst fears are realised, if our already pagan

THE MATURING OF THE EASTER PEOPLE 1975-1983

society becomes increasingly pagan and Marxist, then future Catenians, living in Great Britain, may well look back to the faithfulness of present-day Catenians, consider the priceless heritage handed down by them, and express themselves with the same heartfelt gratitude.

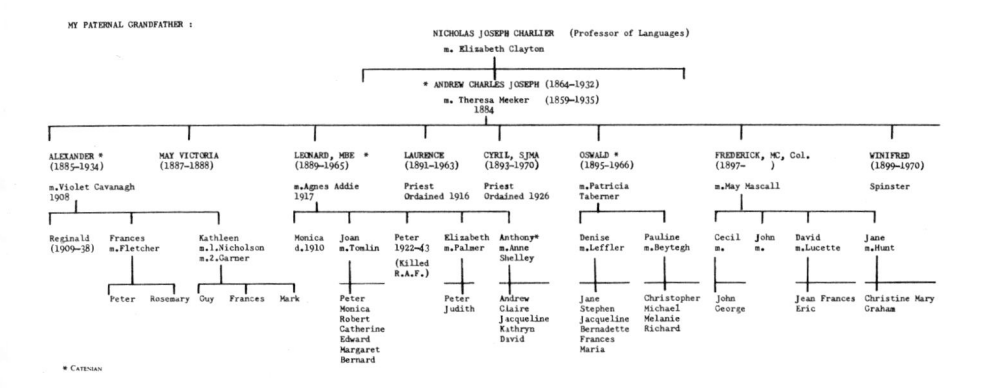

MY PATERNAL GRANDFATHER:

NICHOLAS JOSEPH CHARLIER (Professor of Languages)
m. Elizabeth Clayton

* ANDREW CHARLES JOSEPH (1864-1932)
m. Theresa Meeker (1859-1935)
1884

ALEXANDER *	MAY VICTORIA	LEONARD, MBE *	LAURENCE	CYRIL, SJMA	OSWALD *	FREDERICK, MC, Col.	WINIFRED
(1885-1934)	(1887-1888)	(1889-1965)	(1891-1963)	(1893-1970)	(1895-1966)	(1897-)	(1899-1970)
m.Violet Cavanagh 1908		m.Agnes Addie 1917	Priest Ordained 1916	Priest Ordained 1926	m.Patricia Taberner	m.May Mascall	Spinster

| Reginald (1909-38) | Frances m.Fletcher | Kathleen m.1.Nicholson m.2.Garner | Monica d.1910 | Joan m.Tomlin | Peter 1922-43 (Killed R.A.F.) | Elizabeth m.Palmer | Anthony* m.Anne Shelley | Denise m.Leffler | Pauline m.Beytegh | Cecil m. | John m. | David m.Lucette | Jane m.Hunt |

| Peter | Rosemary | Guy | Frances | Mark | Peter Monica Robert Catherine Edward Margaret Bernard | Peter Judith | Andrew Claire Jacqueline Kathryn David | Jane Stephen Jacqueline Bernadette Frances Maria | Christopher Michael Melanie Richard | John George | Jean Frances Eric | Christine Mary Graham |

* CATENIAN

Index

Across Trust, 108, 192, 215
Addly, Thomas J., 148
Africa: Circles in, 45, 92, 172, 199–205
Ahearn, Raymond, 214
Alden, Geoffrey, 202
Albert, King of the Belgians, 46, 54, 98
Almond, Bro., 169
Amigo, Archbishop Peter, 44, 119, 149
anti-Catholicism, 1, 4–5, 13, 14, 15, 40, 41–2, 49, 123–4, 134–5, 157, 168
Apostleship of the Sea, 108
Apostolic Blessing, 42, 77, 222–3
Arnold, Laurie, 165, 174, 177
Aspell, Dennis, 198, 205
Assumption, Little Sisters of the, 175, 216
Aveling, Fr, on Aims and Objects, 49, 52
Ayers, Laurence, 201, 204–5

Badman, Bro., 199
Bainbridge, Tony, 66
Baines, Bernard, 44
Baines, Thomas, 42, 44, 68, 76, 81, 84, 85, 110, 149
Baker, Jimmy, 55, 127, 200
Banks, Tom, 166
Barrett, Bob, 175, 223
Barry, Bro., 165
Barton, 95
Battle for Schools: (1905) 7; (1908) 137; (1920s) 21; (1943–4) 21; (1945–53) 21, 155–8, 164, 166–8
Beales, Professor A.C.F., 164
Beck, Archbishop Andrew, 168, 179–82
Beda College, 21, 46, 49, 73–8, 108, 113, 139, 176, 217, 223
Benedict XV, Pope, 75
bigotry, 5, 14, 41, 44, 68, 124, 134, 135, 156
Bilsborrow, Bishop John, 2
Birmingham, 101–2, 140, 141; St Gerard Hospital, 70; White Horse, Congreve Street, 56
Blackburn: Castle Hotel, 38
Blackburn, Richard, 216
Blackpool: Royal Hotel, 48
Bodkin, Bro., 137
Boniface, W.G., 162, 163
Bourne, Cardinal Francis, 2, 12, 15, 30, 32, 42, 49, 67, 68–9, 71, 74, 75–6, 77, 141
Bournemouth: St Peter's School, 167
Bowden, H.D., 52
Bowen, John, 147, 159, 191, 192, 207
Bower, Alfred, Lord Mayor of London, 134, 140
Bower, Cdr, M.P., 157
Bowyer, J.M., 190

Boyle, Alderman Dan, 23, 27, 29
Bradford: Victoria Hotel, 45
brancardiers, 175, 190, 216
Branigan, J., 41
Brennan, J.E., 46
Briggs, Percy, 124, 142
Bright, Bishop Humphrey, 155
Brindle, Bishop Robert, 47
Bristol: Grand Hotel, 48
Brosch, Richard, 43–4, 46, 47, 48, 49, 54, 55, 56–9, 60, 61, 62, 66, 68, 69, 72, 77, 81, 82, 102, 113, 125, 142, 162
Browne, Douglas, 211
Browning, Jack, 207, 208, 214
Burns, Bob, 48, 173, 199
Burns, Leo, 67, 163
Burns, Tom, 11, 12, 20
Burton, Bishop George Ambrose, 141, 142
Bushell, Bro., 42
Bussy, Christopher, 193, 221
Butcher, George, 65
Byers, Bro., 34

Callaghan, Bro., 69
Callaghan, John, 31, 107
Caraman, René, 42, 54, 55
Cardiff: St David's Cathedral, 151; St Illtyd's School, 137–8, 166, 168
Carroll, Bro., 166
Carus, Alex, 127, 178, 200–1
Casartelli, Bishop Louis Charles, 2, 4, 6, 7, 8, 9–10, 11, 12, 14, 16, 17–18, 19, 20, 21, 22, 23, 27, 30, 31, 32, 33, 34, 35–8, 39, 41, 42, 43, 49, 62, 67, 68, 70, 76, 121, 122, 139, 142, 143, 165
Cash, Edward, 46
Cashman, Bishop David, 174, 187–8, 193
Caswell, Bro., 147
Catalinks, 218, 219
Catena: conceived by Birmingham Brothers, 57; editors: James Watson, 56; Richard Brosch, 59, 61, 162; Sydney Redwood,17, 44, 59, 162; L. J. Sullivan, 59; Bernard Kirchner, 59, 162, 181, 188; Leo Simmonds, 60, 162, 189
Catena Trustees Limited, 118
Catenian Association:
academics as Catenians, 137; Aims and Objects, 20–1, 49–50, 52, 59, 108, 121–31, 141–3, 164, 174, 187–9, 212, 219, 224; Annual General Meetings, 77, 82, 83, 85, 104, 169; (1909) 26; (1916) 51; (1923) 77, 85; (1924) 77; (1925) 77; (1931) 126; (1932) 60; (1937) 143; (1947) 164; (1948) 64; (1949) 79; (1950) 161; (1951) 169, 178; (1952) 170–1; (1955) 179; (1957) 64; (1958) 105; (1960) 64; (1961)

177, 179; (1963) 35, 177, 187–8; (1965) 94, 182; (1966) 94, 187–8; (1970) 186; (1971) 87–8; (1977) 212, 214; Anthems, 42, 52; apathy, 73, 136, 149–50, 172, 211; Armed Forces, Catenians in, 151; Association Officers: Grand Chamberlain, 51; Grand Director, 83, 84, 85, 86, 87, 90–1, 94, 97; Grand President, 27, 35, 38, 39, 42, 43, 44, 45, 46, 47, 48, 50, 51, 56, 61, 62, 64, 68, 69, 76, 77, 79, 83, 84, 85, 93–4, 97, 147, 150, 168, 173, 196; Grand Secretary, 31, 33, 41, 51, 56, 58, 60, 64, 71, 77, 82, 93, 95–7, 100, 103, 104, 111, 170, 173, 196, 210; Grand Treasurer, 44, 51, 110; Grand Vice-President, 51, 57, 76, 86, 103; attendance at meetings: decline in, 73, 82, 136, 145, 172; increase in, 159; benevolence, 49, 52, 91, 107–20; Benevolent Board: 34, 52, 73, 93, 107, 110–12; Benevolent Fund, 31, 73, 108, 109–10, 112, 113–14, 116, 117–19, 120, 121, 139, 169, 187, 211; 'Brothers', 25, 26, 27, 88–9; capitation fees, 119, 211; Caravan Club, 129; Caravanning Fellowship, Catenian, 220; ceremonial, 89; *see also* ritual; charitable and social work, 49–50, 61, 62, 70, 112–20, 140–1, 175, 190–2, 215–16; charge to candidate for initiation, 21; Children's Fund, 61, 77, 109, 112–15, 116, 117–18, 119, 126, 127, 139; 'Chums, the', 12, 17, 18, 19, 20, 23, 25, 26, 27, 28, 29, 30, 31, 34, 35, 37, 43, 45, 53, 95, 96, 107, 221; Chums' Benevolent Association, 17, 35, 36, 38, 139; Circle Council, 63; Circle Officers: 88–9; Chamberlain, 51, 174; Guard, 26, 186; President, 63, 88; President's Marshal, 51; Secretary, 51, 57, 61, 72, 89, 95; Treasurer, 51; Tyler, 26, 51; Vice-President's Marshal, 51, 186; clubs proposed, 72, 128; Constitution, 18, 27, 48, 51–2, 82–5, 88, 89, 100, 104, 107–8, 121, 126, 127, 173; councillors, 70, 140, 165, 215; Covenant system, 119–20; cricketers, 137; enrolment fees, 119; entertainments, 133; expansion, 27, 28, 31–3, 41–5, 47–8, 53–4, 66–7, 68, 98–9, 132, 172; slow-down in, 53, 85, 132, 210–11; renewal of, 160–1; overseas, 198–209; families, 112, 221–3; foundation date, 16–18; Golfing Society, 129, 220; Grand Almoner suggested, 111; Grand Benevolent Board, 52, 108, 110–12, 115–16; Grand

227

INDEX

Circle, 35, 39, 51–2, 36, 74, 75, 76, 81, 82, 83, 84–5, 95, 109, 122, 126; Grand Council, 27, 34, 38, 43, 44, 45, 46, 48, 51, 52, 56, 57, 58, 59, 61, 62, 63, 64, 72, 74, 76, 77, 80, 81, 82, 83, 84, 85, 86, 87, 88, 89, 90, 91–3, 94, 96, 97, 100, 101, 103, 105, 107, 108, 109, 110, 113, 115, 116, 118, 119, 122, 125, 126, 131, 136, 141, 142, 145, 152, 153, 154, 155, 162, 168–9, 170, 173, 174, 177, 179, 180, 181, 182, 185, 186, 187, 192, 193, 194, 195, 196, 198, 199, 200, 202, 203, 204–5, 206, 207, 208, 211, 212–13, 218; 'Group, the', 104, 152, 160, 206–7, 208; Head Office, 51, 71, 84, 174, 211; move to London, 105, 161–2; initiation, 25, 30, 35, 39, 130; Ireland, Catenians in, 205–6; justices of peace, 71, 139, 163, 215; Ladies' Evenings, 34, 61, 160, 217; lapsation, 26, 127–8, 137, 169, 172–3; Link Clubs, 72, 128, 211; Mayors and Lord Mayors, 27, 35, 41, 42, 45, 46, 50, 61, 70, 73, 139–40, 165, 166, 175, 215; meetings, character of early, 25, 26; conduct of, 25, 31, 89, 169; membership, decreasing, 172–3, 186, 210–11; honorary, 170; increasing, 66, 160; Membership Officers, 210; motto, 27, 60; musical evenings, 25, 133; outings, 61, 62, 71, 133, 217; Parliament, Members of, 70, 140, 165–6, 175, 190, 301; Past Presidents' Clubs, 64–5; Pilgrimage to Rome, 77; political activities, 11, 70, 140, 155, 157, 165–6, 175, 190; prayer groups, 213; President's Sunday, 61, 71, 126, 129, 154; priests, 'Catenian', 46, 77–8, 122, 176, 217, 223; Provinces, 45, 48, 51, 53, 72, 82, 85–7, 185; (No. 1), 85, 86, 162, 170; (No. 2), 72; (No. 3), 179 (No. 6), 175; (No. 7), 72, 87, 112–13, 175; (No. 8), 85; (No. 9), 85; (No. 11), 87, 162, 163, 176, 198; (No. 12), 85, 161, 162; (No. 13), 85, 86, 161; (No. 14), 86; (No. 15), 86; (No. 16), 86; (No. 17), 86, 87, 211; (No. 18), 87; (No. 19), 87; Provincial Councils, 82, 83, 85, 86, 89–91, 94, 152; Provincial Officers, 82–3, 86; Provincial rallies, 62, 129; public office, Catenians in, 70, 124, 139–40, 162–3, 164–6, 175, 201, 214–15; Redundancy Officers, 187, 211; Reorganisation Commission (1970), 87–8, 186, 195, 196, 203; Requiems, 71; resignations, 26, 127–8, 169–70, 172–3; Retreats, 71, 154, 176; ritual, 26, 31, 34, 35, 61, 136, 169, 173–4, 186; Rules, 18, 27, 51, 173, 186, 213; 'Salute', 26, 169, 174; Scotland, Catenians in, 46, 60–1; Signs and Passwords, 26, 107, 124, 135–6, 169, 174; social intercourse, 21, 25, 26, 128–9, 164–5, 183, 189, 217–18; spiritual dimension, 130–1, 176, 213; sportsmen, 137; 'style', 42, 52; subscription, annual, 20, 108, 109, 168–9, 170, 211; title, 69, 70–1; veto, power of, 83, 168; visiting, inter-Circle, 60, 61–2, 129, 134, 147; wartime activities (1914–18), 53–4; (1939–45), 145–58; widows, 218–19; wives, 189, 217–18

'Catenians do nothing' (allegation), 50, 57, 76, 78, 164, 165, 174, 187–8

Catholic action, 20, 49, 69, 73, 93, 121, 130–1, 141–4, 154, 164–5, 176, 188–90

Catholic Education Council (1905), 7, 41

Catholic Evidence Guild, 70, 213

Catholic Federation, 10, 11–12, 14, 17–18, 20, 32, 41, 143

Catholic Handicapped Children's Fellowship, 197, 215

Catholic Housing Aid Society, 190

Catholic Huts campaign, 54

Catholic Marriage Advisory Council (C.M.A.C), 163, 165

Catholic Parents and Electors Association (C.P.E.A.), 41, 46, 155–7, 166, 174

Catholic Pharmaceutical Guild, 175

Catholic Prisoners' Aid Society, 57, 141, 175, 190

Catholic Social Guild (C.S.G.), 43, 70, 78, 79, 80, 165

Catholic Teachers' Federation (C.T.F.), 41, 156, 165, 175, 179

Catholic Trade Unionists, National Confederation of, 12

Catholic Women's League (C.W.L.), 59, 96, 163

Catholic Workers' College, 43, 47, 49, 78, 79–80, 139, 190

Catholic Young Men's Society (C.Y.M.S.), 5, 50, 101, 102, 141

Caunter, Lionel, 31

Chamberlain, George Henry, 54

Chaplaincies, University, 176, 177, 178–84, 192, 197, 213

Charity Officers, Association of, 119

Charlier family, 57, 223

Cheam: St Anthony's Hospital, 108, 163, 175

Cheshire Homes, 109, 190, 216

Circles:
Ashton-under-Lyne, 28, 29, 215; Axminster, 190; Beckenham, 112; Birkenhead, 215; Birmingham, 42, 43, 47, 48, 54, 56, 60, 66, 70, 71, 72, 101, 102, 125, 126, 128, 137, 160, 176; Birmingham, City of, 66; Birmingham Midland, 132–3, 147, 199; Blackburn, 27, 29, 34, 36, 38, 73, 139–40, 213, 221–2; Blackheath, 44, 151, 160; Blackpool and The Fylde, 24, 48, 138, 166; Bolton, 47; Bournemouth, 45, 54, 61, 62, 71, 117, 138, 140, 141, 165, 166, 167, 175, 207, 218, 219; Bradford, 45–7, 61, 71, 77, 110, 123, 157, 199; Brighton, 44, 46, 47, 175; Bristol, 48, 117, 141, 217; Bristol, City of, 48; Bromley, 44, 112, 113, 145, 191; Bromley and Beckenham, 112, 176; Brooklands, 126, 215; Bulawayo, 45, 200–1, 202–3, 203–4, 220; Burnley, 138, 140, 161, 198; Burton-upon-Trent, 47; Cambridge, 36, 61, 70, 138, 216; Cardiff, 48, 62, 67, 70, 138, 140, 157, 159, 167; Cardiff, City of, 134; Carlisle, 67, 150; Cheshire North, 126, 127; Chesterfield, 47; Chichester, 151; Chorley, 47, 215; Colchester, 221–2; Copperbelt, 201, 202, 203; Cork, 206; Cornwall, Duchy of, 160, 222; Coventry, 54, 71, 140, 147, 160, 167; Coventry, City of, 54; Croydon, 44, 67, 137, 157, 165, 175; Derby, 47, 67, 70, 163; Doncaster, 152, 166, 218; Dublin, 44, 205–6; Durham, 220; Ealing, 159, 161; Eccles, 27, 215; Edinburgh, 33, 34, 36, 60, 68, 137, 148, 165, 217; Epping Forest, 148, 151; Epsom, 119, 175, 215; Exeter, 45, 85, 166, 215–16; Fife St Margaret, 186; Fleet, 175; Fleetwood, 161; Glamorgan North, 150, 216; Glasgow, 46–7, 66, 125, 133, 138, 151, 222; Glasgow Strathclyde, 66, 78; Glasgow South, 160; Gloucester, County of, 143, 163; Greenock, 159; Guernsey, 152, 208; Halifax, 216; Harrogate, 53, 200; Harrow, 48, 157, 175; Hastings, 44, 146, 166, 175; Hong Kong, 80, 152, 208; Huddersfield, 192; Hull, 36, 40, 55, 138; Isle of Wight, 215; Jersey, 198, 199, 201; Kent, 44; Ku-Ring-Gai, 207; Lancashire, 72, 126; Lancashire North, 137, 222; Leeds, 12, 29, 31, 32, 33, 34, 36, 51, 61, 73, 138, 148, 151, 157, 166; Leeds, City of, 160; Leicester, 47, 154, 167, 217; Leigh Lancashire, 153, 160, 222; Liverpool, 25, 33–5, 36, 38, 47, 48, 52, 53, 54, 66, 72, 126, 128, 138, 141, 151, 161, 222; Liverpool, City of, 221, 222; Liverpool South, 213–14; London, 27, 30, 31, 33, 34, 35, 36, 37, 40, 42, 47, 48, 49, 50, 51, 68, 69, 74, 75–6, 79, 95, 107, 125, 128; London Belgravia, 215; London Charterhouse, 48, 65, 66, 149, 191; London, City of, 42, 44, 59, 68–9, 76, 94, 110, 149, 216, 229; London North, 48, 68, 149, 159, 221; London Northern Heights, 48; London North West, 48, 223; London South, 44–5, 67, 71, 76, 110, 149, 215, 221; London South West, 133, 175, 190–1; Loughborough, 47; Lusaka, 202–3; Macclesfield, 152, 222; Maidstone, 160; Malta, 80, 92, 208; Manchester, 12, 16, 18, 22, 23, 25, 26, 27, 31, 32, 34, 35, 36, 39, 41, 43, 46, 47, 48, 57, 68, 71, 76, 81, 82, 86–7, 95, 96, 97, 107, 124, 126, 127, 133, 138, 139, 141, 154, 165, 166, 217, 221; Manchester City, 66, 70, 100; Manchester North, 86; Manchester South, 53, 56, 71, 86, 126, 154, 163, 187; Mansfield and The Dukeries, 47; Margate, 146; Melbourne, 207; Middlesbrough, 54, 61, 138, 157; Mid-Essex, 145; Mid-Herts, 217; Mid-Surrey, see

228

INDEX

Sutton Mid-Surrey; Newcastle-upon-Tyne, 32, 33, 34, 35, 36, 38, 49, 51, 61, 66, 70, 71, 77, 79, 82, 125, 149; Newport Gwent, 48, 67, 110, 133, 138, 151, 157, 168; Northampton, 53, 54, 141; North Middlesex, 66; North Wales, 100, 152–3; Norwich, 141; Norwood, 44, 151, 157, 159; Nottingham, 47, 48, 49, 67, 125, 135, 138, 141, 164, 218; Nottingham, City of, 47; Oldham, 160; Orpington, 215, 221; Oxford, 137, 153, 160, 216; Paisley, 148; Perth, City of, 207, 222; Peterborough, 47; Plymouth, 36, 45, 67, 85, 135, 148, 151, 216, 218; Portsmouth, 45, 62, 138, 147–8, 151, 159, 161, 218; Preston, 45, 48, 77, 140, 151, 160, 217; Preston South, 216; Purley, 160, 215, 223; Ramsgate, 146–7, 176; Reading, 45, 62, 141; Richmond and Twickenham, 133; St Helens, 47, 143, 163, 215; Scunthorpe, 152; Sheffield, 57, 148, 151, 222, 223; Shrewsbury, 119, 139, 148, 167; Southampton, 45, 54, 61, 62, 71, 138, 148, 157, 175, 222; South Bucks, 148, 152; Southend-on-Sea, 47, 168, 216; South Essex, *see* Southend-on-Sea; Southgate and District, 48, 146; Southport, 53, 125, 157; Stockport, 152, 222; Stockton, 153; Stoke-on-Trent, 45, 70, 79, 175, 190; Stratford-on-Avon, 217; Sunderland, 66, 151; Sutton Mid-Surrey, 44, 71, 157, 175; Swansea, 48, 67, 70, 85, 129, 133, 216; Sydney, City of, 207; Thames Valley, 19, 44, 223; Thanet, 132; Torbay, 45, 85, 216; Tynemouth, 160; Tyneside, 79; Vale of Evesham, 208; Wallasey, 66, 138, 149, 164; Walsall, 157; Wandsworth and Putney, *see* London South West; Warwickshire North, 147, 159, 190; Waterloo, 133; Westerham, 221; West Essex, 61, 164, 168; West Kent, 112, 136, 153; West London, 59, 66, 137; West Middlesex, 145, 215; Westminster, City of, 157, 216; West Surrey, 151; Weybridge, 19, 153, 164, 190, 215; Wigan, 47, 71, 190, 217; Wimbledon, 19, 44, 54, 163; Winchester, 45, 160, 175; Worthing, 124; Yarmouth, 105; York, 61, 132; Yorkshire, 54, 61; Zambia, 80; Zimbabwe, 80
Clark, Philip Lindsey, 105–6
Clarke, Bro., 166
Coakley, Brian, 120
Cockshutt, Dennis, 215
Coggan, Frank, 201
Coker, Pat, 212, 214
Collins, Bishop Richard, 32, 34
Commercial and General Intelligence Committees: *see* 'Service'
Compendium of ritual and procedure, 169, 174
Conference of Catholic industrialists, 43, 79
Conlon, Bro., 189
Conrad, Alfred George, 175, 188

converts, isolation of, 24
Cooper, Jack, 213
Coppinger, Bro., 204
Cornwell, Reg, 215
Corrigan, Bro., 24
Cosgrove, Hubert, 120, 149, 155
Cotter, Fr Sylvester, 217
Cotter, Bishop William T., 44
Cowderoy, Archbishop Cyril, 181, 183
Cowgill, Bishop Joseph Robert, 31
Cox, Joe, 93, 118, 120, 145, 186, 187, 203, 207, 216
Craven, A., 139
Critchley, Bro., 165
Crotty, Paddy, 190
Croydon: Josephite College, 6
Crusade of Reserve, 10, 61, 141, 163
Cunningham, Bill, 174
Curtis, Alban, 183
Cuss, Francis, 188

Dabinett, Sid and Maureen, 218
Daly, Bernard, 181, 186
Daly, Jim, 189
Davies, Llewellyn, 183
De Profundis, 44, 61, 71, 84, 169
de Roma, Norbert, 206
Delahunty, J., 16, 95
Denver, Bro., 95
depression, economic, 72–3, 75–6, 103–4, 109, 113, 116, 118, 125, 132, 187, 210
Deverall, Freddie, 146
Dix, G.L.P., 49, 52, 71
Dixon, Bro., 137
Donovan, Michael, 183
Doran, Teddy, 53, 54, 56, 71, 126
Downey, Francis, 149
Downey, Archbishop Richard, 50, 52, 143
Doyle, Fr J.C.B., 176
Driscoll, Bro., 168
Dublin: Gresham Hotel, 198
Dunn, James, 190
Dunn, Bishop Thomas, 68
Dunn, Sir W.H., 35, 42, 139
Durnford, V.M., 40, 44, 51; first Grand Treasurer, 110
Duval, G.F., 46
Dwyer, Archbishop G.P., 181, 217

Ecclesiastical Commisions, Report on, 194–5
Edmundson, Bro., 166
Edridge, Dr Ray, 71
education, 5–8, 11, 12, 14, 23, 112–13, 114, 117, 118, 129, 137–9, 155–8, 166–8, 174
Education Act (1870), 11; (1891), 7; (1902), 1, 7, 137; (1907), 13, 41, 137; (1944), 41, 131, 155–6, 157–8, 166
Educational Institute of Scotland, 165
Ellis, Bishop Edward, 164
'élitism', accusation of, 99
Emblem, Bernard, 119–20
Eucharistic Congress (1908), 14–15; (1933), 104
Everest, Bro., 163
Exworthy, W.A., 41, 156, 157
Eyre, John, 207, 212

Faith and Light Pilgrimage 1969, 191
family, the, 21, 24, 25, 130–1, 219–20, 221–3
Farrell, George, 216
Farrelly, Fr John, 217
Farrelly, William, 215
Father Hudson's Homes, 42, 56, 70, 141
Fattorini family, 45–6
Faulkner, Ray, 223
Faupel, Bro., 212
Fearnhead, Alderman, 47–8
Feeney, Victor, 149
Finan, J.J., 41, 156, 164
Fitzgerald-Hart, E., 12, 32, 45, 51, 70
Fitz-Gibbon, Denis, 130
Fitzsimons, G.W.G., 165, 190
Fitzsimons, James, 165
Flynn, Fred, 163
Flynn, George, 53
Foggin, Dr George, 32–3, 38, 39, 46, 47, 51, 54, 57, 62, 81, 122
Forde, Paddy, 211
Forest Hill, S.E.23: Cabrini House, 215
Fox, Bro., 70
Francis, Tom, 215
Fraser, Bro., 62
Freemasonry, 18, 19, 25, 62, 64, 72, 123
French, Bob, 214
friendship, Catenian gift for, 24, 50, 127, 183, 223
Fyans, Alderman, 16, 18, 48
Gallacher, H., 206
Garner, Archbishop John, 204
Garner, Victor, 204
Gaskin, Cyril, 220–1, 223
Gaskin, Jimmy, 52
Gasquet, Cardinal Aidan, O.S.B., 71, 74–5, 76
Gaynor, Canon, 67
Gibbons, John, 12, 16, 17, 19, 23, 30, 31, 36, 39, 42, 69
Gilroy, Cardinal Norman, 207
Glanville, Bro., 147
Glithero, Richard, 191–2
Glynn, Brian, 215
Glynn, James, 215
Godfrey, Cardinal William, 164, 177, 179
Godwin, Len, 175–6
Goodier, Archbishop Alban, S.J., 45, 75, 77
Goodier, Alderman Oswald, 45, 69, 75, 76, 77, 82, 123
Gordon, Bishop William, 12, 31–2, 34
Gormley, Jack, 223
Gosling, Vincent, 56–7
Gottelier family, 112–13, 114
Graham-Green, Bro., 163
Grasar, Bro., 152
Gray, Cardinal Gordon, 213
Green, F., 95
Gregory, Michael, 175
Griffin, Cardinal Bernard, 147, 154, 163, 167, 175, 178
Griffiths, Gerry, 215
Grobel, Cyril, 165, 181
Guardians of the Poor, Catholic (1906), 11

229

INDEX

Hailwood, Augustine, 70, 140
Hains, G., 147
Hall, Dr Jimmy, 147
Hall, Martin, 147
Hall, Pat, 191
handicapped, the, 21, 62, 108–9, 190–2, 215–16
Handicapped Children's Pilgrim Trust (H.C.P.T.), 112, 190–2, 216
Harris, George, 115, 127, 174, 182
Harty, G.A.N., 192
Harvey, Tom, 315
Healy, Paddy, 207
Heenan, Cardinal John Carmel, 178–9, 183, 193–4
Hegarty, Fr Bernard, 176
Helmore, Richard, 60
Hems, Leonard, 199
Hendren, 'Patsy', 137
Hennessy, Christopher, 194
Hensler, Thomas Gordon, 42, 68, 138
Heyburn, Bernard, 44, 110
Heyburn, Edward, L., 44, 110, 162
Hierarchy, English, 73–4; Low Week Meetings of, 69, 177, 179, 180, 181, 194; Restoration of (1850), 4–5, 87; Centenary (1950), 166, 213
Hierarchy and the Association, 69, 74, 75–6, 142–4, 164, 174, 177–84, 193–5, 212, 213
Hierarchy, Scottish, 164, 213
Hildred, Glen, 64, 79, 155, 164
Hinckley: St Peter's College, 6
Hinsley, Cardinal Arthur, 143, 149, 153–4
Hipkin, Harry, 186
Hogan, Edward J., 27, 28, 29, 30, 31, 35, 37, 39, 42, 43, 44, 46, 48, 51, 57, 81, 84–5, 134, 198
Holden, Richard, 27, 29, 34, 38, 39
Holland, Bishop Thomas, 213
Holloway, Cliff, 207
Holman, Abbot, 194–5
Holohan, Michael, 38
Holt, Charles, 17, 19, 24, 39
Holt, Frank, 24–5
Hopkins, Luke, 216
Hosanna House, 108, 112, 191–2, 215
Hume, Cardinal George Basil, 212
Hurst, Thomas, 176
Hussey, Geoffrey M., 204, 205
Hutton, Bro., 43, 47

Ilsley, Archbishop Edward, 43
Irving, Dan, 13
isolation, Catholic, 60, 67–8

Jacomelli family, 32, 36, 37
Jenkins, Douglas, 87, 207
Jennings, Desmond, 220
John Paul II, Pope, 213
Johnson, J.M., 192
Jones, J. Trevor, 36
Jones, Stanley, 187
Jordan, W.C., 16
'Jumbulance', the, 49, 93, 108, 112, 192, 215
Justice and Peace Commission, 213

Kanc, Bro., 177
Kearney, Bro., 153
Kearney, Dr Basil, 178
Kearney, William, 222
Keast, Walter, 155
Keating, Bishop Frederick William, 69, 70, 141
Kelly, Cuthbert, 131, 164
Kelly, Paul, 42–3, 44, 77, 79, 80, 94, 154, 163, 167, 182, 221
Kelly, Peter, 153
Kenny, Alderman, 27
Kevill, Thomas Halliwell, 47–8, 68, 112, 123
Kiely, Bishop John, 67
Kimberlin, Bro., 157, 167
King, Archbishop John Henry, 45, 157
King, Mike, 215
Kirchner, Bernard, 59–60, 131, 162, 164, 188, 196
Kirk, Rex: quoted, 186
Knights of Columbus, 69, 122, 149, 198
Knights of St Columbanus of Ireland, 96, 104
Knights of St Columba (K.S.C.), 46, 50, 61, 69, 70, 96, 123, 141, 165, 171, 205, 206
Knights of the Southern Cross (K.S.C.), 198, 206, 218
Koolhoven, Bro., 176

Laity, role of, 3, 7–8, 9 -10, 49, 60, 62, 68, 122, 139–44, 172, 177–8, 179, 183, 193–5, 212–14, 224
Last, Dick, 44, 218–19
Laverty, R.H., 147
Lawler, Jack, 120, 170–1
Leach, Bro., 166
Lednicki, H., 149
Lee, Charles, 201
Lee, Hugh, 70, 108
Leeds: St Bede's Grammar School, 46
Lees, Bro., 95
Le Fèvre, F.W., 46, 77–8, 176
Le Jeune, David, 176
Leo XIII, Pope, 2, 11, 73, 78, 142
Lescher, Edward, 74, 75–6
Lewis, David, 216
Lindsay, Bishop Hugh, 108
Little Sisters of the Poor, 175
Liverpool: St Francis Xavier's school, 6; Xaverian College, 6
Lloyd, Frank, 108, 116, 188, 189, 191
Local Education Authorities (L.E.A.s), 7, 13, 166–8
Locan, Tom, 12, 17, 18, 19, 21, 23, 24, 25, 26, 28, 30, 31, 33, 35, 36, 43, 53, 62, 95, 107
Lomas, Frank, 34, 35, 93, 122, 127, 152, 174, 177, 181, 188, 203, 222
Lomas, John, 35, 152, 222
London: Bridge House Hotel, London Bridge, 44; St Charles's, North Kensington, 6; St John and St Elizabeth, Hospital of, 108; Stanley Hall, Tufnell Park, 48; Tyburn Convent, 175
Longford, Lord, 153
Lourdes, Catenians and, 62, 108, 175, 190–1, 215, 216
Lynskey family, 34, 35, 55, 72
Lythgoe, Dom Raymond, O.S.B., 67

McCabe, Alderman Sir Dan, 23, 41,
42, 50, 53, 54, 55, 62, 69, 70, 98, 124, 139
McClean, Bishop John, 213
McClelland, Bro., 165
McDermott, Joseph, 27, 28–9, 30–1, 32, 33, 34, 35–6, 38, 39, 42, 43, 46, 51, 67, 95, 107, 139, 215
McDermott, Richard, 28
McDonald, Archbishop Andrew Joseph, 60–1
McInnes, Frank, 166, 167
McIntyre, Archbishop John, 50, 101, 102
Macken, H.J., 198
McLachlan, Tom, 160
McLaughlin, Canon, 67
McMahon, John, 17, 24, 39, 107
McMurray, Joe, 18, 64, 88, 105, 189, 210
McNabb, Jim, 187, 211
McNulty, Bishop John Francis, 47
Maguire, Dr Peter (father and son), 207, 222
Mahon, Simon, 189, 190
Malley, Harold, 147
Malone, Sir Patrick Bernard, 30–1, 70, 140
Maltby, Edward, 214
Manchester: Albion Hotel, 22, 27, 30; Ardwick, 140; Cenacle Convent, 154; Free Trade Hall, 8, 22, 23; Horniman Repertory Theatre, 22; Ingham's Hotel, 22, 25; Midland Hotel, 22, 34, 39; Morning Star Hostel, 213; St Anne's, Ancoats, 21, 41; St Bede's, 6, 8, 9, 10; St Mary's, Mulberry Street, 22, 39
Manning, Cardinal Henry Edward, 3, 6, 7, 10, 11
Manual of Procedure, 89, 186
Margate: Xaverian College, 6
Martin, Bro., 166
Martin, Charles, 215
Martin, J.A., 147
Mather, Denis, 93
May, Raymond, 204
'Meals on Wheels Service', first, 175
Melvin, Sir Martin, 43, 56, 58, 101
Mercer, John, 213
middle class, Catholic, 2, 5, 6–7, 20, 25, 30, 40, 69, 81, 99, 122, 123, 139
Middlesbrough, diocese of, 12, 213
Miller, Miles, 222
Millers, Bro., 34, 38, 39, 95, 107
Minghella, Eddie, 215
Mitchell, Bill, 220
Molony, Sir Joseph, 94
Molyneux, Jack, 213
Moorhead, Terry, 214
Moran, Archbishop Patrick, 74
Moran, Dr, 198
Morris, Jim, 214
Morrison, John, 216
Mostyn, Archbishop Francis, 67
Multiple Sclerosis Society, 109, 175
Munich, Charles J., 42, 48, 75, 222–3
Munro, Dennis, 222–3
Murphy, Gerald, 189
Murphy-O'Connor, Fr Patrick, 175
Myers, Bishop Edward, 146
Myers, Reggie, 44, 149

INDEX

National Catholic Congress, (1910), 32; (1920), 74; (1923), 102
National Confederation of Catholic Trade Unionists, 12
National Council of Directors of Vocations, 189
National Pastoral Congress (1980), 62, 213
Nazareth Houses, 61, 112, 141, 148, 190, 216
Neville, V., 29, 32, 39
Newcastle-upon-Tyne: St Cuthbert's Grammar School, 38
Newman, Cardinal John Henry, 3, 7, 22, 188
Nulty, Bishop, 41

Oakamoor: Cotton College, 138
O'Brien, H.F., 16, 70
O'Brien, Bishop James, 217
O'Brien, W.J., 16, 19, 21, 26, 31
O'Callaghan, John, 217, 218, 219
O'Connell, David, 151
O'Connor, Fr Dan, 217
O'Connor, Fr Liam, 217
O'Dea, William, 41, 69, 71, 81, 108, 156
O'Donnell, Bro., 166
O'Donnell, Clare, 22
O'Donnell, John, 12, 16, 17, 18, 19, 21, 22, 23, 25, 28, 30, 31, 32, 34, 35, 36, 37, 38, 39, 41, 42, 43, 45, 46, 48, 49, 51, 53, 57, 62, 81, 84, 85, 86, 95, 107, 121, 122, 139, 164, 166
O'Donovan, John, 164
O'Hea, Fr Leo, S.J., 78
Ohly, Sidney, 183
Oldham, Father, S.J., 143
O'Leary, Canon Maurice, 163
Ollard, Bros., 70, 166
O'Roake, Hugh, 213
Our Lady of Good Counsel, Society of, 140
Our Relevance Today (Tanner), 130
Owen, Bro., 146

Paines, H. Wilfred, 36, 152
Palethorpe, Charles, 54
Palmer, Victor, 64–4, 151, 155, 176–7, 188
Parker, Bro., 199, 208
Parker, Bishop Leo, 36–7
Patterson, Bro., Major, 163
Pearson, Keith, 93, 210
Peckston, Bro., 205, 206
Pegge, Bro., 48
Pemberton, Bro., 166
Pendergast, Frank, 12, 16, 17, 18, 19, 20, 21, 23, 26, 28, 29, 30, 35, 37, 43, 44, 62, 95, 165, 186
People of God, 178, 187, 214
Pepper, Bernard, 45, 199–201, 202–3, 204, 205, 206
Pepper, W.O., 45, 199
Perceval, Sir Westby, 42, 71, 110, 125
Petit, Bishop John, 106, 177, 179
Peyton, Edmund, J.P., 70
Phillimore, Professor John Swinnerton, 46–7, 137
Pius IX, Pope, 73
Pius X, Pope, 2, 74
Pius XI, Pope, 77, 102, 142
Pius XII, Pope, 189

Plater, Fr Charles, S.J., 50, 78
Plater College, *see* Catholic Workers' College
Politi, Jack, 86, 154, 176
Poor Clares (Colettines), 190
Porter, Pat, 190, 191–2
Poskitt, Bishop Henry John, 166–7
Preston: Catholic College, 6
Priestly, Formation, Commission on, 189, 213
priests and Association, 20, 122, 143, 174
prisoners, aid to discharged, 175, 190
Purnell, Bro., 140, 168

Quick, Herbert, 149
Quick, Sidney, 44, 191, 196

Rankin, Richard, 35
Ratcliffe College, 6, 32
'Recognition, Methods of', 25–6, 136
Recollection, Days of, 154, 176
Redwood, Sydney, 17, 36–7, 44, 59, 63, 79, 108, 143, 145, 162
Reeve, Fr C.G., 176
Registration Societies, 11, 12
Reid, Agnew, 216
Renewal Movement, 213
Rerum Novarum, 2, 78
Reynolds, Bro., 107
Rhodesia, 199–205
Rice, Anthony, 119
Richards, Bob, 199
Ridgers, Bill, 191, 215
Ross, Leonard, 119, 167
Rees, Peter, 119–20
Rossi, Hugh, 190, 214–15
Ross-shire, Catholic isolation in, 60
Rotzinger, Mr, 67
Rourke, John, 175
Rowbottom, Bro., 95
Rudman, Frank, 16, 17, 37, 60, 86, 101–2, 104–5, 126, 137, 151, 152, 154, 160–1, 162, 170–1, 176, 178, 186, 195
Rudman, Gerard, 159
Rye, Alan, 160, 175, 179
Ryan, Dr J.J., 124

St Augustine, Society of, 43
St Disinas, Society of, 62, 108, 175, 190
St Francis Leprosy Guild, 108–9, 190
St Helens: Royal Raven Hotel, 47
St Vincent de Paul, Society of (S.V.P.), 5, 32, 43, 50, 55, 61, 70, 108, 141, 190, 215
'salariat', 69, 81, 133
Salisbury (Zimbabwe), 199, 201, 202, 203, 220
Samaritans, 190
Sampson, Michael, 213–14
Sandham family, 137, 222
Sandy, Henry T., 42, 43, 47, 57, 62
Savage, Dr T., 46
Save the Children Fund, 215
Sxanlon, Archbishop James Donald, 78, 176
Schmitt, Bishop Adolf, 201
schools
boarding, 5–6, 7; elementary, 7, 62; grammar, 7, 62; middle-class, 7; secondary, 48, 61, 62, 70, 129, 137–9, 155–8, 166–8, 174; Battle for Schools, *see* Battle

Scott, Phil, 220
Seagar, Kenneth, 191
Serra Movement, 108, 188, 189, 216–17
'Service', 72, 84, 124–6, 187, 211–12
Service Committees, 48, 125–6, 127, 129
Shacklady, Basil, 215
Shaughnessy, John, 47, 66, 110, 126
Shaw, Jock, 86
Shee, Dr, 199–200
Sheehan, Mrs Catherine, quoted, 16–17, 19–20, 23
Sheffield: King's Head Hotel, 51
Sheffield University, 179
Shelmerdine, Roger, 175, 190
Sheill, Charles H., 41, 156, 165
Sheldon, Bro., 58
Shepherd, Joe, 31, 34, 35, 37, 38, 39, 41, 42, 45, 46, 47, 48, 51–2, 54, 59, 62, 71, 82–3, 84, 85, 95–6, 97–101, 102–3, 108, 112, 122, 153, 170, 185, 195
Shippey, Bro., 107
Signs of the Times, The (Casartelli), 9
Simmonds, Leo, 60, 162, 189, 190
Skinnider, Dr, 148
Skipton: St Stephen's, 45
Skivington, Francis, 42
Smallbone, A.E., 211
Smith, Gordon, 141
Smith, John, 218
Society for the Protection of the Unborn Child (S.P.U.C.), 215
South Africa, 201, 203–5
Southend, 146, 168; St Bernard, Convent of, 168
Stanford, Bro., 152
Stevens, Pat, 213
Stoke-on-Trent: Douglas McMillan Home, 190
Stone, Bro., 139
Stroud, D.A., 44, 67, 69, 136, 146, 150, 157
Sullivan, Dan, 164, 175
Sullivan, H. Bernard, 46, 165, 208
Sullivan, J.A., 46
Sullivan, L.J., 59
Sweeney, Dr Plunkett, 206, 207
Swift, Joe, 207
Sword of the Spirit, 43, 154–5
Sykes, Sir Mark, 40–1, 55, 140
Synott, Walter, 48, 76, 81, 83, 85, 90, 123–4, 125, 139

Taggart, John (father), 34, 55, 157
Taggart, John (grandson), 164
Taggart, Pat (son), 34, 55, 72, 80, 93, 122, 128, 142, 143, 154, 177, 218
Tait, John, 17, 25, 30, 36, 85
Talbot, Mgr Gilbert, 3
Tanner, Laurie, 30, 89, 93, 103, 105, 130, 173, 174, 177, 181, 182, 185–6, 192–3, 194, 195–7, 200, 206, 210
Taverner, Bro., 168
Thompson, Alderman, 27, 139
Thorndike, Reg, 215
Tickle family, 45, 148, 223
Time for Reappraisal of Catenian Potential, 188
Tindall, Edward, 200
Tindall, Freddie, 148, 159
Tindall, J.A., 200
Tolkien, J.R.R., 137, 153, 160

231

INDEX

Tonks, Jim, 207
Tordoft, G.J., 190
Trades Union Congress (T.U.C.), 155–6, 158
trade unions, 11, 12, 17, 20, 78, 79, 139
Tressider, Bro., 163
Turnbull, Bro., 70, 140

Universe, The, 30, 37, 41, 43, 49, 56, 58, 177, 194
University Catholic Students Association, 129
Urwin, Bro., 166
Ushaw: St Cuthbert's College, 6, 9

Vatican Council, Second, 60, 122, 174, 177, 183, 185, 189; Decree on the Laity, 193, 214
Vaughan, Cardinal Herbert, 2, 10–11, 73, 74
Vickerstaff family, 222

Vincent, Bro., 166
Vincent, P.A. Clark, 119
Vinculum Association, 45, 200

Wall, John, 216
Walsh, Dermot, 161
Walsingham, first Pilgrimage to, 141
Ware: St Edmund's, 6
Watson, James, 56
Webb, J.B., 43, 56, 58, 220
Webster, T.L., 126
Wehrle, Karl, 70
Weidner, Bro., 55, 70
Welfare Committees, 117, 219
Wells, W.T., 166, 190
Welsh Circle, first, 67
West, Stan, 211
Weybridge: St George's, 6
Wheatley, John (Lord), 165, 166, 188
Whiteside, Archbishop Thomas, 34, 67
Whittle family, 17, 18, 26, 107
Wilding, Richard, 34, 38

Wilkinson, Fred, 220
Wisbech, 70, 166
Wiseman, Cardinal Nicholas, 4–5, 73
Woodruff, Douglas, 157
Woolgar, Bernard, 203
Woolwich: Royal Military College, 6
working class, Catholic, 30, 78
World War I, 24, 38, 40, 48, 53, 54, 109, 198
World War II, 16, 24, 25, 44, 47, 104, 116, 145–53, 159
Worlock, Archbishop Derek, 176, 194, 213
Worswick, Mr, 17
Wright, Gerard, 216
Wutack, Bro., 167

Xaverian Colleges, 6

Year Book, production of, 124
Young, Rowland, 220
youth, Catholic, 129–30